T0250666

ISSE 2015

Lizenz zum Wissen.

Sichern Sie sich umfassendes Technikwissen mit Sofortzugriff auf tausende Fachbücher und Fachzeitschriften aus den Bereichen: Automobiltechnik, Maschinenbau, Energie + Umwelt, E-Technik, Informatik + IT und Bauwesen.

Exklusiv für Leser von Springer-Fachbüchern: Testen Sie Springer für Professionals 30 Tage unverbindlich. Nutzen Sie dazu im Bestellverlauf Ihren persönlichen Aktionscode C0005406 auf *www.springerprofessional.de/buchaktion/*

Jetzt 30 Tage testen!

Springer für Professionals.
Digitale Fachbibliothek. Themen-Scout. Knowledge-Manager.

🔑 Zugriff auf tausende von Fachbüchern und Fachzeitschriften

⊕ Selektion, Komprimierung und Verknüpfung relevanter Themen durch Fachredaktionen

✎ Tools zur persönlichen Wissensorganisation und Vernetzung

www.entschieden-intelligenter.de

Springer für Professionals

 Springer

Helmut Reimer · Norbert Pohlmann ·
Wolfgang Schneider
Editors

ISSE 2015

Highlights of the Information Security Solutions Europe 2015 Conference

Springer Vieweg

Editors

Helmut Reimer
Bundesverband IT-Sicherheit e.V.
TeleTrusT
Erfurt, Germany

Norbert Pohlmann
Westfälische Hochschule
Gelsenkirchen, Germany

Wolfgang Schneider
Fraunhofer SIT
Darmstadt, Germany

ISBN 978-3-658-10933-2   ISBN 978-3-658-10934-9 (eBook)
DOI 10.1007/978-3-658-10934-9

Library of Congress Control Number: 2015951350

Springer Vieweg
© Springer Fachmedien Wiesbaden 2015
This work is subject to copyright. All rights are reserved by the Publisher, whether the whole or part of the material is concerned, specifically the rights of translation, reprinting, reuse of illustrations, recitation, broadcasting, reproduction on microfilms or in any other physical way, and transmission or information storage and retrieval, electronic adaptation, computer software, or by similar or dissimilar methodology now known or hereafter developed.
The use of general descriptive names, registered names, trademarks, service marks, etc. in this publication does not imply, even in the absence of a specific statement, that such names are exempt from the relevant protective laws and regulations and therefore free for general use.
The publisher, the authors and the editors are safe to assume that the advice and information in this book are believed to be true and accurate at the date of publication. Neither the publisher nor the authors or the editors give a warranty, express or implied, with respect to the material contained herein or for any errors or omissions that may have been made.

Typesetting: Oliver Reimer, Großschwabhausen

Printed on acid-free paper

Springer Fachmedien Wiesbaden GmbH is part of Springer Science+Business Media
(www.springer.com)

Contents

Authentication and eID   225

Regulation and Policies   261

Index   305

About this Book

The Information Security Solutions Europe Conference (ISSE) was started in 1999 by eema and TeleTrusT with the support of the European Commission and the German Federal Ministry of Technology and Economics. Today the annual conference is a fixed event in every IT security professional's calendar.

The range of topics has changed enormously since the founding of ISSE. In addition to our ongoing focus on securing IT applications and designing secure business processes, protecting against attacks on networks and their infrastructures is currently of vital importance. The ubiquity of social networks has also changed the role of users in a fundamental way: requiring increased awareness and competence to actively support systems security. ISSE offers a perfect platform for the discussion of the relationship between these considerations and for the presentation of the practical implementation of concepts with their technical, organisational and economic parameters.

From the beginning ISSE has been carefully prepared. The organisers succeeded in giving the conference a profile that combines a scientifically sophisticated and interdisciplinary discussion of IT security solutions while presenting pragmatic approaches for overcoming current IT security problems.

An enduring documentation of the presentations given at the conference which is available to every interested person thus became important. This year sees the publication of the twelfth ISSE book – another mark of the event's success – and with about 22 carefully edited papers it bears witness to the quality of the conference.

An international programme committee is responsible for the selection of the conference contributions and the composition of the programme:
- **Ammar Alkassar** (TeleTrusT/Sirrix AG)
- **John Colley** ((ISC)²)
- **Jos Dumortier** (time.lex)
- **Walter Fumy** (Bundesdruckerei)
- **David Goodman** (EEMA)
- **Michael Hartmann** (SAP)
- **Marc Kleff** (NetApp)
- **Jaap Kuipers** (Id Network)
- **Patrick Michaelis** (AC – The Auditing Company)
- **Lennart Oly** (ENX)

- **Norbert Pohlmann** (TeleTrusT/if(is))
- **Bart Preneel** (KU Leuven)
- **Helmut Reimer** (TeleTrusT)
- **Wolfgang Schneider** (Fraunhofer Institute SIT)
- **Marc Sel** (PwC)
- **Jon Shamah** (EEMA/EJ Consultants)
- **Franky Thrasher** (Electrabel)
- **Erik R. van Zuuren** (TrustCore)
- **Claire Vishik** (Intel)

The editors have endeavoured to allocate the contributions in these proceedings – which differ from the structure of the conference programme – to topic areas which cover the interests of the readers. With this book TeleTrusT aims to continue documenting the many valuable contributions to ISSE.

Norbert Pohlmann   *Helmut Reimer*   *Wolfgang Schneider*

TeleTrusT – IT Security Association Germany

TeleTrusT is a widespread competence network for IT security comprising members from industry, administration, research as well as national and international partner organizations with similar objectives. With a broad range of members and partner organizations TeleTrusT embodies the largest competence network for IT security in Germany and Europe. TeleTrusT provides interdisciplinary fora for IT security experts and facilitates information exchange between vendors, users and authorities. TeleTrusT comments on technical, political and legal issues related to IT security and is organizer of events and conferences. TeleTrusT is a non-profit association, whose objective is to promote information security professionalism, raising awareness and best practices in all domains of information security. TeleTrusT is carrier of the "European Bridge CA" (EBCA; PKI network of trust), the quality seal "IT Security made in Germany" and runs the IT expert certification programs "TeleTrusT Information Security Professional" (T.I.S.P.) and "TeleTrusT Engineer for System Security" (T.E.S.S.). TeleTrusT is a member of the European Telecommunications Standards Institute (ETSI). The association is headquartered in Berlin, Germany.

Keeping in mind the raising importance of the European security market, TeleTrusT seeks co-operation with European and international organisations and authorities with similar objectives. Thus, this year's European Security Conference ISSE is again being organized in collaboration with TeleTrusT's partner organisation eema and supported by the European Commission.

Contact:

TeleTrusT – IT Security Association Germany
Dr. Holger Muehlbauer
Managing Director
Chausseestrasse 17, 10115 Berlin, GERMANY
Tel.: +49 30 4005 4306, Fax: +49 30 4005 4311
http://www.teletrust.de

EEMA

EEMA is a non-profit membership association registered in Brussels. For over 25 years, from the dawn of the digital age, EEMA has helped European companies gain a competitive advantage and make informed technology choices and business decisions. Today it is the place where professionals gather to meet, network and define best practice in the areas of identity management and cybersecurity. EEMA's member representatives are drawn from leading corporate and multi-national end-user organisations, service providers, consultancies, academia, as well as local, national and European governmental agencies

In addition to a regular online newsletter and other information dissemination activities, EEMA benefits its members through conferences, thought leadership seminars and workshops, often in collaboration with partners such as ENISA, OECD, BCS, TDL, LSEC, TeleTrusT, ECP, Chamber of Commerce, CEN/ETSI, Digital Policy, ITU, Alliance, e-Forum, FAIB, FEDICT, IDESG, ISC2, United Nations, Oasis, SANS, SECEUR, GSMA, OIX and the Kantara Initiative. Recent EEMA events include 'Digital Enterprise Europe - Managing Identity for the Future' in London, 'Trust in the Digital World' in Vienna (in partnership with Trust in Digital Life) as well as special interest group meetings on 'Evolution & Future of eSignature & eSeal' and 'Cybersecurity – State of Play' in Brussels.

With its European partners, EEMA also participates in several high profile EU-sponsored projects including STORK 2.0 (Large scale pilot for e-ID interoperability between governments), SSEDIC (Scoping the single European digital identity community), Cloud for Europe (Public sector pre-commercial procurement in the Cloud) and FutureID (Shaping the future of electronic identity).

Visit www.eema.org or contact EEMA directly on +44 1386 793028 or info@eema.org

The EDPS Strategy – Leading by Example

Giovanni Buttarelli · Wojciech Wiewiórowski · Christopher Docksey

Rue Wiertz/Wiertzstraat 60
B-1047 Bruxelles/Brussel, Belgique/België
edps@edps.europa.eu

Abstract

The European Data Protection Supervisor (EDPS) is the independent supervisory authority monitoring the processing of personal data by the EU institutions and bodies, advising on policies and legislation that affect privacy and cooperating with similar authorities to ensure consistent data protection.

The current Supervisor, Giovanni Buttarelli, and Assistant Supervisor, Wojciech Wiewiórowski, were appointed in December 2014 by the European Parliament and the Council of the EU.

At a crucial moment for data protection, the EDPS has presented a strategy for 2015-2019 which identifies the major data protection and privacy challenges over the coming years, defines three strategic objectives and 10 accompanying actions for meeting those challenges and ways to deliver the strategy, through effective resource management, clear communication and evaluation of performance.

His three strategic objectives and 10 actions are:

1 **Data protection goes digital**

    (1) Promoting technologies to enhance privacy and data protection;

    (2) Identifying cross-disciplinary policy solutions;

    (3) Increasing transparency, user control and accountability in big data processing.

2 **Forging global partnerships**

    (4) Developing an ethical dimension to data protection;

    (5) Speaking with a single EU voice in the international arena;

    (6) Mainstreaming data protection into international policies.

3 **Opening a new chapter for EU data protection**

    (7) Adopting and implementing up-to-date data protection rules;

    (8) Increasing accountability of EU bodies collecting, using and storing personal information;

    (9) Facilitating responsible and informed policymaking;

    (10) Promoting a mature conversation on security and privacy.

As a first milestone in implementing his strategy, the EDPS adopted in July 2015 an opinion on the state of the data protection reform, setting out red lines and providing his advice for the on-going legislative negotiations. Building on discussions with the EU institutions, Member States, civil society, industry and other stakeholders, it addresses the GDPR in two parts:

- the EDPS vision for future-oriented rules on data protection, with illustrative examples of recommendations; and

- an annex with a four-column table for comparing, article-by-article, the text of the GDPR as adopted respectively by Commission, Parliament and Council, alongside the EDPS recommendation.

1 Introduction

This is truly a historic moment for data protection.

Over the last 25 years, technology has transformed our lives in positive ways nobody could have imagined. Big data, the internet of things, cloud computing, have so much to offer to enhance our lives. But these benefits should not be at the expense of the fundamental rights of individuals and their dignity in the digital society of the future. So big data will need equally big data protection.

The EU has a window of opportunity to adopt the future-oriented standards that we need, standards that are inspiring at global level.Europe has to lead the conversation on the legal and ethical consequences of the new technologies. This means adopting the data protection reform this year. A modern, future-oriented set of rules is key to solving Europe's digital challenge. We need EU rules which are innovative and robust enough to cope with the growing challenges of new technologies and trans-border data flows. Data protection must go digital.

Data protection will remain a relevant factor in most EU policy areas, and is the key to legitimise policies and increase trust and confidence in them. The EDPS will help the EU institutions and bodies to be fully accountable as legislators, to build data protection into the fabric of their legislative proposals.

To develop a single European voice on strategic data protection issues, the EDPS will cooperate with fellow independent data protection authorities.

2 Data Protection in the Digital Era

Digital technology is an extraordinary catalyst for all forms of social expression and social change. From amusing videos and games to revolutions powered by social media, technology can enable the powerless to challenge the powerful. There is no doubt that technology brings many benefits, both individual and social.

Data protection regulators need to identify the opportunities in terms of prosperity, well-being and significant benefits, particularly for important public interests.

On the other hand, the widespread collection and use of massive amounts of personal data today -made possible through cloud computing, big data analytics and electronic mass surveillance techniques- is unprecedented.

The digital environment is determining:
- how people communicate, consume and contribute to social and political life in the post big data world;
- how businesses organise themselves to make profits;
- how governments interpret their duty to pursue public interests and protect individuals; and
- how engineers design and develop new technologies.

2.1 The International Dimension

Data protection laws are national, but personal information is not. As a result, the international dimension of data protection has, for years, been the subject of much debate.

In such a global scenario, a clear and modern, future-oriented set of rules is also the key to solving Europe's digital challenge.

The popularity of the internet can largely be attributed to the way it has tapped into our social nature. Whether or not new products and technologies appeal to us, together with our desire to stay safe and not appear foolish, determines whether they will have mass appeal. But the widespread collection of massive amounts of our personal information is taking the control of their personal information away from individuals and limiting their ability to engage freely in the digital world.

Big data that deals with large volumes of personal information implies greater accountability towards the individuals whose data are being processed. People want to understand how algorithms can create correlations and assumptions about them, and how their combined personal information can turn into intrusive predictions about their behaviour.

Digital technologies need to be developed according to data protection principles, giving more say to individuals on how and why their information can be used, with more informed choice where relevant. This means we must put an end to opaque privacy policies, which encourage people to tick a box and sign away their rights.

Our values and our fundamental rights are not for sale. The new technologies should not dictate our values, and we should be able to benefit both from the new technologies and our fundamental rights.

One solution is to assess the ethical dimension beyond the application of the data protection rules. Organisations, companies and public authorities that handle personal information are responsible for how that information is collected, exchanged and stored, irrespective of whether these decisions are taken by humans or algorithms. An ethical approach to data processing recognises that feasible, useful or profitable does not equal sustainable. It stresses accountability over mechanical compliance with the letter of the law.

2.2 Forging Global Partnerships

Accountability in handling personal information is a global challenge.

An ethical dimension to data protection involves reaching out beyond the community of EU officials, lawyers and IT specialists towards thinkers who are equipped to judge the medium to long-term implications of technological change and regulatory responses.

The EDPS will work closely with his national colleagues to reinforce cooperation and encourage the EU to speak with one voice in the global fora on privacy and data protection matters.

He will invest in dialogue with IT experts, with industry and civil society to explore how to improve international cooperation, including arrangements for existing and future data-flows, in the interests of the individual.

The EDPS will also invest in global partnerships with fellow experts, non-EU countries, authorities and international organisations to work towards a social consensus on principles that can inform binding laws and the design of business operations and technologies and the scope for interoperability of different data protection systems.

2.3 A New Chapter for EU Data Protection

The EU currently occupies a privileged position as the point of reference for much of the world on privacy and data protection. But for the EU to continue being a credible leader in the digital age, it must act on its own fundamental principles of privacy and data protection, and it must act quickly.

The reform should not slow down innovation, but equally it should ensure that our fundamental rights are safeguarded in a modern manner and made effective in practice, to rebuild the trust in the digital society that has been eroded not least by covert and disproportionate surveillance.

It is vital to make data protection easier, clearer and less bureaucratic, so that it will underpin the digital world now and into the future. Technologies will continue to develop in a manner that is unpredictable even for their designers.

Individuals, public authorities, companies and researchers now need a rulebook which is unambiguous, comprehensive and robust enough to last two decades and that can be enforced as required by the European and national courts as well as by truly independent data protection authorities. It needs to uphold the rights of the online generation growing up today.

In a modernised regulatory framework for the digital economy of the future, big data protection can be a driver for sustainable growth. A solid EU Digital Agenda can build on a solid foundation of modern data protection.

The way Europe responds to the challenges it faces will serve as an example for other countries and regions around the world grappling with the same issues.

3 Accountability of EU Bodies

EU bodies, including the EDPS, must be fully accountable for how they process personal information, because to demonstrate exemplary leadership we must be beyond reproach.

The EDPS aims to be more selective, intervening only where there are important interests at stake or interventions that can clearly lead to an improved data protection culture and encourage accountability within EU institutions, embedded as a part of their day to day good administration, not as a separate discipline.

4 Time for an Entirely New Conversation on Security and Privacy

Public security and combating crime and terrorism are important public objectives. However, unnecessary, disproportionate or even excessive surveillance by or on behalf of governments sows mistrust and undermines the efforts of lawmakers to address common security concerns.

The EU has struggled in recent years to identify effective measures that do not excessively interfere with the fundamental rights to privacy and data protection; measures that are necessary, effective and proportionate. The priority should be a coherent and systematic mechanism for tracking the behaviour and movements of known criminal and terrorism suspects, not the indiscriminate collection of personal data.

Scrutiny of the necessity and proportionality of specific measures to fight crime and terrorism warrant a broad debate. These are principles enshrined in the Charter of Fundamental Rights as applied in the case law of the Court of Justice of the EU, high-level legal requirements of EU law that the EDPS is tasked with safeguarding. As an independent authority, the EDPS is not automatically for or against any measure; but fully committed to his mission of advising the EU institutions on the implications of policies which have a serious impact on these fundamental rights.

By considering the Data Protection Reform as a package, and by considering how existing and future bilateral and international agreements can work in a more balanced way, we have to establish a clear and comprehensive set of principles and criteria which law enforcement and national security must respect when they interfere with our fundamental rights.

5 The Action Plan

5.1 Data Protection Goes Digital

ACTION 1: Promoting technologies to enhance privacy and data protection
- work with communities of IT developers and designers to encourage the application of privacy by design and privacy by default through privacy engineering;
- promote the development of building blocks and tools for privacy-friendly applications and services, such as libraries, design patterns, snippets, algorithms, methods and practices, which can be easily used in real-life cases;
- expand the Internet Privacy Engineering Network (IPEN) to work with an even more diverse range of skill groups to integrate data protection and privacy into all phases of development of systems, services and applications;
- provide creative guidance on applying data protection principles to technological development and product design;
- highlight that data protection compliance is a driver for consumer trust and more efficient economic interaction, and hence can encourage business growth;
- work with academia and researchers in the public and private sectors focusing on innovative fields of technical developments that affect the protection of personal data, in order to inform our technology monitoring activities.

ACTION 2: Identifying cross-disciplinary policy solutions
- initiate and support a Europe-wide dialogue amongst EU bodies and regulators, academics, industry, the IT community, consumer protection organi-sations and others, on big data, the internet of things and fundamental rights in the public and private sector;
- work across disciplinary boundaries to address policy issues with a privacy and data protection dimension;
- initiate a discussion on broad themes which integrates insights from other fields, and coordinate training efforts to familiarise staff with these related disciplines.

ACTION 3: Increasing transparency, user control and accountability in big data processing
- develop a model for information-handling policies, particularly for online services provided by EU bodies, which explains in simple terms how business processes could affect individuals' rights to privacy and protection of personal data, including the risks for individuals to be re-identified
- from anonymised, pseudonymous or aggregated data;
- encourage the development of innovative technical solutions for providing information and control to users, reducing information asymmetry and increasing users' autonomy.

5.2 Forging Global Partnerships

ACTION 4: Developing an ethical dimension to data protection
- establish an external advisory group on the ethical dimension of data protection to explore the relationships between human rights, technology, markets and business models in the 21st century;
- integrate ethical insights into our day-to-day work as an independent regulator and policy advisor.

ACTION 5: Mainstreaming data protection into international agreements
- advise EU institutions on coherently and consistently applying the EU data protection principles when negotiating trade agreements (as well as agreements in the law enforcement sector), highlighting that data protection is not a barrier but rather a facilitator of cooperation;
- monitor the implementation of existing international agreements, including those on trade, to ensure they do not harm individuals' fundamental rights.

ACTION 6: Speaking with a single EU voice in the international arena
- promote a global alliance with data protection and privacy authorities to identify technical and regulatory responses to key challenges to data protection such as big data, the internet of things and mass surveillance;
- cooperate with national authorities to ensure more effective coordinated supervision of large scale IT systems involving databases at EU and national levels, and encourage the legislator to harmonise the various existing platforms;
- maximise our contribution to discussions on data protection and privacy at international fora including the Council of Europe and the OECD;
- develop our in-house expertise on comparative data protection legal norms.

5.3 Opening a New Chapter for EU Data Protection

ACTION 7: Adopting and implementing up-to-date data protection rules
- urge the European Parliament, the Council and the Commission to resolve outstanding differences as soon as possible on the data protection reform package;
- seek workable solutions that avoid red tape, remain flexible for technological innovation and cross-border data flows and enable individuals to enforce their rights more effectively on and offline;
- focus during the post-adoption period on encouraging correct, consistent and timely implementation, with supervisory authorities as the main drivers;
- in the event that the EDPS provides the Secretariat for the new European Data Protection Board (EDPB), allow this body to be ready on 'day one' in close cooperation with national colleagues, in particular by ensuring proper transitional arrangements are in place to enable a seamless handover from the Article 29 Working Party;
- work in partnership with authorities through the EDPB to develop training and guidance for those individuals or organisations that collect, use, share and store personal information in order to comply with the Regulation by the beginning of 2018;
- engage closely in the development of subsequent implementing or sector-specific legislation;
- develop a web-based repository of information on data protection as a resource for our stakeholders.

ACTION 8: Increasing the accountability of EU bodies processing personal information
- work with the European Parliament, Council and Commission to ensure current rules set out in Regulation 45/2001 are brought into line with the General Data Protection Regulation and a revised framework enters into force by the beginning of 2018 at the latest;
- continue to train and guide EU bodies on how best to respect in practice data protection rules, focusing our efforts on types of processing which present high risks to individuals;
- continue to support EU institutions in moving beyond a purely compliance-based approach to one that is also based on accountability, in close cooperation with data protection officers;
- improve our methodology for inspections and visits, in particular a more streamlined method for inspecting IT systems.

ACTION 9: Facilitating responsible and informed policymaking
- develop a comprehensive policy toolkit for EU bodies, consisting of written guidance, workshops and training events, supported by a network;
- each year identify the EU policy issues with the most impact on privacy and data protection, and provide appropriate legal analysis and guidance, whether in the form of published opinions or informal advice;
- increase our in-house knowledge of specific sectors so that our advice is well-informed and relevant;
- establish efficient working methods with the Parliament, Council and Commission and actively seek feedback on the value of our advice;
- develop our dialogue with the Court of Justice of the EU on fundamental rights and assist the Court in all relevant cases, whether as a party or an expert.

ACTION 10: Promoting a mature conversation on security and privacy
- promote an informed discussion on the definition and scope of terms such as national security, public security and serious crime;
- encourage the legislators to practically collect and examine evidence from Member States (in closed sessions if required) that require the collection of large volumes of personal information, for purposes such as public security and financial transparency, which would interfere with the right to privacy, to inform our advice to the EU legislator on necessity and proportionality;
- promote convergence between the different laws on data protection in the areas of police and judicial cooperation, as well as consistency in the supervision of large scale IT systems. This should include the swift adoption of the draft Directive on the processing of data for the purposes of prevention, investigation, detection or prosecution of criminal offences.

6 The EDPS Opinion on the GDPR

The EDPS Opinion on the GDPR is the first milestone in the EDPS strategy. Building on discussions with the EU institutions, Member States, civil society, industry and other stakeholders, our advice aims to assist the participants in the trilogue in reaching the right consensus on time. It addresses the GDPR in two parts:
- the EDPS vision for future-oriented rules on data protection, with illustrative examples of our recommendations; and
- an annex with a four-column table for comparing, article-by-article, the text of the GDPR as adopted respectively by Commission, Parliament and Council, alongside the EDPS recommendation.

The Opinion is published on the EDPS website and via a mobile app. It will be supplemented in autumn 2015 once the Council has adopted its General Position for the directive, on data protection applying to police and judicial activities.

6.1 A Rare Opportunity: Why this Reform is so Important

The EU is in the last mile of a marathon effort to reform its rules on personal information. The General Data Protection Regulation will potentially affect, for decades to come, all individuals in the EU, all organisations in the EU who process personal data and organisations outside the EU who process personal data on individuals in the EU. The time is now to safeguard individuals' fundamental rights and freedoms in the data-driven society of the future.

Effective data protection empowers the individual and galvanises responsible businesses and public authorities. The GDPR is likely to be one of the longest in the Union's statute book, so now the EU must aim to be selective, focus on the provisions which are really necessary and avoid detail which as an unintended consequence might unduly interfere with future technologies.

It is for the Parliament and the Council as co-legislators to determine the final legal text, facilitated by the Commission, as initiator of legislation and guardian of the Treaties. The EDPS is not part of the 'trilogue' negotiations, but legally competent to offer advice to help guide the institu-

tions towards an outcome which will serve the interests of the individual. His recommendations stay within the boundaries of the three texts, driven by three abiding concerns:
- a better deal for citizens,
- rules which will work in practice,
- rules which will last a generation.

6.2 A Better Deal for Citizens

EU rules have always sought to facilitate data flows, both within the EU and with its trading partners, yet with an overriding concern for the rights and freedoms of the individual..

The reformed framework needs to maintain and, where possible, raise standards for the individual. Existing principles set down in the Charter, primary law of the EU, should be applied consistently, dynamically and innovatively so that they are effective for the citizen in practice. The reform needs to be comprehensive, hence the commitment to a package, but as data processing is likely to fall under separate legal instruments there must be clarity as to their precise scope and how they work together, with no loopholes for compromising on safeguards.

For the EDPS, the starting point is the dignity of the individual which transcends questions of mere legal compliance The point of reference is the principles at the core of data protection, that is, Article 8 of the Charter of Fundamental Rights.

1. Definitions: let's be clear on what personal information is
- Individuals should be able to exercise more effectively their rights with regard to any information which is able to identify or single them out, even if the information is considered 'pseudonymised'.

2. All data processing must be both lawful and justified
- The requirements for all data processing to be limited to specific purposes and on a legal basis are cumulative, not alternatives. Conflation and thereby weakening of these principles should be avoided. Instead, the EU should preserve, simplify and operationalise the established notion that personal data should only be used in ways compatible with the original purposes for collection.
- Consent is one possible legal basis for processing, but we need to prevent coercive tick boxes where there is no meaningful choice for the individual and where there is no need for data to be processed at all.
- The EDPS supports sound, innovative solutions for international transfers of personal information which facilitate data exchanges and respect data protection and supervision principles. Permitting transfers on the sole basis of legitimate interests of the controller provides insufficient protection for individual. The EU should not open the door for direct access by third country authorities to data located in the EU. Third country requests should only be recognised where respecting the norms established in Mutual Legal Assistance Treaties, international agreements or other legal channels for international cooperation.

3. More independent, more authoritative supervision
- The EU's data protection authorities should be ready to exercise their roles the moment the GDPR enters into force, with the European Data Protection Board fully operational as soon as the Regulation becomes applicable.
- Authorities should be able to hear and to investigated complaints and claims brought by data subjects or bodies, organisations and associations.
- Individual rights enforcement requires an effective system of liability and compensation for damage caused by the unlawful data processing. Given the clear obstacles to obtaining redress in practice, individuals should be able to be represented by bodies, organisations and associations in legal proceedings.

6.3 Rules which will Work in Practice

Safeguards should not be confused with formalities. Excessive detail or attempts at micromanagement of business processes risks becoming outdated in the future.

Each of the three texts demands greater clarity and simplicity from those responsible for processing personal information. Equally, technical obligations must also be concise and easily-understood if they are to be implemented properly by controllers.

1. Effective safeguards, not procedures
- Documentation should be a means not an end to compliance: a scalable approach which reduces documentation obligations on controllers into single policy on how it will comply with the regulation taking into account the risks, is recommended.
- On the basis of explicit risk assessment criteria, and following from experience of supervising the EU institutions, notification of data breaches to the supervisory authority and data protection impact assessments should be required only where the rights and freedoms of data subjects are at risk.
- Industry initiatives, whether through Binding Corporate Rules or privacy seals, should be actively encouraged.

2. A better equilibrium between public interest and personal data protection
- Data protection rules should not hamper historical, statistical and scientific research which is genuinely in the public interest. Those responsible must make the necessary arrangements to prevent personal information being used against the interest of the individual.

3. Trusting and empowering supervisory authorities
- We recommend allowing supervisory authorities to issue guidance to data controllers and to develop their own internal rules of procedure in the spirit of a simplified, easier application of the GDPR by one single supervisory authority (the 'One Stop Shop') close to the citizen ('proximity').
- Authorities should be able to determine effective, proportionate and dissuasive remedial and administrative sanctions on the basis of all relevant circumstances.

6.4 Rules which will Last a Generation

Directive 95/46/EC, has been a model for further legislation on data processing in the EU and around the world. This reform will shape data processing for a generation which has no memory of living without the internet. The EU must therefore fully understand the implications of this act for individuals, and its sustainability in the face of technological development.

Recent years have seen an exponential increase in the generation, collection, analysis and exchange of personal information. Judging by the longevity of Directive 95/46/EC, it is reasonable to expect a similar timeframe before the next major revision of data protection rules. Long before this time, data-driven technologies can be expected to have converged with artificial intelligence, natural language processing and biometric systems.

These technologies are challenging the principles of data protection. A future-oriented reform must therefore be based on the dignity of the individual and informed by ethics and address the imbalance between innovation in the protection of personal data and its exploitation.

1. Accountable business practices and innovative engineering
- The reform should reverse the recent trend towards secret tracking and decision making on the basis of profiles hidden from the individual.
- The principles of data protection by design and by default are necessary for requiring the rights and interests of the individual to be integrated in product development and default settings.

2. Empowered individuals
- Data portability is the gateway in the digital environment to the user control which individuals are now realising they lack.

3. Future-proofed rules
- We recommend avoiding language and practices that are likely to become outdated or disputable.

7 Conclusion

Facing unprecedented challenges, caused by major technological and social developments, confronted with a complete review of the very foundations of EU data protection law, the EDPS has designed a strategy that in order to be able to make, in cooperation and jointly with the other data protection authorities, the maximum possible contribution to addressing issues which concern human dignity and the basic values of our society. This strategy serves to focus scarce resources on clear priorities and to work in the most efficient way.

Future Ecosystems for Secure Authentication and Identification

Abstract

Username/Password is still the prevailing authentication mechanism for internet based services – but it is not secure! We show how new authentication and identification mechanisms focused on usability and security can change this and which role the FIDO Alliance plays within this new user-centric approach.

Part 1 | A brief outline of the FIDO approach

Malte Kahrs

MTRIX GmbH, Stadtkoppel 23a, 21337 Lüneburg
malte.kahrs@mtrix.de

1 Today's Authentication Infrastructure: Security vs. Usability

In today's authentication infrastructure with dozens of different passwords to remember, most users choose weak passwords or utilize the same e-mail address and password combinations on multiple websites. Thereby online fraud is easier and attackers are able to use the stolen login credentials to log into several websites associated with their victims. In the end online service providers are faced with constantly increasing costs caused by online fraud.

Therefore strong online authentication has become a more and more important requirement. Unfortunately most solutions for strong security are complex, expensive and harder to use – especially with mobile devices. As a result of the poor usability most users/employees don't utilize strong authentication methods if they can avoid it. Enterprises on the other hand have to face huge costs for strong authentication mechanisms and then are tied to one vendor.

So ideally, a future ecosystem for secure authentication and identification has to meet all these requirements from consumers, online service providers and enterprises at the same time: strong authentication methods, privacy, usability as well as interoperability among different authentication devices. In the light of these issues the FIDO (Fast IDentity Online) Alliance was formed in July 2012.

2 FIDO – Simpler and stronger Authentication

The FIDO Alliance is a non-profit organization nominally formed in July 2012 with the goal of revolutionizing online authentication with an industry-supported, standards-based open protocol which not only brings users more security but is also easy and convenient to use. This new standard for security devices and browser plugins permits any website or cloud application to interface with a broad variety of existing and future FIDO-enabled devices.

The core ideas driving the FIDO Alliance's efforts are:
- Making strong authentication secure and easy to use
- Protecting consumers privacy (for more information please see „The FIDO Alliance: Privacy Principles Whitepaper"[1])
- Reducing costs resulting from exposure to breaches for online service providers
- Lowering infrastructure costs and complexity for enterprises

Within the final 1.0 specifications, published in December 2014, there are two FIDO protocols that reflect different use cases – UAF (a passwordless user experience) and U2F (a second factor user experience). While they have been developed in parallel and are separate within the final 1.0 specifications, it can be expected that the two different protocols will harmonize in the future. (For more information on FIDO Authentication and the 1.0 specifications please see „The FIDO Alliance: December 2014 Whitepaper"[2])

Both protocols share common FIDO design principles regarding ease of use and privacy:
- No 3rd party in the protocol
- No secrets on the server side, only public cryptographic keys
- Biometric data (if used) never leaves the device
- No link-ability between services
- No link-ability between accounts

3 FIDO: A short history – From early Deployments to 2015

Ever since the FIDO Alliance was formed in summer 2012 with six founding members it is picking up steam. When in February 2014 the FIDO Alliance issued draft specifications for public review, and in December 2014, the final 1.0 specifications were made available, many big industry players, like Bank of America, Google, Intel, Lenovo, MasterCard, PayPal, RSA, Samsung, Visa and Yubico, have joined the Alliance. Parallel to the work on the specifications already several mass-scale FIDO deployments were launched in the market:

In February 2014 PayPal and Samsung announced the first FIDO deployment, a collaboration that enables Samsung Galaxy S5 users to login and shop with the swipe of a finger wherever PayPal is accepted. The Samsung device is equipped with a fingerprint sensor from Synaptics and to enable the new payment system the Nok Nok Labs S3 Authentication Suite was selected. In September 2014 Alipay followed PayPal.

---

1 https://fidoalliance.org/assets/images/general/FIDO_Alliance_Whitepaper_Privacy_Principles.pdf
2 https://fidoalliance.org/wp-content/uploads/FIDOMessagingWPv1.pdf

In October 2014 the first U2F deployment was launched by Google and Yubico. Thereby Google Chrome became the first browser to implement FIDO standards. As the second factor every compatible security key can be used (e.g. YubiKey or Plug-up-Key).

In February 2015 Microsoft announced it would eventually support future FIDO 2.0 protocols in Windows 10.

In June 2015 the FIDO Alliance introduced a new class of membership for government agencies reflecting the particular interests of governments in securing cyberspace with FIDO authentication and identification.

On June 30, 2015, the FIDO Alliance released two new protocols that support Bluetooth Technology and Near Field Communication (NFC) as transport protocols for U2F. As of August 2015, FIDO specifications 2.0. are under development.

4 FIDO and beyond – Visions for a user-centric Identity Ecosystem

While FIDO focuses on authentication mechanisms, the design principles are based on common visions for a future user-centric Identity ecosystem – as described e.g. from the National Strategy for Trusted Identities in Cyberspace (NSTIC), an US-initiative created by the White House in 2011:

> „The Strategy's vision is:
>
> Individuals and organizations utilize secure, efficient, easy-to-use, and interoperable identity solutions to access online services in a manner that promotes confidence, privacy, choice, and innovation.
>
> The realization of this vision is the user-centric "Identity Ecosystem" described in this Strategy. It is an online environment where individuals and organizations will be able to trust each other because they follow agreed upon standards to obtain and authenticate their digital identities — and the digital identities of devices. The Identity Ecosystem is designed to securely support transactions that range from anonymous to fully-authenticated and from low- to high-value. The Identity Ecosystem, as envisioned here, will increase the following:
> - **Privacy** protections for individuals, who will be able trust that their personal data is handled fairly and transparently;
> - **Convenience** for individuals, who may choose to manage fewer passwords or accounts than they do today;
> - **Efficiency** for organizations, which will benefit from a reduction in paper-based and account management processes;
> - **Ease-of-use**, by automating identity solutions whenever possible and basing them on technol-ogy that is simple to operate;
> - **Security**, by making it more difficult for criminals to compromise online transactions;
> - **Confidence** that digital identities are adequately protected, thereby promoting the use of online services;

- *Innovation*, by lowering the risk associated with sensitive services and by enabling service providers to develop or expand their online presence;
- *Choice*, as service providers offer individuals different—yet interoperable—identity credentials and media"[3]

Therefore it was a logical step that in June 2015 the FIDO Alliance introduced a new class of membership for government agencies with United States NSTIC/NIST and United Kingdom Office of the Cabinet first to join. In other governmental institutions all around the world there are as well considerations on user-centric identity Ecosystems and how therefore the FIDO approach can be combined with identification mechanisms – e.g. from D-Trust, the accredited trust center of the German Bundesdruckerei.[4]

5 Conclusion

The fast evolution which has taken place since the foundation of the FIDO Alliance and the immediate deployments of global players like PayPal, Samsung and Google reflect how pressing the need for such authentication standards has been in the market. With all those joint industries and institutions responding to user demands we expect FIDO clearly to play a major role in a future ecosystem for secure authentication and identification.

---

3 https://www.whitehouse.gov/sites/default/files/rss_viewer/NSTICstrategy_041511.pdf
4 „Authentification and Identification – talking the user into account", Dr. Kim Nguyen, D-Trust GmbH

Part 2 | Authentication and Identification – Taking the User into Account

Dr. Kim Nguyen

Bundesdruckerei GmbH/D-Trust GmbH, Oranienstraße 91, 10969 Berlin
kim.nguyen@bdr.de

1 Introduction

Security breaches in the context of web based services and networks are everywhere, ranging from stolen passwords to the hijacking of complete digital identities. The heartbleet phenomena has shown that even existing protocol frameworks can be used for password exploitations, that even cannot be detected by standard systems.

From a technological perspective, hardware based (two factor) authentication is a good answer to many of these challenges, however one has to concede that a broad acceptance for these mechanisms is clearly missing outside certain small closed user groups.

We argue, that this is not due to the lack of technical functionality, but rather due to the lacking user acceptance.

The game can only be won when a concept can be found in which user acceptance, security, privacy and easy integration can be combined. We aim at introducing such a new concept in this article.

2 IT technology – past and present

From the perspective of today, the availability of IT technology and services can hardly be compared to that of twenty years, ago, maybe even not with that of five years ago.

Today's smartphones, and in fact it is quite hard NOT to receive such a phone with a new mobile contract, are using greater ressources of memory, processing capabilities and support a multitude of interfaces of various types and thus exceed typical PCs as in use only a few years ago.

Furthermore new mobile devices are always connected with the internet, while ten years ago internet connectivity has to be implemented manually via the landline. But even more striking than all these technological dimensions is the focus on usability and applications that sets new benchmarks that need to be met by all the connected technologies as well. For the first time in the history of large scale distribution of IT technology, the user can focus on the application itself – and not the underlying technologies.

The comprehensive usage of smartphones and tablets as a universal channel to perform transactions of various sorts is in many situations already reality, and will certainly become even more dominating for coming generations of users. (even accepting the fact that PCs will still be existing and in use). It is therefore clear that mobile devices of various sorts have already established themselves as a primary digital communication channel and hence as the prevalent key to services of different types.

The user experience that comes along with these new types of mobile devices, i.e. the complete focus on usability and intuitive handling, also has impact on the way how to implement and integrate mechanisms providing more security for the mentioned various services and applications, especially when these security mechanisms rely on hardware token or such like. Token based authentication will only prevail, when a deep integration of these mechanisms in the underlying operating system or applications is guaranteed. Formerly common ways of integration (implying and including installation of additional software components and of reader devices) will no longer be acceptable to users that have been growing up within a application focussed IT world.

Do we need additional security mechanisms at all? This is certainly the cases, and especially so in the case of mobile devices, where most or all applications typically are secured only by username/ password, a mechanism that neither has the required strength (especially if the user chooses to use same passwords over different applications) nor can be secured by the service providers in the appropriate way (every day brings us new indications of thousands and in some cases even millions of stolen passwords). Given the omnipresence of mobile devices in various application scenarios, it is on the other hand clear that more security is needed in order to secure at least critical services (either having a „financial" dimensions, i.e. online banking or payment, or having an „identity related" dimension, i.e. takeover of an identity in a social network).

The new application focussed world of IT users is opportunity as well as challenge for the providers of security tokens and technology: only if these will be compatible both technologically as well with respect to the user experience will they experience a larger acceptance.

3 Our technology – your problem

The offering of companies in the security business is still largely dominated by making available software modules (e.g. antivirus or encryption software) hardware (e.g. firewalls or other appliances) mostly in conjunction with associated tokens (chipcards or other form factors).

Todays offering is therefore still dominated by „technology" and not by „function/application". In this model the potential customer is requested to understand the problem he wants to solve and therefore to purchase the required technology building blocks to deal with this problem using the aforementioned providers.

Therefore in this scenario the providers wants to be seen and understood as provider of technology and not solutions. Furthermore in this context the user is in the end his own solution provider that builds the solution for his specific problem on the basis of the technology building blocks purchased.

However considering the fact that the dramatic increase of mobile usage is mostly based on operating systems like iOS and Android, which are totally focussed on Applications/Apps/solutions, the user here does not have the need to assemble different elements and combine them into one specific configuration. Hence, the main difference with respect to the previous situation, complete functionality and not only technologies are provided.

Considering the acceptance of token-based mechanisms this means in turns:

Not the functionality itself is of importance, but the integration of the token into a larger application context is where the user can experience a significant difference. Technologywise this implies especially that the integration should be both seamless as well as requiring only the absolute minimum of unser interaction. This especially implies that components should be provided either in pre-existing components of the operating system or should be provided server based. Furthermore existing interfacing technologies should be preferred as compared to additional interfaces that are being provided especially by additional hardware components.

The approach of the FIDO (Fast IDentity Online) Alliance, which will be introduced in the next section, follows this approach closely.

4 The FIDO approach

The FIDO Alliance is a non-profit organization nominally formed in July 2012 to address the lack of interoperability among strong authentication devices as well as the problems users face with creating and remembering multiple usernames and passwords. The FIDO Alliance aims at changing the nature of authentication by developing specifications that define an open, scalable, interoperable set of mechanisms that supplant reliance on passwords to securely authenticate users of online services. This new standard for security devices and browser plugins will allow any website or cloud application to interface with a broad variety of existing and future FIDO-enabled devices that the user has for online security. FIDO has gained a remarkable momentum over the last twelve months.

The FIDO falls in two main categories to address a wide range of use cases and deployment scenarios. FIDO protocols are based on public key cryptography and are strongly resistant to phishing.

4.1 Passwordless user experience

The passwordless FIDO experience is supported by the Universal Authentication Framework (UAF) protocol. In this experience, the user registers their device to the online service by selecting a local authentication mechanism such as swiping a finger, looking at the camera, speaking into the mic, entering a PIN, etc. The UAF protocol allows the service to select which mechanisms are presented to the user.

Once registered, the user simply repeats the local authentication action whenever they need to authenticate to the service. The user no longer needs to enter their password when authenticating from that device. UAF also allows experiences that combine multiple authentication mechanisms such as fingerprint + PIN. For details refer to [1, FIDO UAF Architectural Overview].

4.2 Second Factor User experience

The second factor FIDO experience is supported by the Universal Second Factor (U2F) protocol. This experience allows online services to augment the security of their existing password infrastructure by adding a strong second factor to user login. The user logs in with a username and password as before. The service can also prompt the user to present a second factor device at any time it chooses. The strong second factor allows the service to simplify its passwords (e.g. 4–digit PIN) without compromising security.

During registration and authentication, the user presents the second factor by simply pressing a button on a USB device or tapping over NFC. The user can use their FIDO U2F device across all online services that support the protocol leveraging built–in support in web browsers.

The core ideas driving FIDO are (1) ease of use, (2) privacy and security, and (3) standardization. For implementing authentication beyond a password (and perhaps an OTP), companies have traditionally been faced with an entire stack of proprietary clients and protocols.

FIDO changes this by standardizing the client and protocol layers. This ignites a thriving ecosystem of client authentication methods such as biometrics, PINs and second–factors that can be used with a variety of online services in an interoperable manner. For details refer to [1, FIDO U2F Architectural Overview].

4.3 Online Crypto Protocol Standardization:

FIDO standardizes the authentication protocol used between the client and the online service. The protocol is based on standard public key cryptography — the client registers a public key with the online service at initial setup. Later, when authenticating, the service verifies that the client owns the private key by asking it to sign a challenge. The protocol is designed to ensure user privacy and security in the current day state of the internet.

4.4 Client Standardization for Local Authentication

FIDO standards define a common interface at the client for the local authentication method that the user exercises. The client can be pre–installed on the operating system or web browser. Different authentication methods such as secure PIN, biometrics (face, voice, iris, fingerprint recognition, etc.) and second–factor devices can be "plugged in" via this standardized interface into the client.

5 FIDO and beyond – the role of identity based mechanisms

As described in the previous section the FIDO approach focuses mainly on the topic of authentication in two ways, namely u2f (strengthening a primarily username/password based infrastructures) and uaf (replacing password with various authentication possibilities).

For those use cases, where the authentication should also include a token based identification complementing the authentication, typically a Certification Authority (CA) comes into play.

Technically speaking we are referring here to certificate based mechanisms relying mostly on the definitions of the X.509 standard. However we would like to point out here that the main role of a CA lies in fact far beyond these technical considerations, the CA is in fact an institution that provides trustworthy services, amongst which the most prominent is that of reliable ID verification.

This is typically a new point in the discussion of the main properties of a CA, as these discussion mostly focus on technical matters, i.e. how is the certificate produced, how ist he key material handled, how are technical specifications adhered to. As any PKI based authentication mechanism relies on all these matters for its successfull technical completion, all this points are well worth considering, however the core of a „Trust service provider" needs a much broader discussion.

The certificate a CA issues is on the one hand a digital object, that can be used in various technical contexts. However, such a digital object may be produced by almost anyone technically versatile enough to set up the appropriate software and generate his own CA. Technically these certificates do not differ at all from those that are issued by a professional CA, so what is in fact the difference?

The paramount difference is a deeply non-technical one:

The certificate is much more than the digital object representing the certificate, it ist he manifestation of a process which in its core takes a conventional identity (e.g. an identity related to a person on the basis of an ID document) and transform this identity into another one – a derived identity – that is more suitable for usage in the relevant application context (e.g. a X.509 based certificate, a SAML token etc.).

Thus, the trust provided in the manifestation of a certificate etc. is mainly based not on technical issues but on the trustworthiness of the underlying processes, the high quality of the provided ID data as well as on the possibility for third parties to verify the integrity of the provided identity (based typically on technologies like OCSP, ldap etc.)

Only on the basis of such a trusted identification and verification ecosystem can a token integration into applications guarantee the provisioning of trustworthy and verifiable identities.

Different applications and the related transactions will require different levels of trustworthiness, as they typically will have different economic impact and intrinsic value. Hence also different trust levels should be used to reflect this observation in the context of token based authentication and identification within the mentioned identification and verification ecosystem. This is in fact something quite well known as we use such a layered approach to identification and authentication in everyday life: Different identification is needed when buying a house as opposed to entering the gym for the daily workout (to name two rather contrasting use cases), and when transferring authentication and identification from the "analogue" to the digital world, this is something that user expect to recognize in the new technologies as well.

But not only the process of identification and verification is of interest, this holds also for the process of the delivery of the derived identity to the user.

While in the "classical" world, the delivery is mostly restricted to providing the certificate on a suitable physical carrier (i.e. card or another physical token), in the new application- and integration scenarios different ways of delivery come to mind.

This especially refers to the fact, that the user already possesses a physical token, that can be used for authentication purposes (e.g. u2f or uaf enabled), but would like to add identity based mechanisms to the functionality of the token. In this case, a purely digital post-issuance scenario is attractive, in which the process of verification of an identity was already performed successfully (as the user is already known via his user account), or can be performed instantaneous using his ID or eID documents (preferably on the basis of mobile devices, like smartphones).

This is already reality for the German eID card using the sign-me system operated by Bundes-druckerei GmbH and D-Trust as trust service provider (see [2]), which can be used both as a means of identification as well as a carrier for a qualified certificate – in both cases fully digital and without the necessity for the user to handle paperbased documents at all.

The future lies clearly within the integration of various identification ways (resulting in different assurance levels as discussed above), preferably based on mobile usage, as well as new post-issu-ance scenarios, especially using token that are already well established with the user, for example from u2f or uaf authentication scenarios.

6 Conclusion

Summarizing, the future of hardware based authentication will rely on the following facts:

- Gaining user acceptance by deep and easy integration of hardware and software into ap-plications
- Accepting the fact that authentication and identification will need to rely on a layered approach using different assurance levels ranging from simple token based recognition up to identification on the highest level
- Providing means to "upgrade" the functionality as needed in the moment of the interac-tion with an appropriate service

The combination of the existing trust service provider portfolio with new token functionality and token integration offers a unique opportunity to provide strong authentication and/or identifica-tion where and when need arises.

References

[1] https://fidoalliance.org/specifications/download
[2] https://www.bundesdruckerei.de/en/798-sign-me

Encrypted
Communication

The Public Key Muddle –
How to Manage Transparent End-to-end
Encryption in Organizations

Gunnar Jacobson

Secardeo GmbH
gunnar.jacobson@secardeo.com

Abstract

We discuss the business requirements and available solutions for end-to-end encryption in the application areas of electronic mail, instant messaging, file exchange and voice over IP. We will show that many applications today rather fulfil the security requirements of a private user than those of an organization. Our special focus is on the provided key management schemes that often do not satisfy the business needs. Combining encryption products from different vendors can then lead to a public key muddle. For key management a universal X.509 based PKI meets today's business requirements best. We show how the consistent distribution of certificates and private keys to encryption applications on all user devices can be done. This will help to consolidate and automate key management processes leading to reduced operational security costs and high user satisfaction.

1 Introduction

1.1 Public Key Cryptography

Public key cryptography is available for almost forty years, now. Bob can publish his public key so anybody can use it to send him encrypted messages and only Bob may decrypt them using his private key. The promised scenario is that a user can exchange end-to-end encrypted messages with anybody in the world, reliably and without any efforts – from any device of that user. This scenario, however, has not become a reality, yet. What are the reasons?

Besides the ongoing academic discussions about cryptographic properties of asymmetric and symmetric ciphers or hash functions on one side and political interests and leverage on the other side there are two main practical issues that still defer the breakthrough of global end-to-end encryption:

1. The diversity of data formats and protocols using public key cryptography (encryption mechanisms)
2. The variety of trust models and distribution, retrieval and validation methods for public and private keys (key management)

Two major public key encryption standards are being used since their publication in the early 1990s: Pretty Good Privacy (PGP) and Secure Multipurpose Internet Mail Extensions (S/MIME) together with the X.509 framework [CDF+07] [RaTu10] [ITU12]. These standards are rather incompatible with respect to data formats and trust models and limitations of both have been shown up in the past. Many organizations have invested huge efforts in the establishment of X.509 PKIs while PGP is popular for academic and private users. There have been other messaging encryption standards before like X.400 and Privacy Enhanced Mail (PEM), but they did not succeed. On the other hand we see a number of new concepts in the fields of encryption for electronic mail, instant messaging or cloud based file exchange. Most of them are proprietary with new data formats, protocols and key management models and their major features and the consequences of using them are often not well understood.

In the following we will discuss the requirements for end-to-end encryption and its key management from a business perspective and we will show mechanisms and services that will satisfy the needs.

1.2 Business requirements for end-to-end encryption

Two years after Snowden's exposures many IT managers have accepted, that encryption is the only way to prevent from data interception by powerful attackers like intelligence agencies or professional industrial spies. They are also aware of the fact, that meanwhile the attackers place their tools inside the corporate network and that therefore end-to-end encryption of data becomes more and more mission critical. End-to-end encryption (E2EE) means, that a message is encrypted at its source and it cannot be decrypted until it reaches its final destination where it will be decrypted [Shir07]. Solid encryption is also a frequent requirement from compliance regulations like HIPAA, PCI-DSS, SOX or national data privacy laws.

What are the preconditions for a high level of distribution of E2EE?
- Encryption must be legally permissible and must not be bypassed by governmental backdoors.
- Encryption should be done completely transparent to the user.
- The efforts for a public key system should be as low as possible.

So, what are the typical business applications that require end-to-end encryption? In the following the major communication applications are listed:

1. Electronic Mail (e-mail)
2. Instant Messaging (IM)
3. File Exchange
4. Voice over IP (VoIP)

In the following we will discuss these applications, the relevant standards and popular products.

2 Encryption Applications

2.1 Electronic Mail

An e-mail can be encrypted with the e-mail client of the originator and it will be decrypted with the e-mail client of the recipient. Most popular e-mail clients like Outlook, Outlook 365, iOS mail, Mozilla or Notes support the S/MIME standard for this [RaTu10]. S/MIME supports digital certificates for the exchange of symmetric data encryption keys. A TLS encryption (Transport Layer Security) between client and e-mail server cannot offer E2EE, nor is this possible with a secure e-mail gateway (SEG). Here, only dedicated transport connections are encrypted. Access on unencrypted e-mails is possible by the server operators at any time. Fig. 1 shows the E2EE scenario between the organizations A and B and the site-to-site encryption scenario between the organizations C and D.

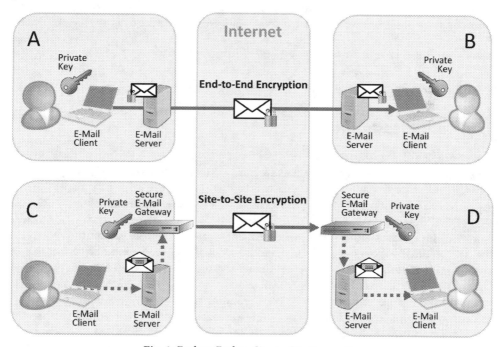

Fig. 1: End-to-End vs. Site-to-Site Encryption

There exist alternatives to S/MIME that are currently not widespread in the business area:
- Pretty Good Privacy (PGP)
- Identity Based Encryption (IBE)
- Dark Mail (DIME)

Pretty Good Privacy (PGP) offers a structured format for encrypted or signed data and a key container format [CDF+07]. It can be used for the protection of arbitrary files as well as for e-mail and message content. PGP requires additional plug-in software for the standard business e-mail clients, therefore its business use is limited to SEGs without E2EE. In the private sector, there are currently new evolvements driven by Google (end-to-end) and Yahoo and national approaches like DE-Mail. Key management is either done by bilaterally exchanging the public PGP keys or by the Web of Trust using so called trusted introducers.

IBE enables anybody to generate a public key from his e-mail address, e.g. "bob@company.com". A trusted third party (Master Key Server) generates the corresponding private key. For this, both the originator Alice and the recipient Bob have to trust the Master Key Server. The goal for IBE was to reduce the complexity of public key management. However it was shown in [FaST06] that the efforts for operating an IBE infrastructure is nearly the same as for a classical X.509 PKI. IBE has the following disadvantages:

- Does not fit with existing PKIs
- Key escrowing is done by the Master Key Server
- Poor standardization
- E-Mail plug-ins required for E2EE

There are further alternative developments for e-mail encryption. One interesting example is the Dark Internet Mail Environment (DIME) or "Dark Mail" covering also privacy of meta data [Levi14]. The protection of the originator and recipient addresses and subject fields is done using new protocols called Dark Mail Transfer Protocol and Dark Mail Access Protocol. Dark mail is a rather proprietary initiative driven by a few companies and currently it has the same disadvantages as IBE except for key escrowing.

2.2 Instant Messaging

Instant messaging (IM) is the spontaneous transfer of text messages ("chat") in a "push" manner. Very popular in the private sector is WhatsApp and in the business sector it is Microsoft Lync, now called "Skype for business". Although a standard exists for IM with XMPP [Sain11], the interoperability of IM products is rather poor as many vendors use proprietary extensions in their products. XMPP specifies E2EE based on PGP or S/MIME [Sain04], however S/MIME is rarely supported by IM products. In contrast, a different encryption scheme called off-the-record messaging (OTR) [BoGB04] is often used which fulfils specific IM requirements like Perfect Forward Secrecy (PFS) [DiOW92]. In OTR the key exchange is done using Diffie-Hellman key agreement and mutual authentication is done using DSA signatures. In order to establish trust in public DSA keys, a manual exchange and check of the corresponding fingerprint is required. This is acceptable in private communication but not for businesses. Table 1 shows the contrary requirements for messaging in a private chat using an IM system and in a business conversation using e-mail.

Besides OTR there are other proprietary developments like Threema or TextSecure. The latter's key agreement protocol has also been integrated with WhatsApp. Here, mutual authentication has also be done by manual comparison of key fingerprints.

The currently most widespread business IM system Lync 2013 does, at the time of this writing, not offer E2EE.

Table 1: Contrary requirements for messaging

Business E-Mail	Private IM/Chat
Non-Repudiability	**Repudiability**
The recipient wants to prove the originator to-wards a third person	In a chat nobody wants that a statement can be used against him.
Key Recovery	**Forward Secrecy**
An enterprise must be able to make e-mails reada-ble under controlled conditions.	Chats are volatile. A compromised key shall not be used for old or future chats.
Organisational Trust	**Bilateral Trust**
Keys must be trusted within the organisation.	Keys are exchanged directly with the partner.
Interoperability	**Proprietary Solution**
Vendor independence and security of investment have priority.	Both parties agree on the same preferred app.
Solution	**Solution**
→ S/MIME	→ OTR

2.3 File Exchange

For the exchange of files with colleagues or business partners similar privacy requirements exist as for the messaging scenarios. End-to-end encryption is a strong requirement and additionally the possibility of recovering encrypted files is important for a business use.

With its Encrypting File System (EFS) Microsoft provides a tool that is built in with the Windows OS. Encryption is transparently done using public keys from the partner's certificates. There exist a series of product alternatives and some of them also make use of certificates. Another alternative is the use of PGP for local file encryption.

The usage of cloud storage systems for the exchange of files but also the synchronization of different devices is more and more being used by company employees. The mobile usage increases rapidly.

A public cloud storage system such as Dropbox, Microsoft OneDrive or Google Drive allows users to store their data on a server in the public cloud and access them, regardless of their location, such as with a smart phone. Public cloud storage systems are especially being used for the spontaneous exchange of data with external partners. Many companies are operating a private cloud storage system, for example on the basis of MS Sharepoint or OwnCloud. These are offering a series of further collaboration services in addition to a server-side document storage. Managed cloud storage systems that are exclusively operated for a company by a provider in the cloud are a further variant.

The storage of data in a cloud storage system has many and sometimes very high risks. The cloud service providers offer security mechanisms for reliable registration, transportation security, encryption, data access, and de-duplication of data. The encryption of the data is done on the cloud storage system itself in the less favorable case. By this, the operator of a public cloud system or the administrator of a private cloud system has access to the keys and thus the data. In the better case, the encryption is done on the user's client. For this, a number of applications exist that perform end-to-end encryption on the devices. Many of these applications use public keys for exchanging symmetric data encryption keys. Popular examples are BoxCryptor or Viivo. However, both public key formats and data encryption formats are rather proprietary in most cases. Even worse, in some products the private key is stored and distributed to other user devices via a server of the product vendor – protected by a mostly weak user password. The vendor may also provide your partner's public keys for encrypting to them. On the other hand there exist some cloud encryption applications that make use of standards like OpenPGP (e.g. SecureZIP) or X.509 and S/MIME (e.g. certDrive).

2.4 VoIP

E2EE for Voice over IP can be provided by the Secure Real-Time Transport Protocol (SRTP) [BMN+04]. The SRTP RFC does not specify key management operations and refers to other standards like Multimedia Internet KEYing (MIKEY) [ACL+04]. MIKEY provides several methods to generate a master key via pre-shared key, public key or Diffie-Hellman (DH) key exchange. For public key based key exchange, X.509 certificates are used. Key pairs and certificates may be generated and provisioned to the phones from a central server. Cisco uses such an approach with X.509 certificates based on their SCCP protocol and their VoIP Unified Communications Manager. As an Alternative to MIKEY the ZRTP protocol has been standardized [ZiJC11]. It promotes DH key exchange and a Short Authentication String (SAS) that has to be compared manually by both peers. Digital signatures based on PGP keys or X.509 certificates are supported optionally. An example product that supports ZRTP is SilentPhone.

3 Key Management

3.1 Requirements on key management

For using E2EE the secure and efficient management of the keys being used is substantial. For E2EE the following requirements have to be fulfilled with respect to the management of public and private keys:
- The recipient's public key must be available anywhere.
- A public key must be definitely assignable to his owner.
- The validity of a public key must be determined free of doubt.
- The owner of a public key should have complete control over his private key.
- Your own private key must always be available there where you need it.
- A private key must be recoverable in case of loss.
- The key management processes must be extensively automatable.
- The method must be interoperable and it must be possible to use different products and services.

There are two major challenges for using public keys:
1. The public key of your partner must be trusted. An appropriate trust and validation scheme is needed.

2. Your private keys and the public keys of all your partners must be made available on your personal systems. Public and private key distribution mechanisms are required.

These challenges and existing solution alternatives will be discussed in the following.

3.2 Trust and validation

Besides it's cryptographic properties, the unambiguous assignment of a public key to his owner, who is often represented by an e-mail address, and the validity of the key are the most important properties of a public key. If someone succeeds to distribute a public key with another user's address, he may be able to read all messages, but not the intended recipient. Such events have been reported in the PGP domain [Schm15]. In order to establish trust in public keys currently different models are being used:

1. Bilateral Trust: The communicating parties Alice and Bob exchange their public keys manually in a reliable fashion, e.g. on a "crypto party". This model is feasible for individuals but it requires too high efforts for organizations.

2. "Web of Trust": Bob, whose public key Alice already trusts, approves the trust in the public key of a further person Dave by signing it. Now, Alice can also trust Dave's public key. There are, however, no reliable mechanisms to check the current validity of a public key. This model is implemented in the PGP world and is useful for private persons but not for organizations that want to govern an organization-wide trust policy.

3. Hierarchical Trust: The trust in public keys is established by a Certification Authority (CA) which is trusted by all users. The CA signs a digital certificate according to X.509 which contains the public key, the owner's name or address and further attributes [ITU12]. A CA can also have a certificate from a superior CA in a certification hierarchy. The validity of a public key can be verified using revocation lists (CRL) or online responders (OCSP). This model is suited well for organizations as it scales up and they can centrally govern all trust issues.

4. Intermediary Trust: Many new applications, mainly in the IM and the Cloud Storage sectors, receive the partner's public keys from their communication service provider (intermediary). Apple iMessage is a popular example for this. The intermediary must be completely trusted, as he is able to decrypt all messages that are transferred through him by passing a faked public key to the client. Organizations should carefully evaluate this model.

An X.509 based hierarchical PKI according to 3. is the preferred trust model for organizations. By using digital certificates they can govern the trust in all internal and external public keys – not only for persons but also for devices and computer services. Often an internal Windows PKI is being used here. The trust in the PKI of other organizations can be established by cross-certification or by participating in a Bridge CA which for example provides a Certificate Trust List. A popular example for this is the TeleTrusT European Bridge CA (EBCA). Another future option for establishing trust is the use of eIDAS Trusted Lists.

CA services are also being offered by commercial providers like Symantec, QuoVadis or Swiss-Sign. They offer Managed PKI services that provide an organization with certificates. The big advantage is, that the corresponding root certificates are already pre-configured in many systems and therefore the individual public key of a user is globally trusted.

3.3 Public key distribution

Public keys may be distributed in different ways. Some typical mechanisms are:

1. Bilaterally: A user may send his public key or certificate via e-mail to his partners. This can be done in combination with a signed e-mail. The partner then has to validate and import the key/certificate manually to his key/certificate store or address book.

2. Using a local directory: Public keys may be stored and retrieved from a directory. A typical platform is Microsoft Active Directory for providing certificates. This is usually limited to organization internal certificates.

3. Using an external key or certificate directory server: An external key or certificate directory server will securely publish your internal public keys or certificates and make them accessible to external partners and it will automatically search the internet for external partner's public keys or certificates. Standard clients may retrieve certificates using common protocols like LDAP or ActiveSync.

4. By your intermediary: As stated before, the communication intermediary can provide you with the required public keys from your partners.

5. Using DNS: DANE provides mechanisms for storing and retrieving certificates from the domain name system using DNSSEC [HoSc12]. OPENPGP defines this for PGP keys.

With respect to the trust requirements of a business the options 4. and 5. are not suited well for an enterprise. Option 1. will put the efforts on the user and therefore E2EE will either be refused by the users or it will cause significant manpower costs. So, a combination of 2. and 3. is a suitable solution for businesses. In [WVHJ] it has been shown, how large organizations successfully use a certificate directory server for frequent E2EE with external partners.

3.4 Private key distribution

In times when users are working on multiple devices where they want to have access to encrypted messages or files, it is important to provide the user's private keys on all his devices. Asymmetric key pairs may be generated either centrally in a trust center or de-centrally at the client. Private keys may be stored either within specific hardware like Trusted Platform Modules (TPM) or smart cards or as a software object within a client's key store. Smart cards have some very positive characteristics: They are highly secure and portable. On the other side they have poor support on mobile devices and they are, together with the required reader and middleware, rather expensive. These are the reasons why many organizations use software keys.

If the encryption application relies on an intermediary for the distribution of the private key to other user devices, as many cloud encryption or IM applications do, then a high level of trust is required in the intermediary and the used technology.

When using digital certificates from a Windows PKI, the key pairs are generated on the Windows client and a certificate request is then sent to the Windows Enterprise CA. By using auto enrollment this can be done automatically and combined with a central key archival mechanism. Now the question is, how will the user be able to decrypt his messages, for example on his iPhone? He could manually export the key from his Windows certificate store as a .PFX file, transfer it to his iPhone and manually import the key into the iOS key chain – pre-assuming, that a low Windows security option allows exporting of private keys. Such a procedure is time consuming, expensive and error-prone. Therefore, a solution is needed, that will help to automate the process. This can be done by a central service that integrates with the key archival mechanism and then automatically "pushes" the encrypted private keys to each user device. This can simply and reliably be performed by using e-mail or a specific web service. At the end the user is able to encrypt and decrypt messages and files on any of his devices. Combined with an external certificate directory server, the user can encrypt for any recipient. We call this desired scenario "any-to-any" encryption.

3.5 Inconsistent key management

If an organization chooses to buy products from different vendors for each of the discussed applications, then a mixture of key management schemes will be the result. Each E2EE application will need a different key pair K_e, K_i, K_f, K_v for a user. These key pairs have to be distributed to all of his devices, see fig. 2. For the key distribution different mechanisms will be used that are provided by an intermediary of the application service or a key server or it has to be done manually by the user. All key management issues like trust, validation, retrieval, recovery etc. have to be solved individually. This will lead to a public (and private) key muddle that causes significant efforts and cost on the operational side and user dissatisfaction on the other side.

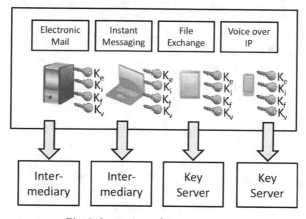

Fig. 2: Inconsistent key management

3.6 Consistent certificate and key distribution

In order to solve the issues discussed in 3.5 the E2EE applications will have to use a common key pair K_a and certificate of the user. The keys and certificates will be stored in a central key store of the operating system, e.g. the Windows certificate store or the iOS key chain. For this, services for the consistent distribution of certificates and private keys are needed, that are being used by all E2EE applications, see fig. 3:

- A certificate enrollment proxy for the manual or automated enrollment of certificates for Active Directory (AD) users from arbitrary internal or external public CAs. This can be enhanced by a key distribution service that "pushes" the private key K_a of a user securely to his mobile devices.

- A certificate directory server for securely publishing internal certificates and automatically finding external certificates in the PKI cloud. It will serve LDAP certificate search requests from Windows or ActiveSync requests from mobile clients.
- A key archive where the user's private keys are stored in encrypted form. Keys may be recovered in case of loss or damage by authorized Key Recovery Agents in compliance with corporate regulations.

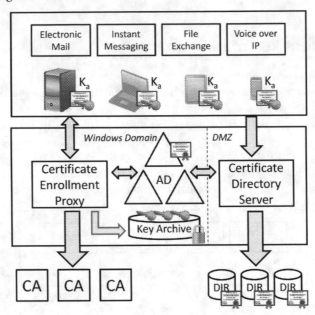

Fig. 3: Consistent certificate and key distribution

4 Conclusion – Cleaning up the public key muddle

We have discussed the end-to-end encryption options in the application fields of electronic mail, instant messaging, file exchange and voice over IP. We have seen that many E2EE applications today rather fulfil the security requirements of a private user than those of a business. In the private area many PGP based applications exist or applications that come with their internal, proprietary key management mechanisms. These key management schemes do not satisfy the business needs for trust, validation, key distribution and recovery. Combining such incompatible products from different vendors will as a consequence lead to a public key muddle that can hardly be managed.

For key management an X.509 based PKI meets today's business requirements best. X.509 certificates are well supported in all popular e-mail products and they are supported by selected products in the other application areas for instant messaging, (cloud based) file exchange and VoIP

There are thousands of companies that have invested in PKI in the last years in order to have a solid and universal key management platform. These companies are highly encouraged to select new encryption products with respect to compatibility with the existing PKI. Furthermore, these companies should invest in automation of their PKI processes in order to save money and gain user acceptance. Companies that already invested in rather proprietary solutions should rethink their strategy, because key-management efforts can explode when adding more such proprietary solutions into the IT infrastructure and users will be frustrated when too much interaction and product knowledge is required.

The discussion shows, that an X.509 based PKI is needed more and more – not only for encryption certificates but also for authentication of users, devices and services or even digital signatures. The fast growing Internet of Things will accelerate this demand for appropriate PKI technology and services.

References

[ACL+04] Arkko, Carrara, Lindholm, Naslund, Norrman: RFC 3830, MIKEY: Multimedia Internet KEYing, IETF 2004.

[BMN+04] Baugher, McGrew, Naslund, Carrara, Norrman: RFC 3711, The Secure Real-time Transport Protocol (SRTP), IETF 2004.

[BoGB04] Borisow, Goldberg, Brewer: Off-the-record communication, or, why not to use PGP. In: Proceedings of the 2004 ACM workshop on Privacy in the electronic society, ACM 2004.

[CDF+07] Callas, Donnerhacke, Finney, Shaw, Thayer: RFC 4880, OpenPGP Message Format, IETF 2007.

[DiOW92] Whitfield, Diffie, Van Oorschot, Paul C., Wiener, Michael J. Designs, Codes and Cryptography, Volume 2, Issue 2, 1992, pp 107-125.

[FaST06] Fay, Schweisgut, Tobias: Identitätsbasierte Kryptografie – Hindernisse auf dem Weg von der Theorie in die Praxis. In: Sicherheit 2006, Gesellschaft für Informatik e.V., 2006.

[HoSc12] Hoffman, Schlyter: RFC 6698, The DNS-Based Authentication of Named Entities (DANE), IETF 2012

[ITU12] International Telecommunication Union: ITU-T Recommendation X.509, Open systems interconnection – The Directory: Public-key and attribute certificate frameworks, ITU 2012.

[Levi14] Ladar Levison: Dark Internet Mail Environment Architecture and Specifications. Dark Mail Technical Alliance, 2014.

[RaTu10] Ramsdell, Turner: RFC 5751, Secure/Multipurpose Internet Mail Extensions (S/MIME) Version 3.2 Message Specification, IETF 2010.

[Sain04] Saint-Andre: RFC 3923, End-to-End Signing and Object Encryption for the Extensible Messaging and Presence Protocol (XMPP). IETF 2004.

[Sain11] Saint-Andre: RFC 6120, Extensible Messaging and Presence Protocol (XMPP): Core, IETF 2011.

[Schm15] Schmidt: Die Schlüssel-Falle – Gefälschte PGP-Keys im Umlauf. In: c't 6, Heise Verlag, 2015.

[Shir07] Shirey: RFC 4949, Internet Security Glossary, Version 2, IETF 2007.

[WVHJ] Wichmann, von der Heidt, Hille, Jacobson: Secure E-Mail Communication across Company Boundaries – Experiences and Architectures. In: ISSE 2009.

[ZiJC11] Zimmermann, Johnston, Callas. RFC6189, ZRTP: Media Path Key Agreement for Unicast Secure RTP, IETF 2011.

Overcoming Obstacles: Encryption for Everyone!

Mechthild Stöwer · Tatjana Rubinstein

Fraunhofer Institute for Secure Information Technology – SIT
Fraunhofer-Institut-Center Schloss Birlinghoven, D-53757 Sankt Augustin

{mechthild.stoewer | tatjana.rubinstein}@sit.fraunhofer.de

Abstract

Confidentiality protection is a request not only for companies but also for private users. Nevertheless the vast majority of users and companies have not adopted strong mechanisms as encryption yet. Lack of awareness may be the reasons for this. But even those companies that know about their risks related to a violation of information confidentiality often abstain from using encryption. As encryption can be applied to different levels of applications it is too difficult for them to develop a coherent strategy including a consistent key management. Another reason is that easy to handle solutions are still missing.

However, companies and private users have no alternative than to integrate encryption mechanisms in their applications if they handle critical and personal related data. To select the appropriate solutions in a first step the specific protection requirements for the data-in-transit and data-at-rest have to be analysed to select the encryption mechanisms that fit to the needs.

Fraunhofer-Institute Secure Information Technology – SIT has tackled the problem and developed a PKI based encryption solution in particular for the target group of inexperienced users to provide them with keys and certificates and an easy to handle application: E4E – Encryption for Everyone.

1 Introduction

Within the last ten years information and communication infrastructures have become one of the most important resources of companies. They are critical for processes with clients and service partners as well as for internal communication. This offers opportunities for companies' business models but also bears severe risks in particular for the smoothly process operations and for the confidentiality of stored and transferred information.

Larger enterprises invest significant parts of their IT budget to improve IT security whereas small and medium sized companies (SME) have difficulties to cope with the challenges. Though they are in the focus of attackers often basic security measures are not in place. To protect sensitive data and intellectual property encryption is a well-established measure which is insufficiently used in particular for E-Mails with confidential contents. According to a survey set up by the German ICT companies' association bitkom only 14% of employees are using E-mail encryption.

65% do not have the technical environment to use this measure. But also at those work places where encryption facilities are available they are not used by 20 % of the employees [1].

Reasons for this may be a lack of awareness related to threats and consequences of attacks, insufficient knowledge of how to handle encryption technologies and no information about appropriate solutions.

This is an alarming result as it may compromise the confidentiality of sensitive business information and the privacy of employees and business partners and put the business success of companies at severe risk.

2 Principles of confidentiality protection

The provision and usage of encryption facilities is part of the confidentiality concept of a company which at least should address the following aspects:

- Access rights should be designed according to the "need-to-know" principle.
- Interfaces to the company's network should be secured by firewall systems.
- Malware protection has to be up-to-date.
- The employees' awareness should be focussed on requirements of confidentiality protection by repeated training events.

The comprehensive use of encryption mechanisms goes beyond these measures and can be focussed on data-at-rest as well as data-in-transit. The following figure shows the targets of encryption.

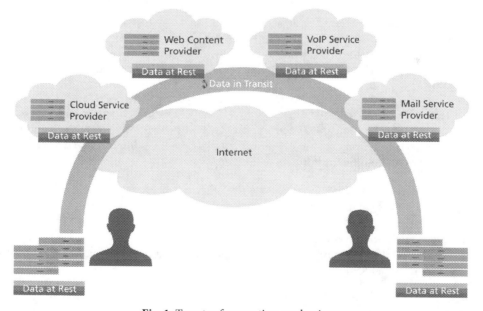

Fig. 1: Targets of encryption mechanisms

---

1 See iX – magazin für professionelle Informationstechnik, 30.6.2014, http://www.heise.de/ix/meldung/Befragung-Stand-der-E-Mail-Verschluesselung-ist-desastroes-2243124.html

Regarding the data-in-transit solutions the encryption mechanisms have to be designed for:
- Instant messaging
- Collaboration applications
- External (and where appropriate internal) Network access
- And in particular e-mail and voice communication

Data-at-rest can be encrypted on the level of
- Storage devices or parts of it
- Files

For all these systems and applications encryption facilities are available. S/MIME basing on PKIs or PGP for e-mail encryption, applications for hard disks' encryption or file encryption using features of office suites – all these options offer a wide range of chances.

But this overview also shows that it is not easy to develop a comprehensive encryption strategy. So many companies use encryption for some applications mostly basing on personal confidentiality estimation but there is no comprehensive view on the confidentiality requirements of the companies' information. This proceeding may cause severe problems:
- There is no companywide policy how to handle business critical or personal data. So neither management nor operative staffs has a directive how to proceed. It depends on personal considerations which mechanisms are used to enhance confidentiality when storing or transferring data.
- Different solutions could be in place which causes inefficient administrative efforts.
- Using encryption means using keys. If there is no comprehensive cryptographic concept there are no companywide agreed mechanisms for key storage to support long-term use and no instruments to control the dissemination of keys. This causes risks for the availability and authorised use of information.
- There are no recovery or emergency procedures which also may cause loss of keys and therefore the loss of encrypted data.
- There are no procedures to improve technology and processes as there are no indicators for monitoring and control.

The data encryption (both data-at-rest and data-in-transit) as a comprehensive managed process has to be integrated into companies' security management procedures. The target should be to establish a well-managed process on a high maturity level that is monitored and controlled by indicators to support continuous business process improvement.

This ambitious target should be on the agenda for larger companies and in particular for those whose business model is highly basing on their ICT infrastructure and those whose infrastructure is considerably exposed to the internet. Smaller companies or even private users will have significant difficulties to implement a coherent encryption strategy with a comprehensive system for managing keys. Development and maintenance of such a complex infrastructure requires a high level expertise that SMEs and private user do not have.

However, at least three steps to secure confidentiality of critical information should be performed [Kr15:51ff]:
1. Evaluation of data protection requirements
2. Threat analysis regarding confidentiality and integrity of transferred and stored data

3. Implementation of appropriate encryption solutions for storage and transfer of information

The example of a small trading firm illustrates the proceeding.

The company is managed by the owner who gets support by two employees. They use a laptop and two office PCs.

Step 1: Protection requirements

The company handles personal data with specific privacy requirements as information about employees or customer related data. It operates with information about its product portfolio, the calculations and suppliers – all data that should be kept confidential to secure the market position of this trade company. They have high protection requirements – appropriate mechanisms to secure confidentiality should be in place.

Step 2: Threads

The company is not a highly exposed organisation or a very attractive target for cyber-attacks. Nevertheless it could be affected by undirected attacks, attacks of unsatisfied employees or unintentional privacy violations by careless handling of files. A specific vulnerability is the mobile equipment. Unauthorized access may happen when the laptop is getting lost.

Step 3: Design of a solution using encryption to enhance confidentiality of information

When critical data as personal data or important business information are transferred they should be encrypted using an easy to handle tool. This requirement is a very specific challenge which is addressed by the "E4E – Encryption for Everyone" system which will be presented in the following.

For stored data different encryption tools should be used, e.g. encrypted USB sticks or tools for disk or container encryption to prevent unauthorized access.

3 Main obstacles for using encryption

The considerations above show that implementing a comprehensive encryption strategy requires a lot of specific know-how and mechanisms that have to be targeted at divers units. But even for SMEs which do not have this comprehensive approach technology which is available for an effective end-to-end encryption is not in use. This has mainly the following reasons [Her13:7ff]:

- Cryptographic keys are not available. There are very few organizations that provide users with trustworthy keys to encrypt e-mails. SMEs or private users have difficulties to find a provider of certificates that offers a low cost and trustworthy solution.
- Companies as well as private users handle a variety of e-mail applications (e.g. MS Outlook, Thunderbird, and diverse Webmail portals) with very different system architectures and interfaces. Most of the users are not experienced enough to activate encryption functionalities within these applications. In some cases this is even not possible (e. g. Webmail portals).
- For encrypted communication a sender needs the public key of the addressee. Up to now there is no infrastructure that supports the widely distribution of keys.

- The concept of using a pair of keys for asymmetric encryption is not intuitively comprehensible and for users with little IT knowledge not easy to understand. The commonly used metaphors describing the usage of a key to open access are not valid for the case of asymmetric encryption which makes it very difficult to communicate this concept. [Gaw06]

So there are two main obstacles that prevent unskilled users from using encryption technologies: the lack of keys and corresponding infrastructure and insufficient usability of available solution.

4 E4E – a contribution for problem solving

Seeing the demand for applications enhancing confidentiality of handled information Fraunhofer-Institute for Secure Information Technology – SIT – started a project providing non-experienced users with an easy-to-use encryption application following the principle of "usability by design". "Volksverschluesselung" – "E4E-Encryption for everyone" is a solution developed and operated by Fraunhofer SIT aiming on this target group. The application can be handled only with a few clicks and with no additional support.

The "E4E-Encryption for Everyone"-Solution includes client (E4E-Software) and server (PKI) components. Client software is actually running on Windows 7 or 8 and can be downloaded online. It is fully configured to acquire and install a new user certificate. A wizard supports users at every step of the process.

To increase the security quality of the digital certificates the user is required to identify him/herself. Current version of the software allows using a German Identity Card (nPA) but the authentication module can be flexible replaced with other acceptable proofs of identity, like Post IDENT or a personal authentication certificate issued by a trustworthy certificate authority.

E4E-Software permanently stores the current status of the user and selects the appropriate step to process further. If e.g. the certificate was successfully downloaded, the user jumps to the computer configuration screen to be able to install his certificate in his email client or browser.

The E4E-Software provides following features (figure 2):

1. Key generation and obtaining a personal digital certificate. The authenticated user generates a key pair locally. The keys will be securely stored in a key store on the user's computer. The user is not confronted with the certificate storage mechanisms – all keys will be automatically encoded and decoded with his Windows master password.

2. Configure user computer to encrypt/sign contents with the digital certificate.

3. Key and certificate management to export, import or revoke certificates.

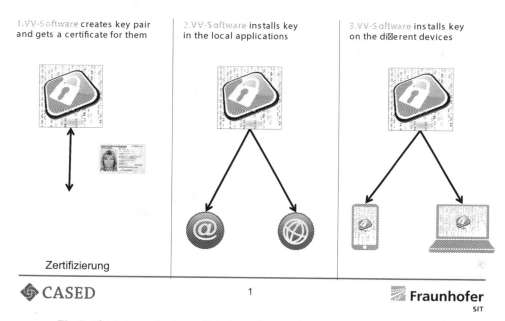

Fig. 2: Obtaining and using a digital certificate with E4E-Encryption for Everyone

The following sections give a short overview of these features.

4.1 Key generation

The system operates as follows:

- After having started the application, the e-mail address and identity of the applicant are verified. In order to verify the applicant's identity, the new German identity card is used, providing a secure, quick and easy procedure. At present, other ID-procedures are checked regarding security and usability.
- First name, surname, and title will be extracted from the personal ID card used for identification. Afterwards the cryptographic keys are generated on the user's PC without any configuration required from the user.
- Automatically, the public part of the key pair is certified with class 3-certificate by a trustworthy PKI run by Fraunhofer SIT.

4.2 Computer configuration

It is a real challenge for a non-expert user to associate the generated certificates to his email account [Fr12]. E-mail clients neither have any common interface nor standard procedure to install certificates. Applications and operation systems use different certificate stores and the user is not aware where these stores are located. E4E-Software takes control over this certificate installation process and

- Integrates the keys and certificates into the e-mail systems, the browsers and other cryptographic applications of the client without user interaction. Current version support integration with MS Outlook, Internet Explorer, Chrome, Firefox and Thunderbird. Figure 3 shows the computer configuration screen in the E4E-Software.
- Distributes certificates to other systems of the user as smartphones and tablets in a very user-friendly way.

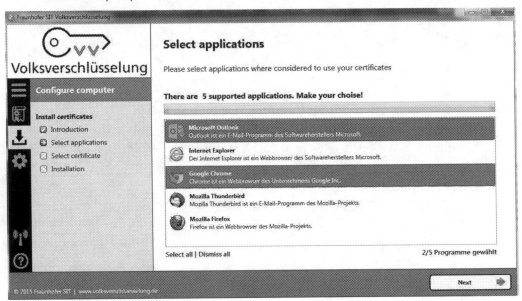

Fig. 3: Certificate Installation, Step 1: Select application to install certificate

4.3 Key management

The E4E-Software supports the user during the entire certificate validity period. The user will be timely notified if the certificate is soon to expire, or if the provide cryptographic algorithms are not considered secure any more. Since the certificates are encoded and stored in the local database they can be easily exported, imported or revoked (see figure 4) without been lost in comprehensive cryptographic concepts such as certificate store, asymmetric encoding and signing. All these operations are assisted by a wizard that leads the user through an entire management process.

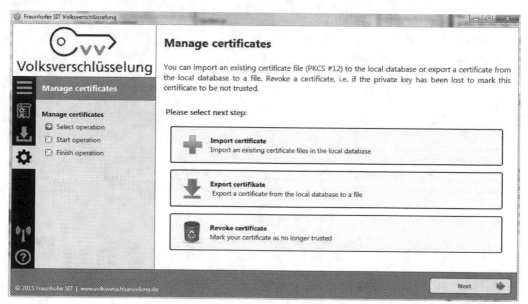

Fig. 4: Manage certificates in E4E-Software

4.4 Server components –PKI

Apart from political problems, a lack of usability is the main reason for the failure of public key infrastructures. There are a lot of usability problems that people are confronted with when trying to use a PKI [BAL05]. Usability issues stayed in the focus of E4E server component's design.

The central component of the application's infrastructure is a secure PKI that is realized by the open source software EJBCA that provides users with certificates and management support. Due to security reasons the CA will be managed offline. An online Registration Authority (RA) is responsible for accepting income digital certificates request. The RA component verifies and stores these requests and envelops them as Certificate Request Message Format (CRMF)-messages. The CA obtains messages through Certificate Management Protocol (CMP).

A directory service publishes certificates (if the user wants to), thus distributes keys to communication partners. The private part of the key pair will never be disclosed and always remains with the user.

Companies who want to run their own PKI can easily adopt this solution and integrate it into their enterprise IT environment.

4.5 Obstacles for encryption addressed by E4E

In chapter three four main obstacles have been identified that prevent users from applying encryption to enhance confidentiality of their information. E4E contributes to solve these problems:

1. No encryption keys available
   Fraunhofer SIT is a non-profit independent research institution developing the E4E-En-

cryption for Everyone -Software. E4E-Software generated "class 3"-keys which are secure and free of charge for a private user.

2. Heterogeneous system environment [Gar05]
   E4E-Software automatically installs certificates into the commonly used e-mail-applications and browsers such as MS Outlook, Thunderbird, Firefox, Google Chrome and Internet Explorer (s. figure 3).

3. Missing public keys
   Distribution of keys is a challenging task of an asymmetric encryption. "E4E-Encryption for Everyone" publishes produced certificates if the user confirmed it. Thus if the sender configured the E4E-Encryption for Everyone directory service, he can load the encoding certificate of the recipient.

4. Concept of asymmetric encryption is hard to comprehend as appropriate metaphors are missing
   The user interface can be handled intuitively, all process steps are supported by a wizard, so inexperienced users easily implement all components they need and use them for their applications.

The solution of Fraunhofer SIT intends to overcome the obstacles for using an end-to-end encryption by providing non-expert users with an easy to use system for confidential communication. This is a chance for a wide range of users, to protect their critical data, and to secure privacy.

All developments are open source. This makes the solution very flexible for developers and companies who want to run their own PKI. It can be adapted to specific requirements and because of the open interfaces integrated in existing environments.

5 Conclusion

All public discussions about targeted access to private information by intelligence services or economic espionage show that it is an important concern of companies as well as of private users to keep their (business) information confidential. In particular for SMEs it may be crucial for the existence of their companies. Encryption is still the strongest measure to secure confidentiality of data. Whereas larger companies with staff that is well-experienced in handling IT-security issues are able to build up complex infrastructures for confidentiality and privacy protection, smaller companies and private users are very reluctant to use encryption mechanisms. They need information about solutions and best practice examples how to apply these instruments. And – because of the complexity of this topic – they need support. Organisations and state funded initiatives that represent the interests of SMEs as chambers of commerce, SME associations, and economic development organisations should bring this topic on their agenda and start awareness campaigns and support SMEs with practical information.

Besides that, applications that fit to the needs of SMEs and private users have to be developed. The Fraunhofer SIT solution is a step in this direction. It provides non-experienced users with keys and certificates and an easy usable procedure to implement them in the system environment. This is a contribution to increase the proportion of encrypted information and by this enhancing the level of confidentiality protection.

References

[Bal05]   D. Balfanz, G. Durfee, and D.K. Smetters: Making the Impossible Easy: Usable PKI. Security and
            Usability. Chapter 16; O'Reilly Media, 2005

[Her13]   M. Herfert et al.: Privatspärenschutz und Vertraulichkeit im Internet, Darmstadt (2014)

[Kr15]   R. Kraft, F. Weber, M. Stöwer et al.: Vertraulichkeitsschutz durch Verschlüsselung; Strategien
            und Lösungen für Unternehmen, Darmstadt (2015)

[Fr12]   A. Fry, S. Chiasson, A. Somayaji: Not sealed but Delivered: The (Un)Usability of S/MIME Today;
            Annual Symposium of Information Assurance & Secure Knowledge Management (2012)

[Gar05]   S.L. Garfinkel, R. C. Miller. Johnny 2: a user test of key continuity management with S/MIME
            and Outlook Express; In Proc. of SOUPS 2005, ACM Press (2005), 13–24.

[Gaw06]   S. Gaw, E.W. Felten. and P. Fernandez-Kelly: Secrecy, flagging, and paranoia: adoption criteria in
            encrypted email; In Proc. of the SIGCHI Conference on Human Factors in Computing Systems
            , pages 591–600. ACM, 2006.

Securing Enterprise Email Communication on both Sides of the Firewall

Dr. Burkhard Wiegel

Zertificon Solutions GmbH
Alt-Moabit 91d, 10559 Berlin, Germany
info@zertificon.com

Abstract

Prior to the NSA affair [1], the threat to electronic enterprise communication was considered to be beyond the firewall. With the Snowden revelations[2] however and the increased use of mobile devices for business email, the need to secure communication from sender to recipient and within the corporate network has raised the awareness[3] for industrial scale end-to-end encryption.

This position paper explains the risks and pitfalls associated with the existing concepts of end-to-end encryption, presents the obstacles which have to be overcome and introduces alternative approaches to securing enterprise email communication.

Many solutions are available which deliver personal simple client-side encryption but which are limited to S/MIME whilst others combine a client and gateway organizational approach, which incorporate flexible delivery options as well as interfaces for anti-virus, anti-spam and data loss prevention tools.

This paper takes a closer look at the complex issue of creating and distributing the certificates which are required for end-to-end encryption and will introduce alternative approaches for secure end-to-end communication. The reader will learn about the benefits and risks of end-to-end encryption within an enterprise security architecture and will understand which approaches work best for specific environments and user groups.

1 Enterprise Email Encryption Status Quo

1.1 Secure Channel versus Content Encryption

When discussing email encryption the topic of Transport Layer Encryption (TLS) always arises. In Germany, TLS has become a popular and established technology but is often mistaken for a full-blown end-to-end encryption solution. TLS however, only secures the communication between two mail relay servers and not the actual message content. Not only is the message content unencrypted during transport but also whenever it is stored. This includes temporary storage on mail relay servers as well as mid-term to permanent storage in users' server-side mailboxes and archives. Any hackers who can make it through the firewall can simply help themselves to whatever they find. In case of sync, pop or push services emails are also unprotected on the client device. TLS gives the appearance of being secure, but does not deliver enterprise level security. Even VPN and other secure channel methods which secure the transport but not the content have the same security problems as TLS [PfPf11] and [4]. It is always better to secure the message. End-to-end encryption appears to be the only solution which provides real security and confidentiality. After the NSA scandal, security experts who were vocal in the media, called for the comprehensive adoption of end-to-end encryption [5] but never came up with realistic day in, day out solutions which could be rolled-out throughout companies.

1.2 Obstacles to Enterprise End-to-End Encryption

End-to-end encryption has to be considered within the context in which it is used. In its purest form, end-to-end encryption means encrypting the message from the sender to the recipient without any exceptions. The message content is never stored in plain text, neither in the sender's outbox nor the recipient's inbox. Only the sender and recipient have access to the keys necessary to encrypt and decrypt the email. That's the theory and a standard scenario for private users.

For the vast majority of internal and external emails, companies do not usually have any interest in full-blown end-to-end encryption where individual employees hold their own private encryption key.

The situation is similar to the real-world office situation. Employees do not hold the only key to their offices. Instead employees have the right to use a standard key or a copy of their office key. In the same way companies should and must avoid giving employees the only key with which emails can be decrypted. For compliance reasons alone, companies must retain ownership of email content. Without being able to centrally access email content, the whole principle of content filtering and data loss prevention is undermined. Companies can easily lose control of their email or have to roll-out & maintain client-side content filtering solutions. A company wide archiving solution is also meaningless if it is not possible to access the email content, or again, a client side archiving solution has to be deployed for each individual user.

To avoid these issues, companies nowadays keep copies of general or employee keys centrally using a Public Key Infrastructure (PKI). There are multiple ways to realize such solutions which are generally known as Key Escrow [KaPS 02].

In the corporate reality however, end-to-end encryption could be better described as "End-to-MaybeTheEnd". An email sender can never be fully sure that only the intended recipient has access to the private key required for decryption. Not only do key-escrow solutions mean that the decryption key is not held directly by the recipient but centralized gateway solutions mean that emails are decrypted centrally and delivered in plain text to the recipient. This is analogous to the corporate mail room, where clerks open mail, stamp them with a receipt date, sort and deliver mail to the recipient within the company. The recipient never gets to see the envelope and clerks can read the message content. Centralized gateway solutions decrypt the messages using the recipient's private key and forward the plain text email to mail servers which deliver it to the recipient. However, in such a scenario, any email server administrator can access the email content.

A message sender cannot see or determine from the encryption key, if the recipient's email is processed by a Secure Mail Gateway [6] or not. If the message sender's organization also uses a Secure Mail Gateway, neither the recipient nor the sender may even be aware that the message has been encrypted. It is only possible to have full confidence in end-to-end encryption when the sender and recipient personally certify each others certificates and ensure that no other copies exist which again is practicable for private use but is not feasible in a large enterprise or a governmental institution.

The problems with classic end-to-end encryption which have been described, can be solved by taking a different view of the situation. Within the corporate environment, the "end" of the secure communication can be the company itself – the legal entity. Because employees always communicate in the name of the company it is the company itself which can be viewed as the sender and recipient of the secure communication. With such a viewpoint, it is acceptable to define the organization's external boundary as one "end" in end-to-end communication. In addition, as you will soon learn there are reasons why an organization should encrypt emails internally between itself and the employees as well making the whole process an "end-to-end-to-end" encryption (Fig. 1).

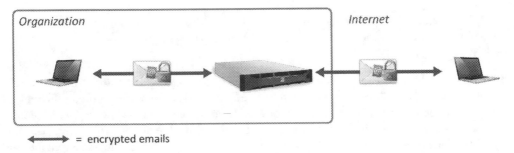

Fig. 1: End-to-End-to-End Encryption

2 Gateway Concepts

2.1 Basic is PKI – Encryption Infrastructure

Modern encryption is based upon asymmetric keys which commonly utilize a Public Key Infrastructure (PKI) such as S/MIME or OpenPGP. Not surprisingly, these two systems are incompatible. Although they both rely on the same cryptographic concepts their trust models are very different. OpenPGP relies on a peer based "web of trust" [7] in which users vouch for each other by signing each others public keys. The more trustworthy signatures a certificate carries the better. What is trustworthy or not is up to the users themselves. S/MIME on the other hand relies on a hierarchical trust model where a higher entity vouches for a lower entity and states how this trust is established (e.g. identity checks). Certification Authorities (CAs) sign the public keys and from that moment on a public key becomes a certificate. The CA publishes the certificate alongside up to date status information relating to the validity of the certificate. Certificate servers such as www.globaltrustpoint.com collate and validate certificates from the CA servers.

S/MIME is supported by all popular email clients and has become the standard in the business world whereas OpenPGP requires 3rd party software and is more popular amongst the few private users who encrypt their emails. OpenPGP is well documented and is open source. Its peer based trust model has a strong social component and cross-signing takes place at popular Crypto Parties [8] which are held regularly at universities, political parties or local IT security networks. S/MIME's reputation was damaged due to widely discussed reports about compromised and undermined Certificate Authorities[9]. The most common CA root certificates are pre-configured in email clients and popular operating systems which speeds up the validation process.

Both S/MIME and OpenPGP use a key pair which consists of an encryption and decryption key. The encryption key is public and must be made available to all email senders whereas the decryption key is private and must be kept very securely. Only the holder of the private key can decrypt messages which have been encrypted with the paired public key.

The public key contains information which is used to check the authenticity and validity of the key with the issuing authority. Regardless of S/MIME or OpenPGP, checking the authenticity, validity & trustworthiness of the key is a fundamental part of the encryption process. Even the most secure encryption algorithm is flawed if the key is not genuine, expired or cannot be trusted. [NiSh03]

2.2 Brute Force PKI Scaling

A basic brute force attempt to implement enterprise level encryption tries to solve the problem of scaling up the public/private key model by automatically issuing a key pair to every external communication partner on an ad hoc basis. In this case, the business acts as a Certificate Authority and vouches for the recipient.

When a confidential email is sent, a brand new key pair is created on the fly. The certificate is sent along with the email or in a separate email. The secure transfer of the private key is a very different matter and for security reasons should better be performed via a different channel.

But a break in the media makes it difficult for the recipient to install the private key in their email client. When recipients are limited to webmailers such as Gmail and are given an X.509 certificate it is simply not possible for them to install the private key. This is a significant problem in B2C communication. If the recipient does not already have a key installed, they are obviously not willing or able to install a key and are not familiar with encryption tools. Does a mail recipient really want to install a key which has been issued by a company for potentially a single one-off communication? It boils down to compromising security versus user acceptance.

The method itself is controversial because it raises security questions about a third party having access to the private key. PKI security standards are not met [NiSh03]. There may also be a flood of keys over the years issued to one person from different businesses which use that technology and each key's validity is limited to communicating with the issuing business. It can neither be officially trusted, nor verified by certificate servers and other email clients. Due to the security and scalability problems there is a very limited number of scenarios where this is an acceptable solution.

2.3 Certificate Management Challenge

It becomes clear that the real challenge for businesses is not the encryption itself, but the management of the private and public keys.

Private keys for employees have to be created, stored, signed, renewed, revoked and kept up to date when staff join and leave the company. This is a critical process to ensure that only employees can communicate in the name of the company. In parallel, the public keys have to be made available to external communication partners and also kept up to date.

At the same time the public keys from communication partners have to be made available to employees [KaLi08]. Throw into the mix the fact that many communication partners may be using OpenPGP keys and the scalability of key management suddenly becomes a problem. Public keys from communication partners have to be searched for, saved, validated and checked against revocation lists in real time following a specified standard [IETF IX]. The certificate management challenge is to automate the full key management and make it fully transparent to employees.

This challenge has been met with Secure Email Gateways and Certificate Servers. Public keys are harvested from incoming mails by the gateway which also interfaces with the certificate server. The server connects to trusted Certificate Authorities and the directories of large corporations to search for and validate public keys by means of Certificate Revocation Lists (CRLs) and Online Certificate Service Protocols (OCSPs). Harvested and validated certificates are cached locally to establish a comprehensive store of valid and trusted public certificates.

2.4 IT-Security and the User

Encryption and security is only guaranteed when it is applied every time it is required. Removing the encryption decision and the key management from employees and making the encryption process automated and invisible guarantees security and compliance. Secure Email Gateways fulfill these requirements and remove compliance responsibility from the end user. These fully automate the key management and use configurable policies to ensure that encryption is applied when it is required. At the same time, users have a degree of flexibility by being able to control the encryption process by adding commands to the message subject or using specialized buttons in the mail client front end. However, this flexibility enhances the fundamental company-wide security policies and cannot undermine the compliance requirements which are guaranteed by the gateway.

Secure Email Gateways deliver a number of key advantages to businesses. Their centralized deployment removes the need for any end-user software and training. Emails are en-/decrypted automatically and all keys and policies are managed centrally. Keys from 3rd parties are checked to ensure that they are valid and employees' keys are made available to communication partners. Depending upon the supplier's solution and the organizational infrastructure the installation can be very straight forward and finished within a few hours. Administration can be very straight forward and some solutions offer rich reporting methods which enable organizations to prove when encryption was applied and supports a better understanding of system efficiency.

But one of the key advantages delivered by Secure Email Gateways, is the ability to communicate securely with any partner regardless as to whether they are using S/MIME, OpenPGP or do not have encryption software installed at all.

2.5 Alternatives for recipients without certificates

Technology is rarely adopted when using it presents high hurdles to the end user. Email communication within the business world has reached such high acceptance because sending an email is as simple as clicking on the send button.

Client-side encryption implies and requires that the message sender knows what encryption method the recipient is using and selects the correct method for each recipient. Secure Email Gateways perform this task for every message sender within the organization and every recipient. Message senders can simply click on the send button to instantly send fully encrypted emails to any recipient with any encryption technology.

This also includes recipients who do not have any encryption technology as is typical in common B2C communication. Password based encryption has become an established alternative to key based encryption when PGP keys or X.509 certificates are not available. Instead the email is delivered to the recipient as an encrypted PDF file or HTML container. Another popular option is a secure web mailer account which can be created on the fly for each recipient for the exclusive secure bi-directional communication between an external contact and an organization.

Only instructional messages to the recipient are communicated using non-encrypted emails whilst the sensitive content is always protected. The security of password-based encryption is equal to PKI based encryption and represents a widely accepted and proven method of secure ad hoc encryption when PKI certificates are not available. In this case, the password is not saved as plain text in the system, but instead as an encrypted hash value. The only security challenge is the initial transmission of the password. To solve this problem different and practicable methods have been developed, including sending the password by SMS. Password based encryption enables businesses to communicate instantly and securely with any recipient with or without PKI keys (Fig 2).

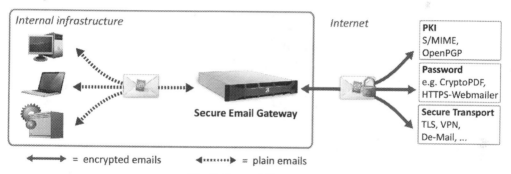

<table>
<tr><td>◄──────►</td><td>= encrypted emails</td><td>◄••••••••►</td><td>= plain emails</td></tr>
</table>

Fig. 2: Gateway Encryption

2.6 Gateway challengers ahead?

Since the NSA affair new Secure Email start-ups seem to be appearing almost every month [10, 11]. But it cannot be assumed that they will be able to revolutionize the situation within a short time frame. The solutions offered by these companies are mostly aimed at end users and not corporations whose special requirements are not usually considered. Instead, the solutions tend to assume that the sender and recipient know each other, trust each other, already communicate with each other and have agreed on a common security provider. An attempt is made to establish closed groups with proprietary systems. Senders and recipients have to use the same software and are restricted to using the devices on which the software is installed. An integration with S/MIME and OpenPGP standards for interoperability is not considered which means a spontaneous and efficient secure communication with businesses using public key infrastructures is not possible.

Some vendors provide secure communication only on certain operating systems. Such restrictions make these solutions very unattractive for the corporate environment.

2.7 Limits of Gateway Security

A Secure Email Gateway acts as an interface to the Internet at which emails are en-/decrypted. Within the company network however, the emails are transmitted in a plain state without any encryption. Secure Email Gateways have become a standard solution for protecting message content between external entities and the organizations boundaries. Until recently the protection offered by a gateway was considered sufficient against industrial and government backed cyber-spying and other prying eyes. But recent events and technological developments mean that security requirements cannot be met by the gateway alone. The internal communication within the organization needs to be protected as well [TiKr07].

First, as has been recently reported in the media [12], the internal network can no longer be considered to be fully protected by firewalls. More and more[13] often, networks are compromised and email data stolen from servers and client devices.

Second, the trend to IT outsourcing means that servers are administered by 3rd parties at off-site locations. Server administrators have access to decrypted messages which are stored in plain text and can easily pass or sell critical data to any interested party.

Finally, with the increase in the use of mobile devices such as smart phones for business communication, the number of devices which are outside the safety of the company network and with which emails are transmitted and stored in plain text is increasing. Even if the connection itself is secured, a hacker with only basic skills can gain access to the message content. If the message itself is not encrypted the content is always at risk.

Therefore the aim is to secure the content itself between the gateway and end users as well as between users. Securing the transport layer with TLS or VPN as mentioned can add some level of protection and investment in Mobile Device Management Systems (MDM) should not be ignored.

However, here only the containing environment is protected and the individual messages are not necessarily encrypted. Manufacturers [14] from the "5-Eyes"[15] countries dominate the MDM market. If protection against government run spying programs is required, or compliance with tighter branch or company requirements is necessary, the aim should always be to encrypt the message and attachments and not simply the transport or storage mechanisms. Foolproof security can only be achieved when the content is secured in transit and of course when it is stored in an encrypted state on the end device.

3 End-to-End Approaches for Enterprises

End-to-end encryption usually means complete content encryption between end devices and also the encrypted storage of the message on the end device. Only the recipient who is in possession of the required key can decrypt and access the message and its content.

As mentioned this highly secure communication method raises a number of problems for businesses. Employees work for the business and the information and communication they generate belongs to the company. In order to support audit compliance, archiving and business continuity, it is imperative that the company can also access the encrypted content should the employee lose the key, be unavailable or refuse to decrypt mails. This is why businesses use PKI based solutions for Key Escrow in order to manage encryption keys and ensure real time and long term access to message content.

In addition to owning and accessing encrypted data, companies need to protect themselves from spam, viruses and phishing attempts despite email encryption. In a true end-to-end encryption scenario where emails can only be decrypted on end devices, the roll-out of distributed content filtering and scanning is simply not scalable or practicable.

A pure client side end-to-end encryption has been available for decades but has never been practical for organizations which led to the development and popularity of email gateway solutions. The original motivation for gateway solutions cannot simply be discarded because of the new risks raised by the increased use of mobile client devices and outsourced system administration.

If gateways are replaced by client-side solutions, the complete functionality (e.g. S/MIME, Open-PGP, Password based encryption, policy enforcement, etc.) provided by the gateway has to be implemented on each and every employee device from desktop computers to smart phones. In case of S/MIME this means that before a single encrypted email can be sent, the client has to find a copy of the recipient's certificate which then has to be validated. The client side effort required for the installation of OpenPGP-clients and password based encryption software, as well as the day to day effort for maintenance, policy enforcement, key acquisition & key validation on each desktop and mobile client is simply not economical. End user training is critical but nevertheless the error rate rises dramatically when each individual employee is responsible for encrypting emails and applying conformance rules.

End-to-end encryption within an organization does not require the wheel to be re-invented. Instead tried and trusted solutions can be enhanced with new functionality.

3.1 Combining internal with external encryption

Two methods are recommended in order to meet an organization's encryption requirements not only with external partners but also within the internal email infrastructure without sacrificing ownership of the company's data and without breaking compliance rules.

"Organizational End-to-End" encryption is a new approach for companies and organizations which is ideally suited to the widespread use by small, medium, and large user groups. Emails are encrypted internally and externally with a re-encryption taking place on the Secure Mail Gateway.

This method is enhanced by "Personal End-to-End" which is analogous to classic client-side encryption and which can be used in parallel with the new organizational end-to-end encryption approach. Personal end-to-end encryption is generally required for a selected set of mails by small user groups such as the board of directors who require highly secure confidential communication without any breaks in the encryption chain. The extra security offered by the personal encryption approach however, does not mean that organizational should be considered insecure.

If fact, organizational mails can generally only ever be accessed by trusted admins whilst the simple usability and comprehensive deployment benefits deliver foolproof security.

The new end-to-end generation uses modern key management services and optional client side software. In terms of efficiency and usability the new generation cannot be compared with the client side solutions from the past.

Only by using centralized modern end-to-end solutions is it possible to deploy end-to-end encryption within a business environment and deliver secure and compliant communication.

3.2 Organizational End2End

Modern Secure Email Gateways with the appropriate extensions combine internal and external email encryption. Emails are transmitted in an encrypted state not only over the Internet but also within the internal company network. For everyday use within a business where content filtering or later access to the content is required, a re-encryption on the gateway takes place. This scenario is ideal for organizations who need to own the message content and is referred to as "Organizational End-to-End".

Organizational End-to-End encryption uses S/MIME within the company's network to encrypt message content. Almost all desktop email clients which can be found in the corporate world such as Outlook and Notes have native support for S/MIME. In addition, the webmail interfaces such as OWA and iNotes provide S/MIME functions or they can be enhanced with plug-ins.

Less clear is the situation for mobile clients. Besides the standard Android, iOS, and Blackberry mail clients, which all have native S/MIME support, there are a raft of other mail apps offered to the business world. Most of them [16] already implement S/MIME or it is on their road-map. Using S/MIME exclusively in the internal company email infrastructure, eliminates the need to install and maintain any other mail encryption software such as PGP or PDF/ZIP-encrypter on clients.

In order to encrypt emails on the clients, organizational end-to-end requires an internal PKI. The X.509 certificates issued specifically for this purpose are not published externally and never leave the company. The relevant infrastructure in companies – for example MS ActiveDirectory and Lotus Domino as well as a wide range of other suppliers – provide proven, out of the box PKI solutions and certificate management for the mail clients. Hence, end-to-end email encryption between employees within a company can be setup with standard infrastructure tools.

The vision behind organizational end-to-end is to securely join the internal encryption world with the external encryption world which is represented by the Secure Mail Gateway. This simple concept is realized by re-encryption on the gateway (Fig. 3). In order for this to work, the organizational end-to-end solution provides all internal S/MIME clients with a valid certificate every time a mail is created with external recipients. Within this context, valid means that the certificate was issued by the internal PKI. The approach eliminates the need to install and maintain any other CA-certificates, CRLs, OCSP configurations on any internal email client. The private key which is required to decrypt the email is stored securely on the Secure Mail Gateway.

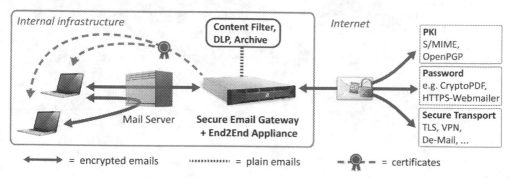

Fig. 3: Organizational End-to-End Encryption

When the S/MIME encrypted mail passes through the gateway it is decrypted and re-encrypted according to the means available for a particular recipient. For example, if the recipient has a published S/MIME certificate, the email is encrypted using the recipient's public key. If no S/MIME or OpenPGP key is available, the gateway can still deliver the mail securely using password based methods, or even secure channel transmission such as TLS or De-Mail [17] (German government sponsored secure email).

The complete process is simply reversed for inbound mails. The gateway decrypts an incoming mail and re-encrypts it with the internal certificate of the employee to whom the email is addressed.

Especially interesting is the extra protection which is offered by organizational end-to-end encryption in outsourcing and cloud based scenarios. Emails are encrypted directly on the client and gateway which means that they are protected when they pass through or stored on mail servers and cannot be read by external system administrators, cloud providers or anyone else who may try to snoop there.

3.3 Personal End-to-End

With the so called "Personal" method, messages are fully encrypted from sender to recipient (Fig. 4). This is analogue to the classic form of end-to-end encryption and is targeted at users with high security needs. Encryption takes place on the client devices and no content filtering can take place. In fact, not even the system administrator can access the message content.

Personal end-to-end is only possible in conjunction with a central key and certificate management validation. In order to avoid high administration costs which arise with client-side installations, it is recommended to establish a homogenous infrastructure using standard technologies such as S/MIME which are supported by email clients out of the box. This comes at the cost of restricting personal end-to-end to recipients who also use S/MIME which makes it only suitable for selected users in certain situations.

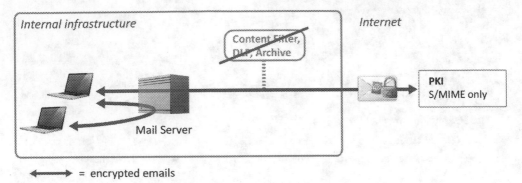

Fig. 4: Personal End-to-End Encryption

Employees can continue to use standard email clients without any extra software although a set of plug-ins deliver a wide range of useful functionality. Even with state of the art technology, security is only good when it is accepted and used correctly by employees.

However without any additional plug-ins, the user alone is responsible for encrypting emails and must be trained accordingly. At the end of the day however, a security risk exists. This risk can be eliminated through the deployment of email client plug-ins which take over the responsibility for activating encryption and for selecting the appropriate encryption method according to central security policies.

In addition, key escrow is supported, which enables even with Personal end-to-end the possibility to access message content in case of emergencies.

4 Conclusion

Public key infrastructures provide the corner stone of secure email communication. It does not matter what encryption technologies the communication partners use or even if they have a method of decrypting messages. Secure Email Gateways can ensure that emails are delivered securely from the employee's computer right to the recipient. For organizations, companies and public agencies that do not use use mobile end devices and do not have any secrets to hide from their mail server admins, a Secure Email Gateway is all they need.

For all others Organizational End-to-End combined with Personal End-to-End delivers a universal solution for secure email communication that protects emails in transit and in rest.

References

[NiSh03]   Ferguson, Niels, Schneier, Bruce. Practical Cryptography, Wiley, 2003, p.323-337.

[PfPf11]   Charles P. Pfleeger, Shari Lawrence Pfleeger. Analyzing Computer Security A Threat/Vulnerability/Countermeasure Approach, Pearson, 2011 p.437-472

[TiKr07]   Harold F.Tipton, Micki Krause, Information Security Management Handbook, CRC Press; 6 edition , 2007, p. 1025

[KaLi08]   Jonathan Katz, Yehuda Lindell, Introduction to Modern Cryptography, CRC press, 2008, p. 316-324

[KaPS 02]   Charlie Kaufmann, Radia Perlman, Mike Speciner, Network Security: Private Communications in a Public World, Prentice Hall, 2002, ebook Chapters 1.10-1.11

[IETF IX]   Internet Engineering Task Force RFC 6818, Internet X.509 Public Key Infrastructure Certificate and Certificate Revocation List (CRL) Profile

A list with Internet links as references

[1]   http://www.dw.com/en/a-chronology-of-the-nsa-surveillance-scandal/a-17197740

[2]   http://www.theguardian.com/us-news/the-nsa-files

[3]   http://www.internationaltradenews.com/interviews/the_nsa_scandal_a_wake-up_call_for_europe/

[4]   https://www.bestvpn.com/blog/6484/the-nsa-prism-scandal-and-how-vpn-can-and-cannot-help/

[5]   http://www.computerworld.com/article/2475978/encryption/snowden-at-sxsw—we-need-better-encryption-to-save-us-from-the-surveillance-state.html

[6]   http://www.techopedia.com/definition/30542/email-encryption-gateway

[7]   https://en.wikipedia.org/wiki/Web_of_trust

[8]   http://www.dw.com/en/cryptoparties-boom-following-nsa-scandal/a-16964049

[9]   https://technet.microsoft.com/en-us/library/security/3050995.aspx

[10] http://www.technologyreview.com/view/518771/the-coming-wave-of-security-startups/

[11] https://www.hubraum.com/news/these-are-the-15-cyber-security-startups

[12] http://www.reuters.com/article/2015/05/15/us-germany-cybersecurity-idUSKBN0O01ON20150515

[13] http://www.zdnet.com/article/cybersecurity-in-2015-what-to-expect/

[14] https://www.vmware.com/files/pdf/info-iech-research-group-vendor-landscape-mdm-suites.pdf

[15] http://www.theguardian.com/world/2013/dec/02/history-of-5-eyes-explainer

[16] https://www.globalsign.com/resources/white-paper-smime-compatibility.pdf, page 8

[17] http://www.cio.bund.de/SharedDocs/Publikationen/DE/Innovative-Vorhaben/de_mail_informationsbroschuere_maerz2012_englisch_download.pdf?__blob=publicationFile

Cloud Security

On Location-determined Cloud Management for Legally Compliant Outsourcing

Bernhard Doll[1] · Dirk Emmerich[2] · Ralph Herkenhöner[2] ·
Ramona Kühn[1] · Hermann de Meer[1]

[1]University of Passau
Innstraße 43, 94032 Passau
{dollbern | kuehnram | demeer}@fim.uni-passau.de

[2]Fujitsu Technology Solutions GmbH
Mies-van-der-Rohe-Str. 8, 80807 München
{dirk.emmerich | ralph.herkenhoener}@ts.fujitsu.com

Abstract

When organisations are outsourcing their data processing to clouds, the cloud providers have to support them in achieving legal compliance. This is particular challenging in globally distributed clouds where the data centres are located in multiple countries with different legislation. Here, the cloud providers have to implement technical constraints based on the legal requirements which apply individually for each cloud customer. In this paper, the legal requirements of cloud customers and their corresponding technical constraints are modelled in a technically decidable and enforceable manner, using information flow control in virtual resource management, and a solution to implement the support of legal requirements in cloud environments is proposed. The solution proposed covers the translation of legal requirements of cloud customers into technical security policies which are applied in virtual resource management of clouds. For these purposes an information model, denoted as the *Cloud Security Matrix*, is defined using the methods of information flow control. In the model, cloud resources (virtual and hardware) are classified and the allowed information flows are defined. The information model is capable to express both location and security constraints including authenticity, integrity and availability. The technical feasibility of a location-based assignment of virtual resources is shown in a proof-of-concept implementation based on OpenStack.

1 Introduction

Legally compliant data processing is one of the key requirements when the outsourcing of data processing to a cloud is considered. Although the cloud customers are responsible for legally compliant processing of their data, the cloud providers (external service providers running the cloud environment) have to provide the technical measures to fulfil all constraints requested by the customers. Particularly challenging are globally distributed clouds where the data centres are located in multiple countries. The key to legally compliant cloud computing is to understand the legal requirements which are applicable to cloud customers and how cloud providers have to implement and operate cloud environments.

The legal requirements which are applicable to cloud customers depend on the types of data processed by them, which are for instance personal data (e.g., according to European data protection law, Art. 7 of the Directive 95/46/EC), data relevant for tax inspections (e.g., according to German tax law, para. 238 of the Handelsgesetzbuch) and data related to sovereign duties and responsibilities of governmental authorities (e.g., in Germany restricted by the German constitutional law, Art. 33 para. 4 of the Grundgesetz). While the cloud customers are responsible for the compliance of the data processing with applicable legislation, the cloud providers have to be able to help their cloud customers to achieve this legal compliance.

A legal requirement that regularly applies is determination and awareness of the geographic location of data processing (also 'data location' [JaGr11] [Chig12], 'data locality' [SuKa11], and 'multi location issue' [ZZX+10]). Here, the cloud providers have to ensure that cloud resources are allocated for the processing of their customers' data only if the location of the data centres hosting the cloud resources are located in admissible countries. An example for legal requirement on the geographic location of the data processing is the European data protection law where the data processing outside of the European Union requires an *adequate level of protection* (Art. 25 para. 1 of the Directive 95/46/EC). Additionally to location constraints, security requirements apply generally for confidentiality, integrity and availability, which also have to be supported by the cloud providers when provisioning cloud resources to their customers.

To support legal compliance in cloud computing, the cloud customers' requirements have to be translated into constraints which are technically enforceable in the cloud's resource management. Technically, the cloud providers have to implement controls – based on the customers' requirements – on how customers' data are transmitted within the cloud and therefore how data centres gain access to customers' data. This is possible by introducing an information model that formally describes applicable constraints derived from legal requirements of the cloud customers and that can be used to ensure the allocation of cloud resources that complies with applicable legislation in predictable manner. A good candidate for doing so is information flow control, because the methods are designed to model access control in a reliable manner and they provide rules that can be enforced in technical systems (e.g., by implementing role-based access control with respect to confidentiality and integrity [Sand93]).

The remainder of the paper is organised as follows. In Section 2, the related work on location-determined data processing in clouds and modelling security requirements in clouds is described. The background necessary to understand the research in this paper is given in Section 3. The information model proposed to address legally compliant cloud computing is presented in Section 4, which is followed by a description of the proof-of-concept implementation in Section 5 and by the conclusion and future research directions in Section 6.

2 Related Work

The need for determining the geolocation of data processing has been identified an open issue in literature [JaGr11] [Chig12] [SuKa11] [ZZX+10]. There is research on in which manner hardware resources have to be assigned in clouds to support legal compliance. Based on a list of countries which provide an adequate level of protection according to European data protection law, it is possible to implement a white listing on secure third countries [TEH+11]. Further, the placement of cloud resources on physical hardware can be attested remotely using trusted platform modules and trusted hypervisors [SSR+12]. Remote attestation is also possible for cloud storage [AlBN12]. Additionally, cloud resources can be tagged and pooled by their geolocation which can be used by cloud providers to place cloud resources in data centres in compliance with location constraints [WaBa13]. There also exist several approaches on considering location constraints in resource allocation algorithms, e.g., location-aware MapReduce [KRG09], colocation of virtual machines [BFB+14] and optimal location in cloud networks [LaSa12]. However, none of these approaches consider legal requirements generally; at best there is an exclusive focus on European data protection law. In particular tax law and governmental requirements of the data processing are not considered. Additionally, none of the approaches mentioned provide an information model which supports the verification and correctness of the decisions made in cloud's resource management. Such verification and correctness are possible to achieve using the methods of information flow control.

Existing approaches on information flow control are based on the ground breaking work of Bell and La Padula [BePa73], Denning [Denn76] and Biba [Biba77], who introduced methods for modelling information flow and the classification of subjects and objects with respect to confidentiality and integrity. Based on their work, models of role-based access control were developed [Sand93]. Adoptions of these methods in the context of cloud computing are considered for software development in platform-as-a-service [BEP+13]. There also are considerations on modelling location constraints with respect to the colocation of cloud resources [ToNH07] and user location [RaKY06]. However, none of the mentioned research considers the modelling of location constraints based on the legal requirements of cloud customers and with respect to the placement of virtual resources to hardware resources in clouds.

Consequently, there is currently no information model that is able to model information flow control based on legal requirements which apply to data processing in clouds to achieve legally compliant hosting of cloud resources in data centres with respect to confidentiality, integrity, availability and location. The approach presented in this paper addresses this research gap by introducing such an information model and shows its feasibility in a proof-of-concept implementation.

3 Background

An important requirement for cloud computing is access control to prevent unauthorized persons reading secret information. This can be guaranteed by an information flow control mechanism. Security classes are the basis for realising information flow control. Information flow control has many advantages: It is possible to control where business or personal data flows, so compliance and security can be enhanced. Furthermore, the sharing between cloud tenants is facilitated. With information flow control a tracking of the data flow is possible to improve accountability.

In 1975, Denning presented four axioms to describe the information flow control within a system [Denn76]:

The first axiom describes the flow relation. The security classes and the flow relation $\langle SC, \rightarrow \rangle$ form a partially ordered set. The second axiom postulates that the set of security classes, denoted as SC, is finite. The third axiom states that a security class has a lower bound L such that $L \rightarrow A$ for all $A \in SC$. The last axiom states that $\oplus$ is the least upper bound operator on SC.

If these axioms are fulfilled, $\langle SC, \rightarrow, \oplus \rangle$ forms a lattice. Denning's model can be used to control the information flow control not only within a system but also between different systems. In this paper, it is shown that these axioms are fulfilled by the developed information model.

A security class being assigned to an object can for instance be named "public", "secret", "confidential" or "top secret". However, a security class may refer to a specific location with special laws to protect personal or business data. For example, such classes can be labelled "EU/EEC" or "Non-EU/-EEC'" or be related to specific countries. Information must not flow from an object of a high security class to an object with a lower security class. If security classes are based on locations one can restrict the countries in which the data processing should take place.

4 Location-based Information Flow Control

To fulfil the demands for providing legally compliant data processing, referring to the location where the data is stored and processed, several additions and modifications to a traditional cloud system have to be made. These cover the implementation of both automatic methods for selecting specific data centres and manual tasks like classifying physical machines with location information and the specification by the user about the kind of data and its constraints which will be transferred to a cloud provider. Therefore the theoretical model and hypothesis which are required are presented in this section.

4.1 Classification of Cloud Resources

Cloud computing primarily relies on the techniques of hardware virtualisation. According to the *NIST cloud computing reference architecture*, service orchestration in IaaS cloud platforms consists of virtual resources utilised by cloud customers, abstraction and control of computing resources by the cloud provider and the hardware resources of the physical infrastructure [LTM+11]. Hardware resources are components of the physical infrastructure located in data centres operated or subcontracted by the cloud providers. Typical hardware resources are servers, storage and communication infrastructure. Additionally, hardware resources are supported by the management infrastructure of the data centres which provides the management functions [Ccit00] such as fault management and configuration management. To utilise hardware resources in clouds, they are virtualised and orchestrated by cloud management using the fabric and management functions [TsSB10]. The management functions create, select and destroy the virtual resources which are running on the hardware resources, while the fabric functions create and provision the virtual instances requested in the cloud service orchestration. In IaaS clouds, cloud services orchestrate virtual resources which are virtual machines, virtual storage, virtual links and network services. Each virtual resource is assigned by the cloud management to a specific hardware resource, resulting in a resource allocation performed by the data centre operating the respective hardware resource.

4.2 Access Model

Based on the classification of cloud resources it is possible to describe information flows in clouds and how the cloud management controls these information flows. In IaaS clouds, cloud customers transfer data to virtual resources based on applications using the virtual resources. The cloud customers decide which data they want to transfer to the cloud and, based on that data, the virtual resources have to comply with legal requirements of the cloud customers. In the cloud, the cloud providers assign virtual resources to hardware resources operated by data centres. Due to the nature of hardware virtualisation, hardware resources have full access to data processed in virtual resources assigned to them. By this, data centres can gain access to that data. Consequently, the assignment of virtual resources to hardware resources results in information flows of the data contained in virtual resources, which is directed to the hardware resources assigned and the data centres which are responsible for operation. From the cloud provider's perspective, each assignment of a virtual resource is equivalent to an information flow caused by the assignment. If the cloud provider seeks to control the information flows on behalf of the cloud customers (in compliance with the legal requirements requested) the cloud provider has to control the assignment of virtual resources. In our model, we use this abstract view on the control of information flow to describe information flows in clouds generally, which we denoted *information flow of virtual resources*. In the model, hardware resources are considered subjects accessing virtual resources, which are considered objects. The cloud management system, which assigns the virtual resources to hardware resources, is considered a multi-level security system that enforces the control of the allowed information flow of virtual resources. In order to achieve legal compliance, the cloud customer's requirements are transformed into security classifications of virtual resources, which are compared with the security classifications of hardware resources. The security classifications of hardware resources depend on the level of protection and level of security provided by the data centres which is operating them.

4.3 Security Classes within Clouds

The security classifications of virtual resources and hardware resources are described in a lattice-based model of security classes. Lattices of security classes are first introduced by Denning [Denn76] in a model which addresses confidentiality. Further, it is possible to describe lattices of security classes addressing both confidentiality and integrity [Sand93]. In our model, we define additional security classes describing availability and location [Same12]. The basic idea is to define a partial order on security properties that are expressed by security classes. For example, confidentiality can be expressed by the following security classes: public, confidential, secret and top secret. As depicted in *Fig. 1a*, these security classes are ordered by their level of confidentiality, and they are applied to subjects and objects. Based on these classes, it is possible to define whether information flow is allowed between security classes or not. For example, confidentiality can be assured, if there is information flow to security classes only of the same or higher confidentiality level. Also, it is possible to define multiple classes at the same level of confidentiality that are considered incomparable and therefore information must not flow between them. For example, this is the case when multiple cloud customers are considered to have secret information that should not be exchanged between these customers. An example is shown in *Fig. 1b*.

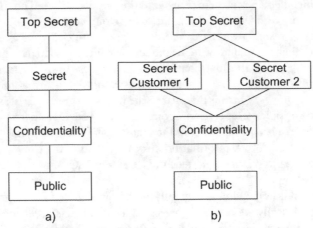

Fig. 1: Examples for security classes using confidentiality.

In our model, we define lattices of security classes on confidentiality, integrity, availability and location, which are described in the following. All sets of security classes described are finite, partially ordered, have a lower bound and a least upper bound operator can be defined.

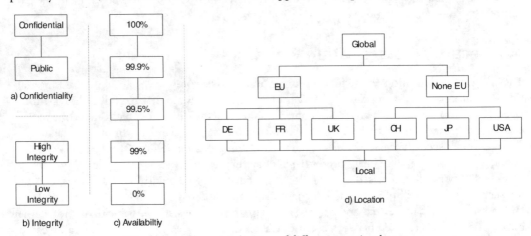

Fig. 2: Exemplary visualization of different security classes.

Confidentiality is considered the requirement that the access to information is limited. Virtual resources (i.e., objects) are classified according to the need of limiting the access to the data processed within. Hardware resources (i.e., subjects) are classified according to their capacity to support access limitations. When applying legal requirements with respect to confidentiality, there are basically two levels of confidentiality: no confidentiality is required and confidentiality is required. The respective security classes are "public" and "confidential". It is possible to introduce additional security classes, e.g., to distinguish virtual resource in those containing personal data and in those containing business data. Such additional security classes make it possible to introduce a finer granular information flow control. *Fig. 2a* illustrates a lattice of two security classes on confidentiality.

Integrity is considered the requirement that information is accurate and consistent. Virtual resources are classified according to the level of integrity required for the data processed within. Hardware resources are classified according to their capacity to support integrity. Integrity can be considered a binary property, where the integrity is required or not. Again, it is possible to introduce additional security classes, e.g., to distinguish between the support of detecting integrity breaches and the support of auto-correction. *Fig. 2b* illustrates a lattice of two security classes on integrity.

Availability is considered the requirement that information is accessible. Virtual resources are classified according to the level of availability required for the data processed within. Hardware resources are classified according to their capacity to support the availability required for the data processed within. A common measure for availability is the asymptotic availability [XiDP04] which is the ration of the time being available and the time of operation. In practice, rations of 99%, 99.5%, 99.9%, 99.95%… are of particular relevance. The lowest bottom security class is "0%" representing the non-availability, and the greatest upper security class is "100%" representing permanent availability. All other security classes are in between and ordered by the ration of availability they represent. *Fig. 2c* illustrates a lattice of five security classes on availability.

Location is considered the requirement that information has to remain within a certain geographic area. In legal regulations, restrictions on the location apply with respect to the location of the recipients of data transfer. Admissible locations for a data transfer can be countries and unions of countries which have a harmonised legislation (such as the European Union). Virtual resources are then classified according to the location restrictions applying to the data processed within. Hardware resources are classified according to their geo-location. The lowest bottom security class is "local" representing that the location is not part of the cloud. The greatest upper security class is "global" representing that the location can be everywhere. *Fig. 2d* illustrates a lattice of 10 security classes on location.

4.4 Cloud Security Information Model

To achieve legal compliance, the virtual resources have to be assigned to hardware resources of data centres that comply with the security requirements of the cloud customers. Typically, the security requirements of the cloud customers derive from legal requirements that apply to the processing of the cloud customer's data. For example, in terms of European data protection law personal data usually have to be processed within the European Union or within countries ensuring an adequate level of protection (Art. 25 para. 1 of the Data Protection Directive). In this example, the location of the data processing is an important criterion for achieving legal compliance. In the model, subjects (i.e., hardware resources) and objects (i.e., virtual resources) are classified using a quadruple (C x I x A x Loc) of security classes with C set of security classes on confidentiality, I set of security classes on integrity, A set of security classes on availability and Loc set of security classes on location. The legal requirements of cloud customers are translated into these security classes. For example, a virtual machine in which personal data are processed according to European data protection law is classified:

```
(Confidential, High Integrity, 99.5%, EU)
```

Fig. 3 illustrates an example of evaluating the potential placement of this virtual machine on four hardware resources located in different countries and with different security classifications.

In this example, the perfect match is the hardware resource located in France, since all security classes of the hardware resource satisfy those of the virtual machine.

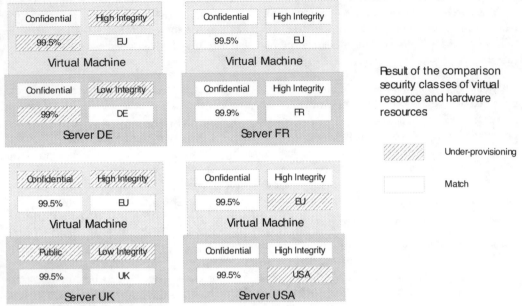

Fig. 3: Example of the placement of a virtual machine on four hardware resources with different security classifications.

4.5 Location-based Resource Allocation

The decision and enforcement of resource location is part of the cloud management software and covers the optimisation of hardware utilisation. To cover the security requirements, it has to be extended to also consider customers' security policies and the physical location of hardware. Therefore, the location information has to be placed on the hardware during the cloud administration process. The decision where virtual resources are hosted depends on the one hand on customer's location constraints for the data processed and on the other hand on the available physical resources. Therefore, the location decision process has to match the customer's location constraints with the location of available physical hardware.

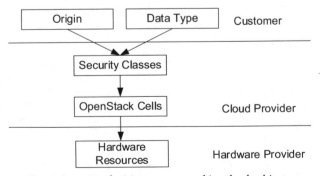

Fig. 4: Location decision process and involved subjects.

An overview on the location decision process is given in *Fig. 4*. This figure also depicts the responsibilities of the involved subjects. The customer's location constraints depend on the data type and the origin of the data to be processed within the cloud. Thus, the decision process starts with the data type and the origin of the data. Based on this information, location security classes are selected by the cloud provider according to the customer's location constraints (e.g., financial data from Germany is only to be processed within Germany). The decision which hardware resource is used is made in a first step by the cloud provider by selecting appropriate groups of hardware resources which are organised via OpenStack cells. In a second step, the corresponding hardware provider selects the hardware resource. For example, the selection of the security class "EU" results in the selection of the hardware resources of data centres which are classified "DE", "FR" or "UK" and therefore are all located within member states of the European Union. Since in regard of the location these locations are treated as equal, a transfer of data between data centres in these regions is allowed.

5 Proof-of-Concept Implementation

In this section, the design and development of a proof-of-concept implementation in the cloud platform OpenStack is presented. The focus of the proof-of-concept implementation is set on the allocation of virtual machines according to location constraints. The implementation is able to enforce the resource allocation based on the customer's selection of the data type and the data origin in compliance with given security policies. For the security policies and in particular the data types and the data origin, it is possible to choose from a predefined list of implementations. In the security policies, the rules on allowed location security classes for specific data types and origins are described using plain XML. The compliance monitoring and reporting was addressed by implementing a logging mechanism and an analytics board. The logging mechanisms create a log file on resource allocation for every virtual instance. The current resource allocation of virtual machines in the cloud is visualised on a world map and it is possible to view the decision details of the log files for every virtual machine. The proof-of-concept implementation was developed and tested in the cloud lab at the site of the University of Passau.

5.1 OpenStack as a Reference Platform

OpenStack is an open source cloud platform offering various features that are necessary to utilise, manage and offer cloud services on visualised hardware infrastructure. It can be considered a reference implementation of an IaaS cloud architecture as defined by the NIST [LTM+11]. Therefore, it has been chosen as a platform for implementing the proof-of-concept implementation of location determined data processing within the cloud.

OpenStack consists of multiple modules. Most relevant for implementing location determined data processing are the modules OpenStack Dashboard for communicating the customer's security requirements, OpenStack Compute for location determined hosting of virtual machines and OpenStack Block Storage for location determined hosting of virtual storage. So far, OpenStack is not able to enforce a location aware resource allocation within a cloud. Therefore, five modifications were necessary which, beside changes of OpenStack Dashboard, OpenStack Compute and its API for creating the proof-of-concept implementation, also cover changes of the logging mechanism and the additional implementation of an analytics board.

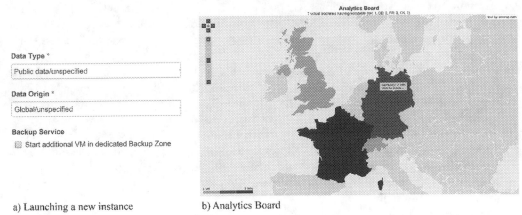

a) Launching a new instance   b) Analytics Board

Fig. 5: Options for selecting the data type, the data origin and the usage of a dedicated backup zone while launching a new instance and the analytics board with the location visualisation on a map.

The OpenStack Dashboard was extended to allow the customer to select predefined or customised security properties for virtual machine instantiation. *Fig. 5a* shows a screenshot of the additional input fields for easy selection of the desired security properties. In the module OpenStack Compute, a location scheduler using XML-based security policies for decision and enforcement of resource allocation based on the usage of OpenStack Compute cells was implemented. Furthermore, the management API of OpenStack Compute was extended to allow the communication of security requirements from the OpenStack Dashboard to OpenStack Compute, so that the user's input can be directly processed and taken into account. To see where the resources are allocated, the logging mechanisms were extended for compliance monitoring and reporting purposes. These special log files are called resource allocation log files and are created during the decision process on allocating a virtual machine. It would not be user-friendly if customers would have to read the log files to know where the current allocation of virtual machines takes place. To represent the information from the log files in an appealing design on a world map and also for compliance monitoring purposes, an analytics board that visualises the current resource allocation of virtual machines was implemented. The analytics board is browser based for a flexible usage and is provided via a HTTP server utilising the amMap[1] library for a graphical representation of an interactive world map. The board offers two different views on the currently instantiated virtual machines: 1) a global view providing general information on all active cells and allocation of the virtual machines and 2) a view on the decision details for a specific virtual machine. A screenshot of the global view is shown in *Fig. 5b*. The map focuses on middle Europe and there are four active cells visible: Germany, France, United Kingdom and Switzerland. The colours of the active cells provide information about the number of virtual machines hosted by that cell. In this example, light green (light grey) means that this cells hosts one virtual machine, two virtual machines are hosted in the dark green (medium grey) cell and the blue (dark grey) cell hosts three virtual machines. The header line above the map also provides brief information on currently instantiated virtual machines and their hosting location. The map can be navigated freely using the mouse or the red control buttons on the upper left corner. Active cells have mouse-over information like the country name and the number of hosted virtual machines. Every active cell can

---

1   The amMap library is free to use and can be found on the Internet: http://www.ammap.com (last accessed: 26.11.2013)

be clicked individually for additional information. The analytics board visualises all information from the resource allocation log files in an easy readable and clear manner.

5.2 Possible Applications

The developed proof-of-concept implementation is able to fulfil the requirements of multiple purposes. Besides the usage for location-determined resource allocation for legally compliant data processing, which has been discussed before, it can also be used to support distributed backup instantiation of virtual resources, e.g., Backup-as-a-Service. It is able to be used not only for providing a backup instance which fulfils the requirements for legal compliance but also can guarantee that the instantiated backup service is located at a different computing centre than the associated virtual machine of the user. Therefore, it's not only able to provide a backup in case of a hardware malfunction like disk corruption of the user's VM, but also is still able to deliver data in case the whole computing centre containing the user's VM is destroyed, e.g., by an environmental disaster like a flood. Otherwise there would be no guarantee, that the backup VM is not located in the same data centre and thereby all of the data is lost irreversible.

Another possible application is the compliance monitoring and reporting which has been demonstrated beforehand with the analytics board. By providing the corresponding log files not only the cloud provider is able to internally check the compliance of its customers' data, but also customers themselves or external auditors can verify the compliance of the processing of data.

6 Conclusion

This paper presented how cloud providers can support their customers in achieving legal compliance during the outsourcing of data processing to IaaS clouds. This is realised by using the methods of information flow control to define an information model in which allowed information flows of virtual resources are modelled based on the security classification of cloud resources. With the information model, it is possible to model information flow control with respect to the security goals confidentiality, integrity, availability and even location. In a proof-of-concept implementation it is shown that it is possible to implement the information model in IaaS cloud platforms using OpenStack as an example. For customers it is important to know how their data are processed in the cloud and if security requirements are fulfilled by the cloud provider. An important aspect is that the location of the hardware resources is determined which defines whether the data processing takes place in a valid location. The feasibility of this approach is demonstrated in a proof-of-concept implementation, showing that it is possible to assign location information to the hardware resources and assign virtual machines in compliance with legal requirements of the customers. Furthermore, it provides a comfortable way for both cloud providers and cloud customers to visualise the locations of virtual machines in the cloud.

Future research directions are to investigate how this approach can be adapted to SaaS and PaaS cloud computing platforms. A particular challenge is to deal with multiple levels of service level agreements (those of customers and those of service providers). Another direction is to investigate how our model can be applied to multi-cloud scenarios, where each cloud provider has own security classifications of hardware and virtual resources. Further, an open issue is how cloud providers can provide reliably evidence on performed data processing like it is needed for inspections and audits with respect to security standards (e.g., in the context of an ISO 27001 internal audit).

References

[AlBN12] Albeshri, Aiiad and Boyd, Colin and Nieto, Juan Gonzalez: Geoproof: proofs of geographic location for cloud computing environments. Distributed Computing Systems Workshops (ICDCSW), 2012, pp. 506-514.

[BEP+13] Bacon, Jean and Eyers, David and Pasquier, T. et al.: Information flow control for secure cloud computing. Network and Service Management, IEEE Transactions on, 2013, pp. 1-14.

[BePa73] Bell, D. Elliott and La Padula, Leonard J.: Secure computer systems: mathematical foundations. The MITRE Corporation, Technical Report MTR-2547 Vol. I., 1973.

[BFB+14] Baig, Mirza Basim and Fitzsimons, Connor and Balasubramanian, Suryanarayanan et al.: Cloudflow: Cloud-wide policy enforcement using fast VM introspection. Proceedings of the 2nd IEEE International Conference on Cloud Engineering (IC2E), 2014.

[Biba77] Biba, Kenneth J.: Integrity considerations for secure systems. DTIC Document, Technical report, 1977.

[Ccit00] CCITT Recommendation M.3400 – TMN management functions. Telecommunication Standardization Sector of ITU (ITU-T), 2000.

[Chig12] Chigozirim, Ajaegbu et al.: Towards building a secure cloud computing environment. International Journal of Advanced Research in Computer Science, Elsevier, 2012, pp. 166-171.

[Denn76] Denning, Dorothy E.: A lattice model of secure information flow. ACM, Communications of the ACM, 1976, pp. 236-243.

[JaGr11] Jansen, Wayne and Grance, Timothy et al.: Guidelines on security and privacy in public cloud computing. NIST special publication, 2011, p. 144.

[KRG09] Kozuch, Michael A. and Ryan, Michael P. and Gass, Richard et al.: Tashi: Location-aware cluster management. ACM, Proceedings of the 1st workshop on automated control of datacenters and clouds, 2009, pp. 43-48.

[LaSa12] Larumbe, Federico and Sansò, Brunilde: Optimal location of data centers and software components in cloud computing network design. Proceedings of the 2012 12th IEEE/ACM International Symposium on Cluster, Cloud and Grid Computing (ccgrid 2012), 2012, pp. 841-844.

[LTM+11] Liu, Fang and Tong, Jin and Mao, Jian and Bohn, Robert and Messina, John and Badger, Lee and Leaf, Dawn: NIST cloud computing reference architecture. NIST special publications, 500, 2011, p. 292.

[RaKY06] Ray, Indrakshi and Kumar, Mahendra and Yu, Lijun: LRBAC: a location-aware role-based access control model. Springer, Information Systems Security, 2006, pp. 147-161.

[Same12] Kai Samelin: Modelling Secure Cloud-Computing. University of Passau, Master's thesis, 2012.

[Sand93] Sandhu, Ravi S.: Lattice-based access control models. IEEE, Computer 26(11), 1993, pp. 9-19.

[SSR+12] Sassu, Roberto and Smiraglia, Paolo and Ramunno, Gianluca et al.: D2.4.2 Initial Component Integration, Final API Specification and Frist Reference Platform. Tclouds Projekt, 2012.

[SuKa11] Subashini, S. and Kavitha, V.: A survey on security issues in service delivery models of cloud computing. Journal of Network and Computer Applications, 2011, pp. 1-11.

[TEH+11] Tordsson, Johan and Elmroth, Erik and Henriksson, Daniel et al.: D1.2.2.2 – OPTIMIS Detailed Design. Technical Report, Optimized Infrastructure Services (OPTIMIS). FP7 Integrated Project, 2011.

[ToNH07] Tolstrup, Terkel K. and Nielson, Flemming and Hansen, René Rydhof: Locality-based security policies. Springer, Formal Aspects in Security and Trust, 2007, pp. 185-201.

[TsSB10] Tsai, Wei-Tek and Sun, Xin and Balasooriya, Janaka: Service-oriented cloud computing archi-
          tecture. In Information Technology: New Generations (ITNG), Seventh International Confer-
          ence on, 2010, pp. 684-689.

[WaBa13] Waltermire, Karen and Bartock, Mike: Trusted Geolocation in the cloud, technical demonstra-
          tion. National Institute of Standards and Technology (NIST), 2013.

[XiDP04] Xie, Min and Dai, Yuan-Shun and Poh, Kim-Leng: Computing System Reliability. Springer,
          Computing System Reliability: Models and Analysis, 2004.

[ZZX+10] Zhou, Minqi and Zhang, Rong and Xie, Wei and Qian, Weining and Zhou, Aoying: Security and
          privacy in cloud computing: A survey. In Semantics Knowledge and Grid (SKG), Sixth Interna-
          tional Conference on, 2010, pp. 105-112.

Cloud Deployments: Is this the End of N-Tier Architectures?

David Frith

Building A8, Room 1003a/b
Cody Technology Park, Ively Road,
Farnborough, Hampshire, GU14 0LX
david.frith@info-assure.co.uk

Abstract

Current Architectural Patterns (APs) outline good security practice. However such patterns are often generic and whilst useful at a reference level often relate to obsolete technologies, are static in nature and limited in scalability. Newer dynamic computer, network and storage virtualisation methods are in use both within data centres and wider cloud infrastructures. They rely on solutions such as Software Defined Networking (SDN), Network Functional Virtualisation (NFV), the dynamic movement of Virtual Machines (VMs) and hybrid cloud mechanisms combined with e-identity and trust services; methods that are not reflected within current N-Tier architectures and render static models redundant. This paper outlines the tools and methods involved in the management of such technologies and covers possible methods and checklists for their management that correspond to these more agile, lightweight and dynamic deployments.

1 Present N-Tier architectures

Traditional architectural patterns are based on the N-Tier model. They are typically applied to specific business scenarios as used by solution architects and system integrators. N-Tier refers to a multi-tier model based on client-server methods of computing. Traditional N-Tier incorporates a 3 tier model extensible to incorporate further tiers as necessary. The standard 3 tiers include:

- A Presentation Tier to authenticate users and incoming content as and if required. Authenticated and/or un-authenticated traffic is routed to a variety of systems typically with web hosting and application content served; the processed data is then delivered back to the clients augmented by any data from the subsequent tiers.
- A Business Logic Tier handling requests as needed from the Presentation Tier. It provides dynamic content and the further validation of requests. It also provides an interface to the next, the Data Tier. Typically the business logic involved can be provided by middleware using web services or standard data calls using SQL, ODBC and/or JDBC queries. This middle-tier therefore contains most of the application logic and handles the translation of client calls into database queries and then back again to the client.
- The Data Tier typically has no access to or from the top Presentation Tier or by any traffic unmediated by business logic. Separate database accounts may exist for external and internal users and are often combined with further access controls separated by function.

Via this model the presentation, the application processing (business logic) and the data management are all separated. Through such an architecture, data functionality and applications are distributed across the multiple tiers and handled individually.

The characteristics of the Tiered architecture approach include:
- Where the threat is perceived to be higher it is contained. Tiers may incorporate separated trust domains and/or DMZs with barrier controls comprising firewalls at the layer 3, application and web levels in combination with intrusion prevention measures; all to restrict attacks propagating through the tiers.
- Each trust domain is separated from the others by suitable physical and logical barriers that may include sets of firewalls, proxy servers, encryption/decryption offloading and the use of content inspection.
- Accounting, monitoring and reviewable audit data are taken from components across the environment with events collated, consolidated and reviewable within designated SIEM devices and offline repositories.
- All external End User Devices (EUD's) either managed or unmanaged are presumed to be compromised and are authenticated, then allowed or denied particular levels of access as required.
- Web components, applications and Content Management Solutions (CMS) are configured with specific lockdowns to reduce attack surfaces. Static content is favoured over the dynamic as far as possible by application designers who typically implement such functionality into their solutions directly rather than externally.
- The tier/s containing the middleware handle the essential tasks of load balancing, resource management, security and transactional integrity which have the effect of insulating programmers from many of the intricacies of operating systems and database applications.

N-tier architecture, by partitioning software and systems, enables flexibility through a building block approach. It facilitates infrastructure design and further growth by clearly separating the various tiers that make up an overall solution, increasing its maintainability and scalability. Network bottlenecks are minimised through the application layer as erroneous data is not transmitted to subsequent tiers or back to the EUDs, only the data needed to handle a particular task is propagated.

Traditionally when the loading on a particular tier increases, instead of continually outgrowing and replacing single-servers, low cost machines are added to accommodate expanding workloads. This is known as 'scaling out' where computing power is added incrementally using pools of affordable parts. By partitioning systems and applications into front-end, middle tier and back-end layers, N-tier architecture supports a more standardized, building block approach to application design. Hardware and software for presentation, application and database functions can be scaled independently (Intel). It allows organisations to increase performance and availability gradually and inexpensively. An example being Google's development of its own applications and functions for load balancing, remote management and new server deployment using affordable components to create scalable computing environments.

N-Tier architectures then tend to be based on generic functions incorporating the good practice principles of segmentation, defence in depth, least privilege and authentication at first entry. An example being the walled garden concepts as used for remote access to provide a controlled environment and sanitised data back to users. N-Tier patterns are also typically supported by the identity, time synchronisation, provider management and the monitoring and auditing component patterns that they require.

2 N-Tier architectural issues

However N-Tier architectures often require significant alteration before being of use. Being static generic models they require customisation for implementation into specific scenarios. They reinforce a perimeter-focused and malware-prevention bias which can result in siloed based approaches where systems cannot, or do not share business-relevant data effectively or communicate freely. The end-to-end traceability of data flowing through both individual servers and each tier is a challenging task for the provision of sufficient resourcing, this is combined with requirements for minimum latency and rapid deploy-ability and time constraints. Any continued use of N-Tier architectures presents four major challenges:

- The growth of software based infrastructures co-existing with and gradually replacing their physical equivalents. This includes the rapid take up of SDN, NFV and Software Defined Storage (SDS). Implementations using such software based architectures offer high levels of dynamic compute, network and storage virtualisation and flexibility.
- This move to software is linked to the growth of dynamic architectures, the rapid movement of Virtual Machines (VM's)[1] and the Virtual Networks (VN's)[2] and the storage that accompanies them as they are altered, moved and dynamically placed around the infrastructure. Traditional N-Tier architectures are often rigid, complex and vendor-specific and as such often prove ill-suited for such agility and suboptimal for the heavily mobile and virtualised environments that use them.
- The growth of hybrid cloud architectures including measures such as Cloud Brokering and Cloud Bursting. Hybrid cloud incorporates the movement of data from one providers cloud to another bypassing traditional tiering and extending boundaries by offloading workload.
- Datacentre automation is augmented through specialist algorithms implementing optimal and intelligent workload placement. Many current operational models incorporate physical network provisioning which is slow compared with workload virtualisation. However in practice many VMs also remain static due to the high operational costs of movement and the issue of potential downtime.

Architects and designers are therefore currently constrained by the static nature and limitations of N-Tier architecture. Protocols tend to be defined in isolation, each set to solve a specific problem without the benefit of conveying fundamental abstractions. This has resulted in a primary limitation: complexity. Large provider infrastructures such as those used by Google, Yahoo!, and Facebook are classed as hyper-scale and are required to provide high-performance, low-cost connectivity incorporating many hundreds of thousands of servers. Such scaling cannot be provided manually. Multi-tenancy further complicates the task, as the network must serve groups of users with different application and performance needs. This can introduce latency with every addi-

---

1   VM and hosting parameters can be automated by methods to review system configuration and self-management. Such an approach is explored within a paper on Discovering Correctness Constraints for the Self-Management of System Configurations (Yi-MinWang).
2   VN's are required for communication over provider networks when shared by many tenants. VN's offer methods to enforce predictable environments and shared settings with providers to gain greater reliability. This is explored within the paper Towards Predictable Datacenter Networks (Hitesh Ballani).

tional switch 'hop' contributing to potential packet loss. In contrast to client-server applications where the bulk of the communication occurs between one client and one server, hyper-scale applications often require access to multiple databases and servers simultaneously. It creates a flurry of 'east-west' or horizontal server to server traffic within the same tier. This being a different model to the traditional 'north-south' traffic patterns where the data flows all the way down and back up the topology to get to its destination, the added barriers between the tiers adding further latency.

An interim answer to this problem is to implement a collapsed (2-tier) architecture with a front end user tier based on leaf switching and a combined business logic and data tier acting as a central spine implementing distribution and core switching to a combined business logic and data tier.

However even a collapsed architecture combined with the extensive use of leaf switching may result in bottlenecks, as with massive horizontal scaling working across thousands of machines in unison causes latencies. This is further aggravated by the tiered barriers included and exacerbated when the VMs remain relatively static due to the perceived operational risks of service disruption. It is also in direct contrast to business need whereby applications for accessibility and availability purposes need to be distributed dynamically across multiple VMs and exchange traffic flows as needed, ad-hoc. Management tools also need to be optimised to migrate and rebalance these server workloads as the physical end points of the flows change often and rapidly. This challenges many of the aspects of traditional networking, hosting and storage from addressing schemes and namespaces to the notion of segmented and routing-based designs.

3 The growth of software based infrastructures

At the network virtualisation level SDN and NFV usage creates a network environment analogous to what compute virtualisation has been subject to over the past decade. The Open Networking Foundation (ONF) defines SDN as a network architecture where network control is decoupled from forwarding and is directly programmable (FAQ's). SDN enables centralised command and control to be combined with the automated provisioning of virtual network functions. The system making the decisions about where traffic is sent (the control plane) is separate from the underlying systems that forward or inspect it. SDN requires methods for the control plane to communicate with the data plane:

- The Control Plane uses central policy engines such as OpenDaylight Manager an SDN controller to push policies Southbound to enabled OpenFlow devices (the Infrastructure Plane) or Northbound to the software applications (the Data Plane).
- The Data Plane is where the applications reside accessible through Open Source API's. Typically such applications are available through repositories such as SourceForge or vendor based ecosystems. SDN applications can provide logical switching, routing, firewalling, load balancing, VPN, QoS, monitoring and other typical networking applications. By this method previously hardware based appliances can now be rendered purely in software with all the ease of configuration and agility that this implies.
- The Infrastructure Plane comprises OpenFlow enabled infrastructure including Switches, vSwitches, blade servers etc. Multi-purpose infrastructure replaces the previous single purpose devices from well know vendors with the networking, application and SDN functionality taking place virtually.

The SDN architecture is therefore:

- Directly programmable with network control decoupled from forwarding functions.
- Agile with the ability to dynamically adjust to meet changing needs.
- Centrally managed with the network intelligence based within the SDN controllers.
- Programmatically configured to manage, secure, and optimise resources using automated SDN programs and self-amending data paths.

Tools such as VMware NSX and Nuage Networks VSP (Virtualized Services Platform) support the aforementioned Control, Data and Infrastructure planes combined with the ability to integrate with Cloud platforms such as CloudStack and OpenStack and development and support environments such as Kubernetes and Mesos.

Within the area of Infrastructure as a Service (IaaS) SDN virtualised networking, virtual computing (VM's) and virtual storage are deployable as elastic resources. Infrastructure can be dynamically allocated to each application in combination with built in security incorporating Moving Target Defence (MTD) algorithms to periodically hide or change key system or network properties. One approach using MTD incorporates evolution-based algorithms, which based upon previous incidents periodically change system attack surfaces. These algorithms are based on value and domain mutations to intermittently change parameters and system attributes (David J. John). Another method is OpenFlow Random Host Mutation (OFRHM) whereby OpenFlow controllers frequently assign altering parameters such as random virtual IP addresses to confuse attackers. The real IP remains untouched, with the IP mutation completely transparent. Named hosts are reachable via the virtual IP addresses acquired via DNS, but real IP addresses can be only reached by authorised entities (Jafar Haadi Jafarian). Such MTD's are used as a technique in detecting and mitigating botnets, worm propagations and Distributed Denial of Service (DDoS) attacks. Protocols such as FlowVisor are used by hardware resources for both production and development purposes and for separating monitoring, configuration and Internet traffic. Others such as FlowChecker validate new OpenFlow rules deployed within a slice of network or computing resource to ensure that each application has its own logical topology.

NFV uses the technologies of IT virtualisation to provide entire classes of security functionality. These functions are treated as building blocks which can be connected or chained to create sets of secure services. Virtualised Network Functions (VNFs) are created which consist of VMs and distributed NFVs running vendor applications or VNF Components (VNFCs) such as firewalls, intrusion prevention, content filtering or secure tunnel termination functions. NFV is an SDN for security. A management layer allows the horizontal scaling out (east-west) and tiering down (north-south) of VNFC instances across the infrastructure.

Service chaining allows multiple VNFs to be used in logical or time based sequences to deliver services. Security workflows are also increasingly automated and orchestrated for rapid and multi layered security responses incorporating deception based measures to obfuscate, block and implement kill chains[3]. For example Access Control Lists (ACLs) are deployable across the infrastructure and can be configured to timeout after a set period (e.g. 6 months) saving manual re-working. Another pattern may include a Quality of Service (QoS) application configured to dynamically allocate bandwidth for a VoIP (Voice over IP) service; both can be deployed instantaneously across the environment with equally rapid teardown when sessions are complete.

---

3 Such models include the Lockheed Martin 'Cyber Kill Chain' model (2011) and a number of variants such as CREST.

Both SDN and NFV solutions overlap. However to offer combined functionality requires central orchestration and management systems that take operator requests associated with a VNF or OpenFlow message and translate them along with the configuration needed to bring functions into operation within a common ecosystem. The combined management, monitoring and integration of SDN, NFV and Software Defined Storage (SDS) being an ongoing area of development.

SDS comprises a component of an overall Software Defined Data Centre (SDDC); this combining virtualised storage, server, networking and security resources. It is the storage virtualisation equivalent of SDN allowing software to manage the policy-based provisioning of data storage independent of any hardware. Functionality is provided for the virtualised deduplication, replication, thin provisioning, snapshots and backup and automated protection and recovery functions. SDS being implemented via appliances within a SAN, via scaled-out NAS solutions, or through Object-based storage. Such storage virtualisation can be used to provide the datafication capabilities needed to transform bulk gathered data into new forms of value as driven by analytics. This however is combined with the replication of data throughout an Infrastructure via distributed processing creating once again the issues of tracking, management and security but this time applied to storage. Big data solutions also create greater bandwidth needs since their handling requires massive parallel processing by thousands of servers all requiring bidirectional connectivity. The rise of such mega datasets also fuels the constant demand for additional network capacities. The operators of hyper-scale data centres face the challenging task of scaling infrastructure to previously unimaginable sizes whilst creating and maintaining high levels of any-to-any communication.

4 The growth of dynamic architectures

The overall shift from equipment-based solutions to a service-based approach results in a demand for collapsed architectures, dynamic machine migration and the use of algorithms to control intelligent VM placements. Measures to overcome static N-Tier model limitations have included the development of a number of scale out practices. These are based on the East and West requirements of keeping workloads local and include the use of horizontal scaling, dynamic clustering, and affinity rules as detailed below.

The use of horizontal scaling refers to the scaling out of infrastructure within a single tier. It provides the ability to connect multiple hardware and software entities to work as single logical unit, therefore providing the ability to increase capacity.

Similarly, the use of dynamic clustering involving load balancing and high availability providing a greater level of redundancy and data sharing. It allows easy scalability for horizontal growth by allowing individual servers to be taken offline for maintenance or replacement without compromising service. However this being at the expense of potential over-provisioning. Distributed workloads horizontally scaled at the hyper-scale can result in dozens of sub-tiers, each with hundreds or even thousands of VMs working in unison requiring workload distribution tools. Tools such as VMWare's vSphere Distributed Resource Scheduler (DRS) or Citrix's XenServer Workload Balancer used to balance the workload, however at the risk of pushing them apart, across the network and so introducing further latencies.

Affinity Rules are settings which record the relationships between two or more VMs and/or their hosts. They are designed to provide a balance between scaling and clustering methods to keep workloads together and in establishing rules between the top talkers. The rules defining the common talkers such as web, application and database servers can require for example common residence on the same host or through the use of vSwitches further constrain communications. They can include:

- VM to VM affinity rules to ensure that certain VMs always reside in close proximity. Therefore if a particular web VM is vMotioned to a different host, other associated VMs such as application and database VM's move correspondingly.
- Host to VM affinity rules to ensure that certain workloads always run on the same physical machine; perhaps because a particular application is tied by licensing to a certain CPU, e.g. in the case of Windows Server Datacentre 2012 or because a VM is a current vSphere host. Such rules ensure that these VM's are never migrated to unsuitable hosts.
- Anti-affinity rules whereby certain VMs cannot run on the same host. This could be the case for multiple Windows Domain Controllers where the configuration and policy data they hold needs to remain available at all times.

Whilst the use of the above methods provide a measure of control for short time periods they need to contend with transient VM behaviour right across the environment including across tiers. The placing of unneeded constraints detracts from the dynamic capabilities offered. Whilst affinity rules provide a certain level of mitigation, for large, complex, hyper-scale architectures where hundreds of applications are present across multiple tiers, complex inventories of multi layered affinity rules are required. These traditional approaches attempt to optimise a system wide measure of performance through average response times, throughput, server load etc. This optimisation is performed by a centralised algorithm. The current and future complexity of resource allocation problems however makes it impossible to define an acceptable system wide performance set of metrics through the use of centralised or consensus based algorithms which prove impractical within a dynamic system owned by multiple organisations (Donald F Ferguson).

5 The growth of hybrid cloud

A hybrid cloud is an integrated service which uses both private and public clouds to perform different functions for the same workload. One hybrid cloud service is a Cloudbroker acting as a trusted intermediary between a purchaser of cloud services and the available sellers. A Cloudbroker may act as a Cloud Aggregator, distributing services across multiple cloud providers in an effort to be as cost-effective as possible. This is enabled via a set of common RESTful API's and User Interfaces (UI) to hide complexities allowing the customer to use their service as if purchased from a single vendor. The cloud broker may also act a Cloud Enabler providing the customer with additional tools such as data deduplication, a variety of encryption methods, data migration and further Data Lifecycle Management (DLM) assistance. Via Cloud White Label Services the broker can act as a Cloud Agent, selecting providers on behalf of the customer and integrating their sets of services together, distributing the customer workload between many providers.

A further extension to the various cloud brokering methods listed above involves Cloudbursting, the provision that customer applications housed within one cloud can burst into other separate clouds as their demand for computing capacity spikes. It is essentially a Pay As You Go approach typically used in deployments where a certain application running within a private cloud bursts into a public one.

Services from CloudSwitch, IBM and F5 Cloudbursting allow the seamless movement of workloads to a public cloud of choice such as Amazon EC2, Rackspace or Google Compute. The application moved to the public cloud can then free up local resources for more business-critical or compute intensive applications. However applications with complex delivery infrastructures, particular integration needs or security and regulatory compliance demands may not be good candidates. The potential for incompatibilities between different environments and the limitations of management tools may further complicate matters.

6 The automation of the datacentre

Datacentres as shown through the growth of software, dynamic and hybrid based architectures exist as increasingly automated environments. Through the implementation of intelligent placement methods and decision making analytics VM infrastructures can be managed towards a desired state. This being a state in which application performance is assured whilst the infrastructure is utilised as efficiently as possible and workload demand is best satisfied by infrastructure supply (VMTurbo, June 2015). Such a state can take into account the complex needs and cyclical nature of workloads along with their associated resource consumption needs with rules to ensure:

- That the use of scheduling and threshold mechanisms are adhered to for VM placement.
- The use of benchmarking implementations to recover server unused capability and to provide a measure of VM rightsizing.
- Allowances and flexibilities are taken into account for the utilisation of machine resources.

The algorithms for VM placement decisions can have a marked improvement upon workload performance. This can be a measure of throughput, CPU usage or completion cycles with potential gains of 70% compared to the randomly allocated placements used traditionally (David Erickson) Indeed, such principles can be taken further to one of supply and demand. This is to abstract such placement into one of the commodities bought and sold, as explored by Yemini on Economic Models for Allocating Resources in Computer Systems[4] . As the resource allocation and optimisation needs grow, the number of permutations also grows exponentially. Yemini's research showed that a local optimum could be found by approximating resource consumers and providers as buyers and sellers in a market place. Therefore at any given time a finite supply of CPU, memory, drive space and other resources are counter-balanced by the demand of VMs and their applications. Loads fluctuate in real-time as demand changes according to utilisation rates; this forces workloads to constantly shop around for better placements, the aim being to maintain an environment in a dynamic equilibrium. This method of usage breaks from the traditional approach of threshold management, predictive analytics and root cause diagnostics by shifting the focus from data analysis to real-time brokerage.

However there is a challenge in managing such environments where hundreds of applications each with dozens of tiers are distributed across thousands of VMs sharing hundreds of hosts, data stores, and network devices. Scheduling engines within tools such as VMTurbo Operations

---

4 Resource allocation complexity due to decentralisation and heterogeneity is also present in human economies. There are similarities between complex distributed systems and human economies and competitive economic models can provide algorithms and tools for allocating resources in distributed computer systems. Yemini explores the use of allocation and pricing models as well as economic models based on flow control, load balancing and data management.

Manager[5] can be used to map the relationships between all the resources required. The engine uses topological probabilities to define different levels of traffic flow. Such engines build network traffic matrices to dynamically define each group of highly communicative VMs into a vPod. When the demand overtakes resources within a local environment, the vPod is migrate-able as a whole cohesive unit to a more suitable set of resources. The vPod consumes resources from a dPod or a pool of resources physically located close together. The dynamically defined vPods self-manage the trade-off between network, compute, and storage needs automatically migrating themselves to the most economic dPod whilst simultaneously maximising workload performance and resource utilisation. When communication needs between vPod members subsides, it disaggregates until further demand drives it back together. The desired state is therefore continually shifting and constantly monitored and amended by the scheduling engine through real time analysis and corresponding action.

Such compute virtualisation patterns have been implemented within experimental cloud projects such as CloudLab and Chamaleon incorporating dynamic machine migration and in encrypting VM data and striping it across multiple locations and jurisdictions. Such methods being used to create the de-perimeterisation, resource pooling and intelligent workload placement measures across clusters as outlined.

The possible use of controls incorporate methods of dynamic authentication and authorisation. This can be combined with localised security measures including the implementation of adaptive security and workflow orchestration defences as explored below.

7 Identity Relationship Management (IRM)

The increasing trend of IT consumerisation is having a profound effect on current enterprise architecture as greater levels of mobile and personal devices access cloud environments. The pressure to accommodate such personal devices in a fine-grained manner whilst protecting data, intellectual property and compliance requirements is resulting in greater demands being placed upon identity and access management solutions. Such tools are traditionally corporate facing and often classified under the umbrella term of Identity Access Management (IAM). IAM solutions being subject to greater demand and are being expanded/morphed into newly titled Identity Relationship Management (IRM). IRM incorporates the shift from a closed and protective authorisation approach to an open, evolving one. It includes the use of open source solutions that link cloud with traditional enterprise infrastructures. These hybrid models typically include a customisable on premises component combined with cloud services to handle user identities across the entire environment. Vendors such as Oracle IRM Fusion Middleware services and the ForgeRock OIS (Open Identity Stack) being extensible across cloud, social, mobile, and enterprise environments. Solutions such as Bridge Service Provider Edition (Bridge SPE) provide the customisable components that reside on premises and handle the user identities between hybrid cloud and on-premises.

IRM solutions offer the needed trust service patterns required for identity federation, identity assertion and identity sourcing with the integration of users, partners, third parties, collaborators

---

5 Operations Manager is a control platform that uses supply and demand principles to model the data and resource requirements on economic markets. Applications, VMs and container based workloads act as the buyers of the compute, storage and fabric selling agents working out placement, sizing, and stop/start decisions among themselves.

and customers into a cohesive framework. For the management of customer identities this encompasses a drastic increase in scale and complexity. For example an existing IAM solution may include several thousand employee identities compared with an IRM solution that could scale to millions. Additionally such identities represent an audience that is not captive to the enterprise or requiring traditional internal-facing security needs.

IRM incorporates both the identities of consumers and artefacts as well as the implementation of Internet scaled, dynamically intelligent, borderless and modular components. The value is provided in the relationship and in particular what an identity represents. IRM solutions contain the provision to scale and adapt to demands without requiring major downtime or overhauls and provide the ability for agile and nuanced responses through different authentication mechanisms dependent on the fraud and mobile risk management patterns presented.

Trust services can make use of third parties such as Identity Providers and Assurance Hubs in addition to the on-premises solutions outlined. Flexible provisioning management can make use of the wide variety of Identity, Entitlement and Access (IdEA) solutions in use. These can then be combined with a variety of authentication methods which can be chained and federated to share identities across domain boundaries.

Embedded into identity federation requirements is the need to provide effective methods of endpoint validation. The FIDO (Fast IDentity Online) Alliance provides a set of solutions for open, scalable and interoperable authentication mechanisms, designed to supplant password methods and to securely authenticate the users of online services. Methods such as Universal Second Factor (U2F) protocol and the Universal Authentication Framework (UAF) allow for the combination of biometrics such as fingerprint and iris scanning, voice and facial recognition with existing solutions such as Trusted Platform Modules (TPM), USB security tokens, embedded Secure Elements (eSE), smart cards, and Near Field Communication (NFC) authentication. FIDO is a device-centric model; when authentication occurs the device registers the user to a server by sending a public key. To authenticate the user, the device signs a challenge from the server using the private key that it holds. The keys on the device can be unlocked by a local user gesture such as a biometric with public-key cryptography used to secure the credentials and ongoing connectivity.

IRM can integrate both with external providers and internal systems such as HR, CRM and ERP instances and when combined with adaptive authorisation and the assessment of authentication based risk can provide the security and the scoring metrics needed (e.g. IP addresses, the device types used for access, location, idle times) for additional security layers. e-Identity measures include the validation, verification, repair and revocation of identities which are reusable across services and use open standards based plug-ins and connectors. By such methods identity security is abstracted as well as made more scalable and robust.

8 Adaptive Security

At the technology level patterns can incorporate the use of Adaptive Security Policies (ASPs) applicable to compute, network and storage environments and implementable down to the granular level of the individual workloads. Solutions such as Illumio ASP can be used in the context of workloads to enable the nano-segmentation of applications down to individual VM, server, and running process levels. ASP decouples security from the underlying infrastructure relying on graph theory[6] to build live interactive maps of the applications and traffic to highlight policy violations, monitor and inspect for suspicious activity and to identify changes in real-time, communicating remedial actions as necessary to Policy Enforcement Points (PEPs). ASP solutions can automatically enforce end point protection implementing access rules to block malicious traffic. Additional tools can unify the responses from multiple vendors into one holistic security plane. Solutions such as CSG Invotas Security Orchestrator provide the automation of security workflows to unify such defences. Multi layered responses can be combined with deception based measures and counter attack orchestration.

Security can be made continuously enforceable, adapting to changing application needs and providing instant encryption to data in motion and ad-hoc data flows as they traverse endpoints. Policies are definable by their workload role, application, location and/or environment, these being configurable through automatically flagged rules which can be translated into actionable templates and/or manually configurable actions. These rules are then implemented by policy servers to the individual ASP agents and nodes. A major change with this model of real-time adaptive security is the shifting of authorisation management and policies to an on-demand service for the policy enforcement.

Compute containers can provide another layer of complication as they are moved throughout the cloud environment and require infrastructure analysis software to review their service relationships and develop measures to allow for container removal, reallocation and reconfiguration; this whilst still retaining security policies and operational requirements and allowing such containers to run within a wide variety of domains. Container applications such as Docker allow applications to be assembled into packages along with their dependency mappings. Such containers comprise standardised units for software development along with subsequent automated deployment. Resources can be isolated, services restricted, and processes provisioned across multiple containers sharing the same kernel, but with each constrained to only use a defined amount of resources, e.g. CPU, memory and I/O. The purpose of container usage being to simplify the creation of highly distributed systems, allowing multiple applications, workload tasks and processing to run autonomously on a single physical machine or across multiple VMs. Such an automated management layer can combine cloud provisioning with big data analytics to review, analyse and take actions against potential threats, particularly those based upon stealthy Advanced Persistent Threat (APT) and Advanced Evasion Technique (AET) based attacks.

9 Checklist controls

The dynamic, agile and changeable architectures illustrated cannot be mapped to N-Tier models. The provisions for remote access walled garden environments, multiple tiered barrier controls or the traditional methods of serving web content do not meet current requirements for agility, timescaling or workloads. Agility requirements instead of architectural patterns are to be developed based on architectural principles and checklists which as a first outline may include:

---

6   Graph theory is the study of graphs and mathematical structures used to model pairwise relations between objects. It uses the concepts of a vertexes (or nodes), edges (or arcs) and loops, degrees, adjacencies, paths, circuits, planars and connected components. It includes Euler Paths a theorem based on when such paths and circuits exist through adjacency matrices as presented through the work of a variety of algorithms to find a shortest path.

- Data in transit and data in rest protection are enabled by default through defined templates for encryption, integrity components and recommended ciphers. Keys being held in client control, independently or through escrow services.
- The minimisation of latency between workload endpoints by the keeping of such workloads and the reservation of network resources local.
- Enforced separation between consumers at the compute, network and storage layers with independently validated, provider validated and customer validated controls enforced at all the layers between them.
- Allowing for workload mobility and the provision of tools to customers allowing them to manage their levels of service.
- Providing independent validation of service design through external testing, qualified reviews and the use of assured components.
- Making monitoring easy through a templated based approach and the use of pre-defined processes for protective monitoring, auditing and incident management.
- The security of virtualised infrastructure (Virtual Machines, Virtual Networks and Virtual Storage) being independent of their movement and overall management.
- Supporting 'Tenant vMotion' for Cloudbursting again through templated based approaches for cloudbrokering and management.

Further work is required to develop the design patterns needed to incorporate overall generic security principles such as least privilege, segregation of duties, defence in depth and an economy of mechanism in promoting simple and comprehensive design.

Additionally patterns are to be explored to include defence in depth measures such as signature based infrastructures which can ensure that components are tagged, tracked and locatable up to a level of Exabyte scaling; this to provide independent and verifiable audit trails and real-time detection. Other work is required around the integration of Threatcloud services, threat intelligence frameworks and maturity models such as the Business Intelligence model and common threat Intelligence lifecycles. Overall such patterns need to be integrated with common frameworks such as SABSA (Sherwood Applied Business Security Architecture), TOGAF (The Open Group Architecture Framework), Zachman and others such as SOMF (Service Oriented Modelling Framework) and SOMA (Service Oriented Modelling and Architecture) for developing service based business systems.

10 Conclusion

N-Tier architecture is too slow, too static and too suboptimal to function effectively in a world of dynamic architectures. Network heavy workloads place considerable strain on current architectures. Topology and traffic-matrix awareness are needed for VM placement decision-ing, to improve application performance and to eliminate potential bottlenecks. Such cloud deployments facilitate an end to N-Tier architectures.

Management tactics using horizontal scaling, dynamic clustering and affinity rules force organisations to choose between network latency and compute and storage latency, a trade-off which cannot be statically controlled. Current solutions typically become rigid, complex and vendor-specific with mobility limited by physical topology and manual provisioning. This ties an increasingly dynamic virtualised world back to an inflexible one, dominated by dedicated hardware and rigidly adhered to tiered controls. These are barriers to optimising capacity and utilisation. Manual provisioning and fragmented management interfaces limit the ability of organisations to rapidly deploy, move, scale and protect applications and data.

To unlock the full value of virtualised infrastructure and cloud services a move to a simpler, automated and predictable delivery set of mechanisms are required to provide enhanced security, a greater control in maintaining a healthy infrastructure state and in consistent service delivery. Further work is required to fully expand on the checklists and methods described here and to provide new cohesive models of dynamic security that map to the dynamic architectures outlined.

References

David Erickson, B. H. (n.d.). Using Network Knowledge to Improve Workload Performance in Virtualized Data Centers. Stanford University.

David J. John, R. W. (n.d.). Evolutionary Based Moving Target Cyber Defense. Dept. of Computer Science Wake Forest University.

Donald F Ferguson, C. N. (n.d.). Economic Models for Allocating Resources in Computer Systems.

FAQ's, O. N. (n.d.). https://www.opennetworking.org/about/faqs

Hitesh Ballani, P. C. (n.d.). Towards Predictable Datacenter Networks. Imperial College London.

Intel. (n.d.). Building a Better e-Business Infrastructure.

Jafar Haadi Jafarian, E. A.-S. (n.d.). OpenFlow Random Host Mutation: Transparent Moving Target Defense using Software Defined Networking. University of North Carolina.

VMTurbo. (June 2015). Approaches to Cloud Management.

Yi-MinWang, E. K. (n.d.). Discovering Correctness Constraints for the Self-Management of System Configurations. Stanford University.

Secure Partitioning of Application Logic In a Trustworthy Cloud

Ammar Alkassar · Michael Gröne · Norbert Schirmer

Sirrix AG security technologies
Im Stadtwald, Geb. D3.2, 66123 Saarbrücken, Germany
{a.alkassar | m.groene | n.schirmer}@sirrix.com

Abstract

Cloud computing based scalable applications or software services (Software-as-a-Service) offer many new opportunities for provisioning and the usage of IT services. Not without risks: sensitive and even mission-critical information and personal data will be stored and processed outside the direct control of the cloud user. Cloud administrators may access those data. Trustworthy Cloud services may only be built upon a strong basis of a trusted cloud infrastructure, separating users from each other and administrators from user data. The cloud model of "Software as a Service" (SaaS), combined with the innovative methods of strict separation of roles and trusted components proposed in this paper is a big chance for higher security in enterprises, especially for SMEs. This is currently been explored in the project SPLITCloud (Secure Partitioning of application Logic In a Trustworthy Cloud) in Germany. An innovative use case in the area of meter data management demonstrates how future trusted SaaS infrastructures and services may look like.

1 Introduction – Cloud Services and Security

Cloud computing offers many new opportunities for provisioning and the usage of IT services. The spectrum ranges from providing virtual IT infrastructures (Infrastructure-as-a-Service) over pre-configured computer systems (Platform-as-a-Service) to scalable applications or software services (Software-as-a-Service). These new opportunities are not without risks: sensitive and even mission-critical information and sometimes personal data will be stored and processed outside the direct control of the cloud user. Ultimately, the users of the cloud service must trust the fact that the availability of data, compliance with national and European data protection obligations and confidentiality of business secrets could be guaranteed uncompromisingly. The primary inhibitor for adopting the cloud is protecting sensitive information. This dilemma regarding "opportunities", especially for small and medium enterprises (SME) all across Europe, and "risk defence" have to be solved to push SaaS and help companies to benefit from cloud services, without gambling unforeseeable risks.

The main question arising for SaaS cloud providers of complex software solutions is to what extent existing software applications and system architectures can be converted into highly secure cloud concepts. The key focus is manageability and deployability in a system that decouples the administrator from the processed sensitive customer data, without making significant intervention to the programming model of the base system. Novel highly automated maintenance and test procedures are required in order to achieve this requirement of decoupling in the systems while maintaining a very high data quality.

This paper gives an overview of the capabilities of a framework that enables strict separation of roles in accessing data within SaaS, which is currently been explored in the project SPLITCloud (Secure Partitioning of application Logic In a Trustworthy Cloud). Furthermore, it will outline how this will be validated to confirm the practicability by implementing meter data management (MDM) as an example application.

1.1 The Project SPLITCloud

In the project described in this paper, the SPLITCloud framework is developed, i.e., an architecture, which protects Software-as-a-Service (SaaS) compliant to data privacy and data security requirements. Through dedicated application virtualization and partitioning of data storage in different virtual compartments (so called Trusted Virtual Domains (TVDs) [AlHu09, CLMS+10]) the SPLITCloud framework will provide a secure and trusted separation of administrative roles between manufacturers, providers and users of the software. Thereby the data of the users is protected effective from access by other users as well as from the access by administrators (covering accidents and insider attacks) of the cloud service and the cloud infrastructure this service is based on. At the same time secure mechanisms and interfaces are provided that allow the service provider and the software manufacturer to perform the necessary support and maintenance tasks of the cloud infrastructure and the software.

The SPLITCloud architecture is not limited to a particular service, but represents an architecture for any kind of software, whether Enterprise-Resource-Planning (ERP) or Customer-Relationship-Management systems, office applications or more specialised software, such as Meter Data Management. As a pilot application, we evaluate and measure the SPLITCloud framework on meter data management (MDM), a pioneering and challenging application in the field of the smart grid. In the energy sector the term MDM is used to describe an IT application in the field of smart metering. In the specific media MDM is often understood directly as part of a "smart metering system". As such, MDM is "the central data management of smart meters".

In addition, the project aims to develop advanced next generation concepts, which will allow extensions of the SPLITCloud architecture to mobile devices and mobile application scenarios.

Innovation of the approach

The SPLITCLoud project closes a central gap in practical oriented implementation of security research and solutions. In research projects in context of cloud security primarily the security of pure cloud infrastructure (IaaS) solutions or the security of specific applications was investigated so far. In contrast, the SPLITCloud project is developing a general framework, which can be used to secure Software-as-a-Service (SaaS), regardless of the specific application. This makes SPLITCloud distinct from other work and projects, such as the CipherCloud platform [CC14].

1.2 Objectives

The aim of the SPLITCloud framework is the security of SaaS, insofar that sensitive data in the cloud can be processed as safe and privacy-compliant as in a company's own IT infrastructure.

Important objectives are:

- Strict isolation of SaaS users: The data of different users can be effectively isolated from each other. With users, different organizations are meant, independently using the same service running on one infrastructure / hardware.
- Isolation of user data from cloud provider and software vendor: The user data are isolated from access by the administrators of both, the service provider and the software vendor (if not the same company).
- Software maintenance by the software vendor: Despite the isolation of the user data from the cloud service provider, he is responsible for software maintenance and able to do this, possibly with assistance of the software vendor. For this purpose, appropriate and secure mechanisms are needed.

For this purpose, approaches, methods and solutions for the following scientific questions are developed:

- How can security of services be anchored in hardware security features?
- How can the operation and migration of virtual machines, providing a service, be carried out, while maintaining the verifiability of this service?
- How can a cloud infrastructure and a cloud service be development, which is secured against the (most) malicious insiders (especially privileged administrators)?
- How can data protection legislation, in particular the concepts of the three privacy protection goals transparency, intervenability, non-linkability, and the privacy-by-design approach (see [RoPf09], [RoBo11]) be reconciled with the use of (secured) cloud service offerings?
- How could scalability of a trusted management component be ensured?

The overall objective:

The overall goal of the project SPLITCloud is the realization of secure and privacy-compliant separation of responsibilities (see Table 1-1) for Software-as-a-Service, by implementing:

- dedicated application virtualization and
- distribution of data into Trusted Virtual Domains (TVD).

Table 1: Separation of Responsibilities within the SPLITCloud Framework

	Cloud infrastructure	Application code	User data
Software vendor		X	
Cloud provider	X		
User (Organization)			X

As the project lead Sirrix AG (security technology provider) is collaborating with Intel Collaborative Research Institute for Secure Computing at TU Darmstadt (security research), Independent Centre for Privacy Protection Schleswig-Holstein Germany (ULD) (data privacy commissioner), Schleupen AG (software provider), and Verizon Deutschland GmbH (cloud provider) to reach these goals. This contribution will show the outcome of the SPLITCloud project from the first year of the project, such as the challenges and requirements that have to be fulfilled to build a trustworthy SaaS cloud framework, an innovative approach for a trusted cloud infrastructure and separation of administrative roles using Trusted Virtual Domains (TVD). Moreover, we present and discuss a modular security framework approach that can be used to realize such SaaS in order to fulfil the requirements of the customers regarding data privacy and data security. This security framework is based on a security kernel [Sirrix15] approach that has been developed within various other projects, e.g. [EMSCB], [OpenTC], [ASSS+06].

2 Background: Cloud Scenario and requirements

The common Cloud scenario means outsourcing of IT infrastructures, such as servers and storage. Systems are running in datacenters off-premise. In Cloud Computing this is done by using IaaS, which involves virtual infrastructures that are owned by Cloud providers. Customers which require isolation from other customers, which may be competitors, or to be compliant with policies for segregation of duties (isolation of management-, sales-, development-departments, etc.), need strict isolation of data in the cloud. This is described in e.g. [CaHo09], [GrSc11]. Figure 1 shows the situation within nowadays typical SaaS cloud infrastructures. The service runs within virtual machines with no user isolation at the infrastructure level. This is typically implemented by access control within the service. Additionally, administrators have access to user data, especially those administrators who maintain the service itself, and not the infrastructure. Either administrators from the cloud provider or external administrators from the software vendor, a subcontractor from the perspective of the cloud user.

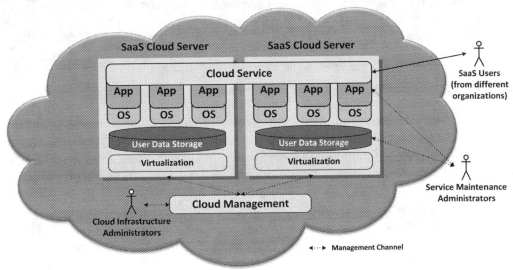

Fig. 1: SaaS-Cloud-Infrastructure architecture today: no isolation of users, user data and administrators

3 SPLITCloud Framework Approach

In the SPLITCloud project we are developing an approach that enforces both, user isolation and the isolation of the user data from administrators, on the infrastructure as well as the service level. Therefore, the technical implementation of the project goals takes place on two levels. At the application level, we implement a strict decoupling of software (application code) and data (user data). This reflects the different responsibilities shown in 1.2. The responsibility for the maintenance of the software is up to the software vendor, but sovereignty over the user data remains with the user. On the infrastructure level, the data of different users are isolated from each other and from the SaaS provider. Several technologies are used here. User-specific encryption in order to protect stored data, and virtualization in order to protect the data during processing. To implement these mechanisms in a secure and trustworthy way, it requires a trusted infrastructure that is storing key material securely, enforces the encryption and provides a secure interface for maintenance by the cloud provider. The SPLITCloud architecture is shown in Figure 2.

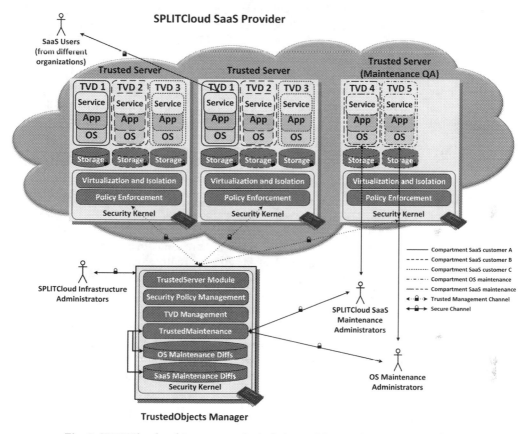

Fig. 2: SPLITCloud architecture – strict isolation and Service Maintenance without access to user data

Virtualization is standard technology within the infrastructure of a cloud provider to achieve a decoupling of the physical resources. Scalability of cloud offerings is based on this technology and it allows on-demand provisioning and billing of virtual and physical resources. The maintainability and availability of this infrastructure benefits of the possibility of migration of virtual resources across physical resources and thus hardware failures can be managed and compensated easily. By virtualization a clean isolation of virtual machines can be implemented, which are running the software. A separation of users can be implemented by separation into different instances of the same virtual machine – the reference machine (reference VM).

On the one hand virtualization is an effective way to ensure user isolation at runtime, but on the other it only inadequately protects against insiders, in particular administrators of cloud providers. In order to fulfill their duties, those typically require access to the host operating system on which virtualization is built on. Furthermore, service administrators need also to have access to the operating system (OS) running inside the virtual machines in order to maintain the software therein. To regulate this access within the trusted infrastructure a security kernel [GrWi12], [Sirrix15] is used. It provides the virtualization layer and security services on a hardened system and controls the interfaces to maintain the system (Trusted Maintenance). With these controlled interfaces administrators do not have privileged access to the system and the virtual machines anymore. The integrity of the hardware and of the security kernel is ensured by Trusted Computing technologies, such as a Trusted Platform Module (TPM) [TPM11], so that manipulations at this level can be excluded. A remote attestation of all cloud infrastructure server platforms on which the application is running is made possible by a trusted cloud infrastructure management, so that tampering or errors in the cloud infrastructure, which would cause data protection and security issues, can be detected.

The encryption of data raises the question of key management. To protect the data even from the cloud provider, the keys may not even be accessible by the cloud provider in an unprotected state. Here we need a trustworthy cloud infrastructure, as developed by Sirrix in the EU-FP7 project TClouds [TClo11]. This is based on Trusted Computing technology [TCG15] that offers a hardware anchor for secure storage of key material and provides the basis for integrity checks of the platform used within the infrastructure. This allows implementation of the concept of Trusted Virtual Domains (TVDs) [CLMS+10], separated virtual security zones in a shared physical infrastructure. Each user is assigned a unique TVD. Data is transparently encrypted specific for each TVD. For the maintenance of service-related software within the virtual machines by service administrators a separate TVD is provided. In this TVD the user data is not accessible, but merely test data. By separating software and data, the administrator can update and test the software in the reference VM within a separate TVD. The necessary maintenance includes optionally a migration of data when, e.g. data formats or database structures have changed. This process must be performed in the runtime environment of the customer area with the user data. Therefore, the administrators should first carry out a QA process using test data. New instances of the reference VM then can be started in the customer area.

The desktop systems of the administrators are also based on a trusted platform capable of TVDs, so unauthorized information flow between separated users and insider attacks can be prevented.

3.1 Trusted Cloud Service Infrastructure

The SPLITCloud framework is technically based on a trusted cloud infrastructure. Our solution is based on the following technologies:

1) Hardware-based trust anchors in each platform enable to ensure verifiable platform integrity at any time. We use Trusted Platform Module (TPM) chips in servers (TrustedServer) and client PCs (TrustedDesktop) which are part of the trusted infrastructure (TI) to implement a secure boot mechanism that prevents a platform from booting, if it is not in a predefined good state. Platform integrity is crucial for enabling secure data processing and trustworthy handling of secrets.

2) Trusted Virtual Domains (TVDs) are used to define security zones within the virtualized infrastructure. At the border of each security zone, policy enforcement points strictly control all information flows. A policy can, for example, define that when data leaves a TVD, it must be encrypted.

The infrastructure would then take care of automatically encrypting all data when crossing TVD boundaries. This encryption at infrastructure level happens transparently to the user, so he must not himself configure or implement encryption of his data. One of the most crucial benefits of TVDs is that they are lightweight logical constructs of the virtual infrastructure, which means they are very flexible, they can be quickly created and deployed, and it is easily possible to have disposable TVDs for temporary maintenance tasks involved in administrative processes.

3) TURAYA™ SecurityKernel: Each platform runs a security kernel and a hypervisor which allows running multiple sandboxed applications isolated from each other on the same hardware. Every so-called "compartment" is assigned to a particular security zone (TVD). Compartments of different TVDs can reside on the same physical machine without affecting each other's security properties.

Information flow policies define what happens to data crossing TVD boundaries. Policy enforcement is implemented by various integrity-checked security services residing within the security kernel on each trusted platform (Figure 3).

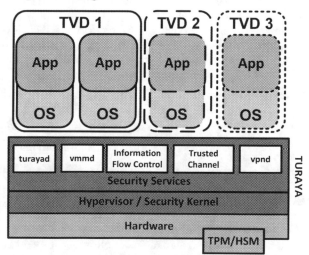

Fig. 3: TURAYA™ SecurityKernel and TVDs

The TURAYA™ SecurityKernel is a security architecture that was developed on the func-tional requirements of the Common Criteria [HASK08]. Its goal is to provide a small security platform, which is hence comprehensive, stable and possible to validate. As the security kernel runs at a higher privilege level than the compartments themselves, it can enforce mandatory policies which cannot be circumvented by anything running inside the compartments. By default, the trusted infrastructure provides transparent encryption of data whenever it crosses a TVD boundary. This means that, when data leaves a compartment (and with that, a TVD), for example, it is stored on an external USB device or a remote server, the data is automatically encrypted and can only be decrypted by a system with access to the original TVD owning the document.

4) TrustedObjects Manager (TOM): The TOM is a management component within the trusted infrastructure (TI). This component allows to define all security policies and to manage all connected platforms within the infrastructure. Different TOM administrators can manage network policies (TCP, UDP layer and ports), TVDs, information flows for communication between TVDs, virtual networks, users, etc. All those configuration information will be pushed to an appliance on start via the management channel (Trusted Channel) in a secure way. Then those will be enforced on the appliance via security kernel. TOM allows uploading and management of compartments (virtual machine images). Templates can be generated and linked to a TVD and VM image. Out of those templates compartments can be created, which then can be pushed to TrustedDesktop or TrustedServer appliances.

3.2 Integration of Mobile Devices

While mobile devices can be integrated seamlessly "as is" into the proposed framework, it is worth to think about a comprehensive concept that provides a higher level of security into an overall system. Having the Trusted Virtual Domains with strict separation of roles, provides the technical basis for providing Information Flow Control [DeDe77] on data throughout the whole system. Compared with so-far deployed Access Control policies, it protects data wherever it is stored, transported or processed over its whole lifetime. However, this requires to extend the TVD concept gapless to the edges, the devices. It is foreseeable that mobile devices will play an important role as an access platform for secure cloud services in the future. It is therefore necessary to develop concepts, which make it possible to extend the security level, achieved by cloud TVDs also to mobile devices and thus, to strictly enforce this separation of data derived from possibly different TVDs. These can utilize hardware-based security anchors, which become popular on mobile platforms, such as microSD-based smart card solutions or Trusted Execution Environments (TEE), which is part of ARM TrustZone and available in most high-end smart phones and tablets. BizzTrust™ by Sirrix could be a technical solution to realize such an integration into the SPLITCloud framework, as it is already fully integrated into the central TOM management.

4 Applying the Framework to Meter Data Management as a Service

To validate the SPLITCloud approach and to confirm the practicability of specific applications, we are implementing meter data management as an example application. This application has all the features for which the SPLITCloud architecture is designed.

Particularly sensitive data is processed, which must be protected from unauthorized access. The application highlights the need for privacy compliant cloud applications because integration of cloud applications is been pushed in critical infrastructures such as the smart grid, driven from economic constraints, due to the high volume of mass data and the regulation of charges for market participants. In the energy sector the term meter data management" (MDM) is used for many years to describe an IT application in the field of smart metering. In the specific media MDM is often understood directly as part of a "smart metering system". As such, MDM is "the central data management of smart meters."

MDM is also referred to as "a database for providing multiple metering systems to multiple data applications." Basically it is valid to say that MDM consists of particularly performance-intensive, volume-driven, complex to integrate and expensive processes and related IT applications. This view is often documented with project experience from overseas and northern Europe. From the perspective of process organization MDM is incorporating all processes that can be specifically attributed to the role "counter value management". A counter measures electric power consumption or power input.

From the perspective of the project, MDM is the role-specific management and processing of counter values that are detected and provided as count or time series at arbitrary intervals by a remote meter reading (Automatic meter reading (AMR), Head End System) from communication-capable meters from producers and consumers in all divisions. The pilot application MDM from the new software generation of Schleupen AG is based on a service-oriented architecture (SOA). Within this service architecture new services are to be implemented to support TVD-based concepts, which automate previously manual executed administrative processes to allow separation of the data and administrator roles.

MDM is a suitable pilot application in particular because of its complex deployment processes within the different types of repositories and databases used. Even after a strict separation of administrative roles, the deployment must be automated and quality assurance must be possible. The database and repository structure in Schleupen.CS 3.0, which must be ready for the pilot application within the TVD concept, consist of many subject-specific databases and repositories, such as Packet- and DeploymentRepository as part of the EnterpriseServiceBus (ESB) and the Microsoft ServiceBus.

A possible implementation of the MDM scenario in different TVDs consist of different SaaS customers in different TVDs of different modules of the MDM service, such as presentation servers and database servers. A proven core concept is information flow control on a network and protocol level between those TVDs, enforced by the security kernel. This is used in the MDM application for a strict separation of data collection on the one hand and for other use by different customers or groups of users on the other hand.

5 Outlook / Future Work

In the first phase of the project the requirements and use cases regarding cloud services and trusted cloud infrastructure including management solutions are defined, in the second phase the technical components, which will realize the SPLITCloud framework, will be developed, together with the pilot application MDM. In the third phase this will be evaluated within a field study at Verizon. In this field study, the applicability of the developed functional components and the pilot application MDM will be tested and fulfilment of the defined security targets will be evaluated. Thereby, an evaluation of the cloud infrastructure framework in the context of data privacy and data security in a cloud environment as well as an evaluation of the pilot application in the context of data privacy within smart metering takes place.

Future work will include technical solutions to include mobile application scenarios and evaluate the framework against other applications such as ERP solutions and new data privacy regulation within the EU.

6 Conclusion

The SPLITCloud architecture provides security, regardless of the security of individual applications, which means, the solution aimed in this project can be used to host any cloud application, and thus long-term use is possible. A cloud service user no longer has to trust the application that it protects data from users of other organizations, in particular from administrators, by properly implemented access control mechanisms. Instead, users can rely on the trusted cloud infrastructure that it isolates the data of different organizations with one another as well as data from the staff of the cloud provider, particularly administrators. The overall system now must be certified only once, rather than – as by today – every application that is provided for an organization in the cloud, would be needed to be certified individually. It is to be expected that there will be no performance loss compared to today's approaches, as they are also based on virtualization within the cloud infrastructure.

Main innovations and perspectives: An effective separation of data and the roles in the cloud context opens up new fields of application such as the processing and storage of sensitive metering data for the control of a smart grid. There, the secure availability of information is of great importance for service security and today's SaaS did not provide such guarantees in terms of insider attacks by administrators. The future use of this metering data and relevant processes for management of this information in the trustworthy cloud will serve the economically necessary process efficiency.

Acknowledgements

Thanks to all SPLITCloud partners for substantial and very helpful input to this section.

The research provided in this paper is partly funded by the German Federal Ministry of Education and Research in the project SPLITCloud (www.splitcloud.de) under grant no. "16KIS0048K".

References

[AlHu09]   Ammar Alkassar, Rani Husseiki: "Data Leakage Prevention in Trusted Virtual Domains", In: proceedings of Information Security Solution Europe Conference (ISSE '09), Brno (Czech Republic), 2009

[ASSS+06]   A. Alkassar, M. Scheibel, C. Stüble, A.-R. Sadeghi, M. Winandy: "Security Architecture for Device Encryption and VPN", In: proceedings of Information Security Solutions Europe (ISSE 2006).

[CaHo09]   Catteddu, Daniele; Hogben, Giles: Cloud Computing – Benefits, risks and recommendations for information security, European Network and Information Security Agency (ENISA), 2009. Available online at: http://www.enisa.europa.eu/act/rm/files/deliverables/cloud-computing-risk-assessment/at_download/fullReport

[CC14]   Information Protection Overview, Technical White Paper, 2014, http://pages.ciphercloud.com/rs/ciphercloud/images/CipherCloud%20Technical%20Whitepaper%20v2.5.pdf

[CLMS+10]   L. Catuogno, H. Löhr, M. Manulis, A.-R. Sadeghi, C. Stüble, M. Winandy: „Trusted Virtual Domains: Color Your Network", Datenschutz und Datensicherheit (DuD), 2010, pp. 289-298.

[DeDe77]   Dorothy E. Denning and Peter J. Denning. Certification of programs for secure information flow. Comm. of the ACM, 20(7):504–513, 1977.

[EMSCB]   European Multilaterally Secure Computing Base, http://www.emscb.de

[GrWi12]   Michael Gröne, Marcel Winandy, "Applying a Security Kernel Framework to Smart Meter Gate-ways", In: proceedings of Information Security Solutions Europe Conference 2012 (ISSE 2012), Brussels, October 2012

[GrSc11]   M. Gröne, N. Schirmer: "From Trusted Cloud Infrastructures to Trustworthy Cloud Services", In: Proceedings of Information Security Solutions Europe (ISSE 2011), 2011

[HASK08]   Sirrix AG: High-Assurance Security Kernel Protection Profile (EAL5), according to the Common Criteria v3.1 R2, 2007, certified by German Federal Office for Information Security (BSI), 2008.

[KKSW+08] H. Kurth, G. Krummeck, C. Stüble, M. Weber, M. Winandy: HASK-PP: Protection Profile for a High Assurance Security Kernel, 2008, http://www.sirrix.com

[OpenTC]   Open Trusted Computing, http://www.opentc.net/

[RoPf09]   M. Rost, A. Pfitzmann: Datenschutz-Schutzziele – revisited. In: DuD: Datenschutz und Daten-sicherheit 6/2009, p. 353-358.

[RoBo11]   M. Rost, K. Bock: Privacy By Design und die Neuen Schutzziele – Grundsätze, Ziele und Anfor-derungen. In: DuD: Datenschutz und Datensicherheit 1/2011, p. 30-35.

[Sirrix15] Sirrix AG security technologies. TURAYA.SecurityKernel. 2015 http://www.sirrix.com/content/pages/securitykernel_en.htm

[TClo11]   Trustworthy Clouds (TClouds) – Privacy and Resilience for Internet-scale Critical Infrastruc-ture, coordinated by Technikon Forschungs- und Planungsgesellschaft mbH, 2011, http://tclouds-project.eu/

[TCG15]   "Trusted Computing Group", http://www.trustedcomputinggroup.org

[TPM11]   Trusted Computing Group (TCG), TPM Main Specification, Version 1.2, Revision 116, March 2011.

Doubtless Identification and Privacy Preserving of User in Cloud Systems

Antonio González Robles[1] · Norbert Pohlmann[1] ·
Christoph Engling[2] · Hubert Jäger[3] · Edmund Ernst[3]

[1]Institute for Internet Security
Westfälische Hochschule, Gelsenkirchen
{gonzalezrobles | pohlmann}@internet-sicherheit.de

[2]Institut für Rechtsinformatik, Universität des Saarlandes
christoph.engling@uni-saarland.de

[3]Uniscon GmbH
{hubert.jaeger | edmund.ernst}@uniscon.de

Abstract

Present paper addresses the common challenge of compliant verification of electronic identities (eID) with legal certainty. The latter is of particular importance for banks, financial institutions, and public authorities. To ensure confidentiality, provider-proof cloud systems are a technical solution. However, they must also ensure privacy for communication from system to system.

With this document, we shall highlight, based on said challenge, our motives and pinpoint the objective of the Verifi-eID research project and its implementation. We shall then address legal considerations, followed by commonly applied provider-proof cloud security and identification measures. Lastly, we shall illuminate a possible solution, followed by a summary.

1 Motives

When information is exchanged or business is done online, being able to identify all users unequivocally and securely is imperative [Kros14]. Certified security allows bank customers, for example, to be able to verify whether they are actually accessing the proper website when conducting financial transactions. In turn, banks verify clients' actual IDs up front via prior face-to-face identification by demanding their user IDs and passwords, followed by remote access user confirmation for transaction. In doing so, banks inevitably recognize the mandatory user information and transaction content. Yet today's customary cloud computing authentication methods have multiple serious drawbacks: Large-scale cloud providers can all access a user's confidential data, not to mention metadata. The latter even includes file names and types. Providers are also able to distinguish who accesses which files. Normally, providers cannot exclude that internal staff, e.g. a system administrator, accesses data without authorization. Storing or processing confidential or personally identifiable third-party data, in particular, does not comply with strict German data privacy legislation.

In contrast, provider-proof cloud services pose an advantage. These exclude any possible staff access via technical means. In other words, provider employees have no way of accessing entrusted data or metadata at any time whatsoever. The downside, however, is that these providers cannot know the accessing person's actual identity and, consequently, unequivocally verify digital IDs beyond doubt. Yet this is indispensable, for example, for financial transactions.

The objective of the Verifi-eID project, which is supported by the German Federal Ministry of Education and Research and conducted by the Westfälische Hochschule Gelsenkirchen, the University of Saarland and the IT security and provider-proof cloud experts Uniscon, is to find a way in which users can remotely authenticate their ID with the requested due privacy and manage assigned documents (files, images, etc.) safely in compliance with applicable law alike.o have consistency throughout the papers in the book please use for the Title and Headlines uppercase first letters in important Words and lowercase letters for fill words.

2　Verifi-eID Project Mission

Named project partners' mission is to provide a solution enabling provider-proof service users to be able to trust digital IDs. The focus of research is a method in which parties can unequivocally verify each other's identity securely and without having to reveal their identity to the cloud provider, so that their privacy is ensured.

Instead of the cloud provider, identity verification is performed by a reliable third party (Trusted Third Party). What's more, the Verifi-eID system must also be able to verify online IDs of legal entities and digital objects, such as files or images. In addition, the target solution must provide compliant legal certainty upon ID verification. The procedures and methods in development are integrated into a demonstrator, in order to test how the technically and legally secure solution can be used by the applicant.

3　Legal Considerations

Compliant and legally certain implementation per demonstrator must consider several legal aspects. These concern – besides German privacy law – also European identification directives and, finally, law of evidence regulations.

Let us begin with the legal basics of identification. The German Act on Identity Cards and Electronic Identification (Personalausweisgesetz, PAuswG) provides a foundation for the digital identification of persons. However, it is arguable whether the Trusted Third Parties (TTP) concept may be implemented pursuant to this act. Under Section 21 (2) No. 2 PAuswG, authorized access to nPA (new German ID card) data is not granted, if the purpose consists of "commercial transmission of the data" [Möll11, marginal number 15]. The German identity card and electronic identification law provides no direct solution to identification of digital objects. Yet, since ID cards are designed as "secure signature creation devices", files can be signed modification-proof. On the other hand, the purpose of said signature is to identify its creator, and this allows the cloud provider to draw conclusions.

The EU Regulation (EU) No. 910/2014 (eIDAS-VO), in force since 9/17/2014, introduces a new method of identification. Its actual directives come into effect as of 7/1/2016. The Regulation is directly enforceable, applicable and legally binding in the respective EU member countries [Roßn15, p. 359].

The so-called electronic seals mentioned in Section 3 nos. 25-27 of Regulation (EU) No. 910/2014 are new. Named seals are pseudonymous (alias) "signatures" that may be used by legal entities only [Roßn13, p. 70; Quir13, p. 22]. They do not concurrently describe who the corporate body is but rather only ensure the data's authenticity [Sosn15, p. 831]. To date, this was not possible under German law. The Regulation provides that electronic seals are categorized according to degree of trustworthiness: simple, advanced, and qualified electronic seal. As with signatures, said seals can be verified by Trusted Third-Party (TTP) services (Section 3 No. 16 Regulation (EU) No. 910/2014). Trusted services (which the Regulation refers to as "Trusted Service Providers") evidently implement the TTP concept in person, since the Regulation does not stipulate any restrictions, as is the case with the German Act on Identity Cards and Electronic Identification (Personalausweisgesetz, PAuswG). To provide compliant legal certainty, identification (authentication) must even withstand courtordered inspection [Borg11, p. 243]. Prima facie evidence is a possibility. The latter (rebuttable presumption) specifies that, to prove a position, one may infer from previous experience. A good example is rear-end collision: The mere fact that a vehicle collision accident occurred from the rear indicates that the back driver either didn't keep a safe distance or was distracted. No such wealth of experience with identification exists to date. However, owing to how the new ID card is devised, regular presumption, that authentication is merely possible upon possession of an ID and knowledge of the PIN, is justifiable [Borg11, p. 234; Borg10, p. 3338]. For this reason, authentication is only performable by the owner of the card or a third party given the respective PIN [Borg11, p. 234; Borg10, p. 3338].

Yet this is only applies to a limited extent for activity carried out after identification and, hence, situations in which the ID is used to prove that the identified user is the actual author of the respective activity [Borg11, p. 247 ff.]. Consequently, the integrity (i.e. authenticity in terms of authorship / lack of modification) of digital objects cannot be verified reliably per prima facie evidence if the files are not signed. For the time being and pursuant to Regulation (EU) No. 910/2014, the aforementioned principles of prima facie evidence are transferable to signatures and seals. However, since the Regulation also dictates that the EU member states must, in turn, recognize the IDs of other EU countries, it remains questionable whether prima facie evidence of definitely national design is sustainable. Moreover, pursuant to Section 25 and 35, qualified electronic signatures and seals are subject to special evidence provisions. According to Section 2, a qualified electronic seal shall enjoy "the presumption of integrity of the data and of correctness of the origin of that data to which the qualified electronic seal is linked". Thus, Regulation (EU) No. 910/2014 provides an important and applicable legal basis for legally certain identification of individual persons, legal entities, and data.

4 Cloud Service Provider Security Measures

If personal data is stored or processed in a cloud, a German customer must be able to reassure himself locally in advance (i.e. in the data center), and on a regular basis thereafter, that compliance is observed pursuant to Germany's Federal Data Privacy Act (Federal Ministry of Justice and Consumer Protection 2003). After all, it is risky for a user to outsource data to online services and data centers, where it is stored and may be accessed by third-party beneficiaries. Cloud applications that process data, e.g. within the framework of software as a service (SaaS), and are used by parties obliged to legal confidentiality, in particular, provide information during processing. After all, a cloud provider can access a database through the application server.

4.1 Common Security Technologies

Security aware cloud application providers apply both technical and organizational measures, to safeguard against internal and external attacks via web application. Organizational measures, such as the two-man rule or role based access control, are often applied for data that is unencrypted during processing (e.g. the German DE-Mail).

End-to-end content encryption is also often applied as a technical measure, to complicate access pursuant to § 203 of the German Penal Code StGB (e.g. Wuala).

Named protection measures prevent access to content. They do not prevent access to metadata.

Hitherto existing Unicast systems must disclose the recipient's e-mail address to the provider, for the provider to be able to forward data correctly. Hence, communication service providers are able to access connection data. Yet connection data is defined as personal and personally identifiable data. In other words, it, too, is subject to data privacy.

4.2 Advanced Technologies

To date, there are four state-of-the-art privacy protecting technologies:
- Accurate adherence to organizational protection measures, to protect metadata
  (Example: IT baseline protection catalogues based on this method)
- The Multicast approach
  (Example: The Freenet project[1])
  This approach is currently rather suited for narrow band applications, since it requires high processing power and high access availability from its network users.
- Application of mix networks
  (Example: The security software TOR[2])
  Owing to long transmission delays, this approach is currently also rather suited for narrow band applications.
- Sealed Cloud technology, which is based on three essential requirements: Performance, necessary security, and convenience.
  (Example: The web service IDGARD[3])

We shall take a closer look at the latter approach in the following. What makes Sealed Cloud technology so unique, is that a set of purely technical measures prevents access to content and metadata. Mere organizational measures along the first line of defense no longer sufficiently protect against external cybercrime or internal attacks. Hence, IT security experts recommend excluding the human risk factor. The following sub-chapter commits itself to cloud provider "proofness".

---

1 e. g. http://www.freenet.de, abgerufen am 21.07.2015 15.00.
2 e. g. https://www.torproject.org, abgerufen am 21. 07.2015 15.06.
3 e. g. https://www.idgard.de, abgerufen am 21.07.2015 15.07.

4.2.1   Cloud Provider-proofness per Sealed Cloud

The technical measures, developed to meet the aforementioned four basic requirements (performance, necessary security, convenience), consist of the following:

- **Security Measures during Data Connection to the Data Center**
  In order to avoid having to install special software, user device to Sealed Cloud connection occurs via classic SSL encryption. Only strong ciphers (encryption algorithms, e. g. AES 256), i.e. with long keys and no known implementation weakness, are accepted in the process. Since no private key should be accessible on the server side, it is calculated on demand. A browser add-on and apps for mobile devices protect against man-in-the-middle attacks and alert the user of fake digital certificates. With a one-time password generator or a numerical code sent via text message, user data is protected per 2-factor authentication.

- **Security Measures against Data Access during Processing**
  Components that process unencrypted data are located in the so-called data clean-up area. Mechanical cages are equipped with electromechanical locks for the purpose. Further, all electronic interfaces are limited to granting only the user access; direct administrator access is not possible. None of the underlying components dispose of persistent memory. The electronic interfaces and electromechanical components of the cages dispose of numerous sensors that instantly trigger an alarm upon attempted access. This alarm instantly triggers data clean-up. In other words, user sessions on the respective servers are automatically routed to unconcerned segments, and all data in the affected segments is deleted. To ensure deletion, power to the servers is disconnected for 15 seconds. Accordingly, a respective procedure occurs before technical maintenance.

- **Security Measures during Storage**
  The principle of sealing also includes special key distribution. According to the scientific project report [Jaeg13], the provider disposes of no decryption key, neither for database protocol decryption, nor for decipherment of data in the file systems.
  The keys for the protocols in the database are derived from user name and password hashtags. The instant the hash values are determined, user name and password are dismissed. At the end of a session, the determined hash value is also deleted. An exclusively volatile meta-mapping server operates within the data clean-up area, so that no application usage information can be deducted from the foreign keys in the database. The application is able to map data structures within the server yet without the infrastructure provider or the application provider being able to access them. Any access attempt automatically triggers the mentioned data clean-up. However, since the server disposes of volatile memory only, high availability postulates, first of all, redundant configuration in a cluster and, secondly, in the event that the entire infrastructure should fail, gradual data restoration per active user sessions.

- **Further Metadata Protection Measures**
  Communication regarding traffic is intensity dependently "randomly delayed", so that no metadata conclusions may be drawn from the traffic. In addition, communicated file siz-

es are increased to the next higher standard size, so that metadata cannot be computed through time or size correlation, either.

5   Identification in a Cloud Scenario

Today's cloud systems offer services on behalf of a company, so their employees or customers can use the externally hosted service. They also offer cloud services to customers (single users or huge user groups, such as those of companies) directly. Using and offering cloud services entails several implications. The first requires that the cloud provider identify and unequivocally authenticate the user during registration and, in the latter case, usage of the service. The second implication demands user privacy is not breached in a cloud context (i.e. remaining operator-proof). Identification of cloud users opposite cloud service providers is mandatory.

Rapid development of cloud system technologies entails multiple features: cloud service users can, among others, invite new users that are not yet registered to the pertinent service in question. This requires that registered users must also be able to securely identify the users they invite to the (hired) cloud service.

This allows us to arrive to the following crucial conclusions: It is imperative, first of all, that the user is identified securely opposite the cloud service provider and, secondly, towards a further still registered cloud service user. Last but not least, the cloud system operator should not be able to compromise both users' privacy.

The following sub-chapters are committed to the applied identification methods of cloud service users opposite cloud service providers, on the one hand, and other cloud service users (still registered users and new ones), on the other hand. This is followed by a conclusion listing the challenges that result from the aforementioned so-called "crucial aspects".

5.1   User Identification opposite Cloud Service Providers

Current advanced technology based cloud systems offer identification and authentication methods that go beyond using only username and password. They offer modern two-factor authentication that ensures legitimate access to resources. These methods are, for example, based on SMS pass codes with one-time password generators or PIN protected smart cards.

Further far-reaching ID and authentication methods applied, e.g. in cloud (operator-proof) systems, consist in the Vodafone Secure SIM (VSS) and the German National Identity Card (neuer deutscher Personalausweis, nPA) using pertinent pseudonym (alias) eIDs. Recommendable German National Identity Card (nPA) based identification and authentication solutions are listed on the website of the German Federal Ministry of the Interior. These are, among others, the Trusted Cloud project SkIDentity and the provider OpenID.[4]

Identification and authentication per Vodafone Secure SIM (VSS) and the German National Identity Card (nPA) entail further-reaching implications insofar, as that they certify that the electronic identity used is assigned to a true existing legal entity or person. Mobile phone operators have been registering customers long since to mobile numbers, which comes along with face-to-face

---

4 http://www.personalausweisportal.de

identification per official state-issued ID. What's more, legal entities (persons) are also officially granted German IDs, used by the systems to rely on commensurate pseudonym (alias) eIDs.

Owing to strict German legislation (§ 19 PAuswG, the Act on Identity Cards and Electronic Identification, also known as Personalausweisgesetz) (German Federal Assembly 2009; Federal Ministry of Justice and Consumer Protection 2009), cloud system providers currently dispose of no scientifically and technologically proven method with which to remotely access a user's physical (legal) identity during initial registration. Thus, cloud providers can merely verify whether the same electronic identity (eID) is used persistently, without knowing the actual identity, disclosed by an unequivocal combination of first name, last name, birthdate, birthplace, address, etc.

5.2 User Identification opposite Other Users

Nowadays, cloud system providers offer the user (customer) the feature to be able to invite external users, i.e. users that are not yet registered with said provider, to join the hired service. As in the preceding sub-chapter, for user-to-user communication, it is also imperative that the user inviting the third party is able to unequivocally identify this latter user. Current methods commonly used for this purpose are based on identification via SMS and/or e-mail.

This kind of identification merely ensures that one existing user simultaneously applies a mobile number and e-mail and that these are allocated to the assigned account pertinent user invitation. From then on, the inviting user has the certainty that the same still registered user accesses the service for collaboration at all times.

The inviting cloud service user does not receive any information relating to the true legal entity (person) behind the mobile phone number and e-mail account. However, in certain cases, the user may want certainty as to the real identity in terms of personal information, such as first name, last name, birthdate, birthplace, address, etc. In the latter event, as in 5.1, it is necessary that users be (ideally mutually) identifiable unequivocally

The consideration in present sub-chapter leads to an additional problem. It pertains to the privacy between communicating users. The user ID methods mentioned in 5.1 depend on the cloud service provider. Therefore, the privacy of the two users is not protected.

5.3 Subsequent Challenges

The goal of present subchapter is to summarize the resulting and yet to be achieved objectives.

Security considerations examined to date as per provider-proof cloud systems, as well as the imperative of unambiguous user identification opposite cloud providers, comprise the following issues, which must be solved in the course of the project:

- Unequivocal identification
- of users by cloud providers
- of users by other users
- Privacy protection of multiple users opposite cloud providers

Measures to be taken to solve the above are highlighted in chapter 6, "Solution".

6 Solution

Secure cloud services allow its users to identify themselves via user name and password and, optionally, 2-factor authentication (2FA). Named second factor may consist, e.g., in a pass code, which is sent to the user via SMS or another channel. However, the second factor may also be a one-time, non-recurring password created by the one-time password generator or smart card the user possesses. The latter communicate per SAML protocol or similar standard solutions with the ID provider on the one hand and, on the other hand, with the respective cloud service.

With the Sealed Cloud based Web service IDGARD, provided by the corporate business partner Uniscon, the second factor consists either of a one-time password generator the size of a credit card (IDGARD Login Card), an SMS Pass Code, or a Vodafone Secure SIM (VSS) and its respective connection via SAML protocol. What's more, nPA connection per 2FA alias was also demonstrated at the CeBIT 2012 fair by means of the Trusted Cloud project SkIDentity. The Institute for Internet Security works with the first OpenID provider[1] disposing of nPA based authentication per alias. The public is offered this service at www.personalausweisportal.de[2].

The basic structure of the solution is depicted in Figure 1 and relies on a Trusted Third Party, to protect user privacy.

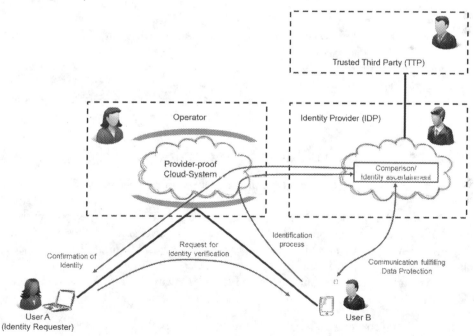

Fig. 1: Verification scenario. The uniqueness of this scenario is a situation often to be expected in the future, in which the cloud service provider cannot and does not wish to identify Users A and B yet named users must be able to verify each other's identity reciprocally.

However, said authentication method merely proves that the digital ID logon is invariably performed by the very same user. It does not substantiate whether first name, last name, address, or place and date of birth provided by the user are actually identical to the data that identifies the user unequivocally.

A fundamental security measure consists in meticulously detailed rights management for compliant ID verification of digital objects. The exact technical measures can only be developed in the course of the research project. Yet two basic principles of Sealed Cloud technology are essential. They are combined with further measures, to verify an unequivocally identified user whose privacy is protected.

6.1 Privacy by Design

The principle "privacy / data protection by design" is based on the insight that building in privacy features from the very beginning of the design process is preferable to attempting to adapt a product or service at a later stage. Involving them in the design process considers the full lifecycle of said data and its usage.

- Minimize: The most basic privacy design strategy is MINIMIZE, which states that the amount of personal data that is processed should be restricted to the minimum amount possible.
- Hide: This strategy states that any personal data and respective interrelationships should be hidden from plain view.
- Separate: States that personal data should be processed in a distributed fashion, in separate compartments, whenever possible.
- Aggregate: this fourth design pattern states that personal data should be processed at the highest level of aggregation and with the least possible detail in which it is (still) useful.
- Demonstrate: This strategy requires a data controller, in order to be able to demonstrate compliance with the privacy policy and any applicable legal requirements.

6.2 Trusted Third-Party Identity Verification

Use of pretty much any Internet service on the market requires application of a digital Trusted Identity (TId) [GoRoPo14], since this postulates identification of the actual person. The definition of Trusted Identity requires that the accompanying legal identity (person) must match unambiguously. Customary user name / password based authentication to determine the identity of a person is generally based on information provided by the user himself. Applied procedures are often based on e-mail, SMS, or sometimes even postal verification. Yet these procedures are unsatisfactory and far from meeting the offered services' security requirements. Subsequential user identities are often referred to as soft digital identities.

With common cloud concepts and traditional Internet services, the legal person and service provider are only close to each other in exceptional cases, so that personal face-to-face identification opposite the service provider is rarely feasible. Identification serves to verify identity describing attributes. Personal identification relies on visual verification of an official state-approved identity card issued by the respective state for a verifiable natural citizen. In Europe, commonly used national IDs provide electronic identities (eIDs) that unify associated attributes pursuant to ISO/EC 24760 and, in this case, unequivocally represent the natural person. Said attributes consist, among others, of first name, last name, birthdate, birthplace, postal address, etc.

Electronic identification that relies on the new German ID card (neuer Personalausweis, nPA) is of special interest, because it incorporates two essential requirements that must be met, to be able to refer to an identity as digital Trusted Identity (TId). The first implies that the registration process, performed by a trustworthy entity, ensures verification of the natural person. The second is the feasibility of secure, strong user-side attribute authentication which qualifies the eID.

Named Verifi-eID project shall investigate a solution that unequivocally verifies actual user identities and relies on a digital Trusted Identity, as provided by the new German ID (nPA). The nPA applies pertinent eID, ensures cloud system provider-proofness and, what's more, expanding user-to-user privacy, in order to exclude the cloud provider. The elaborated solution will be at least on a par with locally performed face-to-face identification.

7 Conclusion

The project's target solutions for legally certain, compliant ID verification in provider-proof clouds tap the full potential of cloud computing user groups that don't exploit today's services due to data privacy concerns. Verifi-eID allows users to exchange confidential business data online or even store and process particular personally identifiable data (e.g. that of medical practices or law firms) per cloud computing.

Acknowledgment

This work is part of the project "Rechtssichere Verifikation elektronischer Identitäten in betreibersicheren Cloud-Systemen" (Verifi-eID)", which is funded by the German Federal Ministry of Education and Research (BMBF). The content of this article is solely in charge of the authors and reflects in no way the BMBF's opinion.

References

[Borg11, p.] Borges, Georg: Rechtsfragen der Haftung im Zusammenhang mit dem elektronischen Identitätsnachweis, 2011, Baden-Baden (Nomos).

[Bogr10, p.]Borges, Georg.: Der neue Personalausweis und der elektronische Identitätsnachweis, NJW 2010, 3334-3339.

[FelPoh10] Security Analysis of OpenID, followed by a Reference Implementation of an nPA-based OpenID Provider. In: Norbert Pohlmann, Helmut Reimer und Wolfgang Schneider (Eds.): ISSE 2010 Securing Electronic Business Processes.

[FelPoh10] Security Analysis of OpenID, followed by a Reference Implementation of an nPA-based OpenID Provider. In: Norbert Pohlmann, Helmut Reimer und Wolfgang Schneider (Eds.): ISSE 2010 Securing Electronic Business Processes.

[GoRoPo14]González Robles, Antonio; Pohlmann, Norbert: Identity Provider zur Verifikation der vertrauenswürdigen digitalen Identität. In: Peter Schartner und Peter Lipp (Hg.): DACH Security 2014. Bestandsaufnahme – Konzepte – Anwendungen – Perspektiven. New edition. Frechen: Horster, Patrick.

[Jaeg13] Jäger, Hubert, et al.: A Novel Set of Measures against Insider Attacks – Sealed Cloud, in: Detlef Hühnlein, Heiko Roßnagel (Ed.): Proceedings of Open Identity Summit 2013, Lecture Notes in Informatics, Volume 223.

[Kros14]   Kroschwald, Steffen: Verschlüsseltes Cloud Computing. In: Zeitschrift für Datenschutz (ZD) 2014, p. 75-80.

[Möll11, marg. nr] Möller, Jan: Kommentierung zu § 21 PAuswG in: Hornung, Gerit/Möller, Jan (Hrsg.): Passgesetz Personalausweisgesetz – Kommentar, 2011, München (C.H. Beck).

[Quir13, p.] Quiring-Kock, Gisela: Entwurf EU-Verordnung über elektronische Identifizierung und Vertrauensdienste – EU-weite Interoperabilität – Anspruch und Wirklichkeit, DuD 2013, 20-24.

[Roßn15, p.] Roßnagel, Alexander: Der Anwendungsvorrang der eIDAS-Verordnung – Welche Regelungen des deutschen Rechts sind weiterhin für elektronische Signaturen anwendbar?, MMR 2015, 359-364.

[Roßn13, p.] Roßnagel, Alexander: Entwurf einer EU-Verordnung über elektronische Identifizierung und Vertrauensdienste – Neue Regeln für elektronische Sicherheitsdienste, ZD 2013, 65-725.

[Sosn14, p.] Sosna, Sabine: EU-weite elektronische Identifizierung und Nutzung von Vertrauensdiensten – eIDAS-Verordnung – Ein Überblick über die wichtigsten Inhalte und deren Konsequenzen für Unternehmen, CR 2014, 825, 831.

Industry 4.0 and Internet of Things

Industry 4.0 – Challenges in Anti-Counterfeiting

Christian Thiel[1] · Christoph Thiel[2]

[1]FHS University of Applied Sciences St. Gallen,
christian.thiel@fhsg.ch

[2]University of Applied Sciences Bielefeld
christoph.thiel@fh-bielefeld.de

Abstract

As part of the evolution of industrial production and automation processes referred to as industry 4.0, new developments in information technologies such as the Internet of Things and cloud computing grow together with real (physical) objects and classic industrial processes. In production processes following the Industry 4.0 approach large amounts of data are generated from RFID's, sensors, embedded systems, the components itself to be manufactured, the machines, but also of the management and control functions of computer units. They contain information about the production process, place, time and condition of the product to be produced, even on the design documents and used materials and parts. By an unauthorized derivation of these information (in the simplest case by just observing the production facilities), the entire production process and the properties of the material produced can be disclosed. This simplifies the work of pirates and calls for new approaches to protect against counterfeiting and know-how loss.

In our work we identify new requirements on Industry 4.0 processes and production facilities. These requirements comprise both the protection of the whole production process and the usability and cost effectiveness from the different viewpoints of all stakeholders down the supply chain. We match these requirements with existing protective measures and close existing gaps. For that we develop new protocols and propose adaptations of existing processes and components.

1 Introduction

Counterfeiting and piracy have a strong impact on businesses and the global economy, jeopardizing investments in creativity and innovation, undermining recognized brands and creating consumer health and safety risks ([VDMA13]). Counterfeiters are producing fake foods and beverages, pharmaceuticals, electronics, auto parts and everyday household products. By 2015, the International Chamber of Commerce ICC expects the value of counterfeit goods globally to exceed $1.7 trillion. That's over 2% of the world's total current economic output ([ICC11]).

This problem has grown hand-in-hand with globalization of the economy. Along with trade liberalization, the growth of sophisticated logistics networks and information sharing through data networks and the Internet has dramatically increased the volume of products and information moving around the world. The value chains have become increasingly global and longer both geographically and in the number of value chain links, i.e. players in the value chain like raw materials and component suppliers, transport operators, and landlords and property or infra-structure owners. Consequently, these trends have also created significant challenges for rights holders in detecting, investigating and stopping the flow of counterfeited and pirated materials. In particular, it is much more difficult for rights holders to know, manage, and control every play-er (chain link) involved in their value chains and to see their every transaction. Players of a value chain face similar challenges with their sub-players, e.g. suppliers and customers (cf. [CGM+12]).

This situation has exposed a number of value chain vulnerabilities, and criminal agents have seized the opportunity to exploit them (cf. [ICC11]). As a result of this, reliance threats to value chains have attracted more attention, including the threat of intentional tampering during de-velopment, distribution or operations, or the threat of substitution with counterfeit (including cloned or overproduced) components before or during delivery.

To make things even worse traditional industrial processes and modern technologies of informa-tion technology have started to grow together. An ongoing industrial revolution referred to as the fourth industrial revolution, or short 'Industry 4.0' initiates the conglomerating of the horizontal integration of inter-corporation value networks, the end-to-end integration of value chains, and the vertical integration of factory inside (which is called smart factory). While still in the begin-ning it is obvious that Industry 4.0 will lead to new challenges in fighting against counterfeits.

It would be difficult in a single paper to cover all facets of counterfeiting and product piracy. Here we will not discuss the different kinds of potential damages nor give detailed technical descrip-tions of the possible approaches of counterfeiters. Thus the emphasis of this paper is to illustrate the impact of Industry 4.0 on counterfeiting and product piracy by discussing new challenges in comparison with the pre Industry 4.0 era and describing showcase threats and possible counter-measures.

2 Counterfeiting in the pre Industry 4.0 era

One of the most interesting questions in the context of counterfeiting and product piracy is, where counterfeiters and product pirates do get the know-how to counterfeit or copy products as they do, i.e. the know-how about the products and the necessary production processes. In general the counterfeiter or pirate is applying one or more of the following five approaches to get and use this kind of information:

- Reverse engineering: The product itself contains a lot of information. One way to imitate a product is therefore reverse engineering. The more technologically sophisticated the products are and the more difficult product features can be understood by disassembly, all the more challenging is reverse engineering. For example hard to understand man-ufacturing processes (such as in heat treatment processes) could hinder the successful product creation. Or an original product could not be disassembled without simultaneous destruction.
- Industrial espionage: Illegal direct attacks on know-how or information through industri-al espionage (hacking, corruption of insiders, etc.)
- Loss of know-how: The right holder or company loses know-how via former personnel, clients, or suppliers.
- Competitive Intelligence: Outflow of corporate knowledge that is not protectable by in-dustrial property rights. Offender try systematically to obtain information about objec-

tives, strengths and weaknesses, tactics, risks and opportunities, products and services, sales channels and sales success as well as new developments, pending property rights and technologies of the companies which should be copied.
- Overbuilding: That means the foundry or system integrator in charge of manufacturing the devices produces more of them than originally specified by the designer.

According to [VDMA] most right holders point to reverse engineering as a means of gaining know-how. Forty-two percent of companies believe that imitating the products needed no specific information. Frequently, counterfeiters copy protected brands or designs (color, form etc.). The third most common source of information (at 31 percent) lies in the loss of know-how, e.g. via former personnel, clients, or suppliers

Measures which may take the right holder or Original Equipment Manufacturer (OEM) to prevent the copyist / pirate of his projects are grouped under the term reduction of imitation attractiveness ([Neem07]). This includes all measures that seek to ensure that the potential pirate no longer wants to imitate resp. clone the product of the original provider, e.g. technical or organizational concepts making the reproduction to expensive, to complex or even impossible. When the potential pirate has decided to imitate resp. clone, he will – additionally to the information gathered so far – try to acquire the necessary know-how of the innovator. This includes both the product know-how and the necessary process know-how. Measures of the innovator who are trying to hinder this process, are listed under the term aggravation of know-how acquisition. This includes all measures that obstruct the pirate in his intention to acquire the necessary know-how about the products and the necessary production processes.

Following the successful know-how acquisition the pirate has all the theoretical knowledge necessary for the manufacture of the product and will try to reproduce the product with his own resources. Measures that try to limit this are referred to as measures to aggravation of reproduction.

After a successful reproduction the pirate will begin with the marketing of the produced imitations. Also in this phase, the Innovator has opportunities to hinder the offender in his activities. Measures of this kind will be treated under the term aggravation of marketing.

There are some process approaches that have been created for the purpose of deriving concepts to protect against product piracy ([VDMS13], [Meiw11]). These guidelines offer solutions in the form of a structured procedural model, designed to reveal the requirements and possible protective means for relevant key areas of businesses.

Among the technical solutions are marking technologies to differentiate the plagiarism from the original, or constructive protection technologies making the reproduction of devices, machines and control systems more difficult and therefore preventing possible attacks by pirates. Therefore most concepts focus on (cf. [VDMA13]):
- Product identification: Identification technologies comprise visible and invisible security features aimed at proving product originality and authenticity. Examples include holograms, data matrix codes, RFIDs, special printing methods, or added materials.
- Detection and authentication of protected products: This refers to devices, equipment and systems able to recognize, read, check and verify the originality of security features.
- Tracking and tracing systems: Systems to track and trace products through the supply chain and the entire lifecycle with unique security markers.

- Embedded security: Know-how protection in the form of controlling software, electronics, and data stored in intelligent technical products.
- Technical know-how protection: IT-based technologies for protecting sensitive construction, production, or business know-how.

None of the above-mentioned traditional procedures, methods and projects takes into account the special challenges of Industry 4.0. The existing measures and methods are not designed for intelligent, networked systems and therefore not applicable without adjustment.

3 Industry 4.0

The underlying concept of Industry 4.0 is to connect embedded systems and smart production facilities to generate a digital convergence between industry, business and internal functions and processes. Industry 4.0 refers to a fourth industrial revolution (following water/steam power, mass production and automation through IT and robotics) and introduces the concept of "cyber-physical systems" to differentiate this new evolutionary phase from the electronic automation that has gone before. According to [KaWH13] in the future businesses will establish global networks that incorporate their machinery, warehousing systems and production facilities in the shape of Cyber-Physical Systems (CPS). In the manufacturing environment, these Cyber-Physical Systems comprise smart machines, storage systems and production facilities capable of autonomously exchanging information, triggering actions and controlling each other independently.

CPS-based ad hoc networking enables dynamic configuration of different aspects of business processes, such as quality, time, risk, robustness, price and eco-friendliness. This facilitates continuous "trimming" of materials and supply chains.

Smart products are uniquely identifiable, may be located at all times and know their own history, current status and alternative routes to achieving their target state. Digital product memories will collect data from manufacturing, logistics, use and disposal and make them available for the product and process optimization. Even while they are being made, they will know the details of their own manufacturing process. This means that, in certain sectors, smart products will be able to control the individual stages of their production semi-autonomously. Moreover, it will be possible to ensure that finished goods know the parameters within which they can function optimally and are able to recognize signs of wear and tear throughout their life cycle.

A factory owns several physical and informational subsystems, such as actuator and sensor, control, production management, manufacturing, and corporate planning. It is essential to have vertical integration of actuator and sensor signals across different hierarchical levels from the actuator and sensor, control, production management, manufacturing and execution and corporate planning levels right up to the enterprise resource planning (ERP) level to enable a flexible and reconfigurable manufacturing system (connection between plant floor, shop floor and top floor). By this integration, the smart machines form a self-organized system that can be dynamically reconfigured to adapt to different product types.

A precise coordination takes place not only between all processes within a company, but also between all the companies involved in the value chain. The availability of current data from all relevant production processes allow the rapid and precise reacting even to unforeseen events outside the company. This horizontal production network is distinguished by a high degree of flexibility and efficiency. And at the same time the adaptability of production allows a very flexible response to market developments.

Industry 4.0 will be characterized by a new level of socio- technical interaction between all the actors and resources involved in manufacturing. This will revolve around networks of manufacturing resources (manufacturing machinery, robots, conveyor and warehousing systems and production facilities) that are autonomous, capable of controlling themselves in response to different situations, self-configuring, knowledge-based, sensor- equipped and spatially dispersed and that also incorporate the relevant planning and management systems.

As a key component of this vision, smart factories will be embedded into inter-company value networks and will be characterized by end-to-end engineering that encompasses both the manufacturing process and the manufactured product, achieving seamless convergence of the digital and physical worlds.

Industry 4.0 use case scenarios relating e.g. to "net- worked manufacturing", "self-organizing adaptive logistics" and "customer-integrated engineering" will require business models that will primarily be implemented by what could be a highly dynamic network of businesses rather than by a single company.

Companies will in future form dynamic networks, from which they will – order and product specifically – unite their capacities to virtual production communities.

This will raise a number of questions regarding financing, development, reliability, risk, liability and IP and know-how protection.

Companies involved in networks will – to a limited time period – merge production capacity to virtual production platforms. In essence, the networks have to be based on trust between the parties and will therefore often remain closed to the outside. Sometimes, they are supplemented by new companies that bring previously covered inadequately special skills. In this way the major manufacturers continue to maintain their traditional suppliers, but also use the opportunity to regularly expand their network to new companies. Thus, they can respond flexibly to special customer requests in individual projects. However, this mainly closed chain approach will reduce the expected flexibility of value networks and limits the potential to already existing supply chain concepts. Additionally many supply companies are members of multiple networks and platforms, thus increasing their job opportunities.

The flexibility in the networking of the entire value chain is based on the high speed of data exchange between the parties. Just so they can coordinate their processes in near real time with each other. Networking requires an effective fight against numerous security risks: industrial espionage, fraud, manipulation and even terrorist activities are a threat to networked systems for a long time.

4 Challenges and Threats

The horizontal integration of inter-corporation value networks, the end-to-end integration of value chains, and the vertical integration in smart factories driven by Industry 4.0 is giving target points to challenging threats on all levels, from plant floor to the top floor. First we summarize main challenges posed by Industry 4.0, which generalizes [CGM+12]:

- Complex nature of virtual production communities with not only globally distributed but also fast changing value chains
- Lack of common guidelines for achieving and measuring the degree of protection against counterfeiting and product piracy
- Absence of tools, processes and controls to help measure statistical confidence levels and verify protection against counterfeiting and product piracy across value networks and value chains
- Ineffective methodologies and technologies for end-user verification of products (i.e. lack of appropriate approaches, methodologies, and tools to evaluate products by the customer)
- Lack of broadly applicable tools, techniques, and processes to detect or defeat counterfeiting and tampering in systems
- Lack of coordinated approaches to preserving integrity of products from production to deployment

While recognizing explicit threats should be part of an in-depth security and risk management approach of the company or right holder here we just want to mention some important generic threat categories arising from the mentioned challenges brought by Industry 4.0.

1. External third parties but also partners in the corporate network can try to use the network connection and to get access to enterprise data or even to technical design documents, process descriptions and trade secrets, by which they could copy the components produced by the company easier. In the classic supply chain management this threat existed already at the level of the top floor (ERP systems were already linked for example by EDI). But now, new attack options arise through the interlinked plans floor and top floor levels that were previously usually barely protected. Using the network all connected systems at these two levels can be accessed and attacked. Conversely, there are links of the technical systems to business applications. Manipulated control systems could be used to access production know how and business information. Unfortunately, most common industrial automation systems in operation were designed to operate in "friendly" environments, from which no attacks against their higher-level function were expected. As a result, these systems and their components on their own are not able to ensure security objectives. Many in industrial automation used protocols for programming and monitoring of controls and for the exchange of production data work in plain text, without encryption or other mechanisms for confidentiality, integrity and authenticity.

2. An attacker could try to get physical or logical access to CPSs or to programmable logic controllers (PLC) as a typical representative of an IT system of the shop-floor level. The attacker could try to read the system software of which could give him important information for counterfeiting. Or he could try to manipulate the firmware or software in such a way that the production systems implement weaker protection mechanisms within the products. [FiSc12] discusses the way in which attacks on hardware and software in embedded systems can occur. A counterfeiter will thereby split the system piece by piece into its individual components, identify the used components (product teardown), then analyze the system (systems analysis) and rebuild a circuit with the same or equivalent components. The required firmware can be read from the original and recorded in the replica. The firmware usually involves the most know-how (e.g. algorithms). Protecting

firmware is thus often in the foreground of anti-counterfeiting. Nevertheless effective protection against data espionage or reverse engineering of software products requires a certain amount of hardware support [FiSc12], i.e. hardware mechanisms that provide software with a secure execution environment. So hardware is the last line of defense before damage is done – if an attacker compromises hardware then every sole software security mechanisms may be useless. Later in 2014 several survey paper (e.g. [RoKK14], [CoBo14]) systematizes the knowledge in hardware security and design protection in the microelectronics industry, including a classification of threat models (hardware Trojans, IP piracy and IC overbuilding, reverse engineering, side channel analysis and counterfeiting), state-of-the-art defenses (design obfuscation, IP watermarking, IP fingerprinting, IC metering, split manufacturing IC camouflaging, IC information leakage reduction, key based authentication, noise injection secure-scan, physical unclonable functions PUF / unique IDs and aging sensors), and evaluation metrics for important hardware-based attacks.

3. The manipulation of CPSs could even be done before the assembly of the production machine itself. Thus we have to consider security in the hardware supply chain (e.g. of PLCs): Information and Communication Technology (ICT) products are assembled, built, and transported by multiple vendors around the world not always with the knowledge of the acquirer. Abundant opportunities exist for malicious actors to tamper with and sabotage products, ultimately compromising system integrity, reliability, and safety. A counterfeiter could try a two-step attack to the products of a right owner: he could tamper with the manufacturing facility by attacking its supply chain and exchanging some components. The manufacturing facility will be built together with manipulated components which could cause it to produce less protected products during operation stage. Organizations acquiring hardware, software, and services are not able to fully understand and appropriately manage the security risks associated with the use of these products and services: Threats range from insufficient acquirer practices to lack of visibility into the supply chain.

4. [KKDG15] examines the system protection for CPSs and identifies new requirements referring to the use and support of CPS-specific properties, such as the ability to self-optimization and automatic learning. These skills of CPS offer new possibilities of system protection, but at the same time new targets for counterfeiters appear.

5. Compared to classical products the new smart products contain considerably more information and details of their own manufacturing process. This knowledge could be used by a counterfeiter and has to be protected for example by the known embedded system protection techniques. But there are additional information leaks which could be accessed by an attacker in case the smart product consists of several components each of which is part of an extend service and sends its information to its manufacturer. Even if this information are encrypted the attacker could get some information about the components based on the network traffic.

6. Like in the pre Industry 4.0 era companies or right owners have also to assure the knowledge protection by all players of the value chain (chain links) and by theirs production systems. They have to find answers to the question how to assure that all players reach a comparable security and protection level. To be more formal, companies or right owners have to handle threats to the integrity of value chains to an extent to which consistency of actions, values, methods, measures, principles, expectations and outcome is achieved.

7. Closed networks can be protected through specially designed security architectures with-
    out major difficulties. Unfortunately the security applications required in open networks
    work often at the expense of real-time capability. For example we consider the following
    scenario: Before companies can open their server for data from the Internet of things, they
    must be analyzed in foreclosed server departments for malware. These data quarantine in-
    evitably leads to delays and reduces the potential for optimization of data communication
    in real time.

5 Protective measures

Based on the challenges and threats posed by Industry 4.0 several high level key areas for protective measures can be identified, e.g.:

- Measures to ensure that dynamic value network and value chains are fault tolerant and can
  recover from failures and attacks that compromise chain links
- Measures to model, define and evaluate trust in whole value networks resp. value chains
- Measures to achieve authenticity, both component and chain link authenticity
- Utilizing automated tools to identify transaction patterns in the value networks to effec-
  tively identify high-risk behavior patterns inside the value network, and to deter the entry
  of counterfeits and pirated works into the value chains
- Developing and implementing standards and codes of practice for protecting industrial
  automation and control systems, CPSs, etc.
- Developing and realizing approaches for assessing policy needs on a global scale
- Etc.

There are likely many years of research and development before there will be sufficient powerful
toolsets of measures for all these areas. Here we are shortly going into two examples:

1. When working with trusted links in a value chain along well-defined guidelines and
    standards, the risks of counterfeit products or concerns about the authenticity of chain
    links or components of the product can be minimized. There are a number of elements
    that may be used to build trust in chain links that include: personnel identification and
    authentication; access management; past and current value chain performance etc. But
    based on the experiences in recent years with international standardization in the area of
    electronic identification and trust services nobody should be too confident, that in near
    future there will be a globally accepted trust infrastructure that will permit (legally, tech-
    nically and trustworthy) consistent verification and authentication methods. To bypass
    this shortcoming we are suggesting to use the model of the "web of trust" (for value net-
    works) or "chain of custody" (for value chains, s. [CGM+12]), where chain links confirm
    and verify their trustworthiness mutually. Without going in detail we want to remark that
    properly identifying a chain link is not sufficient for trust building. Obviously addition-
    al "quality measures" have to be involved (e.g. ISO 27000 series certification, ISO 14000
    series certification or ISO 9000 series certification). Aside from mutual link assessment
    there are technical means to consider for trust validation, including technical approaches
    to trust and integrity, such as integrity metrics, digital signatures, and Trusted Computing
    techniques including the Trusted Platform Module (ISO/IEC 11889). Verifying the claims
    of each suppler in a chain is an important, but not necessarily sufficient process step in
    establishing integrity of a supply chain. Claims of certification to standards (such as ISO

9000, ISO 14000, ISO 27000, etc.) need to be authenticated and verified. Records that these claims have been authenticated need to be protected (e.g., with digital signatures or other IT security techniques).

2. In former days Industrial Control Systems (ICS) have been physically separated from other IT systems and decoupled from other networks and thus protected against external influences (This fact sometimes is called 'air gap'). Hence, most common industrial automation systems in operation were designed to operate in "friendly" environments, from which no attacks against their higher-level function were expected. With the introduction of IT systems from the office environment and the increasing networking of ICS also beyond network boundaries (e.g. in a corporate network), these systems are now exposed to additional risks. In contrast to IT infrastructures, as we know from data centers and the office environment, ICS have specific requirements for protection goals availability, integrity and confidentiality. Conspicuously, here significantly longer overall life spans, disregarding automated system updates, a very small number of maintenance windows, real-time requirements and warranty claims must be respected in security standards and best practices. Standards and guidelines such as the arising IEC 62443 (Security for Industrial Automation and Control Systems) or the Security Guideline from [PROFI13] have to be coordinated and implemented.

6 Conclusion

Counterfeiting is a problem for many years. Although there are many legal, technical and organizational protective measures the damage caused by counterfeiting is continuously growing. In some areas Industry 4.0 will make the situation even worse. Unfortunately the necessary protective measures such as a globally accepted trust infrastructure that will permit (legally, technically and trustworthy) consistent verification and authentication methods will only be available in years. A possible way for OEMs to protect their products may be on the expansion of their products to smart products. The added value of smart products often lies in the additional services (which must not only be preventive maintenance but could also be the intelligent behavior of the product to the user). If the innovator finds a way to place this intelligence in a cloud service a copy of the product is only useful if it gets access to the cloud service (or a clone of the service). But cloud service can be secured by existing security mechanisms on the control of the right owner.

References

[AS5553]   SAE International: Counterfeit electronic parts; Avoidance, detection, mitigation, and disposition. 2009, URL http://standards.sae.org/as5553/

[AS6081]   SAE International: Fraudulent/counterfeit electronic parts: Avoidance, detection, mitigation, and disposition – Distributors counterfeit electronic parts; Avoidance protocol, distributors. 2012, URL http://standards.sae.org/as6081/

[AS6171]   SAE International: Test methods standard; Counterfeit electronic parts. URL http://standards.sae.org/wip/as6171/

[AS6178]   SAE International: Fraudulent/counterfeit electronic parts; Tool for risk assessment of distributors. 2011, URL http://standards.sae.org/arp6178/

[AS6496]   SAE International: Fraudulent/counterfeit electronic parts: Avoidance, detection, mitigation, and disposition authorized/ franchised distribution. 2014, URL http://standards.sae.org/wip/as6496/

[BoPMB15] Jon Boyens, Celia Paulsen, Rama Moorthy, Nadya Bartol: Supply Chain Risk Management: Practices for Federal Information Systems and Organizations, NIST Special Publication 800 -161, 2015

[CGM+12] Scott Cadzow, Georgios Giannopoulos Alain Merle, Tyson Storch, Claire Vishik, Slawomir Gorniak, Demosthenes Ikono: Supply Chain Integrity: An overview of the ICT supply chain risks and challenges, and vision for the way forward. ENISA, 2012, URL https://www.enisa.europa.eu/activities/identity-and-trust/library/deliverables/sci/at_download/ fullReport

[CoBo14] Brice Colombier, Lilian Bossuet: Survey of hardware protection of design data for integrated circuits and intellectual properties. IET Comput. Digit. Tech., Vol. 8, 2014, Iss. 6, pp. 274–287

[FiSc12] Bartol Filipovic, Oliver Schimmel: Protecting embedded systems against product piracy: technological background and preventive measures. Fraunhofer AISEC, 2012, URL https://www.aisec.fraunhofer.de/content/dam/aisec/Dokumente/Publikationen/Studien_TechReports/englisch/Whitepaper_ProductProtection.pdf

[ICC11] International Chamber of Commerce: Estimating the global economic and social impacts of counterfeiting and piracy. Frontier Economics Ltd, London, 2011, URL http://www.iccwbo.org/Data/Documents/Bascap/Global-Impacts-Study-Full-Report/

[ISO27036]ISO/IEC 27036-3:2013: Guidelines for ICT supply chain security

[IECa]   IEC62443-3-1: Industrial communication networks – Network and system security – Part 3 1: Security technologies for industrial automation and control systems

[IECb]   IEC62443-2-4: Requirements for IACS Solution Suppliers (Draft for Comment)

[KaWH13] Henning Kagermann, Wolfgang Wahlster, Johannes Helbigacatech: Securing the future of German manufacturing industry: Recommendations for implementing the strategic initiative INDUSTRIE 4.0. acatech, Industry 4.0 Working Group, 2013, URL http://www.acatech.de/fileadmin/user_upload/Baumstruktur_nach_Website/Acatech/root/de/Material_fuer_Sonderseiten/Industrie_4.0/Final_report__Industrie_4.0_accessible.pdf

[KKDG15] Daniel Kliewe, Arno Kühn, Roman Dumitrescu, Jürgen Gausemeier: Challenges in Anti-Counterfeiting of Cyber-Physical Systems. International Journal of Social, Behavioral, Educational, Economic and Management Engineering Vol:9, No:5, 2015

[LSMF08] Mikko Lehtonen, Thorsten Staake, Florian Michahelles, Elgar Fleisch: The Potential of RFID and NFC in Anti-Counterfeiting Improving Customs Processes with RFID and NFC Technology to Fight Illicit Trade. Paper WP-BIZAPP-027, Auto-ID Labs White, 2008

[Meiw11] Meiwald, Thomas.: Konzepte zum Schutz vor Produktpiraterie und unerwünschtem Know-how-Abfluss. Dr. Hut Verlag, München 2011, ISBN 978-3-8439-0167-3

[NA11]   NA 060 Normenausschuss Maschinenbau: Zusammenstellung gefährdungsspezifischer Schutzkonzepte gegen Produktpiraterie und unerwünschten Know-how-Transfer. Studie, 2011

[Neem07] Christoph Wiard Neemann: Methodik zum Schutz gegen Produktimitationen: Verlag. Shaker; Auflage: 1, Juni 2007, ISBN-13: 978-3832262716:

[PROFI13] PROFIBUS & PROFINET International (PI): PROFINET Security Guideline Version 2.0. PROFIBUS Nutzerorganisation e.V, Order No.: 7.002, 2013 http://www.profibus.com/nc/download/specifications-standards/downloads/profinet-security-guideline/download/16511/

[RoKK14] Masoud Rostami, Farinaz Koushanfar, Ramesh Karri: A Primer on Hardware Security: Models, Methods, and Metrics. Proceedings of the IEEE Vol. 102, No. 8, 2014, Digital Object Identifier: 10.1109/JPROC.2014.2335155

[VDMA13]VDMA Working Group Product and Know-how Protection: Product and Know how Protection Guidelines / A Generic Process Model for Introducing Means of Protection against Product Piracy and the Loss of Know-How. 2013, 1st edition

Trust Evidence for IoT: Trust Establishment from Servers to Sensors

David Ott · Claire Vishik · David Grawrock · Anand Rajan

{david.e.ott | claire.vishik | david.grawrock | anand.rajan}@intel.com
Intel Corporation

Abstract

Trust Evidence provides a framework for demonstrating the trustworthiness of a device, a system, or a service, a key requirement in managing risk within interactions associated with a broad spectrum of electronic processes (sensor networks, data analytics, ecommerce, etc.) As an addition to authentication and proof of integrity, Trust Evidence comprises a broader range of factors when demonstrating the trustworthiness of a computing device, for example, considering its configuration, software stack, and operational context.

The rapid proliferation of connected devices as part of the new Internet of Things (IoT) era will create an even greater need for Trust Evidence. IoT will bring with it a broader spectrum of device and service types, and more complex distributed architectures for managing data exchange. Devices across the IoT continuum, from servers to sensors, will interact in new ways, sometimes with users in the loop but often times without. With this dramatic increase in number of interacting devices, there is a need for a unified framework to assess risk and to push the boundaries of what is possible and expected when demonstrating trustworthiness.

In this paper, we present relevant results from Intel's university research program on Trust Evidence, which included participants from the US and Europe. The program accumulated approaches that can be broadly applied to emerging technology environments, including the IoT space. And serve as a unifying theory of approaches to trust. The paper will apply Trust Evidence principles to various IoT scenarios to enrich current approaches.

1 Introduction

As the Internet expands to include billions of heterogeneous devices, there is a growing need to develop a usable trust infrastructure that allows interacting systems to better manage security risks. Devices in technology domains like transportation, manufacturing, health care, smart homes and buildings, energy management, entertainment, ecommerce, and e-government, for example, could benefit from the availability of information establishing the relative trustworthiness of interacting systems in real time. Such information (or its absence) could be used to select an appropriate threat posture as interaction is initiated or requested.

We refer to frameworks for demonstrating the trustworthiness of a device, a system, or a service as *Trust Evidence*. As a complement to authentication, Trust Evidence provides additional information about a device for evaluation, potentially comprehending a broad range of system characteristics and operating state. For example, Trust Evidence may be used to demonstrate trustworthy device configuration, software stack integrity, and operational context information.

The rapid proliferation of sensors, lightweight compute devices, and edge gateways, as part of the new Internet of Things (IoT) era, will create an even greater need for Trust Evidence. IoT will bring with it not only a greatly increased number of computing devices, but a broader spectrum of device and service types, and more complex distributed architectures for managing data exchange. Devices across the IoT continuum, from servers to sensors, will interact in new ways, sometimes with users in the loop but often times without. With this dramatic increase in number of interacting devices, there is a need for Trust Evidence to assess risk and to advance the state-of-the-art in how devices interact with one another.

In this paper, we present research results from an Intel university research program exploring approaches to Trust Evidence. In particular, we describe and comment on several notable areas of work: protected software module architectures, data flow tracking, and programming language extensions for generating and evaluating Trust Evidence. As part of the discussion, we point out how they might apply to IoT scenarios, and provide additional pointers where interested readers can go for more information on program research results.

2 Trust Evidence

The need for Trust Evidence starts with the observation that interaction between devices often relies solely on authentication as a mechanism for reducing risk and ensuring that systems trust one another. We believe that this is has two undesirable consequences. First, it leads to decisions on device trust that are highly dichotomous. That is, authentication determines whether an interacting system will be trusted entirety or not. In fact, an interacting system that has passed the authentication step may still pose a risk if the system is under the control of an attacker, or if parts of the system are in an unknown state after being vulnerable to compromise. Conversely, systems that have not been configured with authentication credentials may still be trustable for some types of data exchanges. For example, IoT sensors with no authentication mechanism in a smart city context may still be trustworthy for certain purposes and within certain boundaries, especially if their current state and operational context are well-understood.

A second consequence of all-or-nothing reliance on authentication is that decisions on device trustworthiness take place without considering the operating characteristics of the system or device engaged in the interaction. A device capable of passing authentication may be in a broad range of states and configurations, from carefully managed and recently updated with the latest patches to misconfigured or malware-infected and under the control of a malicious entity. There is a need for more information that identifies the state of the device, its operating characteristics, the integrity of its operating system and software stack, the versioning and configuration of its applications, and so on. User authentication, in particular, may be highly disconnected from such considerations since users may readily be able to prove membership to a particular domain but unaware that their system has been compromised or misconfigured in various ways. In most cases, the user is not equipped to make judgments regarding the operating characteristics of their device and its software (e.g., knowing whether malware is present), nor may the user be in the loop as devices interact independently or in an automated manner.

While the definition of Trust Evidence is an open research problem, some examples that help to illustrate possible approaches include:

- Evidence that a device or a platform is running a good configuration (a weak configuration or a configuration that was modified without authorization implies risk),
- Evidence that the hardware or the software did not generate deviations from normal behavior (unusual patterns are indicative of abnormal operation),
- Evidence that a device makes use of defined security levels (a predefined security level for a device or an application provides additional guidance for trust establishment),
- Evidence that a device employs mechanisms and policy for the protection of secrets (e.g., evidence that secrets are not stored in software elevates the security properties),
- Evidence of data certification in a message or protocol (if a medical device or sensor was certified, it can be trusted to a greater degree),
- Evidence of negative events and remediation (a device or application undergoing remediation implies monitoring and management which implies greater trust)

Two related issues to consider with Trust Evidence are *freshness* and *longevity*. Must Trust Evidence be consumed immediately to be of value in assessing risk, or is there a shelf life allowing it to be stored and then updated periodically? Perhaps frameworks exist that allow Trust Evidence to be archived by a third party and then updated periodically or on demand under various circumstances. Or, perhaps a given framework works by providing a preponderance of Trust Evidence taken over a period of time and archived in a historical manner.

2.1 Research Initiative

Intel collaborated with university researchers in two rounds to better understand possible avenues for developing Trust Evidence, and then for developing several approaches that will be described in the subsequent sections of this paper.

The initial round of research (a seedling initiative) included exploratory work by UC Berkeley, University of Washington, University of North Carolina, and Dartmouth College. Researchers considered the problems of trust between consumer devices in home user contexts [DKL13], Trust Evidence for data exchanged over the Internet [CBP+13], the problem of remotely detecting compromises in distributed applications [BCR11], and the language of trust for use by human agents to express requirements and discuss policy [BLO+11].

Based on the results of investigation, a follow-on program was created including KU Leuven, Columbia University, Imperial College London, and Dartmouth College which looked more specifically at the central role of software runtime systems in providing Trust Evidence for interacting systems or devices. Without software runtime integrity, program researchers concluded, there is little basis for trust, even when a legitimate user has provided correct authentication credentials or a system has provided attestation in various ways.

Two key notions were often discussed by researchers as part of the Trust Evidence program initiative for software runtime systems. The first is *intention semantics* [VOG12] which provides a means for software authors, administrators, and perhaps even users to express the intended functionality and correct operation of a deployed system in detail. We believe that if intention semantics could be defined, captured, and used to annotate computer software, both users and developers would benefit. This approach might be applied to user interface designs, systems integration problems, communication protocols, and application-specific domains. Most importantly for our purposes, it could be used for Trust Evidence frameworks that express intended functionality and measure system operating characteristics against expected behaviour. Intention semantics may imply the need for a new language to describe such intention in various ways, something that could be added to existing programming languages, policy languages, and communications protocols.

A second notion is that of software *baselining* [VOG12]. Baselining refers to frameworks for constructing a baseline reference of expected behaviour for executing software. Control-flow baselining is one possible variety and makes the observation that while software can be complex and the number of possible states and execution paths exceedingly large, in practice, critical execution sequences often follow predictable patterns. The software baselining approach asks the question, "Can such predictability be captured and used to provide Trust Evidence for software execution?"

Baselining is closely related to anomaly detection [CBK09] in that it looks to establish a notion of "normal" or "expected" behavior, and then use this to construct evidence that execution paths through the same program sequence either conform or fail to conform to what is expected. It is also related to control-flow integrity (CFI) approaches [ABEL09] which construct control-flow graphs (CFG) from source-code analysis, binary analysis, or execution profiling and then use them to constrain software execution at runtime. This is often done in accordance with explicit security policies incorporated into the structure of the CFG. Baselining, however, is not confined to control-flow approaches, it may be coarser in granularity compared to CFI, and is generally focused on Trust Evidence rather than enforcing legal execution paths.

3 Approaches to Trust Evidence

In this section, we summarize research exploring several approaches to the problem of generating Trust Evidence in software runtime systems. Pointers are provided for further reading and comments are made on the application of ideas to IoT.

3.1 Protected Module Architecture

Researchers at KU Leuven approached the challenge of generating Trust Evidence by developing a protected module architecture that provides robust defense against low-level attacks from software running on the same system. The framework also supports remote attestation for interacting parties looking to assess the trustworthiness of software running on the system.

At the core of the approach is the notion of a *self-protecting module* (SPM) which represents an area of system memory where a code module and its data reside. [SP12] An SPM includes a *public* section where the module's code and other non-confidential data can reside with strong integrity guarantees. A *secret* section holds the module's sensitive data (e.g., cryptographic keys) and provides strict assurance that read and write access is only possible from within the module itself.

Protection of an SPM is provided by enforcing a memory access control model. That is, an SPM has a strictly enforced entry point and known size that protects the module from access by other processes on the system, including the operating system itself. Researchers demonstrate three different implementations of this scheme to prove its practicality. First, their work on Fides [SP12] shows how the memory access control scheme can be implemented using a lightweight hypervisor. The hypervisor supports two virtual machines, a *legacy VM* for the operating system kernel and user applications to run in, and a *secure VM* where protected modules reside and are managed by a basic *security kernel* with rudimentary system features and a fine-grained access control model. The hypervisor effectively prevents system processes from accessing protected modules without strict adherence to the framework access control policy.

Alternatively, researchers show that the architecture's memory access control mechanism can be implemented as a Linux kernel modification. [ASAP13] [SAAP15] In this scheme, an application is divided into *compartments* representing virtual memory regions with special access control properties. A compartment is implemented with the familiar public and private sections, but access control this time leverages the standard MMU found on most processors. The compartment memory region is aligned to a memory page with a specific read-write configuration. Execution by any process will generate a page fault which can then be handled by a special kernel extension to enforce SPM policy control. As a third implementation scheme, researchers also show that the access control scheme can be implemented as a hardware extension to mainstream microprocessors with fairly minimal performance overhead, area requirements, and power demands. [NAD+13]

A prominent feature of the protected module architecture is its attacker model which makes few assumptions about attacker capability limitations. Attackers, for KU Leuven researchers, can execute arbitrary code on the system, whether at user-level or kernel-level. Attackers can also build their own protected modules and make use of the protected architecture for whatever purpose they may have. Even with these capabilities, however, the protected module architecture is able to maintain entry point restrictions, to insure the integrity of module code and data, and to guarantee the confidentiality of secret data. This is true even when the host is malware-infected.

Researchers also consider the problem of compiler support for protected modules. In the Sancus hardware implementation approach [NAD+13], they demonstrate an LLVM-based compiler that compiles standard C files into protected modules automatically using only simple developer hints about which functions should be protected. The compiler assigns each logical entry point a unique ID in the hardware-based scheme, also protecting the runtime stack of the software module by placing it inside the protected section. Registers are cleared whenever a module exits to avoid leaking information, and secure linking is handled using a cryptographic verification scheme with the module's caller.

Generating Trust Evidence for an interacting system may be done at two levels. First, the protected module architecture supports remote attestation and secure communication which allows an interacting system to obtain assurance of module identity and integrity. This is done using a cryptographic hash of the public section for the module, something that forms the basis for a *security report* from the underlying system. [ASAP13] [SAAP15] Additional information in the report includes the layout of the module and a cryptographic signature for demonstrating the report's authenticity. In Sancus [NAD+13], a hardware instruction is provided for computing the MAC of the protected memory region. This is used to create a secure exchange protocol to provide assurance that the correct module is running, including a nonce mechanism to address the problem of information freshness (i.e., replay attacks).

The protected module architecture may also be used to generate Trust Evidence through trust assessment modules implemented using the protection architecture. Modules may be used to examine the state of software applications running on the system. For example, they may sample the call stack of applications or services in order to inspect their control flow. Modules could potentially inspect any part of the system, or provide information summarizing system configuration or state in highly customizable ways. Trusted modules may be designed that communicate with interacting systems and respond to queries of various types.

The protected module architecture is well-suited for IoT applications in a number of ways. First, the IoT context represents a continuum of devices -- from ensembles of low-powered sensors and compute devices to gateway nodes that aggregate data and communicate with powerful server systems residing in the cloud. Researchers have shown that the memory access control can be implemented in a variety of ways (e.g., hardware, kernel-based, hypervisor) and thus is flexible enough to accommodate a variety of device and device software scenarios. To illustrate, light-weight devices may lend themselves to a hardware implementation since platforms are more readily customized and the approach minimizes power requirements. In contrast, server platforms might leverage hypervisor schemes since processors usually cannot be customized but compute researches and processor features readily lend themselves to virtualization.

This implementation flexibility makes it possible to imagine the protected module architecture as a unifying framework across the device spectrum, including new IoT devices that will emerge in the coming years. A standard set of trust assessment modules might be expected on all IoT devices which communicate with a gateway. The gateway could be designed to gather Trust Evidence about device configuration, state, and operational characteristics in order to make a risk assessment before including device data in its aggregation processes.

3.2 Data Flow Tracking

Researchers at Columbia University approached the challenge of generating Trust Evidence from the standpoint of dynamic data flow tracking (DFT), also referred to as information flow tracking. The general idea in DFT is to track data as it is propagated during program execution in order to understand how sensitive information may leak from the program, where vulnerabilities like buffer overflows or questionable string formatting occur, when system configuration values may be corrupted or rewritten, or how data may be accessed or modified by malware running on the same system.

While DFT is a powerful tool for analyzing the trustworthiness of data flows, the problem of performance overhead makes it largely impractical for software runtime environments executing in real time. To address this obstacle, Columbia researchers develop an approach they refer to as *ShadowReplica* [JKK+13]. Their work proposes an efficient technique for accelerating dynamic DFT without the overhead generated by such prior approaches as execution replay and analysis [CGC08], duplicate execution in parallel [CC13], and speculative execution with in-lined analysis [NPC+08].

ShadowReplica relies on several techniques to achieve its performance improvements over existing approaches. First, researchers develop a framework for decoupling DFT analysis from the primary program execution thread. This is done by generating code that is injected into the application binary to enqueue information during runtime into specially designed data structures. These data structures (lock-free ring buffers) avoid the use of performance-crippling locks as the DFT analysis application reads the information in a separate execution thread. Researchers use a dynamic binary instrumentation (DBI) framework to avoid the need for application source code access, so they can operate on unmodified binary applications, and so that instrumentation takes place at the lowest possible level.

In their scheme, DFT analysis involves an initial stage where an application is profiled to extract code blocks (i.e., basic blocks or BBLs) and control-flow information, including the construction of a partial control-flow graph showing how code blocks are connected and how frequently branches are taken. The data is processed to generate optimized code that will be injected into the application binary. A significant contribution of the work is an extensive set of techniques for reducing the amount of data necessary for the DFT analysis thread to achieve good results. Researchers look at ways to reduce the number of addresses that need to be enqueued through intra-block, DFT, and inter-block optimizations, approaches to control flow filtering and consolidation, and optimizations for fast ring buffer checking. In addition, the DFT analysis code employs optimizations in control flow restoration and various DFT operations, including fast address references.

Code injection involves the placement of enqueueing stubs at strategic locations in the application binary to track data and propagate tags. Essentially, stubs provide the DFT thread with the information it needs to accurately perform DFT analysis, for example, supplying control-flow branching decisions and information on when to tag a new address range. Execution of the instrumented binary, along with shared data structures, allows application and DFT analysis threads to run in parallel, ideally on separate cores within the same multi-core system.

Researchers note that many of their techniques can be applied to a variety of memory shadowing techniques including control-flow integrity (CFI) which enforces runtime checks using control-flow graphs (CFGs), monitoring schemes for uninitialized memory segments, and frameworks for tracking memory leaks, heap overflows, and so on.

The results of research demonstrate the performance feasibility of DFT and makes possible its use for the generation of Trust Evidence. DFT-based frameworks might be used to generate report information sent directly to an interacting system certifying key data flow properties or providing detailed profile information. DFT analysis applications might run in protected modules leveraging the KU Leuven framework for ensuring software integrity and supporting attestation.

In the context of IoT, DFT approaches might be used to address the problem of Trust Evidence for data. A DFT-based certification application, perhaps running in the context of a protected module architecture, might be used to provide additional information on the trustworthiness of data coming from an IoT device. DFT trace or analysis information might also be available in a way that allows a gateway to assess the trustworthiness of data sent by an application running on an IoT sensor or compute device. The decoupling of an application thread from its DFT analysis thread, a key contribution of Columbia researchers, opens up the possibility that DFT analysis may be offloaded to a gateway or cloud server. While this would introduce delay, perhaps Trust Evidence need not be instantaneous to be useful. For example, random sampling in tandem with other techniques might be used to incrementally build a case for trust.

3.3 Programming Language Extensions

Researchers at Imperial College London approached the challenge of generating Trust Evidence by developing a programming language extension that allows software developers to express expectations about the results of computation as it proceeds. [HKS13] [HK13] Expectation statements generate numerical trust values which can then be aggregated for broader policy assessments. [HK14] [HK214]

In some ways an expansion on the `assert` statement, researchers develop a rich annotation language allowing a programmer to specify detailed checks on program state and execution path to be checked by the underlying runtime system as the program executes. At the heart of their approach is the `@expect` statement which allows a programmer to define expectation blocks like the following [HKS13]:

```
@expect[max] default 0.1 {
    if (calledBy foo1) setTrustEvidenceTo 0.9;
    if (calledBy foo2) setTrustEvidenceTo 0.3;
    if (sameDomain(@caller)) setTrustEvidenceTo 0.8;
}
method foo(...) { ... } // body of method foo(...)
```

The block places a numerical value in the variable `setTrustEvidenceTo` reflecting the control-flow path of execution at runtime. One can imagine many such statements generating scores for a variety of system execution paths taken and program states, for example, more sophisticated `expect` blocks examining user input, the integrity of sensitive configuration parameters, the sequencing of program operations, or the manner in which system hardware resources are accessed.

The annotation language extension includes a companion `@policy` statement that directs the system to take a particular action based on generated `@expect` values. To illustrate using pseudocode, the code block

```
@policy{
    grant if (localTrust > threshold)
    deny otherwise
}
```

directs the system to deny access or a resource allocation if the value of trust aggregation variable `localTrust` does not exceed `threshold`. The semantics and use of such variables is application-specific and depends entirely on context. This flexibility allows a software developer to focus on whatever states or conditions are relevant and important for assessing the trustworthiness of program execution at a particular point. For example, the integrity of a data structure or the outcome of a series of operations may be crucial for demonstrating trust for a particular security-sensitive region of program logic.

Researchers go on to define an aggregation language capable of collecting the fine-grained outcomes of `@expect` blocks and putting them together to understand the broader picture of trustworthiness across large sections of program operation. They refer to this trust calculus language as *Peal⁺* [HK214] for "pluggable evidence aggregation language". Peal⁺ supports the creation of rules, policies, and policy sets from basic conditions (predicates indicating numerical trust or risk scores) and inequalities (statements comparing scores). Again, the definition of predicates is left entirely open-ended, thus allowing programmers to define application-specific semantics in a flexible and context-specific way. The use of numerical trust values has the nice feature that it supports a wide range of composition and aggregation techniques which can be defined over arithmetic (e.g., addition or subtraction) and other types of operators (e.g., max, min, weighted average).

Researchers, furthermore, develop a tool they refer to as PERLT [HK14] which takes as input Peal+ statements (e.g., policies, policy sets, conditions, domain-specifics) and verification conditions and evaluates them to determine satisfiability. Verification can be handled explicitly through conversion of all references to numerical values and then straightforward numerical evaluation, but at the expense of an explosion in resulting formula length. Or, verification may be handled symbolically through the use of an SMT solver (researchers use Z3) which captures logical dependencies but places constraints on formula complexity.

Trust Evidence in this framework can be packaged for use by interacting systems in a variety of ways. Perhaps the most obvious is to have the system running the instrumented software provide a numerical summary score or brief set of scores to an interacting device. The score represents the outcome of checks built into program code, for example, evaluating program state and execution paths of importance in assessing trust. Another option might be to provide a raw trace upon request and allow the interacting system to evaluate it, perhaps using an undisclosed criteria which cannot be guessed or spoofed by the system being assessed. A third option might be the use of a third party certification system or agent that combines attestation and score evaluation to make a recommendation on trustworthiness.

To see how the program instrumentation framework might apply to IoT, consider an illustrative scenario like dynamic discovery of trustworthy devices. A gateway might require a new IoT devices to present Trust Evidence report scores based on a standardized application built into the operating system or installed at the factory. The application has been instrumented with various system checks and perhaps runs as a protected module per the protected module architecture described previously. The results of assessment are obtained and signed by the underlying runtime system in a way that protects it from software tampering. The gateway uses the assessment, along with other authentication mechanisms, to make a decision on whether the device is trustworthy. Another illustrative scenario might be dynamic risk evaluation. An instrumented application running on your mobile phone might provide periodic updates in the form of numeric values assessing the outcome of various application or system configuration checks. The lack of such Trust Evidence in a public device terminal, for example, may result in a very different threat posture from the same user.

4 Conclusions and Future Work

In this paper, we have described the need for Trust Evidence as the Internet expands to include billions of heterogeneous devices. Trust Evidence provides a framework for demonstrating the trustworthiness of a device or system by providing information on its configuration, software stack integrity, operational context, its management of data security, and other types of descriptive and evaluative information. The rapid proliferation of sensors, lightweight compute devices, and edge gateways, as part of the new Internet of Things (IoT) era, will create an even greater need for Trust Evidence as devices bring new platform and service types, and more complex distributed architectures for managing data exchange.

We described three candidate approaches to Trust Evidence developed by researchers, each looking at the problem in a different way. A *protected module architecture* was described that allows software to execute on a system with robust protections against software-based tampering. [SP12] [ASAP13][NAD+13][DSPV14][SAAP15] An acceleration framework was described that enables dynamic *data-flow tracking* for assessing the robustness of data flow security. [JKK+13] Finally, a *program language extension* was described that supports inline annotations for assessing program state and control flow, and then translating local results to a global assessment. [HKS13][HK13] [HK14][HK214] Each approach offers a variety of ways to generate Trust Evidence and are by no means mutually exclusive. For each, we have commented on possible IoT applications.

Future work may consider a number of areas for making Trust Evidence practical in today's systems, and especially for IoT deployment contexts. Communication protocols are needed that describe how Trust Evidence is requested and exchanged between devices, for example, between IoT sensors and gateways over a wireless network. Standards are needed to better describe the content and format of Trust Evidence, something that requires agreement among technology stakeholders in the IoT space. Both software and hardware support are needed for collecting Trust Evidence in IoT devices and making it available in a way that eludes attack. We believe that the approaches discussed in this paper have important implications for all of these challenges.

References

[VOG12] Claire Vishik, David Ott, and David Grawrock. Intention Semantics and Trust Evidence. *Information Security Solution Europe (ISSE)*. November, 2012.

[CBP+13] Dan Caselden, Alex Bazhanyuk, Mathias Payer, Stephen McCamant, and Dawn Song. Hi-CFG: Construction by binary analysis and application to attack polymorphism. *Proceedings of ESO-RICS*, page(s): 164-181. September 2013.

[DKL13] T. Denning, T. Kohno, and H. Levy. Computer Security in the Modern Home. *Communications of the ACM*, 56(1), January 2013.

[BCR11] L. Bauer, Y. Liang, M. K. Reiter and C. Spensky. Discovering access-control misconfigurations: New approaches and evaluation methodologies. *Proceedings of the 2nd ACM Conference on Data and Application Security and Privacy*. February 2012.

[BLO+11] S. Bratus, M. Locasto, B. Otto, R. Shapiro, S. W. Smith, G. Weaver. Beyond SELinux: the Case for Behavior-Based Policy and Trust Languages. Computer Science Technical Report TR2011-701. Dartmouth College. August 2011.

[CBK09] V. Chandola, A. Banerjee, and V. Kumar. Anomaly detection: A survey. *ACM Computing Surveys*. Vol 41, No 3, (July 2009).

[ABEL09] Abadi, M., Budiu, M., Erlingsson, U., Ligatti, J. Control-flow integrity principles, implementations, and applications. *ACM Transactions on Information and System Security*, Vol 13, No 1 (October 2009).

[SP12] R. Strackx, F. Piessens. Fides: Selectively Hardening Software Application Components against Kernel-level or Process-level Malware. *ACM Conference on Computer and Communications Security (CCS)*. October 2012.

[ASAP13] N. Avonds, R. Strackx, P. Agten, F. Piessens. Salus: Non-Hierarchical Memory Access Rights to Enforce the Principle of Least Privilege. *Security and Privacy in Communication Networks (SecureComm 2013)*. September 2013.

[NAD+13] J. Noorman, P. Agten, W. Daniels, R. Strackx, A. Van Herrewege, C. Huygens, B. Preneel, I. Verbauwhede, F. Piessens. Sancus: Low-cost trustworthy extensible networked devices with a zero-software trusted computing base. *22nd USENIX Security Symposium*, pages 479-494. August 2013.

[DSPV14] R. De Clercq, D. Schellekens, F. Piessens, I. Verbauwhede, Secure Interrupts on Low-End Microcontrollers. *25th IEEE International Conference on Application-specific Systems, Architectures and Processors (ASAP 2014)*. June 2014.

[PJP15] P. Agten, B. Jacobs, F. Piessens. Sound modular verification of C code executing in an unverified context. *Proceedings of the 42nd ACM SIGPLAN-SIGACT Symposium on Principles of Programming Languages (POPL 2015)*. January 2015

[SAAP15] R. Strackx, P. Agten, N. Avonds, F. Piessens. Salus: Kernel support for secure process compartments. *EAI Endorsed Transactions on Security and Safety*, volume 15, issue 3, 30 January 2015.

[PAS+15] M. Patrignani, P. Agten, R. Strackx, B. Jacobs, D. Clarke, F. Piessens. Secure compilation to protected module architectures. *ACM Transactions on Programming Languages and Systems*, volume 37, issue 2, pages 6:1-6:50, April 2015.

[JKK+13] K. Jee, V. P. Kemerlis, A. D. Keromytis, G. Portokalidis. ShadowReplica: Efficient Parallelization of Dynamic Data Flow Tracking. *ACM Conference on Computer and Communications Security (CCS)*. November 2013.

[CGC08] J. Chow, T. Garfinkel, and P. Chen. Decoupling dynamic program analysis from execution in virtual environments. *Proceedings of USENIX ATC*. 2008.

[CC13] Y. Chen and H. Chen. Scalable deterministic replay in a parallel full-system emulator. *Proceedings of PPoPP*. 2013.

[NPC+08] E. B. Nightingale, D. Peek, P. M. Chen, and J. Flinn. Parallelizing security checks on commodity hardware. *Proceedings of ASPLOS*. 2008.

[HKS13] M. Huth, J.H.P. Kuo, A. Sasse, et al. Towards usable generation and enforcement of Trust Evidence from programmers' intent. *Lecture Notes in Computer Science* (including subseries *Lecture Notes in Artificial Intelligence and Lecture Notes in Bioinformatics*), Vol: 8030 LNCS, Pages: 246-255. 2013.

[HK13] M. Huth, J.H.P. Kuo. Towards verifiable trust management for software execution (extended abstract). *Lecture Notes in Computer Science* (including subseries *Lecture Notes in Artificial Intelligence and Lecture Notes in Bioinformatics*), Vol: 7904 LNCS, Pages: 275-276. 2013.

[HK14] M. Huth, J.H.P. Kuo. PEALT: An Automated Reasoning Tool for Numerical Aggregation of Trust Evidence. *Tools and Algorithms for the Construction and Analysis of Systems (TACAS)*. 2014.

[HK214] M. Huth, J.H.P. Kuo. On designing usable policy languages for declarative trust aggregation. *Lecture Notes in Computer Science*. Pages: 45-56, ISSN: 0302-9743. 2014.

Cybersecurity and Cybercrime

Making Sense of Future Cybersecurity Technologies: Using Ontologies for Multidisciplinary Domain Analysis

Claire Vishik[1] · Marcello Balduccini[2]

[1]Intel Corporation
claire.vishik@intel.com

[2]Drexel University
marcello.balduccini@drexel.edu

Abstract

Security experts have difficulties achieving quick vulnerability mitigation because cybersecurity is a complex multi-disciplinary subject that yields itself with great difficulty to traditional methods of risk analysis. In particular, the effectiveness of mitigation strategies depends on an accurate understanding of the relationships among the components of systems that need to be protected, their functional requirements, and of the trade-off between security protection and core functionality. Mitigation strategies may have undesired ripple-effects, such as unexpectedly modifying functions that other system components rely upon. If some of the side-effects of a mitigation strategy are not clearly understood by a security expert, the consequences may be costly. Thus, vulnerability mitigation requires a deep understanding of the subtle interdependencies that exist between domains that are different in nature. This is especially difficult for new technology use models, such as Cloud-based computing and IoT, in which cyber and physical components are combined and interdependent. By their own design, ontologies and the associated inference mechanisms permit us to reason about connections between diverse domains and contexts that are pertinent for the general threat picture, and to highlight the effects and ramifications of the mitigation strategies considered. In this paper, we position ontologies as crucial tools for understanding the threat space for new technology space, for increasing security experts' situational awareness, and, ultimately, as decision-support tools for rapid development of mitigation strategies. We follow with the discussion of the new information and insights gleaned from the ontology-based study of the root of trust in cyber-physical systems.

1 Introduction

Modern processes and technologies are cross-domain, merging together approaches created for different contexts. Complexity is intrinsic. Even activities resulting in identical or similar outcomes – e.g., sending electronic mail, processing identical datasets or payments, using e-commerce applications, or assessing the data quality collected from sensors – could be executed in very different environments, resulting in different risks. Thus, it is sometimes necessary to assume different risk postures in response to similar events or in the course of the same process.

Moreover, computing or physical environments are not the only contexts that influence the nature of vulnerabilities. Economic conditions or regulatory requirements can alter the impact of the cybersecurity risks and therefore lead to changes in mitigation strategies.

This paper uses cyber-physical systems (CPS) as an example environment. Complexity and composition considerations are especially meaningful when analyzing CPS that have computing capabilities, communication (cyber) capabilities, and physical interfaces [. In most use cases, CPS and other systems don't operate in isolation, but rather work in the end to end continuum, extending from edge devices to the Cloud, where data generated by sensors and enriched by processing can be stored. CPS almost always display significant environmental complexity as do multi-device environments in general, complicated by the physical interfaces and use cases that CPS generally enable. Moreover, diversity among CPS is extensive, with seemingly little in common in different CPS contexts. If we compare connected kitchen appliances with transportation systems, or energy systems, they appear to have very little in common, but they draw from similar foundational technologies and deployment processes.

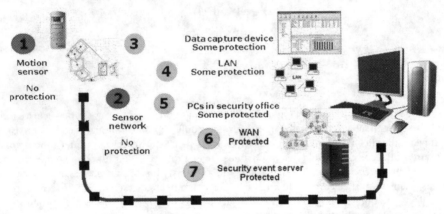

Fig. 1: Security protection and "anonymity readiness" in today's computing environments.

Because of the complexity of processes associated with the use of CPS, one process typically contains multiple operational conditions and levels of security capabilities as illustrated in Fig. 1.

Although the complex processes have a unifying operational goal, the security capabilities are different at different stages of the process. The diversity in security extends to privacy protection.

The diversity and complexity makes it impossible to assess composite risks with traditional techniques [GGIK2015] and to develop mitigations that are broadly applicable rather than context dependent. Ontology-based reasoning can permit us to obtain a multi-dimensional view of the subject, incorporate consistent constraints, understand dependencies, and make informed conclusions about remediation. It could also help the developers to design a nuanced risk posture in new technologies that is better suited to the majority of today's dynamic use cases. Finally, we believe ontologies could be useful in assessing new and emerging technology spaces, for both research and technology deployment, in multi-disciplinary subjects like cybersecurity.

2 Ontology and Complex Multidisciplinary Subjects

2.1 About cybersecurity

Cybersecurity has begun to crystallize into a firmer subject a relatively short time ago. Although definitions of cybersecurity vary, they are not highly divergent and frequently comprise a narrow definition and a broader one. The example of a narrow definition is provided by the National Initiative on Cybersecurity in the US:

> *The activity or process, ability or capability, or state whereby information and communications systems and the information contained therein are protected from and/ or defended against damage, unauthorized use or modification, or exploitation.*

In other cases, a broad definition, including related and non-technical subjects, from economics and psychology to political science and diplomacy is used, for example:

> *Strategy, policy, and standards regarding the security of and operations in cyberspace, and encompassing the full range of threat reduction, vulnerability reduction, prevention, international engagement, incident response, resiliency, and recovery policies and activities, including computer network operations ,information assurance, law enforcement, diplomacy, military, and intelligence missions as they relate to the security and stability of the global information and communications infrastructure.*

Further complicating the issue, cybersecurity characteristics for IT systems, the best studied cybersecurity area, are different from the emerging characteristics of cybersecurity when applied to different environments, such as cyber-physical systems (CPS). While the researchers have defined cross-cutting considerations that apply to most cybersecurity environments, the science of cybersecurity is not sufficiently advanced to create a unifying theory of cybersecurity foundations. As a result, every new context (such as CPS) tends to develop its own cybersecurity approach that shares similar technologies and governance models with adjacent contexts, but creates its own body of knowledge. Cybersecurity approaches for energy sector (e.g., smart meters) differ superficially from the approaches adopted in transportation (e.g., smart cars), leading to the fragmentation of cybersecurity and slower adoption of productive techniques. In new areas, the technology community tends to focus on niche context driven issues because they are easier to analyze and to avoid studying broadly applicable phenomena. Consequently, literature describing cybersecurity R&D in energy space draws very little content and engages in little collaboration with the researchers focusing on transportation, although technologies used in both contexts are very similar.

An ontology-based approach could permit researchers and practitioners to link together disparate content that draws from similar premises [IBN+15], allowing technologists to reuse, share, and propagate knowledge, in order to create a field of cybersecurity that is broader in scope and more theoretically sound.

2.2 About ontology

One of the main goals of the field of Knowledge Representation (KR) is the study of methodologies and tools that enable capturing knowledge accurately, compactly and so that information can be easily added and updated. Acknowledging the importance of the design principle of separation of concerns, KR researchers typically separate knowledge specification from the associated computations. This yields a *declarative specification* (as opposed to the traditional *imperative* one), in which knowledge is specified by statements that say what is true (or false) in the domain of interest, without stating how, algorithmically, statements should be combined and their truth propagated. Rather, the semantics of the representation language defines the meaning of those statements in precise and unambiguous (usually, logical) terms. For automated computation, general-purpose algorithms, often called *inference engines*, are separately defined, which embody the semantics of the language. Thanks to this separation, the meaning of a *knowledge base* can be determined independently of the particular algorithms used, and alternative algorithms can be adopted to fit specific practical needs (e.g., performance on given kinds of knowledge).

An ontology is a hierarchical specification of a set of objects from a domain of interest, of their properties and of their relationships. As such, ontologies enable a principled organization of knowledge. For example, a simple ontology may specify that laptops and desktops are kinds of computers, that computers and smartphones are kinds of computing devices, that all computing devices are equipped with a CPU, and that computers and smartphones are disjoint classes of objects (i.e., something cannot be a computer and a smartphone at the same time). Additionally, the ontology may specify that "John's workstation" is a laptop. Specifically designed ontological languages enable the encoding of such knowledge in an accurate way.

The true power of ontologies, however, comes from the fact that ontological languages are associated, through their semantics, with inference mechanisms that make it possible to perform automated, provably correct reasoning about the elements of an ontology. Inference mechanisms are related, for example, to expanding the class-subclass relationships into ancestor/descendant and – importantly – to determining how properties and relationships are propagated through the hierarchy specified by the ontology, i.e., how classes inherit their ancestors' characteristics. In the computer ontology described earlier, inference mechanisms can conclude, for example, that laptops are computing devices and that, as such, they inherit the properties of the latter. Hence, it is possible to infer that all laptops are equipped with a CPU and that "John's workstation" is equipped with a CPU. Fincally, because computers and smartphones are disjoint classes, it is possible to conclude that "John's workstation" cannot be classified as a smartphone.

By applying inference mechanisms, one can often derive information that was not immediately evident from the original specification of the ontology, and the reasons for such derivation can be clearly pinpointed and explained automatically.

Notable similarities exist between ontologies and (relational) databases, which in fact can be viewed as their precursors. Like ontologies, databases are declarative specifications of objects and of their properties and relations. From a conceptual perspective, however, ontologies are characterized by a more uniform and thorough encoding of knowledge. For example, information about computing devices can indeed be encoded using a relational database, but the meaning (i.e., the semantics) of the relations themselves remains implicit and external to the database. Thus, while the database may well contain a relation (represented by a table) called "kind-of" that holds between laptop and computer, the meaning of such relation – e.g., its transitivity and the inheritance of properties from classes to their sub-classes – is not part of the specification and must be provided separately to draw inferences.

2.3 Reasoning about multidisciplinary connections using ontologies

The general-purpose, hierarchical nature of ontologies, their broad applicability, and the fact that all relevant information is encoded in an explicit, machine-accessible way, make ontologies prime candidates for formalizing multidisciplinary knowledge and for reasoning about the underlying connections.

An interesting example of a multidisciplinary ontology is that of [PFCS14], in which a multidisciplinary ontology of epidemiology is developed in order to enable a uniform annotation of epidemiology resources and the integration and sharing of data about global epidemiological events.

A further example is that of [BaLR14], where the authors discuss how an ontology could be used for the development of a discovery network linking databases of materials scientific data. Such a "Layered Material Ontology" would enable connecting multidisciplinary knowledge ranging from matter and materials to performance and design (see Fig. 2), and asking queries spanning across domain boundaries, such as asking for metal alloys that are suitable for a given kind of design.

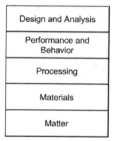

Fig. 2: Structure of the Layered Material Ontology proposed (courtesy of [BaLR14]).

From an organizational perspective, when tackling multidisciplinary knowledge, it is useful to divide the formalization in upper ontology and (multiple) domain ontologies. An upper ontology is an encoding of the concepts that are common across all disciplines of interest. In the context of securing cyber-physical systems, for instance, an upper ontology might define the high-level concept of system component, with its refinements of computational device and physical device, and the concept of vulnerability. Additionally, a relation "vulnerable-to" might be used to associate a system component with its known vulnerabilities.

A domain ontology formalizes a specific knowledge domain. The concepts captured by a domain ontology are typically specified as specializations of concepts from the upper ontology. In reference to the previous example, a domain ontology of smart grids might describe SCADA systems as kinds of computational devices, power generators as types of physical device, and list a number of vulnerabilities specific to the smart grid. Relation "vulnerable-to" could then be used to indicate the specific vulnerabilities of smart grid components. Similarly, a domain ontology of automotive systems might describe the ECU as a computational device, a brake actuator as a physical device, and use relation "vulnerable-to" to specify the vulnerabilities of the various components of an automotive system. Inference can then be applied to propagate relevant properties and relations throughout the ontology. For example, suppose a new vulnerability is discovered, which affects certain system components. Obviously, one can check which components are directly vulnerable. However, one may also want to define the notion of a component being "affected by" the vulnerability either because it is directly vulnerable to it or because it is connected to some other component that is affected by it. Inference can now be used to identify, across the ontology, any component that is affected, even remotely, by a vulnerability (more details on this topic will be provided in the next section).

This representation and reasoning framework becomes especially useful in situations in which knowledge from multiple fields must be taken into account at the same time. Consider the task of assessing the vulnerabilities of an electric car. The example ontology discussed in the previous paragraph would allow one to study vulnerabilities that may come from coordinated exploits affecting both the power system and the braking system (e.g., one could automate the search for scenarios in which a central control component becomes overloaded when elements in the power *and* braking subsystems are caused to misbehave). Such a model can be incrementally extended by adding domain ontologies for other car subsystems. By replacing the braking system ontology with an ontology modeling a navigation system or a weapons system, one could study the vulnerabilities of combat ships. What is essential to note is that, in all of these cases, multidisciplinary knowledge can be incrementally and seamlessly integrated and sophisticated questions about the systems being modeled can be answered by means of general-purpose inference mechanisms, without the need to develop dedicated algorithms.

3 Case Study: Root of Trust in CPS

3.1 General information about the project

The Cyber Security Research Alliance, Inc. (CSRA) is an industry-led, non-profit consortium focused on research and development strategy to address evolving cyber security environment through partnerships among government, industry, and academia. This effort was established in response to the growing need for increased public-private collaboration to address R&D issues in cyber security.

CSRA has identified several priority areas crucial for improving security in cyber-physical systems through the input at the CSRA/NIST Workshop on Cybersecurity for Cyber Physical Systems, held April 4-5, 2013. Almost all of the study sessions acknowledged the need for the common vocabulary and reasoning mechanism to unify currently available research and technology to reduce fragmentation of CPS space. The lack of common terminology and combined assessment of work in adjacent fields was considered one of the main inhibitors of research due to the diversity of CPS contexts and the multidisciplinary nature of the field. As a result, best practices and research advances are not always shared and applied across relevant CPS contexts.

Following the workshop, CSRA set up a pilot project to build a subset of an ontology focusing on cybersecurity for CPS. The project covered the subject of the root of trust in CPS. Teams from two universities – George Mason University and Drexel University – participated in the pilot and built the foundations of the ontology.

The participants in the pilot project surveyed the field, prioritized technologies, identified gaps, and defined ontology approaches that could be adjusted for CPS contexts. Seed ontologies were built by both groups of the participants. They included terminology, information on research already done, R&D groups active in this area, and other relevant information. The reasoning process identified and prioritized gaps that need to be addressed. The project addressed the discovery of cyber security technologies protecting CPS at different stages of development. The results of the project have been used as a tool for subsequent phases of research in COS security addressing research gaps, evaluating research results, directions of technology adoption and commercialization, e.g., as a reference point in the work of the NIST Public Working Group (PWG) on cyber-physical systems. The outcome of the project helped multidisciplinary teams investigate solutions in perspective of real-world trade-offs for protection, detection and response to cyber-attacks on CPS.

We provide information on one of the project deliverables below.

3.2 Building the ontology

The RoT ontology is divided into an upper component, which provides concepts relevant to all cyber-physical systems, and domain ontologies for the specific domains, including smart grids, transportation, and healthcare. Key elements of the upper component are the notions of *cyber-physical system concepts*, *cyber attacks*, and *countermeasures*. The latter two classes are divided in further domain-independent concepts, such as *malicious* and *non-malicious threats* and *cyber defense methods* (e.g., *preparation* and *detection*). Although there is an obvious relationship among the three top components of the upper ontology, to ensure breadth of the ontology we have included in it elements as exhaustively as possible, independently of whether they are currently related to other elements from the ontology. For example, instances of cyber attacks have been included independently of whether it is currently known how to use them against cyber-physical system. Domain ontologies provide further specializations of the three top components. Next, we focus on the smart-grid domain ontology, SG.

The development of the SG ontology was guided by the principles outlined in [LNB+15]. Information was obtained from subject matter experts and from various published sources, including [WaLu13], [NIST10], and [CMGS12]. Fig. 3 gives an overview of the upper component and of the SG domain ontology.

Fig. 3: RoT ontology – upper component and SG domain ontology

At the root of the SG ontology is the concept of *energyCPSInfrastructureComponents*, which acts as a superclass of any concept related to the energy CPS infrastructure and enables expanding the ontology to other energy cyber-physical systems beyond smart grids. Directly under it is class *smartGridInfrastructureComponents*, which constitutes the root concept for smart-grid components. The organization of its subclasses follows an organizational paradigm that is intended to be applicable, with relatively small changes, to multiple knowledge domains. According to this paradigm, concepts are classified in one of:

- *devices*
- *interfaces*
- *protocols*

For example, in the case of our smart grid domain, the class of *devices* comprises *sensors* and *pumps*. Other notable subclasses include:

- *scada*
- *historian*
- *masterTerminalUnitMTU*
- *remoteTerminalUnitRTU*

All of these classes represent key devices of the smart grid infrastructure; the SCADA system, for example, acts as a central governor of the infrastructure, communicating with, and controlling, all remote equipment. There are also classes for key subsystems, such as telemetrySystem and transmissionSystem.

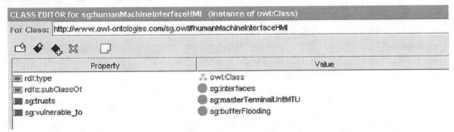

Fig. 4: Class humanMachineInterfaceHMI and relations trusts and vulnerable_to

The most fundamental relation defined by the ontology is the trust relationship, informally denoting the fact that one component trusts another. Intuitively, if a trusted component is affected by a cyber threat, the trusting component will also likely be affected, either directly (e.g., by being compromised) or indirectly (e.g., because it takes as credible false information that is fed to it from the affected component). The fact that a component is vulnerable to a certain threat is encoded by relation vulnerable_to. Fig. 4 shows a sample class and the corresponding definitions of the relations. More specifically, we see that human-machine interface (HMI) "trusts" the master terminal unit and that the HMI is vulnerable to buffer flooding.

3.3 Insights obtained from the ontology

The RoT ontology makes it possible to answer a number of important and nuanced questions related to the assessment of the weaknesses of the infrastructure, including:

- What elements does a given component (e.g., SCADA) trust?
- In turn, what do these elements trust?

- What vulnerabilities does this component have?
- What is impacted by a given vulnerability?

Although conceptually simple, these questions involve a rather substantial amount of reasoning. Consider for instance the last question, useful in a scenario in which a vulnerability is discovered and one wants to determine all components that are put in danger by this vulnerability. Generally speaking, the components that are directly affected by the vulnerability are to be identified (using relation *vulnerable_to*), and then the information must be propagated recursively (through relation *trusts*) to all components trusting the vulnerable ones either directly or indirectly. If the infrastructure includes only a small number of components, then the answer may be straightforward. However, in larger infrastructures answering the question may be more challenging due to more complex trust chains.

With traditional approaches, answering these questions would likely involve implementing a different algorithm for each of them, algorithms (and corresponding data structures) that are made non-trivial by the variability of the concepts that need to be represented. The adoption of an ontology-based formalization makes it is possible to accomplish all of this by stating the questions in a declarative fashion (i.e., by specifying what one is looking for, rather than how to find it) and without the need for implementing ad-hoc algorithms. This is achieved thanks to the general-purpose inference mechanisms associated with the ontology and to powerful query languages. For instance, the components that may be affected by an attack targeting integrity can be found by means of the query shown in Fig. 5.

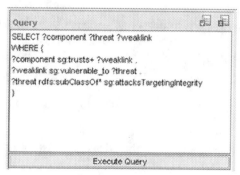

Fig. 5: Sample query

Intuitively, the query asks the inference mechanism to find all triples of the form such that is a "trust element" of , and it is vulnerable to , where is, in this example, a type of attack targeting integrity. Similar queries allow one to identify all trust elements of a given component and to determine the starting points of the corresponding trust chains, which can be viewed as the *roots of trust*.

Fig. 6 shows the output of a query requesting the trust elements of SCADA.

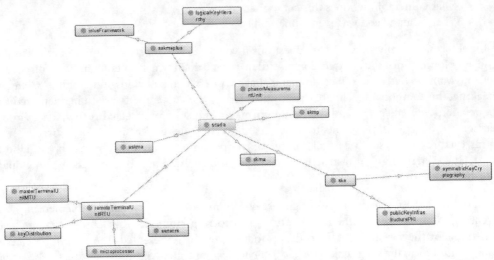

Fig. 6: Trust elements of SCADA

4 Conclusions and Future Work

The review of research literature focusing on cybersecurity in different CPS contexts shows commonalities in approaches among different types of systems, although collaborations among scientists focusing on different contexts remains minimal Similarly, interactions between different domains in cybersecurity, e.g., safety, reliability, and security proper, are limited, although they are reflected in recent literature, e.g., [SMSG15]. Various approaches have been tried to facilitate greater flow of ideas among different contexts and enhance multidisciplinary collaboration, but the nature of synergies remains difficult to assess, and the results difficult to evaluate.

We believe ontological reasoning could be instrumental in fostering a consistent emerging technology space, helping realize broadly applicable ideas in a field of research, and maximize the ability to bring these ideas to practice.

The pilot project for CPS root of trust helped the research teams to identify approaches to creating knowledge representations for a specific, but complex field. The tools created as a result assisted the research community and practitioners to form a multi-dimensional view of emerging subjects, identifying gaps, priorties, and affinities with adjacent fields[1].

The project paved the way for continued research in ontologies for emerging fields. Further work will include broader analysis with a larger number of contexts as well as the creation of focused analysis tools specialized for R&D, research funding, or deployment in new areas of technology.

---

1   See http://www.cybersecurityresearch.org/news_and_events/press_releases/pr_20150106.html for more information.

Bibliography

[FKWL11] Ashfaq H. Farooqi, Farrukh A. Khan, Jin Wang, and Sungyoung Lee. 2011. Security require-ments for a cyber physical community system: a case study. In *Proceedings of the 4th International Symposium on Applied Sciences in Biomedical and Communication Technologies*(ISABEL ,11). ACM, New York, NY, USA

[GGIK15] Dieter Gollmann, Pavel Gurikov, Alexander Isakov, Marina Krotofil, Jason Larsen, and Alexander Winnicki. 2015. Cyber-Physical Systems Security: Experimental Analysis of a Vinyl Acetate Monomer Plant. In *Proceedings of the 1st ACM Workshop on Cyber-Physical System Security*(CPSS ,15). ACM, New York, NY, USA, 1-12.

[BaLR14] Balduccini, M., LeBlanc, E., & Regli, W. C.: Towards a Content-Based Material Science *Discovery Network. In: 2014 AAAI Workshop for Discovery Informatics*, 2014.

[CMGS12] Cichonski, P., Millar, T., Grance, T., and Scarfone, K.: Computer Security Incident Handling Guide. National Institute of Standards and Technology Special Publication No. 800-61, 2012.

[IBN+15] Iannacone, Michael, Bohn, Shawn, Nakamura, Grant, Gerth, John, Huffer, Kelly, Bridges, Robert, Ferragut, Erik, and Goodall, John. 2015. Developing an Ontology for Cyber Security Knowledge Graphs. In *Proceedings of the 10th Annual Cyber and Information Security Research Conference*(CISR ,15). ACM, New York, NY, USA

[LNB+15] LeBlanc, E., Nguyen, D., Balduccini, M., Regli, W. C., Kopena, J., and Wambold, T.: Military Ontologies for Information Dissemination at the Tactical Edge. In: *1st Workshop on Formal Ontologies for Artificial Intelligence (FOfAI15)*, 2015.

[NIST10] National Institute of Standards and Technology. *Guidelines for Smart Grid Cyber Security. NIST IR-7628, 2010.*

[PFCS14] Pesquita, C., Ferreira, J. D., Couto, F. M., and Silva, M. J.: The epidemiology ontology: an ontology for the semantic annotation of epidemiological resources. In: *J. Biomed Semantics*, 5(4), 2014.

[WaLu13] Wang, W., and Lu, Z.: Cyber Security in the Smart Grid: Survey and Challenges. In: *Computer Networks*, 57(5), 2013, 1344-1371.

[SMSG15] Christoph Schmittner, Zhendong Ma, Erwin Schoitsch, and Thomas Gruber. 2015. A Case Study of FMVEA and CHASSIS as Safety and Security Co-Analysis Method for Automotive Cyber-physical Systems. In *Proceedings of the 1st ACM Workshop on Cyber-Physical System Security*(CPSS ,15). ACM, New York, NY, USA, 69-80.

How the God Particle will Help You Securing Your Assets

Roger Bollhalder[1] · Christian Thiel[2] · Thomas Punz[3]

[1]Fernfachhochschule Schweiz (FFHS), Switzerland
roger.bollhalder@ffhs.ch

[2]FHS University of Applied Sciences St. Gallen,
christian.thiel@fhsg.ch

[3]Itecor, Switzerland
t.punz@itecor.com

Abstract

Since the first computer worms emerged in the late 1980s cyber threats constantly grew in sophistication, impact and scale. However, as cybercrime has become more sophisticated, so has the security against it. Today, reliable and efficient security incident management requires tools highly integrated into the corporate landscape, sophisticated detection mechanisms, highly-trained security specialists and a robust process framework to adequately react on identified threats. This paper shows how approaches taken by the teams finding the Higgs boson at CERN can help solving the problems faced in corporate security incident detection. Cyber security management is a huge and rapidly evolving area of corporate IT and this paper can't claim to present the complete answers to the challenges. It does, however, identify the main challenges faced when implementing a Security Information and Event Management system (SIEM) and point out feasible approaches to address these challenges.

1 The LHC challenge and how was it solved

The standard model of particle physics describes the properties of leptons, quarks and bosons including their interactions. The Higgs boson was the last predicted but not discovered particle within the standard model.

The first extensive search for the Higgs boson was conducted at the Large Electron–Positron Collider (LEP) at CERN in Switzerland in the 1990s. At the end of its service in 2000, LEP had found no conclusive evidence for the Higgs. Fermilab in the United States continued the search until the Large Hadron Collider (LHC) at CERN was available in March 2010. The LHC was designed specifically to either confirm or exclude the existence of the Higgs boson. It was built in a circular tunnel of 27 km length near Geneva and is one of the world's most complex experimental facilities to date. On 4 July 2012 both of the CERN experiments announced they had independently discovered a previously unknown particle. On 14 March 2013 CERN confirmed that evidence strongly indicated that the particle is indeed one of the predicted Higgs boson flavors.

2 How does the LHC challenge apply to IT Security

There are distinct differences between the search for the Higgs boson and security related incidents but there are also a surprising number of similarities. Physicists and security specialists both need a model to guide their efforts, funding for the work must be obtained, stakeholder requests must be fulfilled, data has to be collected, enriched, processed and analyzed and the correct conclusions must be reached and acted upon.

2.1 IT Security Threat Model and Stakeholders

The Standard Model of Particle Physics is the physicist's equivalent of the IT Security Threat Model. Both attempt to describe the universe and thus guide future efforts; be it research or IT Security. The aim of the Threat Model is to collect and holistically assess all (IT Security) threats the company is exposed to. By mapping threats to assets a landscape of risk exposure develops.

Technical prerequisites are a risk assessment method suitable for the company and a Configuration Management Database (CMDB) showing the assets of the company. From an organizational point of view, it's imperative to identify and involve the stakeholders. Typically, IT Security Monitoring will be governed by the Chief Information Security Officer, IT Risk and IT Forensics.

Then, high-level use cases are described and mapped to the Threat Model. Use cases can be as straightforward – although not necessarily easy – as 'Remediate Virus infections' or 'Defend against DDoS', highly complex like 'Detect changes to systems made by unauthorized persons or without approved change request' or on first sight only loosely connected like 'How and when is IT Forensics allowed to access log data'.

One more step is required to complete the picture: the target state defined by Threat Model and use cases is compared with the security implementation to identify gaps and determine the extent of these gaps. The gaps and the risks associated to them allow prioritization, planning and finally budgeting of IT Security-related activities.

Sustainable security mandates that this is not just a one-time-exercise but either a continuously maintained framework or at least regularly reassessed.

2.2 Data Collection

2.2.1 How does a detector at the LHC experiment look like

The Compact Muon Solenoid (CMS) detector is a multipurpose detector used to study a variety of physical processes. It has an onion-like structure consisting of specialized sub detectors placed inside a superconducting solenoid, which provides a 4 T magnetic field. The layers track the paths of particles and measure the kinetic properties of leptons, hadrons and photons. All properties of CMS and its sub detectors, its structure, their layering and accuracy are tuned to the research questions in the context of the standard model.

2.2.2   How does an IT security solutions setup look like

IT security is not measuring particles but how an electronic or physical being (i.e. a user or an employee) moves through a company, its IT systems and its data. To this end, multiple detectors are deployed and operated. For instance, a badge system at the entrance registers that a person is physically inside the building. Subsequent badging points or a smart NAC solution can track the position of a person further. A solution for user behavior analytics can check if today's behavior of a user is suspicious and how one behaves in contrasts to one's role peers.

Like in experimental particle physics conscious selection of 'detectors' (Can it collect relevant data? How much of it? What are the restrictions of the technology and are they acceptable based on the risk appetite?), their sensible placing and a continuous maintenance are crucial in order to be able to come to meaningful conclusions.

2.3   Data Processing and Enrichment

2.3.1   How did the LHC experiment process data

The LHC is operating with an effective proton bunch crossing rate of 32 MHz, producing about a billion proton-proton collision events per second. Only 100 to 200 carefully selected events per second can be captured for later analysis and each of these events is overlapped by more than 20 overlapping proton-proton events in the same bunch crossing. The big challenge is to create a rejection filter, called trigger, which will remove about 10^7 events and keep only the most important and relevant events that are required to answer the research questions.

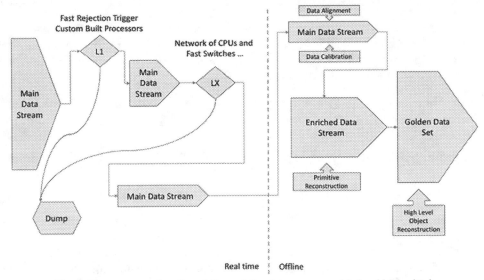

Fig. 1: The event rate is reduced (in real-time) to a manageable level by multiple triggers. At a later time, error correction, enrichment and identification of research candidates lead to the Golden Data Set used to perform the actual research.

The trigger system is comprised of multiple layers as can be seen in Figure 1. The first layer of custom-built processors executes decisions within 2.5-3.2 μs but use only a limited set of detector information to identify the most promising events. This first trigger reduces the actual data rate to about 100 kHz (i.e. hundred thousand events per second). Subsequent triggers leverage a network of several thousand commercial CPUs, enabling the fast execution of algorithms that require gradually more detector information and achieve a further reduction down to 150-200 Hz, which is the desired data rate. With a typical event size of 1.5 MB this results in an annual data volume of approximately 10 PB.

2.3.2 How can an IT security solution process data

IT Security shares the problem of high data volume within a short time. However, dropping data to focus on most promising events is usually not an option. Therefore, events must be captured in real-time and – at least partially – also processed near-real-time.

This is achieved by a Security Event System (SEM) which captures, stores and analyzes events, thus allowing near-real-time analysis which enables security personnel to take defensive actions. To cope with more sophisticated attacks and to reduce the number of false positives a Security Information System (SIM) can be used to further analyze and present information. Security Information and Event Management (SIEM) products combine SIM and SEM. Important capabilities of a SIEM are aggregation of data from multiple sources, correlation of events following defined rules, alerting on specific situations or thresholds, data presentation in dashboards, retention of data for legal requirements or later analysis and the ability to search logs based on specific criteria.

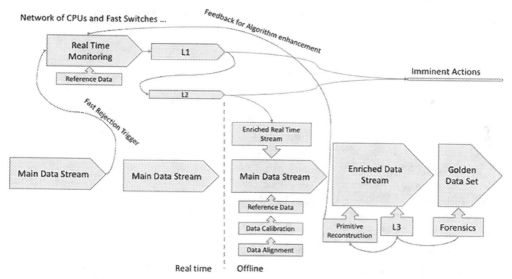

Fig. 2: In contrast to the LHC event data handling an IT Security event stream typically must not dump events. Similar to the fast rejection trigger L1 of the CMS detector, only events required for the real-time analytics logic are piped though the real-time monitoring solution which is comparable to the high level trigger LX. The events are processed by the first level SOC L1 and eventually escalated to the second level SOC L2. Finally, third level SOC L3 and IT Forensics perform offline data analytics. A feedback for algorithm and selection thresholds allows SOC L3 to improve the real-time monitoring solution and the fast rejection trigger. The area of each arrow represents the amount of data to be processed.

Challenges when implementing a SIEM are to ensure all devices continuously send their complete log data, the SIEM can process and store the data and that the data is normalized. Normalization brings differently formatted data into a comparable form, i.e. ensures time is always in GMT and that information like system or user name is reliably stored in the respective fields of the database. It's advisable to also categorize events at this time because this allows for flexible aggregation and correlation afterwards. Although not required by the SIEM it might be required to store the received raw data for legal purpose.

After the data is available and processable the SIEM capabilities come into play: aggregation summaries (counts) of event data (e.g. number of failed logins in a given time) and correlation – the brain of a SIEM – which uses static data (e.g. CMDB), predefined filters and rules to put different events and event types into a relationship. Thus, the SIEM draws conclusions and raises alerts if conditions are met or thresholds are reached. One of the biggest challenges for the operators of the SIEM is to detect suspicious events without generating too much false positives and without missing too many malicious events.

Contrary to the LHC data processing, a typical SIEM performs more granular data processing and supports near-real-time alerting as some security incidents require immediate action, usually by a level 1 Security Operation Center.

2.4 Data Analysis

2.4.1 How did the LHC experiment analyze data and come to conclusions

The previous chapter on data collection described how the main data stream was reduced to a manageable level by using L1 and multiple LX filters. This reduced the main data stream to the most promising candidates and – more importantly – made the data available for later offline processing.

In a first stage, offline processing corrects or enhances the data by considering measurement errors due to age, temperature, crystal transparency or synchronization of detectors. The raw data is preserved for a possible reprocessing and the processed data is added to the data stream. This enriched data stream is then used to perform a primitive identification called reconstruction. Examples are the reconstruction of electron candidates, positrons candidates, muon candidates and so on. These primitives are then added to the data stream and are available for reconstruction of composited high level objects, where the primitive candidates are the final state particle of the hidden interaction (see Figure 4 and Figure 5). This golden data set contains the best and most enriched data and is used by the scientists for their research (see Figure 1).

2.4.2 How can an IT Security organization analyze data and come to conclusions

A well-tuned SIEM already detects many security risks but using the CERN approach and enriching the captured log data with further information enhances the added value of a SIEM significantly – even if this enrichment cannot always be performed immediately. Figure 2 shows a possible data pipeline by applying IT Security requirements on the processing shown by Figure 1.

A traditional SIEM could check whether access to a server originates from a known workstation. With data enrichment, however, it could answer much more sophisticated questions like: Should the user have administrative access to this server at this time? Are tools and commands being used a normal behavior, based on past behavior of the user or other users with similar roles? Do tools or commands used pose any known threats?

Answering such advanced questions not only requires the availability of reference data like HR database or a CMDB but also from workflow and ticketing tools and even external data like information on vulnerabilities. Also, trending information is a big help to identify unusual behavior but must be calculated and stored beforehand to be available when required.

Consequently, the enriched data stream is not available to a level 1 Security Operations Center (SOC) but used by level 2 SOC specialists, data analytics (SOC L3) or IT Forensics. Knowledge gained from the use and analysis of enriched data should be used to continuously improve the granularity and accuracy of the rules used for real-time alerting, thus improving the efficiency of SOC L1. It's imperative to attract and retain competent L2 and L3 specialists and to define accountabilities. Errors will occur as most of the analysis work is performed by humans and efficient processes and continuous measurement of the output minimize the error rate.

3 SIEM Architecture Approaches and Data Routing

A single SIEM may not deliver the performance or flexibility required for a bigger company. This chapter presents approaches to achieve flexibility, performance, or both.

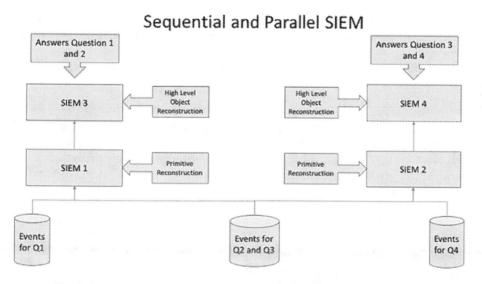

Fig. 3: One option to combine a sequential and a parallel SIEM architecture. First a parallel architecture, followed by a sequential architecture approach.

The capacity of a SIEM instance is limited and organizations with large log and reference data volume will easily outperform a single-box solution. Load-balancing, as generally used to cope with overload, will not work for a SIEM as events would be arbitrarily distributed between the instances and none would have the full picture; i.e. a use case like 'alert on 5 false logins' could not be reliably covered. However, a parallelized SIEM architecture (SIEM 1 and SIEM 2 in Figure 3) where different SIEM instances analyze different use cases increases performance without losing the full picture.

Increased flexibility, as well as the option of not revealing sensitive information abroad or to e.g. SOC L1, is achieved by structuring the analytical algorithms so that they can be processed sequentially. Events are first fed into SIEM 1 where they are analyzed and enriched with supporting information and aggregated to SOC L1 Security events (aka primitive objects or primitive reconstruction in the physicist' world) of lower complexity and level of detail. Subsequently, these primitive objects are fed into SIEM 2 where additional enrichment and logic (aka high level object reconstruction) will collect more detailed information and detect more complex security events like advanced persistent threats. The flexibility is bought with an increase of data volume as primitive objects created in SIEM 1 will be duplicated in SIEM 2.

Combining sequential and parallel SIEM architecture achieves both flexibility and performance. Figure 3 shows a parallel tiered SIEM improving performance followed by a sequential SIEM. The reverse order is also possible but less common as performance is usually the more pressing driver for using multiple SIEM instances.

4 Data security analytics from the legacy perimeter approach to Big Data

Collection of data on a large scale and analysis of historical trends allows security staff to identify the time when an attack started and how the attacker progressed to take control of the company's systems. Historical correlation in the database can identify attacks even if the original attack was not detected by the SIEM, provided enough captured, processed and adequately enriched data is available.

Another advantage of Big Data is the efficiency of queries; trained specialists can execute complex queries easily and receive results in a timely fashion. If, for example, multiple people within the organization are targeted by spear-phishing attacks, a traditional email security appliance would most likely detect and stop this attack. Big Data long-term historical Security Analytics, however, could give deeper insight into the attack and determine that the phishing attack originated from a specific Facebook account and specifically targeted individuals in the organization's accounting department.

Even real-time analysis and attack detection is possible by streaming the traffic, i.e. analyzing data online without doing historical correlations. This is a tool to identify more pressing attacks that appear suddenly, whereas batch processing is better suited for analyzing long-term trends.

Contrary to traditional SIEM detection in the big data approach is not based on signatures or static correlation rules but on dynamic comparisons to normal baseline behaviors for individuals or groups that have similar job functionality and requirements. Behavior outside the normal baseline may indicate attacker activity. Big Data security analytics technologies allow to capture more data and to perform multi-variable Security Analytics.

5 Data Analytics

5.1 Use Case – LHC Physics

One use case concerning the Higgs search was the need to discriminate the ttbar background (see Figure 5) from the decay of the Higgs into two bosons (H®WW signal) (see Figure 4) which is suppressed by a factor of 40. The final state signatures of both particle decays are nearly identical and given the fact that the H®WW channel can also be accompanied by jets from underlying processes the two signatures indeed seem identical. The true positive is not distinguishable from the false positive by analyzing the final state of such an event.

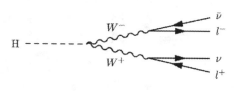
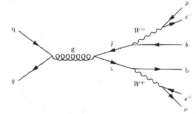

Fig. 4: The Higgs decay into two W bosons.

Fig. 5: The decay of a top and anti top quark pair into two W bosons and two jets caused by the bottom and anti bottom quark.

Fortunately, there are much more properties bound to a particle decay: for instance, every particle has kinetic properties such as transverse energy (ET) or transverse momentum (PT). On the event level one has missing transverse energy (MET), an opening angle ($\Delta\Phi$) between particles and an invariant mass (m_{ll}).

All these parameters, used together, result in a multidimensional phase space where the best discriminator to separate true from false positives can be determined. As the loss of some true positives is acceptable in physicist's research the best discriminator is 'good enough' to identify the most promising candidates for research.

5.2 Use Case – IT Security

While it is ok to cut away some true positive events during false positive discrimination in physics doing this in IT Security means missing threats and possibly taking inacceptable risks.

It's not uncommon that initial deployment of a SIEM is managed by a SOC L1 and L2 team without a L3 Security Analytics team. Being focused on timely reaction to security events SOC L2 tend to focus on false positive reduction. However, false and true positives are often not easily distinguishable as the second graph in Figure 6 illustrates. Simply cutting away all false positives (Cut a) will remove some true positives. This is only ok if done in a conscious and informed decision to accept the risk. Therefore, decisions on rule tuning should be the responsibility of a L3 Security Analytics team independent from day-to-day SLAs. Another advantage of Security Analytics is that by use of the analytics cluster L3 can perform studies and expand the view with more available data on the events (enrichment). This adds additional dimensions to the phase space allowing identification of a discriminator perfectly separating the true and the false positives from each other (see first graph in Figure 6). The results of these studies must be fed back to the selection triggers and real-time analytics content as well as the primitive and higher object reconstruction algorithms, thus improving efficiency of both the SIEM and SOC team.

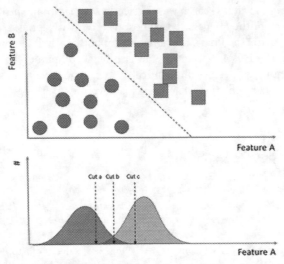

Fig. 6: The lower diagram show to distributions for an arbitrary feature A. The red distribution represents the true positive and the blue distribution the false positive distribution. Both distributions have an overlap and a simple cut on one dimension would not lead to an accurate separation. The upper figure adds an additional arbitrary feature to the dame distributions. One can see now that both distributions can we separated perfectly.

It's not sufficient to design and specify an effective SIEM; it must also be operated competently and diligently. Effective detection of actionable intelligence requires analysts with strong analytical and statistical skills, detailed understanding of application design and behaviors and the ability to notice behaviors which are anomalous. Security monitoring is a resource intensive task and no vendor on the market claims to reduce the demand for skilled human analysts.

While automated, intelligent analytics are an important component of new Security Analytics platforms, they can't replace human judgment. They just spotlight areas where human judgment, with its unique organizational and domain expertise, should be applied. In essence, Security Analytics systems help SOCs scale their threat detection capabilities in ways that weren't possible before, helping analysts to make sense of incidents in time to make a difference in the outcome of an advanced attack.

Therefore, Enterprise Security Intelligence as the collection of data from all potentially security-relevant IT systems in the enterprise and the security teams' knowledge and skill are required to achieve risk reduction.

Building a SOC still starts with threat modeling according to the basic threat modeling process:

1. What threats does the organization care about? E.g. intellectual or customer data loss, compliance, etc.
   - Prioritized based on impact

2. What would the threat look like?
   - How it would access and exfiltrate confidential data
3. How would we detect/ block the threat?
   - Required machine data and external context
   - Searches or visualizations that would detect it
4. What is the playbook/process for each type of threat?
   - Severity, response process, roles and responsibilities, how to document, how to remediate, when to escalate or close, etc.

5.3 Data Analytics Framework – LHC Physics

Even though the trigger systems examine the most crucial properties of events and event fragments, due to processing time limitations this examination is neither detailed nor accurate.

The full raw event information is stored on discs and available for slow offline processing. This processing is done by a data analytics framework able to reconstruct basic physical objects (candidate selections) from raw digital information delivered by the detector readout electronics. Information correction due to alignment and calibration information is performed before basic primitives can be identified among the candidates. Basic primitives are input for the reconstruction of high level objects; such as jets or particles not visible for the detector.

The software module for every primitive reconstruction is designed, implemented and maintained by a dedicated group of domain experts. There might even be different algorithms or fixed input parameters for the reconstruction of the same primitive object. Every single one of these different approaches is available as an independent module that researcher can stack into a data processing queue.

The final goal of the analytics framework is to answer the well defined questions. To accomplish this, the background must be efficiently separated from the signal, i.e. the signal must be significantly larger than the background.

A well configured stack of reconstruction modules might provide a good result for one question, but might not be suitable for another.

Using the modular approach and the production of collection candidates enables the different domain expert groups to stay in full control of the analytics pipeline and enables the single physicist to achieve a reproducible high quality analysis, where he only needs to focus on the facet of the analysis he is working on.

All code of the modules is handled by a versioning system and release management.

5.4 Data Analytics Framework – IT Security

The whole data analytics framework in IT Security may follow the same principles and design patterns as for its counterparts at the LHC (see Section 4.3). More important for IT Security is the implementation of a proper RACI model and its enforcement. A possible high-level RACI is provided in Table 1.

Table 1: Example RACI supporting an agile and sustainable Security Monitoring and Analytics Service.

	Governance	Service Manager	SOC L3	SOC L2	SOC L1	SIEM Operation	IT Forensics	IT Operation
Service Governance	A	R	C	C			C	
Create and maintain Threat Model and Use Cases	A	R	R				R	
Continuously collect complete log data, retain the data as required by company and legal requirements		A				R		R
Normalize and enrich log data		A	R					
Create, maintain and continuously improve monitoring rules		A	R					
Monitor SIEM console and handle immediate reaction to standard security incidents, escalate more complex security incidents		A	I	I	R			
Handle complex security incidents, invoke serious incident management		A	I	R				
Proactively analyze log data to minimize false positives and to identify patterns not yet considered in the rule set		A	R					
Support in handling of complex security incidents		A	R	C				
Manage reaction to serious incidents	I	A	R	I				
Perform forensic analysis		I	I				A/R	

Legend: R – Responsible, A – Accountable, C – Consulted, I – Informed

6 Conclusion

Getting the technical part right is challenging but added value, i.e. risk reduction and management, will not be achieved unless the surrounding aspects like threat and security event management are implemented sustainably and efficiently. The technical approach presented here is almost infinitely scalable but experience shows that it's sensible to start with covering high-risk infrastructure first and only iteratively expand to other parts of the company as soon as a stage of expansion was successfully and sustainably completed. It has been demonstrated that well established and understood methods of experimental particle physics can be mapped to the young field of IT security. Both fields have much in common and it is possible to adapt already developed and established solutions to IT security problems.

References

Spiropulu, M., & Stapnes, S. (2008). LHC's ATLAS and CMS Detector. *International Journal of Modern Physics A* , 4081-4105.

CMS Collaboration. (2007). CMS Technical Design Report, *Volume II: Physics Performance, volume G34. Journal of Physics*, 995-1579

CMS Collaboration. (2006) CMS Physics: Technical Design Report, *volume I of Detector Performance and Software. CERN.*

Proximity-Based Access Control (PBAC) using Model-Driven Security

Ulrich Lang[1] · Rudolf Schreiner[2]

[1]ObjectSecurity LLC
San Diego, CA, USA
ulrich.lang@objectsecurity.com

[2]ObjectSecurity Ltd.
Cambridge, UK
rudolf.schreiner@objectsecurity.com

Abstract

Unfortunately, well-established classic security models for access control are often not sufficient anymore for many of today's use cases and IT landscapes, including for example Internet of Things (IoT) and big data analytics. Access control (and security/privacy in general) requirements and implementations have frequently become very different, and more challenging, compared to conventional enterprise or internet-facing IT environments. More sophisticated approaches based on fine-grained, contextual, dynamic access control are required. This paper focuses on "Proximity Based Access Control" (PBAC), a particularly advanced access control approach that can implement flexible, proximity-based, dynamic, contextual access. PBAC, together with Attribute Based Access Control (ABAC) and Model Driven Security (MDS) is used to express and enforce such security and privacy requirements. Section 1 motivates the need for advanced access control for many of today's environments. Section 2 first introduces ABAC, then section 3 discusses PBAC within the context of ABAC. Section 4 introduces MDS. Finally, section 5 presents a detailed Intelligent Transport Systems (ITS) example of PBAC, implemented using MDS and an extension of ABAC).

1 Access Control in a Changing World

In IT security, there are many well established security models for controlling the access of a *subject*, e.g. a user, to an *object*, e.g. a server. There are for example Discretionary Access Control (DAC) with identity based access control lists (ACLs), Role Based Access Control (RBAC) clustering identities into roles and Mandatory Access Control (MAC) based on the concept of security clearances and labels. In addition, there are also security models based on capabilities or rights. RBAC is a particularly well-established method of access security that is based on a person's role within an organization. Essentially, roles provide a layer of indirection between subjects and objects: subjects are assigned subject roles, and resource permissions are assigned resource roles. A subject can only access a resource if its assigned role matches with the role assigned to the privileges required to access the resource. Furthermore, NIST has described an advanced RBAC model in four layers: flat, hierarchical, constrained, and symmetrical. The NIST model was adopted as a standard ANSI/INCITS 359-2004. In theory, RBAC is a way to provide security because it only allows employees to access information they need to do their jobs, while preventing them from accessing additional information that is not relevant to them (least privilege). In practice, this has turned out to not to always be very effective. Also, RBAC has been criticized for not fitting well to dynamic, non-hierarchical organizational structures, and for causing "role explosion" over time e.g. because contextual and/or delegated security policy requirements had to be captured using many roles.

Unfortunately, these well-established classic security models for access control are often not sufficient anymore for many of today's use cases and IT landscapes. Access control (and security/privacy in general) requirements and implementations have frequently become very different, and more challenging, compared to conventional enterprise or internet-facing IT environments. This is because large amounts of information from many sources is being collected, aggregated, analysed, queried/searched, stored, used etc. – across many stakeholder and trust boundaries, and often including highly sensitive personally identifiable information (PII).

One example is the emerging Internet of Things (IoT), and especially in the Industrial IoT (IIoT) that includes for example intelligent transport systems (ITS), smart grid, and smart cities. The authors have worked on access control and security/privacy for ITS and IIoT for several years under the EU FP7 ICSI R&D project [Icsi15], EU FP6 AD4 [Ad4p06], EU FP6 SWIM-SUIT [Swim09] etc. From a security point of view (vs. ITS billing, for example), individual identities are not really useful in ITS security, especially for end users (vehicle on-board units, OBU) accessing the ITS system. Therefore, DAC does not allow expressing appropriate security policies and is almost unimplementable. First of all, there is the issue of scalability, of identities for all users. Do all OBUs have SIM cards or X.509 certificates? Who is issuing and administrating these identities? This is especially not trivial for non-local cars, an ITS systems has to be able to handle all cars on the road, including such from foreign countries. Secondly, how can these identities be used on the server side? How are ACLs managed, how are huge ACLs enforced on a comparatively small RSU? RBAC, the clustering of identities into roles, which are then used for the formulation of access control policies, is more useful, but on the "service" side of the ITS system. RBAC can be used to control the access of for example road operator employees or police officers. For end user related security, RBAC is again of little use, it would just redirect the problem to another layer, instead of huge ACLs a mapping mechanisms between identities and roles, for example an LDAP server, would be required. RABC also does not solve the issue of the end user identities. RBAC especially is not able to solve the user privacy issue. There is an extended version of RBAC for privacy, adding the concept of a *purpose* to RBAC, but in our opinion, this is still not enough.

Another (often highly related) example is "big data analytics", which dramatically also changes security and privacy requirements and implementations: The (often vast amount of) collected data can now be processed with advanced data mining tools to gain intelligence. From a security point of view, (semantically correct) data labelling/tagging, anonymization, redaction/filtering etc. are critical requirements, as well as data deletion policies. The authors are working on access control and security/privacy for big data analytics (in the context of crime intelligence analysis) under the EU FP7 VALCRI R&D project [Valc15]. Challenges in those use cases revolve around access control policy complexity (and sheer size!), access control requirements going beyond what conventional access control policy approaches can support, challenges around reliability/repeatability/verifiability of policy authoring, implementing, enforcing, monitoring, auditing, and verifying/accrediting.

More sophisticated approaches based on fine-grained, contextual, dynamic access control are required. This paper presents an advanced access control approach that can implement flexible, proximity-based, dynamic, contextual access.

As described in this paper, new access control security models like Attribute Based Access Control (ABAC) and Proximity Based Access Control (PBAC) are able to express and enforce such security requirements, especially together with Model-Driven Security (MDS).

2 Attribute Based Access Control (ABAC)

ABAC can be defined "as a logical access control methodology where authorization to perform a set of operations is determined by evaluating attributes associated with the subject, object, requested operations, and, in some cases, environment conditions against policy, rules, or relationships that describe the allowable operations for a given set of attributes" (source: NIST 800-162 draft 2013 [NIST13]). ABAC has been described in various ways prior to that, and while early references on the subject do not use the same terms, they define many of the same elements of ABAC While ABAC helps achieve greater policy flexibility, it is usually difficult to deploy due to its policy and implementation complexities.

In the ITS context, attributes associated with a subject might for example be the status of toll payments for a vehicle/OBU, but also the classic security attributes like individual identifiers, roles or clearances. Context information might include for example time or weather conditions.

An example standard for ABAC is eXtensible Access Control Markup Language (XACML) [OASI13], which unified the terminology used by various groups working on ABAC concepts prior to 2003, and standardized the elements of ABAC, incl. rules, policies, rule- and policy-combining algorithms, attributes (subject, (resource) object, action and environment conditions), obligations, and advice. It defines a declarative access control policy language implemented in XML and a processing model describing how to evaluate authorization requests according to the rules defined in policies. The reference architecture includes functions such as Policy Decision Points (PDPs), Policy Enforcement Points (PEPs), Policy Administration Points (PAPs), and Policy Information Points (PIPs) to control access. Furthermore, XACML provides a request/response protocol which can be used to mediate communications between the components.

3 Proximity Based Access Control (PBAC)

PBAC in general is access control where information provided to a subject is determined need-to-know based on proximity attributes. In the authors' particular definition, it goes far beyond traditional devices access based on physical proximity:

Proximity-Based Access Control (PBAC) is access control using policies that are based on the relative proximity/distance (calculated by a **distance calculation function**) between one or more **proximity attributes** associated with an accessor and one or more **proximity attributes** associated with an accessed resource. PBAC is not just about physical proximity, but can involve **many proximity dimensions**: Geo-Location/Geospatial; Organizational; Operational; Temporal; Business Process; Security; Risk; Social; Information etc.

For our purposes, these proximity definitions comprise the following general concepts:

- **The proximity aspect** (attributes) considered, which is the attribute(s) used to express proximity. For example, *time, place, causation, influence, order, occurrence, or relation*. A critical requirement for proximity attributes is that they are within a space where a notion of distance exists.
- **The distance function** between two or more proximity attributes. In mathematics, a distance function (aka "metric") is a function that defines a distance between elements of a set. A set with a metric is called a metric space. A metric induces a topology on a set but not all topologies can be generated by a metric. A topological space whose topology can be described by a metric is called "metrizable". Graphs and graph theory can also be used to describe distances (e.g. number of hops across a directed graph).

PBAC goes further than conventional ABAC: it bases its access control decisions on proximity between attributes associated with two (or more) entities, in most cases between subject and object.

PBAC differs technically from non-PBAC ABAC systems in that a relative distance function exists between attributes associated with the requesting subject, the action and/or the requested resource (often also called "object"). The distance functions usually includes distance values in addition to zero values (i.e. equality, no distance, same). For example, a distance or a location related to a point or area, a hierarchical distance or anything else where the concept of a distance can be applied. The policy is determined based on the result of that distance function (see **Fig. 1**).

Many other (non-PBAC) access control attributes and decisioning functions used in ABAC are either only related to the requesting subject, the requested resource, the requested action, and environmental context (see **Fig. 2** for an exemplary non-PBAC subject attribute).

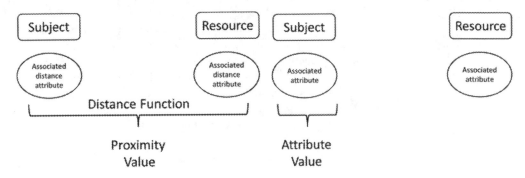

Fig. 1: PBAC Attributes   **Fig. 2:** Conventional (non-PBAC) Attributes

Rich, dynamic, contextual, and generic policies can be expressed and enforced if attribute and calculation services can be made available to the PBAC system: For example, geospatial proximity may not be calculated based on the physical location of the requesting user and the requested resource, but for example based on the geospatial area the user's assigned task pertains to, and the geospatial area the requested information resource pertains to: "*Team leaders can access all resources which pertain to a geospatial area that overlaps at least 70% with the geospatial area associated with the requestor's assigned task*". Or "*crime analysts working on a task pertaining to a criminal can access all resources pertaining to criminals known to be within 2 hops proximity on the criminal social graph*".

PBAC Benefits

PBAC has numerous benefits, including: it helps increase access for those who should have access, while decreasing the 'all or nothing' system-wide access that has caused insider threat issues in the past; and that it enables simpler, more manageable, more intuitive, ore automated, more relevant, more auditable policies.

PBAC with ABAC are very new and innovative approaches for access control, which are most useful for the protection of ITS, Location Based Services (LBS), and other complex applications requiring more than simple identity or role based access control. PBAC with ABAC for access control and information filtering in ITS, both from functionality and implementation point of view will be very beneficial because it allows defining and implementing more appropriate polices, for example the concept of the least privilege, in a manageable way. Using DAC or RBAC, it would be theoretically possible to define fine grained access policies for all stakeholders, but this would be non-manageable. PBAC with ABAC now allows defining and enforcing policies in the terms of the application domain, for example for operators (incl. traffic managers, first responders, police officers etc.) responsible for a certain geographical area in the operator's proximity or in a certain context (emergency or extraordinary situations like bad weather). It also reduces the "brittleness" of the security polices, because they are a less complex and closer to the business functionality of the system, instead a huge number of complex rules nobody understands. Another advantage is the ability to define and implement better user privacy, because information flow can now be controlled in a much more fine grained way.

PBAC Challenges

However, PBAC's challenges include the lack of availability of attribute information sources, attribute reliability, proximity calculation complexity/feasibility, rule complexity, enforceability etc.

First of all, PBAC (with ABAC) is more complex than DAC, RBAC and MAC, and it is difficult to formally prove them. Then, the semantics of the attributes has to be very carefully taken into consideration over the whole security mechanism stack. It has to be clearly defined how an attribute itself and the operations on it are expressed in a security policy (including both the attribute identifier and the attribute information), how attribute information is obtained from a security mechanism or the application platform with sufficient assurance and how the attribute information is processed in order to calculate an access control decision. All this is much more complex than it looks at the first glance. For example, the position of a vehicle per se is well understood and can easily be obtained, e.g. from a GPS receiver in the vehicle. Unfortunately, this information cannot be trusted, because it is supplied from the subject itself and can therefore be manipulated[1]. Positioning information from other sources, e.g. from location within a cellular network, is much harder to manipulate and therefore much more trustworthy. Another way to establish trust in attribute information might be a correlation of different sources.

4 Model-Driven Security (MDS)

MDS generates technical security policy rules and accreditation evidence from models, using model-driven approaches. ABAC/PBAC needs Model-Driven Security because of PBAC's com-

---

1 Unless the client software and the GPS system are in a single trust domain. Even in this case, it would be possible to spoof GPS locations over the antenna, but this is, while demonstrated in the past, out of scope.

plex policy implementation details – it would be too cumbersome and error-prone to manually implement generic PBAC policies.

- In the context of PBAC (and ABAC), Model-Driven Security (MDS) answers the questions: Where do the machine-enforceable access rules come from? Who can reliably and efficiently author and maintain them in the face of dynamic changes? MDS has a number of benefits: simplifies policy authoring; makes policies more generic, human-understandable; reduces the gap between enterprise security policy and technical implementation; automates technical policy creation; reuses information from other stakeholders/sources; improves auditing and accreditation; reduces maintenance complexity; enables rule/attribute interoperability; is based on proven model-driven concepts.

Model-driven security originates from research work since 2002 and is related to the well-accepted concepts of the OMG Model Driven Architecture (MDA). As an example implementation, full model-driven security has been implemented by the authors since 2002 in their OpenPMF ("Open Policy Management Framework") product [Obje15], which uses model-driven approaches to automate the process of translating human-understandable security & compliance requirements into the corresponding numerous and ever-changing technical authorization policy rules and configurations. In addition, it proactively enforces ("whitelisting") decentralized access decisions, and continuously monitors for security incidents (incl. at the application layer). This model-driven security policy automation approach forms a critical part of an effective least privilege implementation for agile SOA[LaSc07, Lang10], cloud[Lang10b, Lang10c,Lang10], and similar IT application architectures. Several sources (e.g. analyst firm Gartner) forecast that model-driven security will have a significant impact as information security infrastructure is required to become increasingly real-time, automated and adaptive to changes in the organization and its environment.

As with most emerging technology approaches, at this time there is no agreed consensus about what model-driven security precisely means. The authors as well as several university and industrial teams have each published their own approaches and presented their own valid definition matching their approach.

The basic underlying idea of most of them is to do one or both of the following two approaches, which, when combined, can be viewed as a form of "round-trip engineering" (the following discussion is based on the authors' MDS approach):

MDS Policy Automation (Model-to-Enforcement Generation)

Definition: Model driven security policy automation is "the tool supported process of modelling security requirements at a high level of abstraction, and using other information sources available about the system (produced by other stakeholders). These inputs, which are expressed in Domain Specific Languages (DSL), are then transformed into enforceable security rules with as little human intervention as possible. MDS explicitly also includes the run-time security management (e.g. ABAC based), i.e. run-time enforcement of the policy on the protected IT systems, dynamic policy updates and the monitoring of policy violations" [Wiki15].

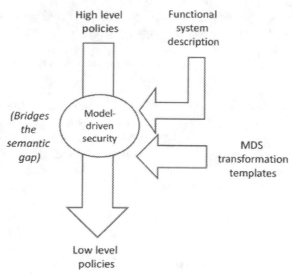

Fig. 3: Model-Driven Security (MDS)

The figure above illustrates "model-driven security (MDS) policy automation" approach at a high abstraction level:

The top shows the inputs, which include high-level security policies captured in (semantic) information models. It also shows the functional system description, which (in a semantic information model) captures information about the environment (e.g. IT systems, applications, users, information flows). Models are best based on a Domain-Specific Language (DSL), so that security policy can be modelled using features specified in the meta-modelled DSL (depicted left, top).

The middle shows the model driven security process to generate low level policies from high-level policies, using model transformations. Customization can be achieved using MDS transformation templates, as depicted. A trivial policy example would be "Interactions in the component deployment model are interpreted as explicit granted access". Roles are only used to split up interfaces into subsets of operations, in order to minimize privileges. From these transformation inputs, MDS then generates a number of explicit access rules that allows the identity of the modelled invoker to access the modelled invocation target. The advantage of this approach is that basic security policies for distributed component applications can be automatically generated without any human interaction or any security-related tags in the models.

The bottom shows the output: a number of technical security rules (e.g. ABAC rules, RBAC configuration files or IP layer filter lists) and other configuration files (e.g. command lines for application start up) for all parts of the application and security infrastructure that reflect the high-level input security requirements at a low level of abstraction and that can be enforced or implemented within the actual system.

The technical security rules are then automatically pushed into the policy enforcement points for enforcement, and policy incidents are monitored. Whenever applications change (esp. the integration), the technical security rules can be automatically re-generated. A video tutorial of this process is available online [LaMu11].

MDS has a number of benefits for ICSI when used correctly, including: reduces manual administration, reduces security risks, increases assurance, simplifies/automates policy authoring & maintenance, reduces the gap between enterprise security/privacy policy and technical implementation, helps save cost, IT agility, reduces complexity, supports rich application security policies, and more.

The authors' MDS implementation (OpenPMF) is implemented in the open source Eclipse IDE and tool kit and uses Eclipse Modeling Framework (EMF), together with model-to-model (M2M) transformations based on the OMG Query View Transform (QVT) operational language, model-to-text (M2T) transformations based on Xtext/Xpand etc. The user of the MDS tool (in this case OpenPMF) will not see any of the model transformation complexity once the MDS tool is installed and configured. All they will see is a development / modelling GUI with some extra features and menu items for the model transformation [Obje08]. In order to be able to exchange models and rules between MDS tools, OpenPMF MDS uses numerous standards, incl. OMG XMI, Eclipse Ecore & EMF, OMG MOF, OASIS XACML, UML, BPMN, BPEL etc.

MDS Accreditation Automation (Enforcement-to-Model Verification)

The purpose of this model-driven security approach is to correlate the inverse direction ("bottom-up"), where "undistorted" models are specified for checking, verification and/or compliance, certification & accreditation purposes: The correspondence between security characteristics of the actual IT landscape with the specified compliance/accreditation models is verified[LaSc09]. In other words, MDS accreditation automation analyses and documents the traceable correspondence between technical security implementation, security policy models, and "undistorted" accreditation models. Due to space restrictions this MDS aspect is not discussed in depth in this paper.

5　Example: PBAC with MDS and ABAC

This section illustrates PBAC with MDS and ABAC through an ITS example. As described, PBAC differs technically from non-PBAC Attribute-Based Access Control (ABAC) systems in that a relative distance calculation function exists between attributes associated with the requesting subject, the action and/or the requested resource.

First, consider the following exemplary (highly simplified and fictitious) ITS example scenario, comprising vehicles on the left, sensors to the right of the vehicles, various servers in the middle, and various user interfaces on the right. The example was implemented using DDS applications. Arrows signify information flows (**Fig. 4**):

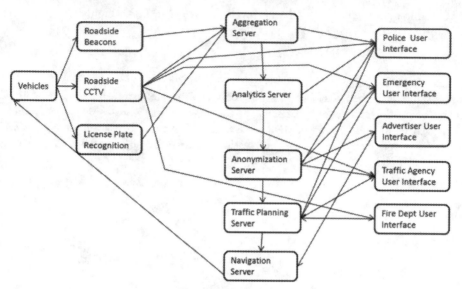

Fig. 4: ITS environment

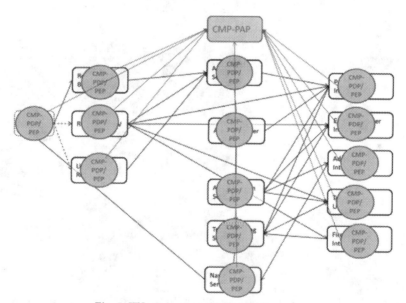

Fig. 5: ITS environment with ABAC runtime

OpenPMF MDS generates machine-enforceable access and logging rules that are enforced by OpenPMF's ABAC runtime infrastructure (**Fig. 5**), consisting of Policy Access Points, Policy Decision Points, Policy Enforcement Points, Attribute Source Services, Calculation Services, and Mapper Services etc. OpenPMF typically deploys a PDP/PEP/PIP combination on each protected node. The following Fig. illustrates the ABAC deployment across this use case, with OpenPMF's ABAC runtime deployed on each node:

Our PBAC example starts with a PBAC **"high-level" access policy** that is highly generic, abstract, and "undistorted" by underlying implementation details:

```
Access is granted to all requestors who are in "80% proximity" to the
requested resource.
```

To illustrate some of the benefits of MDS for PBAC, this example assumes that there is no technical attribute source available for "proximity" in general. In other words, this policy is **not machine-enforceable**. As a consequence, MDS needs to carry out a number of refinement steps. The following (very rough sketch!) illustrates how various ASS/CS/MS are semantically categorized in a metamodel/model:

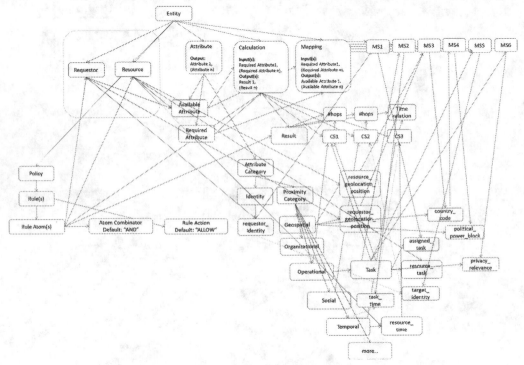

Fig. 6: Metamodel/Model Information Repository

Concrete ASS/CS/MS for the example are illustrated in **Fig. 7**:

The **Metamodel** (and metadata) repositories capture how all **attribute source services (ASS-x)**, **calculation services (CS-x)**, and **mapping services (MS-x)** (for Attribute-Based Access Control, ABAC) relate semantically and syntactically. Attribute Service Sources (ASS) provide the attribute values for a particular decision. ASS have a type (e.g. requestor ID). Calculation services (CS) calculate a result from ASS (in the context of PBAC, several ASS's) – while a trivial CS is "equal", PBAC calculations usually require complex data lookups and calculations (e.g. calculate terrain-dependent geospatial distance between two ASS geospatial locations). Mapping Services (MS) can map attributes into other attributes, e.g. geospatial location to postal address. This allows MDS to traceably, flexibly, and efficiently refine rules and attributes correctly:

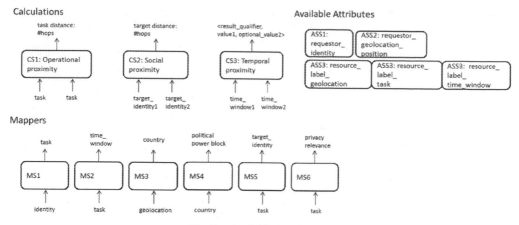

Fig. 7 – Available ASS/CS/MS

1) Rule refinement is done by chaining **rule refinement templates** based on semantics defined in the metamodel, and matching required attributes/calculations with available ones. In the example, rules with "proximity %" can be refined by MDS to four different potential rules with two **required rule elements** (e.g. calculations) that can be runtime enforceable. However, in the example, only "operational" and "time" are actually both **available rule elements** (e.g. calculations) to suffice the template. In this example map proximity as a simple percentage value to several weighted combinations of several proximity dimensions, and further to specific calculation methods for the percentage calculation for each proximity dimension:

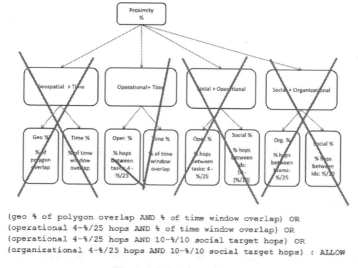

Fig. 8: MDS Rule Refinement

2) Attribute refinement is done by MDS by analyzing the metamodel/metadata to identify mapping paths from **required attributes** to **available attribute services**, using available **mapper services**. As a result of the depicted attributes, calculations, mappers, and refinement templates, exemplary policies like *"privacy-relevant requests are not allowed within the EU"* can be authored, and enforced by a different set of rules and attributes.

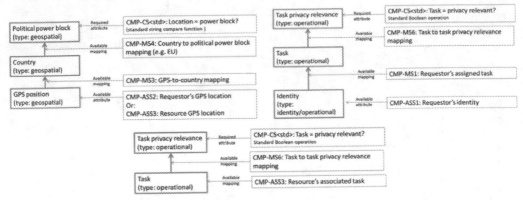

Fig. 9: MDS Attribute Refinement

Generated machine-enforceable technical rules: The machine-enforceable policy rule element automatically produced by OpenPMF MDS for the authored "80%-proximity" would look like this:

```
CMP-CS1(CMP-MS1(CMP-ASS1),ASS3-item-2)<1)AND(CMP-CS3(CMP-MS2(MP-MS1(C-
MP-ASS1)),ASS3-item-3),"CMP-CS3.time-window-difference" )<20%
```

The privacy policy would then look like this (in pseudo notation):

```
CMP-MS4(CMP-MS3(CMP-ASS2))!="EU")AND(CMP-MS6(CMP-MS1(CMP-ASS2))==TRUE)
AND(CMP-MS6(CMP-ASS3)==TRUE)
```

Fortunately, thanks to MDS, humans do not need to be concerned about such technical rule elements.

Functional System Description: MDS can also automatically take information about the protected System of Systems (SoS) into account when generating rules (e.g. application models). In our example, only some SoS nodes could for example process privacy relevant information (PII), and also should only service requests from certain requesting SoS nodes. MDS can then generate specific additional rules (and rule elements) for PDPs protecting those particular nodes, and distribute them to the PDPs. This feature is especially useful in SoS that involve machine-to-machine (M2M) interactions, such as Service Oriented Architectures, Internet of Things, Cloud PaaS/Mashups etc.

Automatic updates are made easy by OpenPMF MDS: This example shows that MDS helps keep access control policy authoring extremely simple and "undistorted", and allows changes to the functional system, the flexible replacement of calculation/attribute services etc. without requiring changes to the edited policies. In other words, MDS may generate different enforceable rules if the inputs change.

Compliance: Because all information in OpenPMF MDS is properly meta-modeled, a model-driven algorithm can analyze whether the actual security enforcement is in line with compliance requirements models.

6 Conclusion

This paper argues that well-established classic security models for access control are often not sufficient anymore for many of today's use cases and IT landscapes, including for example Internet of Things (IoT) and big data analytics. It presents an innovative solution based on a compositing of sophisticated approaches based on fine-grained, contextual, dynamic access control: "Proximity Based Access Control" (PBAC), a particular advanced access control approach that can implement flexible, proximity-based, dynamic, contextual access. PBAC, together with Attribute Based Access Control (ABAC) and Model Driven Security (MDS) is to express and enforce such security and privacy requirements. For PBAC, an extended ABAC is needed to support fine-grained, flexible, contextual, proximity-based access policies. Furthermore, MDS is needed to make ABAC manageable (in general, not just in the context of PBAC). The paper illustrates the approach through a detailed Intelligent Transport Systems (ITS) example of PBAC, implemented using MDS and an extension of ABAC).

References

[LaMu11] Lang, Ulrich and Mullen, John, "SOA IA Demonstrator: Information Assurance (IA) for Service Oriented Architecture (SOA)", demo video tutorial, 2011, objectsecurity.com/soa-ia.html (retrieved 2015)

[Lang10] Lang, U. "Authorization as a Service for Cloud & SOA Applications", Proc. CPSRT 2010, 2nd IEEE Cloudcom, Indianapolis, Indiana, USA, Dec. 2010

[Lang10b] Lang, U., "Security Policy Automation: Improve Cloud Application Security ROI" ISSA Journal, October 2010

[Lang10c] Lang, U. "Cloud & SOA Application Security as a Service" Proceedings of ISSE 2010, Berlin, Germany, 5-7 October 2010

[LaSc07] Lang, U, Schreiner, R. "Model Driven Security (MDS) management & enforcement to support SOA-style agility". Proc. ISSE 2007, Warsaw/Poland, Sept 2007

[LaSc09] Lang, U. and Schreiner, R. "Model Driven Security Accreditation (MDSA) For Agile, Interconnected IT Landscapes", Proceedings of WISG 2009, 2009

[Nist13] NIST Special Publication 800-162. "Guide to Attribute Based Access. Control (ABAC) Definition and. Considerations" (Draft).

[Oasi13] OASIS, "eXtensible Access Control Markup Language (XACML)" Version 3.0. OASIS Standard. 22 January 2013

[Obje08] ObjectSecurity. "Video: OpenPMF seamlessly integrated in SOA tools", http://bpms.openpmf.com (retrieved 2015)

[Obje15] ObjectSecurity. "OpenPMF™ website". www.openpmf.com (retrieved 2015)

[Icsi15] EU FP7 Project ICSI: Intelligent Cooperative Sensing for Improved traffic efficiency, www.ict-icsi.eu

[Ad4p06] EU FP6 Project AD4: 4D Virtual Airspace Management System, http://cordis.europa.eu/project/rcn/74773_en.html

[Swim09] EU FP6 Project SWIM-SUIT: System Wide Information Management – Supported by Innovative Technologies

[Valc15]   EU FP7 Project VALCRI: Visual Analytics for sense-making in Criminal Intelligence Analysis, www.valcri.org

[Wiki15]   Wikipedia. "Model-Driven Security" page. https://en.wikipedia.org/wiki/Model-driven_security (retrieved 2015)

Acknowledgements

Some of the research leading to the positions developed and expressed in this paper has received funding from the European Union Seventh Framework Programme (FP7/2007-2013) through the Project VALCRI, European Commission Grant Agreement N° FP7-IP-608142 and through the Project ICSI, European Commission Grant Agreement N° FP7-ICT-20011-08. Furthermore, this material is based upon work supported by the Air Force Research Laboratory (AFRL) prime contract no. FA8750-13-C-0190. Any opinions, findings, and conclusions or recommendations expressed in this material are those of the author(s) and do not necessarily reflect the view of ARFL or the US government. The concepts described in this paper are patented or patent-pending.

Trust Services

A pan-European Framework on Electronic Identification and Trust Services for Electronic Transactions in the Internal Market

Olivier Delos · Tine Debusschere · Marijke De Soete · Jos Dumortier · Riccardo Genghini · Hans Graux · Sylvie Lacroix · Gianluca Ramunno · Marc Sel · Patrick Van Eecke

DLA Piper, Avenue Louise 106, 1050 Brussels, Belgium
patrick.van.eecke@dlapiper.com

Abstract

This article is summarizing the results of the European study SMART 2012/0001 commissioned by the European Commission..

1 Introduction

1.1 Scope and objectives of the project

The objective of the project was to perform a study to support the implementation of a pan-European framework on electronic identification and trust services for electronic transactions in the internal market.

The Commission adopted on 4 June 2012 a proposal for a Regulation on "electronic identification and trust services for electronic transactions in the internal market". The proposal was adopted on 23 July 2014 by the European Parliament and Council as Regulation (EU) No 910/2014 of the European Parliament and of the Council on electronic identification and trust services for electronic transactions in the internal market and repealing Directive 1999/93/EC[1] (hereinafter referred to as 'Regulation').

In parallel with the ordinary legislative procedure with a view to adopting the proposal, there was a need to:

1. Start working on the analysis of the elements that would help develop secondary legislation (delegated and implementing acts) envisaged in the proposal for a Regulation;

---

[1] Regulation (EU) No 910/2014 of the European Parliament and of the Council of 23 July 2014 on electronic identification and trust services for electronic transactions in the internal market and repealing Directive 1999/93/EC (http://eur-lex.europa.eu/legal-content/EN/TXT/PDF/?uri=CELEX:32014R0910&from=EN)

2. Ensure coherence of the proposed initiative vis-à-vis activities carried out by the European Institutions;

3. Foster take-up of electronic identification, authentication and trust services by raising SME and citizens' awareness on their potential, including leveraging the "Large Scale Pilots" to create a positive understanding and environment for the acceptance and uptake of the new legislative framework.

The main objectives of the study were to:

1. Provide input for devising technical and legal building blocks needed for the preparatory work in the areas envisaged in the planned secondary legislation (delegated and implementing acts) related to Regulation. This objective also included to provide input for standardisation activities related to planned secondary legislation in the Regulation;

2. Monitor the take-up of electronic identification (eID), electronic authentication and electronic trust services (eTS) and evaluate the impact of national and EU legislation (services directive, VAT directive, decisions on "trusted lists" and signature formats, public procurement directive). In particular, the study is supposed to build upon and further develop the results of the studies commissioned by the Commission (IDABC studies) on country profiles delivered in 2009. It also complements and enhances the Impact Assessment report accompanying the proposal for a Regulation and the existing market studies, by collecting additional and updated data and by defining and measuring core progress indicators;

3. Propose a communication strategy and outline an awareness raising campaign to promote the uptake of trusted services by EU citizens and SMEs;

4. Provide technical assistance to the Commission on eID, authentication and eTS in particular by providing thematic technical reports, briefings and analysis.

1.2 Tasks overview

The work was undertaken in the form of five tasks:

1. Task 1 relates to the completion of the legal framework, by studying and proposing building block for drafting secondary legislation;

2. Task 2 and Task 3 focus on stock taking and monitoring of current initiatives in the field of eID and trust services;

3. Task 4 relates to the technical standardisation work required to finalise the normative framework around the Regulation;

4. Task 5 is a broader support task encompassing all areas of expertise, allowing the European Commission to assign ad-hoc tasks to the project team members.

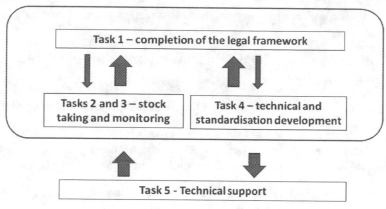

Fig.1: Tasks relations

1.3 Defining building blocks for perfecting the legal framework on electronic identification and electronic trust services

This task aimed to assist the EC in identifying the main expected principles, issues and key points, as well as in executing a reality check on the four technical, legal, economical and societal levels when preparing the secondary legislation associated to the Regulation.

The researchers identified the priorities of the concerned secondary legislative initiatives and discuss their relevance for the correct functioning of the Regulation. According to the scope and the identified relevant key points and issues, the researchers discussed for each secondary legislative act foreseen in the Regulation an implementation **ideal scenario**.

The proposed ideal implementation scenario was further validated by a reality check on the technical, legal, economical and societal levels:

- The **technical reality check** analysed technical aspects of the proposed solution, such as such as technical feasibility, availability of technical solutions or missing / existing / on-going standardisation work and security considerations, etc.;
- The **legal reality check** analysed the feasibility of the applicable secondary legislation to implement the ideal scenario, the EU and national governance, etc. This analysis identified and leveraged on prior legal examples, related good practices in Member States and/or other geographic areas, as well as on non-legal examples when applicable;
- The **economic reality check** analysed business, economic and market aspects, such as the impact on individual service providers and the trust services market in general (both macro-economic impact for the society and microeconomic impact for service providers/ manufacturers;
- The **societal reality check** analysed societal aspects, including notably data protection impacts, but also any other fundamental freedoms that may be implicated by any proposals, including attention for levels of user's readiness and skills to interact with trust service devices like smart cards, eSignature applications, ... and user friendliness of available solutions.

Finally recommendations were provided together with identification of possible next steps and planning.

1.3.1 Building blocks for the establishment and the supervision of Trust Service Providers

Building trust in the online environment is key to economic and social developments.

Increasing trust, trustworthiness and convenience in using (Qualified) electronic Trust Services is the clear aim of the Regulation. It is strongly believed as key factors to expand the adoption of such services and hence the development of electronic transactions in the EU internal market.

The pyramid of trust sketched by the Regulation (and illustrated in Figure 2 is clearly setting up the right foundations in order to reach these objectives.

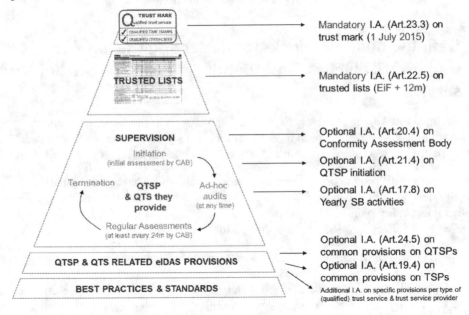

Fig. 2: The pyramid of trust

The present document has detailed the reasons and importance to establish the foreseen secondary legislation, whether mandatory or optional, to further strengthen the foundations of such a pyramid and support the achievement of the Regulation objectives:

- **Trust mark for Qualified electronic Trust Services**: In order to further help the implementing acts on the EU trust mark for qualified electronic Trust Services, foreseen in Article 23.3, to fully implement the fundamental principles organised by the first two paragraphs of Article 23 (i.e. indicating in a simple, recognisable and clear manner the Qualified electronic Trust Services the Qualified electronic Trust Services Providers (QTSPs) provide, and allow users to proceed to a verification, through the corresponding trusted list, of the Qualified status granted to a electronic Trust Service provided by a TSP making use of the trust mark), it would be recommended, as a minimum, to adopt recitals in such acts respectively inviting QTSPs to clearly display the link to the relevant trusted list next to the trust mark and inviting QTSPs to adopt guidelines for using textual information together with the mandated visual. Those latter guidelines for the combination of visual and textual specifications for the EU trust mark for Qualified electronic Trust Services could leverage on the specifications that have already be foreseen in a number of EU legislation such as the guidelines related to the organic production logo of the EU that are introduced by the Commission Regulation (EU) No 271/2010[2] and its use governed by Article 57 of Commission Regulation (EC) No 889/2008. The associated common principles for consumer information (i.e. reliability, usefulness, availability, proportionality) and the relevant societal related constraints (e.g. truthful message that the QTS is trustworthy) should also be addressed.

- **Trusted lists**: The mandatory implementing act should leverage on the maturity of the existing legislation and standards underlying the existing EU Member States and European Economic Area (EEA) countries trusted lists while expanding their current scope to cover all qualified trust services addressed by the Regulation, including nationally defined ones.
- **Supervision**: Establishing the references to standards upon which the competence of the conformity assessment bodies will be accredited and the QTSPs/QTS audit criteria on the basis of which they will conduct their assessments and produce their conformity assessment reports need to ensure an equal treatment to all Qualified electronic Trust Services and Qualified electronic Trust Service Providers over the EU and strengthen their trustworthiness and hence the trust from the market in them and in the trust mark they may use.

European Accreditation (EA) is currently working on the establishment of a Conformity Assessment Body (CAB) accreditation scheme under the framework of Regulation (EC) No 765/2008. That CAB accreditation scheme and the referenced standards would essentially cover a list of standards setting up requirements on CABs, a standard on auditing rules to be followed by accredited CABs when assessing QTSPs/QTSs and one or more standards establishing "outcome based" QTSP/QTS audit criteria against which QTSPs/QTSs assessments shall be carried out and conformity assessments reports shall be produced.

Avoiding the creation of an implementing act that would list reference standards upon which the CAB accreditation scheme shall be established by EA and executed by National Accreditation Bodies (NABs) in the context of Regulation (EC) No 765/2008 would nevertheless require the assurance that the scheme currently established by EA is indeed aligned with the requirements and objectives of the Regulation. To this extent, EA should be invited to establish that CAB accreditation scheme in a way that will:

- Ensure the scheme to meet the Regulation requirements, in particular Article 20.1;
- Not create de facto mandatory standards for QTSPs and the QTSs they provide;
- Truly achieve harmonisation and enhancement of supervision rules all over the EU; and
- Not be restricted to assessing IT security criteria but also encompassing require-ments from the fields of data protection, consumer protection, usability as well as accessibility and inclusion where users' interaction with trust services is concerned.

When this would not be the case, the creation of a short implementing act could be seen as a corrective action. A short implementing act would hence list reference standards upon which

---

2 COMMISSION REGULATION (EU) No 271/2010 of 24 March 2010 amending Regulation (EC) No 889/2008 laying down detailed rules for the implementation of Council Regulation (EC) No 834/2007, as regards the organic production logo of the European Union.

the CAB accreditation scheme shall be established by EA and executed by NABs in the context of Regulation (EC) No 765/2008. Those referenced standards would essentially cover a list of standards setting up requirements on CABs, a standard on auditing rules to be followed by accredited CABs when assessing QTSPs/QTSs and one or more standards establishing "outcome based" QTSP/QTS audit criteria against which QTSPs/QTSs assessments shall be carried out and conformity assessments reports shall be produced.

Under both options, however, no such "outcome based" QTSP/QTS audit criteria standard exists and the European Commission should ask CEN/ETSI to prepare it as a matter of priority, mapping audit criteria against the requirements of the Regulation per type of Qualified electronic Trust Service and which could be used as QTSP/QTS audit criteria and a basis for establishing the resulting conformity assessment report by conformity assessment bodies to assess the relevant TSPs claiming compliance with QTSP/QTS requirements from the Regulation.

- **Common provisions on QTSPs:** The related optional implementing act is similarly useful when aiming to enhance trustworthiness of Qualified electronic Trust Service Providers. When eligible standards would be available as candidates for referencing by an implementing act provided for by Article 24.5, it may also be appropriate to consider a certain period of implementation of such standards before referencing them. Leveraging on existing Commission Decision and updating the references to the appropriate standards should also be considered as part of the approach.
- **Common provisions on TSPs:** It may be appropriate to consider a certain period of implementation of Regulation before elaborating and adopting the related implementing acts. Relying on best practices and existing or future guidance, in particular ENISA guidance, when improved and updated, could be a soft-law alternative to the establishment of implementing acts. When envisaging them, a combined approach should be used defining in implementing acts the security goals (outcome based approach) and successively refer to existing standards. Leveraging on existing processes related to similar due diligence and notification requirements in other EU legislations should also be considered as part of the approach.

The other implementing acts foreseen in the Regulation, supporting specific legal provisions on specific types of QTSPs and QTS, and more generally referencing European or international standards may reveal useful means not only to ensuring a high level of security and interoperability of electronic identification and trust services. They are also beneficial to QTSPs increasing the legal certainty of their QTS implementations. Moreover they will contribute greatly to further increase their credibility and trustworthiness and hence the trust in the whole system.

Considering the aim of the Regulation at increasing confidence in and convenience of online services and in having the market experiencing a real mark of trust, adopting marked TS and massively using digital applications & services, the implementing acts regarding electronic Trust Services chapter of the Regulation are believed to significantly contribute:

- To increase the credibility of the quality and trustworthiness of QTS / QTSPs and the credibility of the truthful message of trust conveyed by trusted lists and EU trust mark for QTSs;
- To support achieving the Regulation aim in enhancing effectiveness of online services in the EU.

1.3.2 Building blocks for enhancing existing electronic signature and electronic seals

This task focuses on the following topics:

- Electronic Signature and Seals levels (security levels determined amongst other by elements such as crypto algorithms, security requirements on the computing environment, level of assurance on the certificate, the signing device quality, etc.);
- Electronic Signature and Seal Creation;
- Electronic Signature and Seals formats and profiles to be handled by public services, (e.g. ETSI formats for Advanced Electronic Signatures (AdES) like XAdES, PAdES, CAdES and ASiC);
- Electronic Signature and Seal Creation Devices (SCDev), in particular protection profiles for Qualfied electronic Signature and Seal Creation Devices (QSCDs), standard for certification, Criteria to be met by Designated Bodies certifying QSCDs, format and procedure for the notification of certified QSCDs by Member States to European Commission.
- Electronic Signature and Seal Validation (in particular how a Qualified Electronic Signatures (QES) can be validated in conformance to Articles 32.1 / 40, minimum requirements on QTSP providing QES validation as per Articles 33 / 40, and more generally how an AdES can be validated),
- Electronic Signature and Seal preservation (possible security procedures and technologies to preserve a QES as per Articles 34 / 40, and more generally to preserve AdES).

1.3.2.1 Interoperability of electronic signatures in public services

(a) Context

The Regulation contains specific provisions aiming to support the interoperability of electronic signatures in public services, and is substantially comparable to the legal framework set up at the EU level in relation to the use of electronic signatures in the so-called points of single contact. Member States have been required to set up these points of single contact as a part of their implementation of the Services Directive, specifically under Article 8 of Directive 2006/123/EC.

In order to support the Member States, the Commission issued Decision 2009/767/EC, as also referenced in the recitals to the Regulation, which contained certain rules on the acceptability of electronic signatures in points of single contact. The Regulation now expands the scope of this rule, aiming to extend its impact to public services in general.

Apart from this broader scope, the Regulation also allows the Commission to establish reference numbers of standards for advanced electronic signatures, which is an element that was not specifically dealt with in Decision 2009/767/EC. In the former Directive 1999/93/EC on electronic signatures, compliance with any such referenced standards shall be presumed to result in compliance with the requirements for advanced electronic signatures, in the sense of the public sector Article 27 and more widely, in the sense of the requirements for advanced electronic signatures as stated in Article 26.

It should be noted that (again, as under the eSignatures Directive 1999/93/EC), this does not imply that compliance with these standards is in any way mandatory or that Advanced Electronic Signatures cannot be created through other means than those described in the standards which the Commission may choose to reference. The purpose of any implementing act would be to facilitate the demonstration of compliance; not to restrict the technical options or to harm the general technological neutrality of the Regulation.

If the Commission should choose to adopt an implementing act, it is likely that the act will focus principally on security features of AdES such as security aspects of the signature, crypto algorithms, security requirements on the computing environment, etc.

(b) Conclusion

The most important conclusion of the present study is to orient the implementing act on existing and wide spread technologies for which proven (i.e. adopted by the market) standards exist. Compliance with such standards shall at first clearly provide conformance with the Article 26 requirements and ideally, shall further enable the identification of the AdES types introduced by the Regulation (i.e. AdES, AdES with Qualified Certificate (AdES_QC) or QES) and should, if possible, allow the identification of the security level ac-cording to a classification scheme.

The proposed technology is Public Key Infrastructure (PKI).

PKI-based AdES (like all AdES), are made of several components: certificate, SCDev and resilience features, each of them being specified in ad-hoc standards. The implementing act will refer to reference numbers of standards specifying:
- Certificates and the policies observed by TSP issuing them;
- SCDev and the procedures, process and policies observed by TSP managing them;
- Electronic Signature formats and forms and the potential additional element of proofs (such as time indication) and the policies observed by TSP issuing these proofs.

Certificates and the policies observed by TSP issuing them should enable the specification of Qualified Certificate while SCDev and the procedures, process and policies observed by TSP managing them should enable the specification of Qualified electronic Signature Creation Device in such a way that AdES_QC or QES can easily be distinguished from other AdES.

A crucial aspect when referring standards for AdES is the insurance that they will be some validation process that will enable the verification of conformity of AdES with regard to these standards, and ideally, in a machine processable way. As shown in the cover document, when conforming to the standards referred to in the implementing act provided for by Article 27.5 (and respectively provided for by Article 37.5 for seal), on electronic signature formats, such a machine processable validation is made possible.

If in addition these standards can further specify additional level of security and assurance on certificates, SCDev and resilience features, so that the classification of AdES into levels would be possible.

The set of standards proposed in annex of the final report is already sorted, as far as possible, in such a way that a quite granular classification can be obtained for each conformant AdES. However, the classification is not easy to map into a simple validation process; beside determination of the fact that an AdES is an AdES, an AdES_QC or a QES, one shall not require stakeholder to make use of the classification scheme, for the sake of simplicity of using AdES in general. To this regard, having a classification scheme in an implementing act per se may even be confusing. Pros and cons need to be carefully discussed.

1.3.2.2 Reference formats of advanced electronic signatures or reference methods

(a) Context

The Regulation refers to an implementing act to list standards for Electronic Signatures formats and profiles to be handled by public services (e.g. XAdES, PAdES, CAdES, ASiC). It may also define an alternative to using these formats (i.e. reference methods where al-ternative formats are used). It will replace (or repeal) Decision 2011/130/EC amended by 2014/148/EU.

(b) Conclusion

It is suggested to build the implementing act on Decision 2014/148/EU (built on Decision 2011/130/EC), with the proposed enhancements. This will benefit from a certain degree of experience, maturity and acceptation by the Member States.

In addition, reference formats of advanced electronic signatures (or reference methods) defined in Decision 2014/148/EU (built on Decision 2011/130/EC) are equally applicable to electronic seals (whose formats are to be dealt in the implementing act provided for by Article 37.5).

The impact of proposed scenario for Articles 27.5 and 37.5 on standards is very limited: those standards only disserve minor improvements (e.g. simplification, readability) and very slight modifications (e.g. terminology introducing electronic seals).

Currently, the Baselines Profiles referred to in the Decision 2011/130/EU (amended by Decision 2014/148/EU, are Technical Specifications (ETSI TS 103 17x). These specifications are in the process of becoming EN:
- ETSI EN 319 122-2 CAdES Baseline profile
- ETSI EN 319 132-2 XAdES Baseline profile
- ETSI EN 319 142-7 PAdES Baseline profile
- ETSI EN 319 162-2 ASiC Baseline profile

1.3.2.3 Reference numbers of standards for qualified electronic signature creation devices

(a) Context

The Regulation refers to an Implementing act to list standards for QSCDs. It should replace the protection profiles for SSCDs listed in Decision 2003/511/EC (ex-CWA 14169). It may be used to list standards for the security evaluation of QSCDs in the perspective of the certification as defined in Article 30.

Throughout the study, a few issues have been identified:

1. The scope of a QSCD is wider than the scope of certification of QSCD. The definition of SCDev, the Annex II point c) and the beginning of recital (56) all together plead for a "wide" scope (i.e. all the elements defined for SCDev for AdES as per Article 26 in the implementing act provided for by Article 27.4).
2. The implementing act described shall cover the requirements for QTSP entrusted for the care of qualified electronic signature creation devices. Distinction should be made be-

tween those cases where (1) only the Signature Creation Application is managed by a QTSP while the signature creation data container is in the hands of the signatory, (2) the cases where the signature creation data container is in the hands of the QTSP while the application resides on the signatory environment, and (3) the cases where the TSP manages both aspects.

3. Transparency that a Qualified electronci Signature Creation Device is entrusted to the care of a Qualified electronic Trust Service Provider.

(b) Conclusion

Firstly, it is important to be able to isolate the requirements for the QSCD components subject to certification from the other requirements that will be used at least as a recommendation (in the case of free environment) or as criteria for the monitoring or supervision of QTSP active in the management of QSCD, even when the signature creation data is in the hands of the signatory.

Because the scope of supervision is broader than the scope of the certification of the QSCDs, if the listed standards enable this distinction, one can ease the QTSP audit process by starting with the certification of the "core" of the device, subject to certification (i.e. either by choosing a device already benefitting from a certification or by performing the certification of the system on the limited scope) and then performing the audit on the whole system (i.e. the environment within which the certified device is implemented, procedures, etc.) for assessing the conformity to Annex II as well as to other Regulation's requirements in matter of provisioning of Qualified electronic Trust Services.

Secondly, it is important to offer the maximum benefit of the regulation to relying parties, by building on the devices lists and offer a validation process that can use them:
- besides the QSCD statement, the TSP issuing Qualified Certificates **should** indicate the type of device (or the certificate number of the device) in the certificate, provided there is a clear way to scope and then identify devices' types and
- the TSP issuing Qualified Certificates **should** revoke or suspend a certificate with a QSCD statement if the device loses it's status.

Thirdly, the statement for Qualified Certificates that the Signature Creation Data is held in a QSCD should be built in such a way that it is possible to indicate that the QSCD is managed (all or partly) by a QTSP with an identification of the provider that would enable a relying party to verify its qualification status according to its Member States trusted list.

1.3.2.4   Standards for the security assessment of information technology products – Qualified electronic Signature Creation Devices

(a) Context

The Regulation refers to an implementing act to list a standard(s) for the security assessment of ICT products (e.g. Common Criteria). The process of certification of products (or services) and accreditation of conformity assessment bodies performing the certification is to be seen as a global concept since the mutual recognition of the certificates cannot be dissociated from the trust and recognition of the conformity assessment bodies.

(b) Conclusion

For what concerns QSCD, an evaluation/certification process based on Common Criteria (CC) seems a natural candidate for an implementing act. In particular, there should be (a set of) Protection Profile(s) (PP) referred to in the implementing acts provided for by Articles 27.4 and 29.2 built and evaluated against Common Criteria (ISO/IEC 15408).

- An important issue to address is the time to market, as there will be some additional time required for the (re)certification of these PPs in such a way that they enter in the interoperable framework of SOGIS-MRA like schemes.

CC shall not be the sole way for the assessment of QSCDs. The important criterion to be observed by a proposed evaluation process is the underlying mutual recognition of the certificates. A track fitting within the umbrella of the Regulation (EC) No 765/2008 shall be envisaged as well.

- This track would be strengthened by having EN 419 203 listed in the implementing act provided for by Article 30.3; this standard would provide consistency between the Regulation (EC) No 765/2008 and ISO 17065 that may be used for the delegated act provided for by the Article 30.4 on one hand, and the security standards for QSCD that would be listed in the implementing act provided for by Article 29.2 on the other hand.
- This second track might be of a particular interest in case of QSCD solutions relying on technical and organisational solutions not covered by CC.
- It would be nice to benchmark similar schemes for the evaluation of cryptographic modules managed by foreign countries (e.g. FIPS) with regard to the selected standards, either for simple comparison, or even better for mutual recognition and / or possible additional alternative to the proposed tracks.

Both tracks however present limitations; time to market and difficulty to activate Article 30.3.b) in particular (beside the fact that both tracks might not exactly be considered a "standard").

Proposed standards shall be such that they do not prevent the activation of Article 30.3.b) in the absence of duly evaluated (or certified in the case of CC) underlying standards for the certification of QSCD. This needs to be clearly stated in the implementing act to prevent a frozen situation where no device can be certified due to a too long time to market for having the duly evaluated underlying standards and/or the impossibility to certify new types of devices because the selected track simply does not support them. It should be made clear in the act that when a QSCD cannot be mapped as the target of evaluation of any available underlying standards, a member state or its designated body should be allowed to propose an alternative standard with security requirements adapted to the QSCD solution en question.

The positioning of such duly evaluated (or certified in the case of CC) underlying standards for the certification of QSCD with regard to standards listed in the implementing act provided for by Article 29.2 needs to be clear (whether there are listed in implementing act provided for by Article 29.2 as well, or provided for by Article 30.3).

1.3.2.5 Specific criteria to be met by the designated bodies

(a) Context

The Regulation refers to a delegated act to establish the criteria to be met by Designated Bodies certifying QSCDs. The act may update Decision 2000/709/EC and provide "SOGIS MRA-like" provisions and/or follow a track fitting within the framework of the Regulation (EC) No 765/2008, setting out the requirements for accreditation and market surveillance relating to the marketing of products (so-called RAMS).

In general, the process of accreditation of Conformity Assessment Bodies performing the certification and the certification of products (or services) is to be seen as a global concept since the mutual recognition of the certificates cannot be dissociated from the trust and recognition of the Conformity Assessment Bodies (in the case of QSCD, the Designated bodies) and the certification scheme they handle.

The scope of this activity is very closely linked to the scope of the the implementing act provided for by Article 30.3, aiming to list standard(s) for the security assessment of information technology products. To a certain extent it also linked to the implementing act provided for by Article 29.2 listing standards against which one can presume conformance to (a part of) Annex II.

(b) Conclusions

A delegated act establishing criteria for Designated Bodies can be based on:
- An enhanced version of Decision 2000/709 and a reference to SOGIS-MRA (to be considered in the implementing act provided for by Article 30.3), itself referring to certified cPPs listed in the implementing act provided for by Article 29.2, and/or
- The Regulation (EC) No 765/2008 and ISO 17065 with references to further elements constituting the QSCD sectorial program (CEN EN 419 203, e.g.), to be considered in the implementing act provided for by Article 30.3, itself referring to standards and PPs (not necessarily certified) listed in the implementing act provided for by Article 29.2.

Both tracks shall allow:
- The automatic recognition of the certification issued by the Designated Bodies;
- Accrediting the competency of Designated Bodies to assess products, processes and services (since QSCD are not limited to "device" in a strict sense).

The advantage of a framework based on the Regulation (EC) No 765/2008 is also that it would cover all the Members States, which is not the case of SOGIS-MRA (as not all the Member States are signatory of this arrangement), while the advantage of a SOGIS-MRA scheme is the immediate availability of the scheme up to certified PPs. However some types of QSCD (e.g. signing server) do not have CC PPs. To this regard, Regulation (EC) No 765/2008 allows for alternatives standards in waiting for QSCD evaluation standards listed in the implementing act provided for by Article 30.3 and QSCD security standards listed on the implementing act provided for by Article 29.2 and may be a quick way to have such (new types of) certified QSCDs. It is a wish that any such "transitional" security standards proposed by a MS can quickly be evaluated under the umbrella of the Regulation (EC) No 765/2008 and the EA as candidates for the QSCD sectorial program; once adopted they would become the de-facto standard. Their peer evaluation is also a pledge of quality.

Finally, nothing forbids having the SOGIS MRA track used under the umbrella of the Regulation (EC) No 765/2008. Indeed, the Certifying Body in SOGIS MRA may well be NAB accredited bodies (within the framework of CC, it is also possible that the evaluating facilities, or labs, are also accredited by the NAB). And obviously, the CC existing PPs for SSCD, e.g., can be very quickly endorsed within a Regulation (EC) No 765/2008 sectorial program. The disadvantage of this "one-stop shop" solution for the delegated act provided for by Article 30.4 is that it imposes some restrictions on the way the SOGIS MRA works today where there is more flexibility for the designation of certifying bodies by the member states.

The need for the list of certified QSCD is necessary by 1st of July 2016, otherwise there are no QSCD for seals and no qualified seals are possible. Indeed, if it is viable for QES thanks to the transitional acceptation of SSCD as QSCD, there is still a problem for Qualified Electronic Seals (QESeals).

The list of certified devices requires:
- (At least one) notified Designated Body; this seems bound to the existence of the the delegated act provided for by Article 30.4 that needs to provide the criteria for designation of Designated Bodies; (at least one) device certified under a process conform to the implementing act provided for by Article 30.3 (that supposes that this act is ready, either with underlying standard(s) listed in the implementing acts provided for by Articles 30.3 or 29.2 against which Designated Body can perform the certification, or by activation of the Article 30.3.b).

The list does not require:
- a Designated Body in every Member State;
- the QSCD standards or PPs listed in the implementing act provided for by Articles 29.2 or 30.3 (the certification is based on the discretion of the Designated Body if Article 30.3.b) is activated).

1.3.3 Building blocks for the extension of the scope of the Directive 99/93/EC to other electronic trust services

This sub-task consisted of identifying the main expected principles, issues and key points, as well as in executing a reality check on the four technical, legal, economical and societal levels when preparing the secondary legislation associated to the "Electronic time stamps" and "Electronic registered delivery services" sections (6 and 7 of chapter III) of the Regulation (EU) No 910/2014. The Regulation articles covered by the present documents are Articles 41 and 42 of Section 6 "Electronic time stamps" and Articles 43 to 44 of Section 7 "Electronic registered delivery services".

According to the scope and the identified relevant key points and issues, the document discusses for each secondary legislative act foreseen in the Regulation with regards to the "Electronic time stamps" and "Electronic registered delivery services" sections an implementation ideal scenario.

1.3.3.1 Time stamps

(a) Context

As to time stamps, the Regulation refers to implementing act to establish reference numbers of standards for the binding of date and time to data and for accurate time sources that should be linked to Coordinated Universal Time (UTC).

One critical issue is the interpretation of Article 42.2 that makes provision of the implementing act. The first sentence of the article recites "The Commission may, by means of implementing acts, establish reference numbers of standards for the binding of date and time to data and for accurate time sources." and induces a reader to understand that the implementing act only refers to the standard for the requirements stated in Article 42.1.a) and .b). However the next sentence recites: "Compliance with the requirements laid down in paragraph 1 shall be presumed where the binding of date and time to data and the accurate time source meets those standards.", but the requirements laid down in paragraph 1 also include the one stated in Article 42.1.c) about the use of an advanced electronic signature or seal applied to the time stamp. Therefore it is unclear if the implementing act actually relates only to Article 42.1.a) and .b) or also .c).

(b) Conclusions

Different applications of the time stamps may have different requirements. Therefore the set of standards referenced in the implementing act should support a broad spectrum of requirements to guarantee that the actual needs of the different applications are satisfied without excessive burden and in line with the necessity principle from data protection law.

According to the current state-of-the art technologies, the best way to bind the date and time to data in such a manner as to reasonably preclude the possibility of the data being changed undetectably is to use the advanced electronic signature or an electronic seal of the time stamp provider. Therefore the signature/seal creation is a critical process that must occur within a secure system and the signature/seal creation data must be adequately protected. For these reasons, requirements similar to those for the qualified electronic signature/seal creation devices (Articles 29 and 39 and Annex II) should also apply to the electronic signature/seal creation devices used by the qualified time stamp provider. One possible group of technical standards specifying the requirements for these devices are the following set of CEN/ISSS Workshop agreements:

- CEN/ISSS CWA 14167-2:2004; Cryptographic module for CSP signing operations with backup – protection profile – CMCSOB-PP;
- CEN/ISSS CWA 14167-3:2004 Cryptographic module for CSP key generation services – protection profile – CMCKG-PP;
- CEN/ISSS CWA 14167-4:2004 Cryptographic module for CSP signing operations – protection profile – CMCSO-PP.

These technical specifications are currently being revised under the EC mandate M/460.

With regards to the data sent to the time stamp provider, with the current technologies there are two possible options: sending the actual data to be time stamped (i.e. documents, signatures/seals or other data) or their digests calculated through a robust and secure hash function. A suitable algorithm can be selected among those listed in the ETSI TS 119 312 Ver. 1.1.1.

Regarding the date/time indication included in the time stamps, its granularity may depend according to different application requirements: the requirements for accuracy are therefore bound to those for the granularity. To satisfy the requirement stated in Article 42.1.b), the provider must synchronize its time source with the international reference time scale Coordinated Universal Time (UTC) within the declared accuracy. If the time stamp provider issues time stamps under different policies with different accuracy requirements, it should use either different time sources, each one synchronized with UTC within the related accuracy, or a single time source synchronized with UTC within the strongest required accuracy.

One possible group of technical standards specifying the format and protocol for the time stamp and the policy requirements for the time stamp provider are the following set of ETSI Technical Specifications:

- TS 102 023 Ver. 1.2.2 – Policy requirements for time-stamping authorities
- TS 101 861 Ver. 1.4.1 – Time stamping profile

These technical specifications are currently being revised under the EC mandate M/460 to become EN (ETSI EN 319 421 and ETSI EN 319 422 respectively).

1.3.3.2 e-registered delivery

(a) Context

As to e-registered delivery, the Regulation refers to an implementing act to establish reference numbers of standards for processes for sending and receiving data.

The objective of the Regulation is to achieve legal effect on the certainty of cross-border e-registered delivery, and to establish qualified e-registered delivery services. National legislation establishing legal equivalence of e-registered delivery and paper registered letter may be present in Member States.

The scope of the implementing act is limited to establishing reference numbers of standards for processes for sending and receiving data. We understand by process 'a structured, measured set of activities designed to produce a specified output'.

With regard establishing such standards, we believe there are the following potential issues:
- In the e-registered delivery field, there are several different working environments and use-cases that need different authentication rules. From UPU (just object and system identification) to legal XML that provides double sender and receiver strong authentication. Each and every use case has its merits and relevance. There is a significant difference between processes in the various different contexts such as B2B, B2C, C2C, G2C etc.;
- A single standard will never be able to address all requirements;
- There are many stakeholders with vested interests, as described in the technical section below. However, few if any of these can be considered open solutions that would not disturb the desired level playing field.

(b) Conclusions

Starting from the position that it is important that e-registered delivery is and remains open to innovation, we conclude that any future scenario should:
- Establish a mechanism that allows European standard organisations and international standardisation bodies as defined in the Regulation (EU) No 1025/2012, to submit a proposal for an e-registered delivery standard to be referenced by the EU Commission;
- Mandate a transparent review of the proposed standard, checking that it does not lack any of the properties required by Regulation (EU) No 1025/2012, in particular:
  a. transparent standardisation process;
  b. open standardisation process, that is accessible by everybody, either through membership to the standardisation committee or through a national standardisation body;
  c. standard publicly available to everybody (free or upon payment[3]).

---

3   CEN and ISO Standards are available only upon payment.

Furthermore, consideration should be given to the fact that innovative solution must have the opportunity to become Qualified electronic Trust Services, even if they solve just specific issues and serve well defined communities. For example the standards, whenever possible, should not address a specific technology.

National legislation may impose restrictive conditions on the delivery of registered e-delivery, like millions of Euro of minimum stock capital, or the possession of a postal licence. This would create national monopolies and force innovative companies to sell to incumbents their innovative solutions, instead of addressing with them directly the market. However such restrictive conditions would make the involved services fall out of the scope of the Regulation and within the scope of the Directive on Community postal services (Directive 97/67/EC, Article 8).

1.3.4   Building blocks for the extension of the scope of the Directive 99/93/EC to mutual recognition of "notified" eIDs

(a) Context

This subtask focuses on the mutual recognition of "notified" electronic IDentification schemes (eIDs). This subtask is from a legal perspective entirely distinct from the earlier 3 subtasks, as eIDs are not considered to be electronic Trust Services under the terms of the Regulation. They fall within an entirely separate chapter of the Regulation, and are unaffected by some of the main principles for electronic Trust Services: eIDs do not have a Qualified service level, they are not subject to supervision obligations, they do not required audits by independent bodies, etc.

Instead, they follow an entirely separate logical model. Member States have the option (but not the obligation) to notify eID schemes applied at the national level to the European Commission. If they choose to do so, then the eID means issued under those schemes must be recognised and accepted by certain service providers in other Member States. The notification by Member States can cover private sector eIDs and private sector eID schemes, and the recognition obligation is not inherently limited to the public sector either. Thus, a broad basis for the mutual recognition of eIDs is created.

Despite this potentially broad scope of application, it is also clear that these provisions are relatively high level, focusing on the results to be achieved, rather than on the steps and processes needed to achieve interoperability.

Details will be addressed in secondary legislation. The Regulation refers to implementing acts to establish "the necessary modalities to facilitate the cooperation between the Member States referred to in paragraph 1 with a view to fostering a high level of trust and security appropriate to the degree of risk. Those implementing acts shall concern, in particular, the exchange of information, experiences and good practice on electronic identification schemes, the peer review of notified electronic identification schemes and the examination of relevant developments arising in the electronic identification sector by the competent authorities of the Member States."

The Regulation also refers to delegated acts "concerning the facilitation of cross border interoperability of electronic identification means by setting of minimum technical requirements".

Recommendations are made with respect to the four implementing acts which are permitted by the Regulation on respectively notification, cooperation, the interoperability framework, and quality assurance.

(b) Conclusions

The main findings and conclusions can be summarised as follows:

Notification

Our team recommends an approach that stresses the importance of a short and pragmatic notification template which focuses on policy information and verifiability rather than on technical details. With respect to the peer review of the notified identification schemes, the review should rely on a consultation based mechanism, in which members of the cooperation group may provide questions or comments to the notifying Member State, inviting it to amend, clarify or revise the notification. The notifying Member State is however not formally required to respond to this feedback, and other Member States cannot block the publication of a notification. However, they do retain the right to dispute the validity of the notification afterwards if they consider it to be non-compliant with the requirements of the Regulation.

(1) Interoperability framework

The team suggests adopting a summary implementing act, outlining only the competences of the cooperation group to decide on certain technical requirements for interoperability and on common operational security standards, and defining a minimum set of person identification data uniquely representing a natural or legal person. Details of the interoperability framework are however highly changeable over time, and should therefore not be enshrined in legislation. The cooperation group should be entrusted with maintaining technical details over time through consensus opinions on which standards and solutions satisfy the requirements of the Regulation.

(2) Cooperation between the Member States

A cooperation group should be set up, consisting of representatives of each Member State, as well as observers from the Commission, Article 29 Working Party and ENISA. A secretariat should be established to support the group on practical matters, and the implementing act should define procedures for the group to adopt 'joint opinions', which are authoritative but non-binding. In this way, the Group can support the establishment and upkeep of the interoperability framework, without impinging on national sovereignty.

(3) Quality assurance

In the team's opinion, a short implementing act should be created that includes a technical annex that specifies the assurance levels. The study team believes that it is crucial in this respect to adhere to international standards, as this is the only way of ensuring future international interoperability (i.e. extending beyond the sphere of applicability of the Regulation) which is clearly an important factor in the area of e-services. Therefore, this annex should be based on the ISO/IEC 29115 standard, and should consist of a specification that uses the three phases defined in this standard (enrolment, credential management, and entity authentication), as this will allow all STORK[4] Quality Authentication Assurance (QAA) elements to be integrated while fully complying with the requirements of the Regulation.

1.4 Monitoring electronic identification, authentication and electronic trust services development and uptake

1.4.1 Context

This task reports upon the development and uptake of electronic Identification and Authentication Services (eIAS), as well as electronic Trust Services (eTS) in the European market and some third country markets. The task consisted of the integration and enrichment of existing materials as well as a continuous monitoring through an Internet-based eID survey and interviews with stakeholders.

The countries included in this study are the 27 Member States and three EEA Countries (Iceland, Liechtenstein, Norway and the forthcoming Member State Croatia). During the period of the study, Croatia became the 28th Member State.

A significant amount of desk research was conducted, analysing input from a.o. the following sources:
- ChamberSign's overview of service provided by their members (www.chambersign.com);
- EFF SSL Observatory[5];
- IDABC Country Profiles;
- SSEDIC surveys[6];
- EC DG ENTR's Digital Signature Server (DSS) project ;
- Results from the various Large Scale Projects (LSPs);
- CENTR, the Council of European National Top Level Domain Registries[7];
- Worldbank's 'Secure Servers' overview (ISBN: 978-0-8213-8996-6 and eISBN: 978-0-8213-9519-6);
- "SME Panel" survey on e-signature[8];
- The European Network and Information Security Market Scenario, Trends and Challenges (EC DG Infosociety, 2009, performed by IDC[9]);
- The State of the Electronic Identity Market: Technologies, Infrastructure, Services and Policies (EC DG JRC, EUR 24567 EN – 2010).

Also, interviews were conducted internally within the study team, and on-line information was collected from PRADO[10] (Public Register of Authentication Documents On-line) and the EU List of Trusted Lists (LOTL[11]).

To ensure all relevant material in the various domains has been captured, the material was distributed to the Member State experts via CIRCABC. Feedback from the experts was obtained

---

4 Secure idenTity acrOss boRders linKed (STORK): https://www.eid-stork2.eu/
5 https://www.eff.org/observatory
6 http://www.eid-ssedic.eu/
7 http://www.internetsociety.org/deploy360/dnssec/statistics/CABforum
8 http://ec.europa.eu/information_society/policy/esignature/eu_legislation/revision/sme_panel/index_en.htm
9 http://ec.europa.eu/information_society/policy/nis/strategy/activities/data_ict_market/index_en.htm
10 http://prado.consilium.europa.eu/
11 https://ec.europa.eu/digital-agenda/en/eu-trusted-lists-certification-service-providers

through this channel, further enriched by the information received after the workshop held on January 29, 2015. The outcome of this task has been used as an input to Task 3.

1.4.2 Conclusions

Building on earlier studies and new input, the developed Country Profiles provide a detailed overview on eID and eTS, including at least the eTS which are part of the Regulation and the approaches in the analysed countries, including national legislations on eTS, on-going initiatives on eTS as well as current and on-going private sector solutions on eTS.

The 31 Country Profiles indicate:

- The presence of a clear market for TSPs. There are 187 listed TSPs identified, over 24 Member States and 3 EEA countries, of which 150 TSPs are issuing Qualified Certificates. Of these, 68 TSPs are issuing time-stamps. With 37 TSP registered, Italy currently has the highest number of TSP in their Trust List.
- An increased use of both mobile solutions and solutions including a central signer.
- A diversified landscape for eID service providers. This is the consequence of the diverging approaches taken by the different countries.

The need for STORK, STORK2 and their 'Levels of Assurance' (STORK QAA). In such a landscape, an interoperability approach such as currently based on Pan-European Proxy Servers (PEPS) appears to be a necessity to further improve the internal digital market. Levels of Assurance are important to facilitate mutual recognition through notification.

1.5 Qualitative and quantitative description and analysis of the eTS market in the European Union

1.5.1 Context

The main objective of Task 3 is to develop a qualitative and quantitative description and analysis of the eTS market in the European Union. The aim is to provide a better insight in today's main market dynamics, without however making theoretical assumptions regarding future market developments. The services covered are those defined in the Regulation, namely electronic signature, time-stamping, registered delivery mail, electronic seal, electronic documents and website authentication, with a special attention to electronic signature.

In particular, the work includes an in-depth analysis and provides updated data on the overall market in the European Union and EEA countries, including market size, market growth rate, competitive intensity, market performance, market trends, key success factors, barriers to entry, value chain, industry profitability.

The work for Task 3 included the following tasks:

1. Description of **providers of eTS technology and services** in the European Union and the characteristics of the offer of products and services (Identify, describe and classify the suppliers of the ETS market. The elaboration of nomenclature analysis should be horizontal and vertical, and will be of national, European and international companies);
2. Description of **eTS products** available on the European Union market;

3. Description and analysis of the **companies that purchase eTS technologies** and services (large companies, SMEs, administrations and other relevant organizations);

4. Collect information and **data usage statistics** on the European eTS market, suppliers of products and services;

5. **Consolidate and integrate** the available information, statistics and data, providing to the Commission a unified view of the supply side of the European eTS market;

6. **Assess the functioning of the eTS market** and formulate recommendations on the challenges of the eTS market;

7. **Devise indicators** suitable to be re-run periodically and one set of measurement;

8. **Define well thought out and justified recommendations** related to the above areas;

9. An **updated assessment** of the eTS market and recommendations for its improvement, in particular in the light of the Regulation.

1.5.2 Conclusions

The market analysis presented in the report was developed in parallel with the policy making cycle, leading to the Regulation. This particular timing implies that the study was made while a number of previously identified recommendations (e.g. related to the need for improved interoperability, for introducing mutual recognition of eID, etc.) were being taken into ac-count in this new Regulation, but before the effect of these legislative improvements can become visible.

At this moment, we can only assume that the eTS market will continue to further develop and that the Regulation will provide for a number of elements that allow for enhancing certain market developments.

The analysis of the eTS market has however pointed out a number of issues and / or flaws that will need to be dealt with for enabling a future monitoring of the eTS market and the evaluation of the impact of the Regulation. Overall, there is currently only very little market intelligence available on the (total size of) the eTS market. Some of the reasons for this are: (1) electronic Trust Services are very heterogeneous and possible market segmentations continue to evolve, which makes it very difficult to delimitate 'the' eTS market. The only eTS for which a clear separate and global market can be distinguished, is website authentication; (2) furthermore, for many larger suppliers, eTS currently only presents a small part of their revenues, but the exact importance of these is not being disclosed; (3) many small start-ups are active in the market, but compiling an up-to-date comprehensive inventory of these is very challenging.

We would like to make the following recommendations for ensuring an improved future market monitoring:

- For monitoring the supply side, some kind of **market observatory**, with the support of the EU 28 Member States, could be envisaged. The aim would be to draw up an inventory of eTS Providers (Qualified and not Qualified) which can be queried on a regular basis with dedicated surveys, with the aim of enhancing the understanding of market developments;

- Regulation (EC) No 1006/2009 (amending Regulation (EC) No 808/2004 concerning **Community statistics on the information society**) includes 'ICT security and trust' in the subjects covered for both enterprises and individuals and households. For monitoring the demand side it could be envisaged to add a number of characteristics (or 'variables') related to eTS to the future Commission Regulations implementing Regulation (EC) No

808/2004. This approach would also allow for the inclusion of official definitions for the variables added. We refer to the overview of indicators for monitoring the eTS market;
- An alternative approach for monitoring the demand side could consist in the set-up of a **Special Eurobarometer- e-Communications Household Survey**. This barometer could focus on electronic Trust Services and include a measurement of the effect of the envisaged large-scale media campaign, the introduction of the "e-Mark U Trust" mark, etc.

1.6 Report on the follow-up of mandate M/460

1.6.1 Context

The purpose of this task was to provide a gap analysis, built on mandate M/460, between the existing technical norms and standards and the preparatory work for secondary acts of the Regulation, as well as electronic identification provisions within that Regulation.

This gap analysis was executed following a three phases approach:
- Phase 1: Identification of the gaps through an update of the existing M/460 gap analysis & worldwide inventory of Electronic Signature standards and adding electronic Identification aspects;
- Phase 2: Analysis how to fill the identified gaps. The analysis carefully evaluates if the gap shall be filled by technical norms or standards, or if it requires legal norms, in the form of delegated acts or implementing acts.
- Phase 3: Recommendations for a new standardisation mandate.

The present gap analysis and the associated recommendations have been built on several inputs. First of all it uses the M/460 existing gap analysis, the worldwide inventory of signature related standards and the specification of a Rationalised Framework for Electronic Signature standards in Europe. But, since M/460 is mainly focusing on Electronic Signature only, also other electronic Identification existing standards and specifications from internationally recognised Standards and Industry Bodies (e.g. ISO, ITU, IETF, W3C, OASIS, etc.), national and sector specific bodies (e.g. national bodies, EPC, Global Platform, etc.) have been considered. In addition, any relevant studies and initiatives (e.g., the former IAS study, IDABC, CROBIES, Kantara initiatives, US NSTIC – National Strategy for Trusted Identities in Cyberspace, EU Large Scale Pilots and ICT PSP projects like STORK, PEPPOL, SPOCS, EpSOS, eCodex and eSENS, etc.) have also been taken as input for the execution of this task.

The study covers the identification of the gaps and the analysis on how to fill these gaps with the amendment of existing technical norms and standards or with new technical norms and standards and the relevant recommendations. It describes an overview of the current version of the existing ETSI/CEN standardisation framework on Electronic Signatures. It further covers the identification of the gaps and the analysis on how to fill these gaps with the amendment of existing technical norms and standards or with new technical norms and standards. It finally provides a summary of the recommendations for a new standardisation mandate.

1.6.2 Conclusions

Based on the gap analysis following recommendations have been made:

1. As to **conformity assessments**, it is recommended to mandate ETSI to: 22 A pan-European Framework on Electronic Identification and Trust Services
   - Ascertain the minimum formal requirements on which an outcome based criteria oriented Conformity Assessment Report (CAR) could be built for each type of QTSP/QTS;
   - Have a NWI to develop a TS standard for such CARs, so that CAB & CAR meet some minimal criteria.

2. As to **advanced electronic signatures/seals**, the development of the new XAdES, CAdES, PAdES and ASiC Baseline Profiles (respectively the forthcoming EN 319 132-2, EN 319 122-2, EN 319 142-1 and EN 319 162-2) should be monitored to ensure that:
   - They address Advanced Electronic Signatures and Advanced Electronic Seals;
   - They leverage on lessons learned from ETSI e-Signature Validation Remote Plugtests conducted during the 03-21 November 2014 period;
   - They take into account the strong demand for simplification of the current specifications.

3. As to the **format and qualified provisioning of qualified certificates, the qualified validation of qualified electronic signatures/seals**, the **qualified preservation of qualified electronic signatures/seals**, the **qualified provisioning of qualified electronic time stamps**, and the **qualified provisioning of qualified electronic registered delivery services** the following is recommended. The complete set of the listed standards (see report) should be developed/finalised to align with relevant requirements from the Regulation, and published:
   - At least under their TS form as soon as possible to ensure that the appropriate set of criteria could be used to build outcome based criteria oriented CAR specifications for ensuring the availability of accredited CABs;
   - When considering their referencing in corresponding optional implementing acts of the Regulation.

While all above recommendations are important, particularly the first one is is essential for an effective, enhanced and harmonised supervision of QTSPs and the QTSs they provide.

Enacting upon this first recommendation is mandatory to ensure availability by 1st of July 2016 of an appropriate model for accreditation of CABs and for conformity assessment reports not requiring de facto mandatory standards for QTSPs. Furthermore close monitoring of the standards produced in the current and future phase of execution of M/460 mandate to meet and support QTSPs/QTSs to meet the relevant requirements of the Regulation in the best delays is an additional recommendation.

1.7 Technical assistance on eID and electronic trust services, including electronic signature

1.7.1 Context

Task 5 was a broader support task encompassing all areas of expertise including assisting the European Commission on the following topics:

- Provide technical support, in particular by providing thematic technical reports, briefings and analysis, to the Commission on eID and electronic trust services, including electronic signatures, electronic seals, time stamping, electronic delivery, electronic documents and website authentication specificities;
- Assist the Commission services while interacting with Member States, European Standardisation Organisations, and the various stakeholders to discuss all issues related to topics developed under "Task 1". To this end, the team provided analysis, briefings, reports or any other support needed in this respect;
- Assist, by providing thematic reports, briefings and analysis, to the work for further development of the legal framework, in particular in implementing the M/460 mandate, the revision of Commission Decision 2003/511/EC5 and the legislative process for the adoption of the proposed Regulation. As well, support, by providing thematic reports, briefings and analysis, provided as needed when carrying international negotiations with third countries;
- Support to outline a wide awareness raising campaign towards European SMEs and citizens, draw up guidelines and recommendations on a communication strategy plan, elaborating proposals on general communication and priority actions aimed at specific media target audiences, and on specific actions aimed at the press as well as on the anticipated impact and coverage figures, broken down geographically and by type of target audience; or finding local relays able to disseminate messages on the benefits of the initiative to local SMEs and citizens;
- Provide "ad hoc" operational and technical support and advice as requested by the Commission.

1.7.2 Conclusions

Throughout the project duration, the European Commission has made use of the Task 5 resources for receiving assistance on the following topics:

1. Drafting of a Communication Strategy Plan;
2. Strategic advice on international trade law aspects;
3. Technical assistance on website certificates;
4. Comments and suggestions relating to the prioritization of the secondary legislation;
5. Ad-hoc questions relating to technical issues;
6. Strategic advice on Levels of Assurance.

Signature Validation – a Dark Art?

Peter Lipp

IAIK, Graz University of Technology
peter.lipp@iaik.tugraz.at

Abstract

ETSI Standard EN 319 102-1 (Procedures for Creation and Validation of AdES Digital Signatures; Part 1: Creation and Validation [2]) is a new standard developed by ETSI during the implementation of Mandate M460 and is currently undergoing the EN approval procedure. The standard covers, as the title suggests, the creation and validation of digital signatures. Some experts, who so far were convinced they understood what needs to be done when validating a signature, are confused. To them the standard is either wrong, not understandable or worst case both. This article tries to shed a light into the approach taken but also discusses why signature validation sometimes gets complex, maybe more complex than necessary, and considers whether this complexity can be avoided.

1 Signature Validation

Electronic signatures are considered the equivalent of hand-written signatures in the electronic habitat. In many countries signature legislation defines requirements an electronic signature has to fulfil to be considered a legal equivalent to a hand-written signature. So it makes sense to look at signature validation in the "real world".

An interesting aspect of signature validation in the paper world is that signatures seem rarely to be validated. One the one hand there may be no need for it – a signature is assumed genuine by default until proven otherwise, especially when the consequences of not checking are minor and/or can be reverted, if necessary. Also, even if one wants to validate a hand-written signature, it turns out to be difficult – extremely difficult indeed. Even if I was in the possession of a specimen to compare to, the signature may look genuine when it in fact isn't – or may look suspect when in reality it is fine. Also, most often there is something else involved that supports the validity signature (and suggests not checking it): a known customer who always sends a signed document once a week; a phone call in advance from a person who is known; other data in the signed document that is only known to the originator. So the signature has rarely to be evaluated on its own.

Digital signatures have an advantage – one can validate them automatically. If e.g. a party sends a signed PDF to another party, the validation of the signature is ideally automated in the business processes. Alternatively the person dealing with that case has to understand, or learn, what needs to be done to validate the signature. If neither of these options is implemented, digital signatures, while validateable, will sometimes be rejected, while a handwritten signature might have been accepted without validation.

In our experience the real-life acceptance of digital signatures improved over the last years, at least in Austria, where more and more people are using the Austrian citizen card, which supports digital signatures. Thus more and more people get in contact with the technology and learn recognizing and accepting (checked or unchecked) a (legally valid) digital signature.

2 Signature Validation and Time

The main reason digital signature validation may get complex is the involvement of time. This assumes that there is a correct and secure signature validation application (SVA) at hand that can correctly parse the formats and do the complex crypto maths calculations. For such a SVA it is usually quite easy to validate a signature shortly after the time the signature has been produced. The closer the time of validation is to the time of signature, the easier in general. What are the reasons for that potential degradation? To discuss this better, lets revisit the basics of signature validation:

Fig. 1: Signed Document

A signature is created using a private key representing the signer. The corresponding public key is certified by an X.509 certificate, binding the public key of the signer to her identity. This certificate contains a signature by the certificate issuer, the CA. This CA may be in possession of another certificate from a superordinate CA, forming a certificate chain up to some trust anchor.

Validating the signature consists, among other steps, of verifying the signature value itself as well as validating the signers certificate. Since the certificate contains a signature, validating the certificate includes a validation of another signature.

In most cases, this process is rather straightforward and easy. It immediately gets more complex if "exceptions" occur:

The certificate may
- have expired,
- have been revoked,
- have been created with an algorithm that is no longer considered secure,
- have been created with a key which is no longer considered secure.

Assuming that at time of the creation of the signature none of these exceptions were the case, validation the signature at the time of signing would have been a no-brainer. The more time passes between creation and validation, the higher the likelihood of these exceptions:

- Expiration may occur any time after signing – but is foreseeable, since the certificate contains the expiration date.
- Revocation may also occur any time after signing. Certificates are most often revoked when people leave the company, lose their smart-card or forget their PIN but rarely for key-compromise or other reasons.
- Expiration of algorithms and key-sizes are mostly long-term issues. When researchers discover weaknesses of algorithms, there is normally enough time to switch to newer, better algorithms or longer keys before these weaknesses can be exploited successfully.

What should the result of the validation of a signature be when the certificate is expired or revoked? A standard validation implementation would just return that fact: expired or revoked – and not consider the signature valid. However, lets look at the legal side. For Europe, Regulation (EU) N°910/2014 on electronic identification and trust services for electronic transactions in the internal market (eIDAS Regulation [7]), adopted by the co-legislators on 23 July 2014, specifies rules for a certain class of signatures: qualified electronic signatures. The regulation states:

Requirements for the validation of qualified electronic signatures
- the certificate ... was, **at the time of signing**, a qualified certificate...
- the qualified certificate .... was valid **at the time of signing**
- ....
- the requirements provided for in Article 26 were met **at the time of signing**.

Fig. 2: Expired or Revoked Certificates

The regulation clearly requires these facts to hold at the time of signing – and not at the time of validation. So, a signature may be perfectly valid, even if the certificate has been revoked, if we can prove that revocation has taken place after the signature has been produced. For validation thus one needs to find out whether the signature has been produced "in time", i.e.:
- before the certificate has been revoked
- before the certificate has expired
- before the used algorithms have become weak
- before the key sizes have become too small

The signature itself will most often contain a time value – but this is unfortunately is a claimed time only and the signer may indeed have inserted a fake signature time. We can now assume that claimed time to be genuine – which in most cases it will be. This assumption also reflects the fact that a claimed time statement on a piece of paper (like "Berlin, Nov. 11th 2015") is equally "precise". Accepting the time as true is in fact a valid approach, taken e.g. by Austria in its eGovernment-implementations.

Alternatively one may require a proof that the signature has indeed been produced before expiration or revocation respectively (proof of existence, PoE). A technical solution for this is the application of time-assertions, e.g. time-stamps.

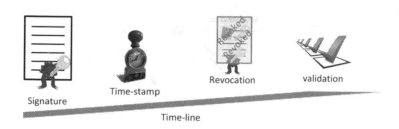

Fig. 3: signature time-stamp

Figure 3 illustrates this concept. A time-stamp is produced after the production of the signature, but before revocation or expiration of the corresponding certicate. The time-stamp will only prove that the signature existed at the time the time-stamp has been created. Such a time-stamp is called signature-time-stamp and ideally should be produced as close to the creation time of the signature. A time-stamp consists of
- a representation of the object[1] (either the object itself or, more likely, a hash of the object)
- a time value
- a signature by the issuer of the time-stamp

When validating a signature that contains a signature-timestamp, it may be necessary to validate the time-stamp. Validating the time-stamp includes a validation of the signature the time-stamp contains. This is again a digital signature associated with a certificate of the issuer. This certificate may
- have expired
- have been revoked
- have been created with an algorithm that is no longer considered secure
- have been created with a key which is no longer considered secure

Déjà vu?

It might turn out that the time-stamp is no longer of any help – unless it has been protected against these issues by another time-stamp as shown in figure 4....

Yes, this is recursive. Since this is again a time-stamp, anything bad that could have happened to the original certificate or the signature-time-stamp holds again and we might want to add another time-stamp to this. Carefully. Additionally, there will usually be other signed objects involved

---

1   in this case the signature

in the validation process, e.g. CRLs and OCSP-responses, which may also need to being protected against any such mishaps. Validating a signature with several time-stamps attached is no longer as straightforward as validating the signature on its own.

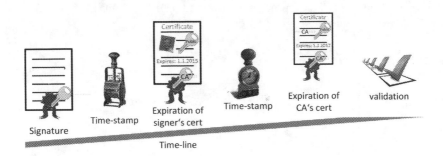

Fig. 4: adding another time-stamp

3 ETSI EN 319 102

In the course of the mandate M460[1] ETSI produced the standard EN 319 102: Procedures for Creation and Validation of AdES Digital Signatures; Part 1: Creation and Validation[2]. This standard specifies procedures for:
- the creation of AdES digital signatures [3],[4],[5];
- establishing whether an AdES digital signature is technically valid.

It defines classes of signatures that correspond to the requirements for validation:
- **Basic Signature:** signature that can be validated as long as the corresponding certificates are neither revoked nor expired.
- **Signature with Time:** proves that the signature already existed at a given point in time.
- **Signature with Long-Term Validation Data:** provides the long term availability of the validation material by incorporating all the material or references to material required for validating the signature.
- **Signature with ArchivalData:** ensures that the validation material provided with the signature is kept preserved for even longer term. This level aims to tackle the long term availability and integrity of the validation material.

Figure 5 shows the building blocks the validation process has been split into. The validation is driven by a validation policy that consists of constraints. The building blocks return status information like PASSED, FAILED and INDETERMINATE that are then combined to a resulting status for the overall validation: TOTAL-PASSED, TOTAL-FAILED and INDETERMINATE.

In short, TOTAL-PASSED is returned only whenever
- the cryptographic checks of the signature succeeded;
- applicable constraints to the signer's identity certication have been positively validated;
- the signature has been positively validated against all validation constraints.

TOTAL-FAILED is only returned when
- either the cryptographic checks of the signature failed,
- or the validation application was able to prove that the generation of the signature took place after the revocation of the signing certificate.

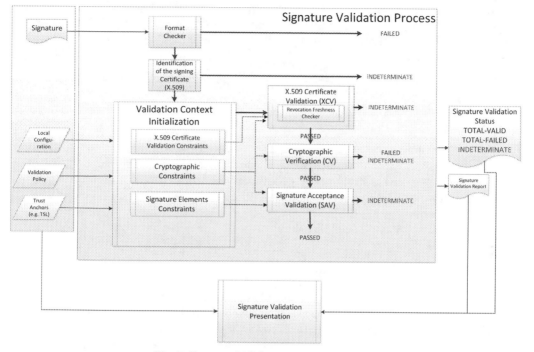

Fig. 5: Signature Validation Process (from [2])

In any other case, the result of the validation will be INDETERMINATE, expressing that the available information was insufficient to ascertain the signature to be TOTAL-PASSED or TO-TALFAILED. This implies that the validation could reach TOTAL-PASSED or TOTAL-FAILED if more information would be available. The status result also contains a sub-indication giving more information on "what's missing".

The validation algorithm described in this standard is capable to validate any of the signature classes and, in case of long-term-validation, where we may face all sorts of complications like expirations, time-stamps and tons of PoEs, also provides the recursiveness required. The design chosen provided in our humble opinion the only way to tackle an algorithm that is capable of correctly handling any extremely complex signature, where all combinations of expirations, revocations and other issues can be handled correctly when appropriate protection measures (time-assertions) are available. Whether such complex life-forms will be found in the signature habitats remains to be seen.

4 Long Term Validation

ETSI EN 310 102 uses building blocks to specify the validation algorithm. When validating "older" signatures, where e.g. certificates have naturally expired, and where time-stamps as proofs-of existence are included, these building blocks will also return INDETERMINATE and the validation algorithm will then try using any existing PoEs to resolve the situation. This may be necessary for any signed element that is required for the overall validation:

- the signature
- time-stamps
- certificates
- certificate revocation lists
- ocsp responses

Thus the resulting long-term validation algorithm intrinsically is recursive, thus somewhat complex and also possibly diffcult to comprehend. The underlying concepts have been described in [6]. It makes use of three building blocks especially designed for long-term validation:

- Past certificate validation building block
- PoE extraction
- Past signature validation building block

4.1 Past certificate validation

The past certificate validation building block validates a certificate chain at a date/time which can be in the past. It requires for each certificate in the chain that it can be ascertained at the current time, or that it can be ascertained using "old" revocation status information (such that the certificate is proven to having existed at a date in the past when the issuer of the certificate was still considered reliable and under control of its signing key). It returns a time value indicating the time when all certificates in the chain have been valid.

4.2 PoE extraction

The PoE extraction building block derives PoEs from a given time-stamp, if the validation of the time-stamp has returned PASSED and either the cryptographic hash function used in the time-stamp is considered reliable at current time or a PoE for that time-stamp exists for a time when the hash function has still been considered reliable. A time-stamp gives a PoE for each data item protected by the time-stamp at the generation date/time of the token.

4.3 Past signature validation

The past signature validation building block calls the past certificate validation building block which will return a time value (when all certificate were valid) and checks if PoEs for the signature exists before that time. If all other constraints can be positively evaluated, past signature validation will return TOTAL-PASSED.

4.4 Long Term Validation

The long-term validation algorithm performs validation for signatures where time-stamps exist. It processes all the time-stamps present. To do so, it

- validates the time-stamp (potentially using the past-signature-validation building block if necessary)
- extract PoEs for all objects protected by the time-stamp Using that information it calls the past-signature-validation building block which will make use of all the PoEs extracted in the previous steps.

5 Reality check and Conclusions

Now having mastered the complexity in theory and having an algorithm at hand that is capable of validating everything correctly, lets look at some interesting scenarios of expired and revoked certificates from a practical perspective.

5.1 Revoked certificate

First: a signature where the certificate has been revoked. Figure 6 illustrates the time-line. We assume that everything else is fine, i.e. the cryptographic checks succeed and any other constraints can be positively validated. An implementation of the validation algorithm then will not return TOTAL-FAILED, since it certainly is possible that the signature is valid. What we would need is a proof the signature in fact existed before the time of revocation, a PoE. Thus the validation result will be INDETERMINATE/REVOKED_NO_POE – which states that the certificate is found to be revoked and indicating that the result of validation might change to TOTAL-PASSED, if a PoE for the signature before revocation time could be made available.

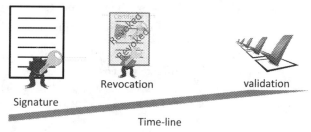

Fig. 6: example scenario

Whether such a proof of existence can indeed be made available to the signature validation application (SVA) is a different story – there may be no such proof or there may be out-of-band proofs that have not been made available in a machine processable form. In any case it would be clearly wrong for the SVA to state that the signature is invalid. Finally it will be a decision to be taken by the user of the SVA to decide to accept or not accept the signature. To be able to do so, the user will need to consider what the real situation is. Three scenarios exist:

1. It is a valid signature that has been created before revocation. We cannot validate the signature, since we are missing the PoE. A time-stamp created in time (before revocation) would have been able to provide that proof.

2. The legitimate user still created the signature after the certificate has been revoked. While this is most certainly a very very bad idea by the signer, the resulting signature could certainly be considered valid (it in the end has been produced by the signer), but we will never be able to technically reach the TOTAL-VALID result. Also, the signer could easily claim that the signature was forged, so we would have difficulties enforcing anything that has been signed.

3. The key was indeed stolen or broken and the signature is forged and not to be accepted. This is the bad case – but we will in the end not be able to differentiate this case from the others.

Excluding the second scenario, which admittedly is a little far-fetched, case 1 and 3 remain. Even if clearly case 1 is more likely than case 3, the decision to accept the signature or not will depend on the business context, the implications of accepting a forged signature or rejecting a valid signature and may also depend on other information available or retrievable by the user that supports the case at hand. The rules the user will have to follow are part of the validation policy in force.

5.2 Expired certificate

Next we will look at the case of an expired certificate, again assuming that we do not have a timestamp available. If we find a signature where the certificate is expired at the time of validation, either

1. the certificate has expired and the signature has been produced by an attacker who somehow got access to that key (whether by key compromise or because the smart card was "left unattended" does not matter). Since the signature has expired before the successful attack, the attack may even not have been noticed. Which, by the way, may happen irrespective of the actual expiration.

2. the certificate has expired and the certificate had indeed been revoked before expiration, but the CA does not keep revocation information after expiration of certificates.[2]

3. the certificate has expired but the signature was actually produced by the owner of the certificate before expiration.

All of these scenarios are possible, but the most likely scenario is scenario 3 – which should not indicate we may ignore the other two. We have discussed the possible scenarios in the previous section. Again, while scenario 1 certainly is a possible one, scenario 3 will still be more likely.

If we know that the CA keeps revocation information available after the end of the lifetime of the certificate, the risk to accept an expired certificate will be low and, on average, the better decision. Of course it would be terribly wrong in scenario 1 however...

5.3 An example

Let us look at a practical example that is not at all unlikely:
- I produced a signature with my Austrian citizen card yesterday.
- Today I lose my Austrian citizen card – revocation is done.
- No time-stamps have been added.

---

2 Most current CAs do keep that information beyond expiration available however.

The scenario described reflects current practice in Austria. When new signature cards are issued, the previous ones loose their validity and any certificate issued for them will be revoked. This is even less critical since the certificate is revoked while I am still in possession of my card. Now: Is my signature still valid? Of course it is. According to the regulation my signature is still valid, since the requirements were met at the time of signing. Not considering it valid would be similar to considering a hand-written signature not valid since the ink meanwhile exceeded its "best before" date.

However, most current implementations of signature validation will not accept the signature and issue an error message. ETSI EN 319 102-1 would return INDETERMINATE/EXPIRED, which is, while not satisfactory, the best we can do in conveying the status of the signature.

So the user depending on the validation result may feel a little lost – and rightly so. The result does not clearly say "Signature is fine" but mumbles something vague as "don't know...". This does not help the user who may need to make a decision now, has no clue what a PoE is – and if, where to acquire one, if at all possible. So our suggestions and conclusions are:

- Do a proper risk analysis for accepting or rejecting signatures with indeterminate validation results and specify your signature validation policy accordingly.
- Try to avoid scenarios where indeterminate results are likely to occur.
- Avoid the need for long-term-validation of signatures.
- When long term validation of signatures however turns out to be unavoidable, consider validating signatures shortly after creation and securely archiving them together with the validation results, a validation report and the material used for validating.

Do not assume technology can be 100% accurate in all cases. With hand-written signatures, the best ink possible cannot ensure there never will be the need for lawyers or the court. Nor can technology for digital signatures. Be prepared.

References

European Commission. Standardisation mandate to the european standardisation organisations cen, cenelec and etsi in the eld of information and communication technologies applied to electronic signatures, 12 2009.

ETSI. ETSI EN 319 102-1: Electronic Signatures and Infrastructures (ESI); Procedures for Creation and Validation of AdES Digital Signatures; Part 1: Creation and Validation. 2015.

ETSI. ETSI EN 319 122-1: Electronic Signatures and Infrastructures (ESI); CAdES digital signatures; Part 1: Building blocks and CAdES baseline signatures. 2015.

ETSI. ETSI EN 319 132-1: Electronic Signatures and Infrastructures (ESI); XAdES digital signatures; Part 1: Building blocks and XAdES baseline signatures. 2015.

ETSI. ETSI EN 319 142: Electronic Signatures and Infrastructures (ESI); PAdES digital signatures. 2015.

Moez Ben MBarka and Julien Stern. Certication validation: Back to the past. In The Eighth European Workshop on Public Key Services, Applications and Infrastructures, EuroPKI2011. Springer-Verlag, 2011.

European Parliament and the Council of the European Union. Regulation (eu) no 910/2014 of the european parliament and of the council of 23 july 2014 on electronic identication and trust services for electronic transactions in the internal market and repealing directive 1999/93/ec.

A Comparison of Trust Models

Marc Sel

Royal Holloway, University of London
Marc.Sel.2013@live.rhul.ac.uk
Marc.Sel@be.pwc.com

Abstract

This article presents a comparative study of trust models, a term often used without a well-defined specification. Nevertheless, most automated enterprise processes rely on it. Examples include Automated Border Control gates, e-Government systems such as Tax-On-Web, electronic banking and money transfer and many more. We first present a short introduction to trust models. We then propose key terms to describe how trust can be established, and illustrate how these terms can be applied. Finally we compare the trust models created by ICAO PKD, EU eIDAS, US FICAM and Bitcoin, and present a conclusion.

1 Introduction

A key part of the development of the electronic society is the introduction of an economy based on electronic transactions and trust, as previously discussed, [1]. We consider trust as a factor that contributes to the taking of a decision. In cases as different as passing a Border Crossing Point, the ordering from a website, making a payment, or starting a medical treatment, trust will play a role in the transactions performed and decisions taken. In this context, an actor is an entity such as a natural or legal person that can act in one or more of trust-specific roles such as trustor, trustee and assessor. The trustor is the entity that is trusting. The trustee is the entity that is potentially trusted. The assessor provides claims about the trustee. Multiple assessors might provide claims about the same trustee. These assessors can have a varying degree of independence from the trustee. Also, a trustee may publish claims about itself. An artefact is a piece of electronic information produced by an actor (e.g. a certificate, an assertion, a time stamp, a claim, a signed document, or a list of trustees for a trustor). Obviously, many other roles can be considered.

Trust is based on elements as the existence (or lack off) of positive outcomes related to similar decisions taken in the past. We may have obtained these positive outcomes ourselves, or we may have learned about them from other sources that we rely on. Other elements include the extent to which some form of transaction-reversal is possible. The product or service provider may offer some form of guarantee or refund. Furthermore a regulator may force the provider to take liability.

Many solutions meet all reasonable expectations with regard to cryptographic trust in a PKI scheme such as appropriate key generation, subscriber registration, certificate creation and distribution, as well as publication of revocation information. All of these can be considered as relevant 'hygienic factors' that are required but not understandable by most end users. As a consequence, these hygienic factors don't necessarily contribute much to the trustor's perception of trust. Elements such as reputation and an assessor's description or opinion on the trustee, formulated in a way understandable to the trustor, may actually contribute equally or more to this perception. Elements that introduce the notion of time into the trust evaluation equation will also contribute to this perception. An end user may trust an organisation more when it has a verifiable history of service provision. The gap between the safeguards that are in operation, and how they are perceived by users is referred to as the trust deficit.

The remainder of this paper is structured as follows. Section 2 elaborates the key concepts and terms we use to describe and compare trust models. In Section 3 we introduce some large scale trust models. This is followed, in Section 4, by a comparison of a selection of those. Section 5 describes related and future work, and Section 6 concludes the paper.

2 Key concepts and terminology

In most if not all instances where trust in electronic transactions is established, the following four types of trust components are involved: computational trust components (such as hard mathematical problems as the Discrete Logarithm Problem or finding points on an elliptic curve), technology components (such as Certification Authority servers, Hardware Security Modules (HSM) and On-line Certificate Status Protocol (OCSP) responders), operating procedures (such as face-to-face registration of an applicant that wants to subscribe to a CA's services) and compliance components. An appropriate combination of these components will yield legal effect.

There are many competing definitions and vocabularies for trust, indicating the concept's importance in many different scenarios and for different stakeholders. In the context of the present article we use the following terms:
- Trust model: a model of multi-party interactions that aims at facilitating a trustor's decision on the basis of metadata and services;
- Trust ecosystem: collection of trust models;
- Mechanism: the mechanism used to bind the participants within the model;
- Actors:
  - Initiator: the actor that took the initiative to create the trust model;
  - Governor/oversight keeper: the actor that governs the trust model and/or oversees it;
  - Operator: the actor responsible for the operation of the model;
  - Assessor: an actor that provides claims about participants;
  - Participants: actors that accept to be bound through the mechanism, this includes
    - Trust Service Providers (TSPs), actors providing trust services such as authentication, signature creation, validation, long term preservation, registered electronic delivery, time stamping etc. In such a context, the TSP can also be referred to as the trustee, the entity that is potentially trusted;
    - Subscribers, actors that subscribe to services offered by TSPs;
    - Relying parties, actors that rely on services offered by TSPs. In such a context, the RP can also be referred to as the trustor, the entity that is trusting.
- Metadata: data provided about the services and data used within a trust model.

3 Large scale trust models

We will now briefly describe some operational large scale trust models, based on computational trust. For an introduction, refer to the IETF's RFC 5217, [2], [3] and [4]. For an introduction to PKI trust calculus, see [5].

3.1 PKI single root model

In this model all participants rely on a single key pair, the root. The root's private key is typically used to sign subordinate public keys, resulting in a certificate chain that can be verified up to the root. The root's private key is usually protected by storing it in trustworthy hardware, and its public key can be verified by for example publishing its hash in a newspaper. Illustrations include electronic banking operating under a public CA or an internal Closed User Group set-up where the bank enrols customers and/or their devices in an in-house PKI, as well as government PKIs. PKI architectures such as the Belgian eID PKI have a single root which is used to protect separate subscriber certificates for authentication and signature. Other approaches to combination exist, e.g. SWIFT combines the SWIFTNET PKI, an application-level PKI, with a VPN PKI. Other large scale single root models include the Credit Card Schemes PKIs, and the European Root Certification Authority (ERCA) PKI architecture for the EU-wide digital tachograph.

3.2 Bridge CA model

In this model CA's are cross certified by a Bridge CA, which acts as an interoperability mechanism for ensuring trust across disparate PKI domains. Such a Bridge CA does not issue certificates to end entities (except those required for its own operations) but establishes unilateral or bilateral cross-certification with other CAs.

The *US Federal PKI Trust Infrastructure* contains the Federal Bridge CA. Successful cross-certification with the FBCA asserts that the Applicant operates in accordance with the standards, guidelines and practices of the Federal PKI Policy Authority (FPKIPA) and of the Identity, Credential, and Access Management Subcommittee (ICAMSC). Levels of Assurance range from 1 to 4, and are based on OMB M-04-04 and NIST SP 800-63-2. Also the *Transglobal Secure Collaboration Program (TSCP)* operates as a Bridge CA, dedicated to the defence industry.

3.3 Trust List model

In this model multiple CA's and their roots coexist at peer level. A list of root certificates is made available typically through a directory. All root certificates are at peer level, there is no hierarchy involved. The list itself may be signed by the publisher. Examples include the ICAO Public Key Directory (PKD), TeleTrust's European Bridge Certification Authority (EBCA), and the European List of Trusted Lists. In the ICAO PKD model, Country Signing Certification Authorities (CSCA) sign certificates of Document Signer Certification Authorities (DSCA). The latter sign the contents of electronic Machine Readable Travel Documents (eMRTD) such as e-passports. TeleTrust's EBCA publishes member registration and certificates via a Trust List based on ETSI TS 102 231. With its signature, the European Bridge CA confirms the origin of members' certificates in the form of a trust list. A similar model is used by the EU List of Trusted Lists (LOTL), which constitutes a supervised oligarchy. The European Commission publishes a signed list containing pointers to the Member State Supervisory Bodies. The latter publish pointers to the actual TSPs under their supervision.

3.4 Mutual Trust model

In this model all participants decide who to trust, and may convey trust information to other participants. While this model has its advantages such as the possibility for the participants to take their own decisions on who exactly to trust, it also places some operational burdens on them, and it scales more difficultly than a single root or oligarchy model. It is used by the Pretty Good Privacy (PGP) email system, and similar systems.

3.5 Other

Many variations of trust models exist. Examples include 'circles of trust' and 'hub models' in healthcare, where delegation is possible. The worldwide telephony system relies on trust between Home Location Registers (HLR) and Visitor Location Registers (VLR) to authenticate local and roaming subscribers.

Various systems introduce privacy features in a PKI setting. For example the Austrian approach to electronic identification includes a 'Source-PIN' (an undisclosed Personal Identification Number) from which sector-specific PINs are derived. The Source-PIN may only be stored on the citizen card, and is thus under the sole control of the citizen. In this manner, sector specific applications (including in the private sector) can derive their own ID numbers without giving them the ability to link data together. The Dutch Parelsnoer Biobank has a trust model that guarantees anonymity which can be conditionally revoked. In Germany, the electronic Personal Ausweiss (ePA) contains three different applications: "electronic identification (eID)", "Biometric application (ePass)", and "electronic signing (eSign)". Each application has its own trust model and is protected against possible misuse by access control mechanisms based on a dedicated PKI.

Furthermore Peer to Peer systems such as TOR, I2P, and Bitcoin have trust models without the concept of a central authority.

4 Comparison of trust models

We will now compare the trust models put forward by ICAO's global PKI Directory, the EU eIDAS regulation, the US FICAM model and Bitcoin's Blockchain trust model for virtual money. For this purpose, we first provide more details about each of these four trust models. Subsequently we compare them.

4.1 ICAO PKD

The ICAO PKD trust model is based on a Memorandum Of Understanding (MOU), signed by all participants. These participants are States issuing electronic machine readable travel documents (eMRTDs) according to the specifications of ICAO Doc 9303. An eMRTD's integrity is protected by a digital signature (referred to as Passive Authentication) supported by the following PKI components:

- Country Signing CA (CSCA): Every State establishes a CSCA as its national trust point in the context of eMRTD's. The CSCA issues public key certificates for one or more (national) Document Signers.
- Document Signers (DS): A Document Signer digitally signs data to be stored on eMRTD's; this signature is stored on the eMRTD's in a Document Security Object.

The States exchange CSCA certificates bilaterally or through the PKD Master Lists. The core trust services of the PKD are operated by Netrust, who publishes this list of CSCA Master Lists, as well as DS certificates and CRL revocation information.

Each State produces its own list of CSCA certificates that is relied on in the inspection process. Compiling this list is based on diplomatic exchanges and subsequent verification processes. A State may countersign its Master List of received certificates as part of the diplomatic exchange. It may publish this Master List to the PKD. CSCA Master Lists are compiled and signed by a dedicated Master Lister Signer. It is at the receiving State's discretion to determine the way it verifies and uses the received certificates.

For completeness, it should be mentioned that other PKIs are involved in eMRTD processing. Issuing States may include biometric features of the document owner and protect the access thereto by Extended Access Control (EAC) certificates. Furthermore, PKIs are used to secure communications between the various elements of the Inspection Systems front and back offices.

4.2 EU's eIDAS

In this trust model, described in [6], States may notify the European Commission of the electronic identity system they operate. As a consequence of this notification, the notifying State's electronic identities become recognised in the other States that already notified. For electronic Trust Service Providers (TSPs) it is possible to qualify their services. This results in supervision of the TSP by a Supervisory Body and in improved legal effect of the usage of these services.

The trust model is based on specifications (EU 910/2014 and ETSI), a compliance mechanism, and services provided by TSPs. The European Commission creates a signed top-level Trust List, referred to as the List Of Trusted Lists (LOTL). The LOTL contains pointers to the Supervisory Bodies in the Member States, who publish their national Trust List (TL). These TLs contain pointers to the TSPs under supervision, and their root certificates.

It can be observed that the eIDAS regulation ('Regulation of the European Commission on electronic identification and trust services for electronic transactions in the internal market', EU 910/2014) introduced the concept of a [Qualified] Trust Service Provider. However, the term 'trust' is not defined in the regulation. Rather, the term 'Trust Service' is defined in Article 3, (16). It can be summarised as electronic service normally provided for remuneration, which consists a.o. of creation, verification and validation of electronic signatures, seals, timestamps, registered delivery services and certificates, as well as certificates for website authentication and preservation services.

4.3 US Federal Identity, Credential, and Access Management (FICAM)

In this trust model, organizations that define a trust framework and certify entities compliant with it are called Trust Framework Providers (TFPs). Once a TFP has been adopted by the FICAM TFS Program, it then has the ability to assess and certify various identity services such as Token Managers, which provide the authentication functions; Identity Managers, which provide the identity proofing and attribute management functions; and Credential Service Providers, which provide a full service capability that combines authentication, identity proofing and the secure binding of token(s) to identity.

Identity services that have been qualified by a FICAM TFS-adopted Trust Framework Provider may optionally apply to the FICAM TFS Program to request approval for the authority to offer their identity services to the Federal Government. Applying to the FICAM TFS Program is optional because some qualified providers may not intend to provide their services to the Federal Government.

The *Authority To Offer Services (ATOS)* for FICAM TFS Approved Identity Services defines the process by which an Applicant, who has been qualified by a FICAM Adopted Trust Framework Provider (TFP) to meet FICAM Trust Framework Solutions (TFS) Privacy and Security requirements, can apply to the FICAM TFS Program to be approved to offer their services to the U.S. Federal Government. The applicant's responsibilities are then laid down in a *Memorandum Of Agreement*.

4.4 Blockchain model

The blockchain is the trust model underlying virtual currencies such as Bitcoin, as well as other innovative concepts such as the DNSChain, an alternative for DNSSec.

The Bitcoin trust model based is based on a combination of Elliptic Curve Cryptography (ECC) and what can be described as emergent convergence amongst peers through Proof Of Work (POW). Nodes compete in first finding a hash of a block of recently completed transactions, the candidate block. The hash should start with a number of zeros. To find such a hash, a certain amount of calculations must be performed, which constitutes the Proof Of Work.

It is inherently a P2P solution with a publicly available reference implementation of the standard node ('full node'). Such a full node includes a wallet, a miner, a full blockchain copy and network functionality. The wallet contains ECC keypair(s) and Bitcoin addresses, which are hashes of public keys. The miner contains functionality to build a candidate block and to compete for finding a nonce that will complement the candidate block's transaction content in such a way that the resulting hash of nonce and transaction content will meet the required difficulty threshold. The full blockchain copy contains all blocks up to the first (`Genesis`) block. When a miner is the first to find the nonce for that candidate block, he can insert a new Bitcoin value of which he is the owner in the version of the candidate block that will become the next block in the chain. In this way the miner is rewarded for his work. Over time, the difficulty of finding the nonce increases because the hash has to contain an increasing number of leading zeros. And the new Bitcoin value that can be inserted by the winning miner decreases. The network functionality consists of P2P functionality to forward transactions and winning blocks within the network.

Reference Client ('Full node')

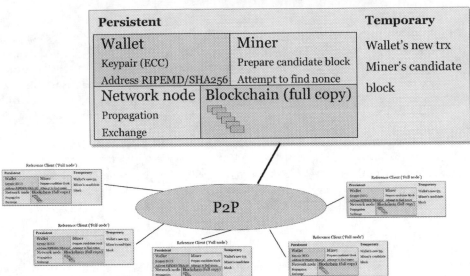

Fig. 1: Bitcoin core model

In this trust model, following components contribute to trust. The Bitcoins include a digital signature with payer identification based on ECC. The publicly available blockchain can easily be verified by everybody, as hashes can easily be checked without a need for significant computing power or any external trust. As the blockchain contains the history of spending, a payee can easily validate that the Bitcoin has not been spent before by the same payer.

4.5 Comparison

The comparison between these four trust models is presented in the two tables below.

Table 1: a comparison of the different actors involved.

	ICAO PKD	eIDAS	US FICAM	Bitcoin (blockchain)
Actor: initiator	ICAO Council	European Commission / European Parliament (legislative)	Fed CIO Council (administrative)	"Satoshi Nakamoto"
Actor: governor/ oversight	PKD Board	EC/EP	OMB	P2P model with reference implementation
Actor: operator	Netrust (SG)	EC and Member States	GSA and TFS program	Individual nodes and exchanges
Actor: assessors	Self-assessment	SB, EA and CABs	GSA-TFPAP, TFP AAs	n/a
Actor: subscribers	Travellers from ICAO members	EU Citizens	C2G/B2G	Anyone
Actor: relying parties	IS of visited countries	Primarily PS	Fed Agencies	Anyone

Table 2: comparison of the other main attributes of these four trust models.

	ICAO PKD	eIDAS	US FICAM	Bitcoin (blockchain)
Objective	Worldwide authenticity of travel document & bearer	Enhance trust in electronic transactions (EU eID and Trust Services) for the Internal Market, for Natural and Legal Persons	US electronic Identity plus management of credentials and access, of NP for Federal Gov	Worldwide dematerialised money (fiduciary)
Mechanism	MOU	EU Regulation (mandatory for Member States) + ESO M460	FICAM Program (ICAM, FPKI, TFS, HSPD-12, FIPS 201) – "rules for participation"	Voluntary participation
Impacts	Participating States	EU-based IdPs that want to have their credentials recognised by MS public sector Relying Parties. TSPs that want their services to have legal effect.	US Fed Agencies and private sector TFPs that want to have their credentials trusted by US Fed Agencies	Payer/payees willing to accept bitcoins
Structuring principle	Participation by eM-RTD Authority (EMA)	Notification for eID (low, substantial, high), discretionary qualification of TS (electronic, advanced, qualified) with supervision	Authority To Offer Services (ATOS) through TFS program for service delivery to FedGov	Mining (finding a hashvalue that meets specific constraints)
Conformity mechanism	Registration procedure and test bench procedure	MS notification of eID to EC/MS SB registration in LOTL, MS SB's TL	TFS ATOS and TFP (OIX, Kantara, …) assessment	n/a
Supporting hw/sw/ standards	ISO/X.509	ETSI/CEN M460	ISPPAP, NIST SP 800 series and FIPS 201 (PIV)	Compliance to reference implementation
Regulations	PKD Regulations	EU 910/2014 + IAs	FICAM (supported by SP 800-63) – FISMA (supported by SP 800-53)	Electronic money regulations
Machine readable information	Machine readable error codes for non-conformant entries in the PKD	LOTL and TLs	TFP metadata	Blockchain
Liability	ICAO MOU Art 6: ICAO exempt, participants for their own errors/omissions	Identity (Art. 11): in X-border trx, notifying MS, issuer, operator of the authentication procedure. Trust Services (Art. 13): TSPs	Identity proofing: CAB, but TFPAP limited to technical compliance	Own responsibility. When using a service provider, some contractual liability may be provided

4.5.1 Similarities

Many traditional large-scale trust models such as ICAO PKD, eIDAS and FICAM are organised as oligarchies, based on some form of a trust list. There is no single root of trust or a hierarchy.

Roles and corresponding accountability include initiator, operator, compliance assessor and participants. Segregation between these roles is common.

From operational and compliance perspectives, multiple layers of actors are involved. In the case of eIDAS, there is the Commission that publishes the LOTL, the Member State Supervisory Bodies that publish their Trust List, the Conformity Assessment Bodies that assess the TSPs. In the case of FICAM there is collection of TFPs and services provided compliant to these TFPs requirements, with compliance demonstrated via ATOS, TFPAP and TFP Assurance Assessors.

4.5.2 Differences

The main differences include:
- While eIDAS aims at establishing legal effect, US FICAM does not. US FICAM's conformity assessment is limited to technical compliance, legal consequences are out of scope.
- While eIDAS includes natural and legal persons, US FICAM is focused on natural persons.
- Most models have been created for a specific purpose in a specific context, and the trust established through them does not easily transfer to other circumstances.

The blockchain model as used by e.g. Bitcoin is inherently different from the other models described, as it is based on a combination of computational trust and a distributed transaction log verifiable by everyone, and no central point of trust. It can also be observed that the liability model is application-specific, and that Bitcoin has no liability model.

5 Related and future work

The exact functioning and role of trust models from vendors such as Microsoft or Adobe, as well as from the CAB Forum could also be analysed in a similar way. The trust models underlying Chinese and Russian trust ecosystems could be a topic of future research, as well as the interoperability between US, European, Chinese, Russian and similar trust models.

It can be observed that both in Europe and in the US, the concept of a Trust Mark is being introduced. Such a Trust Mark aims to provide assurance about the trust provided, by providing information on the conformance criteria and the conformity assessment process followed.

6 Conclusions

On a global scale, transactions are usually performed in an ecosystem that has no default trust mechanisms. The ICAO trust model and its oligarchy is an illustration how global trust can be established. As also illustrated by the eIDAS trust model, oligarchies are a common model for establishing large scale trust.

Large scale trust models such as US FICAM and eIDAS are composed of collections of trust frameworks, with segregation of duties between specifying, assessing compliance and operating the components that implement those frameworks.

Multiple large scale trust models co-exist and trust is being bridged across the individual trust models, as is illustrated by the mutual recognition initiatives by bridge CAs.

The emerging blockchain model is inherently different but holds great potential.

References

[1] Marc Sel. Using the semantic web to generate trust indicators. In Sachar Paulus, Norbert Pohlman, and Helmut Reimer, editors, Securing business processes, pages 106-119. Vieweg+Tuebner, Springer Science+Business Media, 2014.

[2] An overview of PKI Trust Models – Radia Perlman – IEEE Network November/December 1999

[3] NIST-SP-800-39 Managing Information Security Risk Appendix G Trust Models – 2011

[4] The Handbook of Applied Cryptography, CRC Press, 1997, Section 1.11.3 on trusted third parties and public-key certificates

[5] Jingwei Huang and David Nicol. A Calculus of Trust and its Application to PKI and identity management. In Proceedings of IDTrust 2009, April 14-16, 2009 Gaithers-burg, MD, USA. ACM, 2009.

[6] European Parliament DG Connect and European Council. Regulation 910/2014 of the European Parliament and of the Council of 23 July 2014 on electronic identification and trust services for electronic transactions in the internal market and repealing Directive 1999/93/EC. European Commission, 2014. EC 910/2014.

A Reference Model for a Trusted Service Guaranteeing Web-content

Mihai Togan · Ionut Florea

107A, Oltenitei Rd., Building C1, ground floor, Bucharest, Romania
certSIGN
{mihai.togan | ionut.florea }@certsign.ro

Abstract

In this paper we propose a model for a trusted service designed for collecting web information and aiming to guarantee the web content and its presentation format for a long term. The research identifies two usage scenarios: the web content providers that need to prove that certain information was published at a specific moment in time and the end users who visit web pages and may also need to be able to demonstrate later on that certain information was available on-line. The particularities of each scenario are taken into consideration throughout the paper. Both scenarios must tackle a complex problem, related to the dynamic web content, and use long term electronic signature formats (we considered the ETSI's archiving signature formats) and time stamps, in order to guarantee the integrity and authenticity of the information. In both cases, the archiving of the web content will be conducted exclusively by the proposed trusted service, using strong security mechanisms and protocols that preserve the authenticity, integrity and non-repudiation.

1 Introduction

Since World Wide Web was invented over a quarter century ago, it has developed from enthusiastic early adopters in research institutes and Universities to mass market, counting about 3 billion users in 2014, according to ITU's Measuring the Information Society Report 2014 [ITU14]. One of the challenges the web faces today is the ability to guarantee, with a high degree of reliability, the content available to a user at a certain moment of time. This is a complex issue, considering not only the various formats of the content (e.g. text, images, video, voice, etc.), but also the sources of information, from static web pages to database queries and content aggregated from multiple providers. From our knowledge, a complete solution is not available at this moment, although some proposals such as Web ARChive (WARC), Trusted Archive Protocol (TAP), ETSI's CAdES/XAdES formats and ISO 28500 exist and could be of interest in this field [CW03, CAdES, XAdES, ISO28500].

As the technology is continuously evolving, the web content and the way it is presented to the end user are permanently updated. Legal framework, industry specific standards, compliance as well as litigation requirements do not keep pace all the time with ever-changing technology. Nowadays, a significant part of the information is presented directly within the web browser; therefore, a classic approach that involves usage of static electronic documents together with electronic signatures and time stamps is not completely scalable to fulfil this new model. Long term archiving of the content presented on-line is a new challenge. It can use previous established technologies and legal framework, but they need to adapt.

The research described in this paper proposes a model for a trusted service designed for collecting web information and aiming to guarantee for a long term the web content and its presentation format. In this regard, the paper defines the model of a Trusted Third party (TTP) that provides reliable and legal binding web archiving service. In defining of the requirements, the current particularities of the web content were envisaged. The architecture identified for our service includes web crawlers, to identify and collect the content, the central system where the content is stored and the component for archiving the content and guaranteeing for it.

The rest of the paper is organized as follows: in Section 2, we make some considerations regarding the web-content long-term archiving. Section 3 contains the proposal for a trusted service which aims to collect, archive and guarantee the web-content. In this regard, two scenarios are taken into consideration. Section 4 presents some legal aspects provided by the applicable regulations. Finally, conclusions are outlined in Section 5.

2 Long-term Archiving

In certain areas, there are guidelines and requirements regarding the preservation of on-line content, such as the Regulatory notice 11-39 issued in the Unites States of America, by the Financial Industry Regulatory Authority's (FINRA) [RN11-39]. The regulatory notice is related to the obligations of a firm to keep records of communications made through social media depending on whether the content of the communication constitutes a business communication. This clearly stipulates that, for the data published using the IT infrastructure of an organization, it is the responsibility of that organization to capture, preserve and present them in a legally binding/forensically acceptable manner if requested.

When talking about long term archiving, there are two main aspects that must be considered:
1. availability of the information; and
2. preservation of data integrity;

The lifetime of the content from an electronic document can be longer than the lifetime of the storage mechanisms or the data presentation formats. Therefore, a long term archiving solution should cover long term availability of the information, as well as migration of information in new formats, to provide compatibility with the updated hardware and software environment. Several data preservation proposals consider the aspects regarding the data format, but they are not able to guarantee long term data integrity. Nevertheless, an electronic archiving solution must consider several key elements, such as lifetime of storage media, disaster recovery mechanisms, increasing computational power, advances in cryptanalysis of the algorithms and updates of the hardware and software technologies.

A single long term archiving strategy is not available nowadays. Organizations archiving information can choose between several techniques and use either rudimentary solutions, until a clear trend is established, or adhere to one of the proposals that emerges from the working groups with concerns in long term archiving:
- Data replication (cloning) and validating data by comparing several clones;

- Hashing mechanisms;
- A combination between data replication and hashing, such as project LOCKSS (Lots Of Copies Keep Stuff Safe) from Stanford University [LOCKSS];
- Usage of electronic signature and the features CAdES-A and XAdES-A provide for long term archiving [CAdES, XAdES];
- Trusted Archive Protocol (TAP), Evidence Record Syntax (ERS) and Long-Term Archiving and Notary Service (LTANS) from IETF [CW03, RFC4998, RFC6283, BSW09];
- Web ARChive (WARC) format that specifies a method for combining multiple digital resources into an aggregate archival file together with related information;
- Open Archival Information System (OAIS) defined by the Consultative Committee for Space Data Systems and adopted also by other organizations, besides the space agencies.

To be able to easily search and retrieve, the content metadata are used within the archiving systems. Metadata or "data about data" offer a structured way of describing the content to allow data owners and users to interpret and use it correctly. There are numerous metadata standards, specific for different domains. For the on-line resources, Dublin Core Metadata Element Set was defined and maintained by The Dublin Core Metadata Initiative [DCMI].

The requirements for the archiving service are different, depending on the users who use such services and their needs. The basic functionality of such a service is the storage and data acquisition. The service must ensure continuous maintenance and update of archived data, in order to provide access to this data, ensuring their integrity and presentation formats that are compatible for long term preservation. Trusted archiving systems have data storage mechanisms that also ensure the necessary proof of their integrity. Data integrity must be ensured by the archiving system and the service is responsible for providing evidence that this property is guaranteed. The integrity evidence is periodically generated or obtained in such a way as to form a continuous chain that ensures data integrity from their archiving time, until their verification. The evidence can be generated internally, by the archiving service, or it can be obtained from an external trusted service. For example, trusted anchors for an electronic signature can be obtained from a Certification Authority (CA) and time stamps can be obtained from a Time Stamping Authority (TSA).

The adopted standard for web archive container files is WARC. It is an ISO standard [ISO28500] and its main scope is to ensure a file format for web content archiving.

Worldwide, there are many initiatives for archiving web content, with the aim to collect and preserve the web content. Such initiatives include:

- Internet Archive Wayback Machine [IAWM15] is a service for archiving web pages. It also offers a search engine for the approximately 485 billion archived pages. Using the Wayback Machine users are able to access content that is no longer available on the Internet, at least in its original location. Internet Archive project supports and relies on Heritrix crawler [HER15] which is the Internet Archive's open-source, extensible, scalable, archival-quality Web crawler able to archive web content in web specific formats (WARC).
- Aleph Archives [AA15] targets corporations, institutions and governments seeking to keep web content regardless of its format (web, forums, media, etc.). It uses a technology based on distributed crawlers, browser plugin called ArchiView for data access, a performant search engine and near real-time indexing. In addition to these technologies, Aleph Archives developed a set of web monitoring tools called "Web Archiving Bucket" [WAB]. The tools include: WSE – WARC Search Engine, UXTR – Universal Links Extrac-

tor, KEN – Personal Web Archiving, WSDK – Warc Software Development Kit, TRENS
– character encodings convertor. Aleph Archives solution proposes two platforms: KEN –
desktop application and CAMA – ArchiView – web browser plugin that allows accessing,
sharing, searching and exporting archives.

- Another web archiving solution is the one proposed by Hanzo Archives [HA15]. Similar
  to the other two solutions, it collects website content in native format. Hanzo proposed
  three variants of capturing content: Client-side archiving, Transaction archiving, and
  Server-side archiving.

In order to preserve the authenticity and integrity of the archived content several methods are
available:

- Electronic signature – data in electronic form which are attached to or logically associated
  with other electronic data and which are used by the signatory to sign; [REU910].
- Merkle trees – a tree in which every non-leaf node is labelled with the hash of the labels of
  its children nodes [Merk80].
- CAdES-A electronic signature format – CAdES (CMS Advanced Electronic Signatures) is
  a set of extensions to Cryptographic Message Syntax (CMS) signed data making it suitable
  for advanced electronic signature. CAdES- A adds the possibility of periodical timestamp-
  ing of the archived document to prevent compromise caused by weakening signatures
  during long-time storage period [CAdES].

For the proposed solution the, CAdES-A electronic signature format was considered.

3 Proposal for Trusted Service Guaranteeing Web-Content

As the web evolves, the archiving of the web content must follow. It should be approached both
from the archiving policy and supporting technology. These choices should be considered carefully against business objectives, before a design and implementation decision is made. The main
differences lie in the capture and access methods used. We identified two main methods to retrieve and archive the web content:

Site request archiving, where the provider of the web content/ web site owner uses the service of
a TTP to guarantee that at a specific moment of time the web site was presenting a certain content, guaranteeing the format, the authenticity and integrity of the information

Client request archiving, where a user browsing a web site uses the Trusted Third Party (TTP)
to guarantee that a specific web page he was visiting existed in that format at a specific moment
of time.

3.1 Site request archiving

Site request archiving allows the owner of the content to initiate the archiving and preservation
process. Besides collecting and archiving the web content, the solution approaches several specific challenges, generated by the dynamic content that is published on-line, on the one side, and
by the differences between the way the content is presented to the users within the web browser
and the way it is stored within the databases and on the web servers, on the other side. Various

technologies are used nowadays for publishing web content and the interactive web pages are elements to be considered when planning for archiving, in order to allow their preservation and further presentation.

The components of the Site request archiving system provide the following:
- The guarantee that the archived information was collected from a certain web page;
- The information published from different sources and in different formats on a web page is collected and it can be presented in the same integrated format, at any further moment of time, guaranteeing its integrity and authenticity;
- In case of litigation, the information can be presented and recognized in court.

The archiving system will run as a TTP, independent from the web content/ web sites owners. The integrity and authenticity of the archived content is realized through cryptographic mechanisms that are using long term electronic signatures and time stamping. The TTP also provides a service that can demonstrate at a further moment in time the origin of the content and its integrity. The web content/ web sites owners will be able to demonstrate, even in court, that certain content was presented at a certain moment of time on their web site. To achieve these goals the TTP system is offering several other features:
- Web crawler functionalities allowing collecting and secure archiving the web content;
- Automatic archiving of the content from the web site, including detection of updated content;
- Archived information preserves the presentation format from the target web site.

Several distinct modules where designed in order to implement the TTP system:
- **WebCrawler** – collects site content and metadata. It uses Heritrix and stores the content in ARC/WARC archives.
- **LongTimeSignature** – provides long term content authenticity and integrity while binding the archived content with the source web site. It applies CAdES-A detached signatures and time stamps (*signature-time-stamp* and *archive-time-stamp-v3*) on WARC archives.
- **Archive** – provides electronic archiving for the collected information.
- **SignatureUpdater** – periodically updates the information regarding the authenticity and integrity of the content. This monitors the information stored in the archive and refreshes the electronic signatures when required, by adding a new *archive-time-stamp-v3* attribute to the CAdES-A signature. The refreshed content is provided back to the Archive. The signature refreshing policies can be configured.
- **ContentPresentation** – provides information search, retrieval and presentation of the archived content. When presenting the content, it verifies the CAdES-A signatures and provides information about its status.

Each module presents a specific communication interface, allowing communication in a standardized way: the WebCrawler connects to the web site using http protocol, guaranteeing that the content is collected in the same format as presented by the website. From the WebCrawler, the information is stored in files that are transmitted between the other components.

To guarantee the authenticity and integrity of the content, the TTP system uses security mechanisms provided through Public Key Infrastructures (PKI):
- Digital certificates issued by a Certification Authority for electronic signature and secure communication;
- Validation services of digital certificates using OCSP interface [RFC6960];

- Time stamp services according to RFC 3161 [RFC3161];

For legal compliance, the PKI services can be provided by qualified trust services providers according to EU Regulation 910/2014.

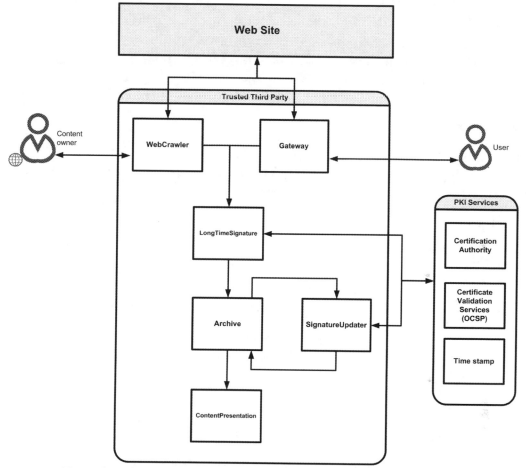

Fig. 1: The architecture of the TTP service for the web-content archiving and guaranteeing

3.2 Client request archiving

Client request archiving allows a user visiting different websites to request the TTP to archive specific web pages, together with all the information that guarantees long term authenticity and integrity as well as the origin of the web page.

Client request archiving has a similar architecture as the Site request archiving, excepting the WebCrawler. This is replaced by a web gateway that allows the user to connect, browse the web pages and generate upon request a screenshot that will be included within the archive. Each screenshot involves rendering the web page and then generating the corresponding image. To archive a certain web page, the user performs the following operations:

1. The user authenticates to the web gateway operated by the TTP, using a digital certificate. Each user shall have his/her own account and user space allocated by the TTP.

2. The user provides the URL of the site and the gateway presents the web page.

3. The user is able to browse the site through the gateway.

4. On user request, the TTP retrieves the web page, generates the image file and initiates the long-time archiving process.

4 Legal Aspects

International, EU and national legislations, industry-specific standards, compliance requirements and other internal regulations of different organizations have impact on what web content can be archived and made accessible either by the organization or by a Trusted Third Party. Besides the technical means to retrieve and preserve the content a key element is the ability to present it to a court of justice.

The EU Regulation No 910/2014 on electronic identification and trust services for electronic transactions in the internal market [REU910] defines the trusted services for electronic transactions.

> 'trust service' means an electronic service normally provided for remuneration which consists of:
> (a) the creation, verification, and validation of electronic signatures, electronic seals or electronic time stamps, electronic registered delivery services and certificates related to those services, or
> (b) the creation, verification and validation of certificates for website authentication; or
> (c) the preservation of electronic signatures, seals or certificates related to those services;

Although the regulation extends the category of trust services from the Directive 1999/93/EC, enforcing the legal value of documents in electronic format, it does not cover an important activity related to the usage of electronic documents, namely their trusted archiving.

Within the EU boundaries, there are several options, in order to establish a new type of TTP offering reliable and legal binding web archiving service:

1. National legislation is established in order to regulate the archiving and presentation the web content before a court. This can help establish national markets, but it lacks international recognition and entails cross-jurisdiction issues. If outside own country, any litigation can become complicated to present and expensive to sustain.

2. Interpret the text of the Regulation No 910/2014 in such way that specific implementations of electronic signatures, electronic seals, time stamp, electronic delivery services or usage of qualified certificates for websites authentication can also provide a complete implementation for a trusted web content legal binding archiving service. As long as the regulation does not envisage from the beginning the implementation of a trusted web

content archiving service, it is improbable that the secondary legislation that is currently under preparation would cover this aspect. Without this, a uniform approach will not be possible, the implementations depending on specific legal interpretations and they will not be able to guarantee smooth cross-border recognisance.

3. Legislation regarding web archiving is established at the EU level. This shall have both legal and technical implications, as it will define a common legal framework across EU and will allow implication of ETSI and other technical bodies with mandate to define a technical baseline that will permit interoperability and standardization.

4. Industry driven approach, with a de-facto technical solution gaining momentum and being recognized across countries.

5 Conclusions

Capturing and preserving web content presents a series of specific challenges, due, on the one hand to the dynamism and continuous update of the published content and, on the other hand, to the differences between the way aggregated content is presented to the end users, which is different from the way information is stored within databases and web servers. Different technologies available today for publishing information on web sites and the permanent interaction between the end user and the web pages are elements that are making difficult collecting of web content in order to archive and present it at a further moment while preserving the format as well as guaranteeing its authenticity and integrity.

In the paper, we proposed the architecture of a TTP able to guarantee the web content. The TTP can act in two different usage scenarios:

1. Web content providers are able to demonstrate at a further moment in time that certain information was present on their web site, in a specific format and at a specific moment of time

2. Users browsing web sites are able to demonstrate at a further moment in time that certain information was presented to them on a web site, in a specific format and at a specific moment of time

From the legal perspective, without a clear legislation the recognition of the archived web content will be difficult, especially in cross-border litigations. Establishing a uniform legislation at EU level can leverage the establishment of TTPs providing reliable and legal binding web archiving service.

Common legislation will help enhancing trust in the online environment, as key to economic and social development, and broaden the scope and applicability of the services defined within the EU regulation 910/2014 as creating electronic content with legal value without establishing a trusted way to preserve and present such information over time may induce weaknesses and lower the adoption rates. Besides this, it can generate enough traction to involve standardization bodies such as ETSI to propose a technical baseline that can create the appropriate conditions for the mutual recognition and interoperability of web archiving across the European Union.

Another approach is the industry-generated adoption, which may be able to promote a generally recognized standard, as well as best practices and a reference model. Such model can be further formalized in a future RFC and/or ISO standard.

Acknowledgements

This work was funded by the Romanian National Authority for Scientific Research (CNCS-UE-FISCDI) under the project PN-II-IN-DPST-2012-1-0087 (ctr. 10DPST/2013).

References

[AA15] Aleph Archives, http://aleph-archives.com/

[BSW09] A. Jerman Blazic, P. Sylvester, C. Wallace, "Long Term Archive Protocol (LTAP)", Internet-Draft, 2009

[CAdES] ETSI TS 101 733, "CMS Advanced Electronic Signatures (CAdES)", 2013.

[CW03] S. Chokhani, C. Wallace, "Trusted Archive Protocol", PKIX Internet Draft, February 2003

[DCMI] The Dublin Core Metadata Initiative, http://dublincore.org/

[HA15] Hanzo Archives, http://www.hanzoarchives.com

[HER15] Heritrix archival web crawler project, https://webarchive.jira.com/wiki/display/Heritrix

[ITU14] The International Telecommunication Union (ITU), "Measuring the Information Society Report", 2014

[IAWM15] Internet Archive Wayback Machine, https://archive.org/

[ISO28500] ISO 28500:2009, "Information and documentation -- WARC file format", 2009.

[LOCKSS] The LOCKSS Program, http://www.lockss.org/

[Merk80] R. C. Merkle, "Protocols for public key cryptosystems". Proceedings of the 1980 Symposium on Security and Privacy, IEEE Computer Society Press, 1980

[REU910] Regulation (EU) No 910/2014 of the European Parliament and of the Council of 23 July 2014 on electronic identification and trust services for electronic transactions in the internal market and repealing Directive 1999/93/EC, 2014

[RFC3161] C. Adams, P. Cain, D. Pinkas, R. Zuccherato, "Time-Stamp Protocol (TSP)", Internet Standard, RFC 3161, 2001

[RFC4998] T. Gondrom, R. Brandner, U. Pordesch, "Evidence Record Syntax (ERS)", Internet Standard, RFC 4998, 2007

[RFC6283] A. Jerman Blazic, T. Gondrom, "Extensible Markup Language Evidence Record Syntax (XM-LERS)", Internet Standard, RFC 6283, 2011

[RFC6960] S. Santesson, M. Myers, R. Ankney, A. Malpani, S. Galperin, C. Adams, "Online Certificate Status Protocol – OCSP", Internet Standard, RFC 6960, 2013

[RN11-39] Financial Industry Regulatory Authority's ("FINRA"), "Regulatory notice 11-39 – Social Media Websites and the Use of Personal Devices for Business Communications", 2011

[XAdES] ETSI TS 101 903, "XML Advanced Electronic Signatures (XAdES)", 2010

[WAB] Web Archiving Bucket, http://webarchivingbucket.com

Authentication and eID

Architectural Elements of a Multidimensional Authentication

Libor Neumann

ANECT a.s., Vídeňská 125, 619 00 Brno, Czech Republic
Libor.Neumann@anect.com

Abstract

Today's ICT environment is significantly different from the environment, where the currently used eID architectures were developed. Mobile devices (such as tablets or phones) are available for anyone today. These devices use advanced application management systems, leading communication mediums and ever-growing range of peripherals.

Attackers have ever-increasing incentives as the assets on the Internet, and specifically in "the cloud", grow in value with the overall growth and development of the Internet. They employ a higher computation force, more sophisticated methods and unique tools. Moreover, these attackers often operate from countries, where the violation of cybercrime laws holds little or no penalty. There is also the increasing risk of a cyber-war.

The paper describes selected elements of a new eID architecture and the experience from their practical implementation. The eID architecture is based on published Distributed Identity Infrastructure (DII) concept, which is remarkable for its fully automated life cycle of electronic identities, user-friendly experience and easy integration to ICT systems.

The presentation deals with two main ideas:
- Replacing the static protection of an electronic identity with a dynamic protection
- Complex protection of the cyber/electronic identity in its whole life cycle (including emergency situations) and the protection of the communication channel itself.

1 Introduction

In recent years, important events took place in the area of ICT, especially in the field of eID. Here are some of them:
- The progress of ICT and the Internet in particular has reached a state, in which the possibilities of the most widely used method of authentication, loginname/password, were definitively exhausted. The reason is that the requirements imposed on a user in real life exceeded human capabilities. This is one of the reasons for significant increase in number of successful cyber attacks.
- There is an apparent shift from understanding eID from authentication alone to an eID ecosystem, it means to the knowledge that the attacker always uses the weakest element of the whole ecosystem. Therefore new methods how to evaluate the quality of the eID ecosystem, such as AAL or QAA, were created [WiBu11, HuLE09].
- There have been successful attacks on manufacturers specializing in security hardware via the Internet or their own internal ICT systems [HuLE09, Zett15].

- The possibilities of attackers, their knowledge and available resources have increased significantly. Also the damage caused by successful attacks has increased significantly. The motivation of the attackers also grows with their increasing success, the volume of investments in the attacks increases.
- There has been a significant spread of mobile devices (smartphones, tablets, etc.). Thus, a significant increase in availability and popularity of computing power in the hands of the user.
- Even though trials have continued for decades and tremendous effort and considerable resources have been invested, no solution of the eID ecosystem or eID technology has managed to replace the use of passwords.

There is an idea to use popular and massively available equipment for a new solution of the eID ecosystem. However this requires a different approach to the challenge.

In the past we published some basic ideas and solutions that are directed towards such goal. This is a fully automated cyber identity securely connected to the real identity of the user [Neum08, Neum12b], a distributed topology of authentication service using the idea of deployment of a universal identity device (UID) [Neum14] and a special universal authentication cryptographic protocol [NeKl11].

To solve the problem, it was necessary to solve other challenges such as:
- Prevention of an attack on the weakest parts of the eID ecosystem
- Change of approach to protection of critical resources of the eID ecosystem, so that it is possible to use commonly available hardware and not rely on specialized "secure" hardware.

The article formulates two basic ideas of eID resources architecture:
- Replacement of static protection of electronic identity with dynamic protection
- Comprehensive protection of cyber identity throughout its life cycle, including the solution of emergency situations and protection of communication channel.

2 Dynamic Protection

Replacement of static defense by movable, mechanized or automated defense is not a new idea. In military field this shift has already been happening for many centuries. Ancient and medieval fortresses and cities protected by walls have been replaced by mobile weapons such as tanks, which are now being replaced by automatic weapons such as e.g. unmanned aircrafts.

It is a new approach in the field of eID. Classical solutions of strong authentication are built on specialized certified hardware. All security features are built into this hardware during the manufacture. Their use is thus limited by security features built-in during their manufacturing.

Such solution has its significant system weaknesses. Here are some of them:
- In case of second factor protection of cryptomaterial it is user complexity and limited security. Regardless of the purpose, the user must enter the second factor every time to be able to use protected cryptomaterial. This leads to unnecessary increase in terms of using the second factor and to the dissatisfaction of the user.

- It also means reduced security in the event of attacker's assault. If the attacker has the hardware in his/her possesion, what he/she must overcome are only the built in barriers of isolated hardware that was developed and manufactured many months or years ago. The attacker can use a variety of side-channel attacks (e.g. analysis of energy supply consumption), including the possibility of attack on manufacturer's information system [HuLE09, Zett15]. If such attack is successful, the attacker cannot be distinguished from an authorized user.

Dynamic protection does not rely on protected hardware. It uses speed, communication and computing power of the standard hardware. It works with higher amount of cryptomaterial, with several keys, some of which have a very short lifetime. Any use of eID will change at least one key. The method of working with many keys is adjusted to potential loss of communication; and evaluation algorithms are able to recognize and tolerate a certain number of failures.

Also, the use of the second factor is dynamic and driven by security context. The second factor is not used to protect cryptomaterial, but to reduce the risk that the eID device is used by unauthorized person. The user does not have to enter the second factor at every start and every use of his/her eID device. The second factor is required only in situations, in which the security risks demand it. For example, when confirming a transactions exceeding corresponding limit.

At the same time the second factor is evaluated dually, i.e. when evaluating it the eID devices cooperate with the server. The second factor is not stored anywhere, not even in encrypted form and values with high entropy are transmitted through the network.

This brings new user experience and new security. It is possible to distinguish between a random attack or a brute force attack from an attack, in which the attacker has the right eID device and tries to break the second factor. The attacker cannot attack the second factor separately; the service provider knows about any attempt and can react accordingly.

3 Complete Protection of the eID Ecosystem

It is a well known fact that security of a whole unit is limited by the weakest element. It is known that authentication is an atomic element of ICT security. Thus, the weakest element of the eID ecosystem limits the overall security of the information system. This applies regardless of whether this element has been or has not been included in the security targets.

On the contrary, elements of the eID ecosystem not included in the security targets are an unknown threat and a great opportunity for the attackers. Here are examples of such often neglected elements:

- Protection of personal data during authentication
- Real capabilities of ordinary end users
- Recovery from emergency situations
- Protection of target assets during remote access.

Recently, the situation has improved slightly by the introduction of integrated quality criteria of the eID ecosystem (AAL[WiBu11], QAA, [HuLE09]). But there still remain some elements of the real eID ecosystem beyond the security targets and therefore outside of the security analysis.

Therefore, a complete protection is important, covering the entire life cycle of a cyber identity, including recovery from emergency situations and protection of communication channel.

The existing eID ecosystems do not expect that there could be emergency situations or they only solve part of the issue of emergency situations. Recovery from emergency situations is omitted most often.

Let's use PKI as an example. The PKI includes CRL/OCSP apparatus. It can only address protection against misuse of compromised private keys (with known weaknesses). It does not address recovery of service in such situation. There is no plan B. This can have disastrous consequences especially when a private key of certificate authority is compromised.

Also, there is no prearranged upgrade procedure of cryptographic algorithms, although it is known that the current cryptographic algorithms will eventually be surpassed and will need to be replaced in the future.

Protection of target assets, which are protected by the eID ecosystem should also be a part of the security targets of the eID ecosystem. This protection has been a natural part of authentication built into the target systems (e.g. PPP/CHAP, SSL, TLS). What is surprising is the finding that modern external authentication systems do not address this issue and the protection of target assets is beyond the scope of their security consideration [Neum13], which means that the problem is left to be dealt with by the integrators. In fact, it is very difficult to solve, in practice it remains unsolved and thus opens up new possibilities for attackers.

Therefore, the issue of protection of target assets is included in the idea of complete protection of the new eID ecosystem, specifically the part of protection that is directly related to authentication; and that is the issue of data channel protection and binding of authentication with data channel protection (data channel binding). The authorization and enforcement of access rights at the application level is still a domain of the target system.

4 Selected Elements of Architecture

Text of the paper does not describe a complete solution. This goes beyond the scope of the paper. It only describes selected elements of architecture, which are designed to contribute to the solution of dynamic protection and also to the solutions of complete protection and which have not been published yet.

4.1 Multichannel Binding

Modern eID ecosystems generally do not address the issues of data channel protection [Neum13]. The point is that it does not suffice to only authenticate the user but it is also necessary to ensure that the data channel, which is set up for access of authenticated user to the target assets, was really used by the authenticated user and not by the attacker, so that the attacker could not seize the outcome of authentication. This is referred to as the "binding".

The issue of secure binding of authentication results with target data channel must respect real limits of widely available software. The situation is not satisfactory. An available solution with sufficient security has not been found yet.

Therefore, three levels of binding, differing in requirements for additional software with different levels of security, have been proposed and an apparatus for automated management and enforcement of the relevant binding method, according to setting by security administrator, has been established.

We will describe in detail the most securely strong level of binding. This is a cryptographically protected data channel (e.g. TLS) interlace with a strong external authentication.

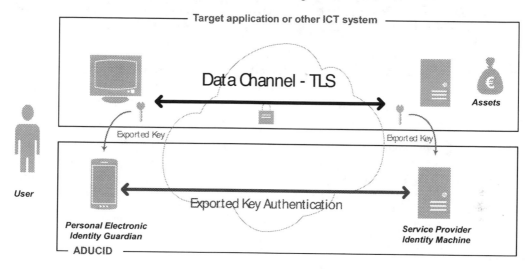

Fig. 1: Data Channel Binding Diagram

A derivative of a data channel internal secret in exportable format (e.g. by RFC 5705), which is calculated at both ends of the data channel independently is used for binding.

This derivative is passed on as a parameter to external authentication that uses it for two purposes:
- To verify the absence of the attacker in the data channel
- To verify the absence of the attacker in the authentication channel

Due to the properties of the authentication protocol [NeKl11] the attacker can thus be excluded of the data channel and also from the authentication channel, except for a theoretical exception that is the presence of an active MITM attacker on both channels simultaneously and at all times in every usage. Even a single case of absence when the attacker is not active on one of the channels is sufficient for its discovery. This also applies vice versa. To completely shut out the attacker, only a single use in environments where it is guaranteed that the attacker is not present on at least one channel, for example in a secure internal network, is sufficient.

4.2 Secrets Anti-copy

A fundamental security challenge of the eID ecosystem is the protection of a secret. If a system solution is based on systematic use of public key cryptography, only a part of the problem is solved. The situation is significantly worse when using a shared secret (e.g. password, OTP).

The use of asymmetric cryptography allows systematically eliminating the need for copying. A single instance of private key is sufficient and therefore it can also solve indisputableness, or more precisely non-repudiation.

The classic approach protects private keys statically either by encrypting on current hardware or by using special hardware (smart card, HSM). Protection of encryption is limited by the quality of the cipher, especially the key and is generally considered to be weaker than protection by special hardware. It is basically a method of authentication of access to the private key, therefore the target authentication is subject to a different authentication.

The idea of dynamic copy protection excludes such chaining authentication. The eID ecosystem protects the private keys against misuse by its own means. In fact copying of the key material itself is not protected but the use of more than a single copy is prevented. At the moment of recognition of existence of multiple copies, any further use of all copies is immediately blocked.

Private (unencrypted) key is accompanied by a dynamic "anti-copy" stack of keys with a very short lifetime. This stack is located on both the client authentication device and on the authentication server.

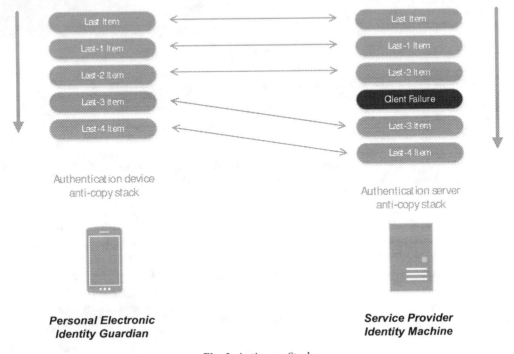

Fig. 2: Anti-copy Stacks

During each authentication is the content of the stack changed. A new shared pseudo-random key is generated, which is then put at the front of the stack and the content of the stack is thus shifted. During each authentication the client authentication device uses all the keys from the stack for additional authentication, which is evaluated by the authentication server according to its stack. Evaluation algorithm also includes recovery from failures (e.g. loss of communication or power during previous authentications), for which the range of failure tolerance can be set by the security manager.

If a disagreement between client and server stack is assessed, which does not correspond to a tolerated failure, the use of eID for all copies is immediately automatically blocked. That is at the first use of a second copy, which cannot be equivalent to a failure of the first copy, the existence of this copy is detected and its use is immediately blocked. Tolerated loss of communication or failure is not the subject of the blockage.

4.3 Self-service Recovery

Part of the full life cycle of eID is not only blocking of the attacker in the event of an emergency situation e.g. in the event of loss of authentication device. In this case a quick and easy recovery of the user from such situation and the possibility of further use of the target service (target service availability for the authorized user) is also important. A similar situation is solved by redundancy. However this idea is not commonly supported in the environment of eID ecosystems. This is another challenge which was addressed.

Fully automatic cyber identity supports the ability to create a replica of the user authentication device. It is not a copy but a different authentication device with independent cyber identity and independent cryptomaterial. This replicated device is linked to the same user account as the original authentication device.

Various scenarios of replicas generation, with the aim of maximum user simplicity while maintaining high security, have been developed and verified. A part of the support of replicas is a wizard that allows the user to generate a replica in several steps in a particular situation that the user wants to use.

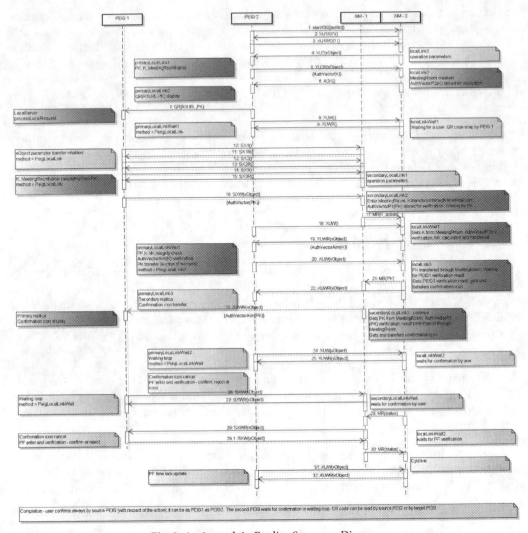

Fig. 3: Anti-attack in Replica Sequence Diagram

Additional dynamic anti-attack is also a part of replica generation. It is using the fact that one user uses two different authentication devices simultaneously to communicate in a given situation via a total of three channels while one channel is directly between devices (not passing via the Internet). The method to exclude the attacker is rather complicated, it uses the dynamics of time, where other secret information is derived from one information by a one-way function and successors are used earlier than predecessors.

In addition to providing a second authentication device of the same user, the result is also a further increase in demands on the attacker. The attacker must be an active MITM simultaneously on both channels used by both replicated devices and at all times.

The chances of the attacker are very small because a multi-channel anti-attack (a part of multichannel binding) is in operation at the same time. The multi-channel anti-attack only gives the attacker a theoretical chance if he/she is active at all times on both the data channel and the authentication channel. The MITM must be always active on the data channel and also on both replicas channels. It is detected by only a single inactivity on a single channel of a single replica. By a single verification at any time on a single replica the attacker may be excluded in the past and in the future.

The user can use the replica either as an alternative authentication device when accessing the target service from a variety of devices (notebook, telephone, tablet) or as a backup in case of an emergency situation, both in case of failure of one of the devices and in case of a loss.

The environment for replicas support allows the user to turn his/her other replicas on and off via online self-service. Therefore when he/she detects a loss, he/she can immediately use his/her replica and disable the lost authentication device remotely. This does not limit an option of classic deactivation by means of administrator (call-center, help-line, ...).

If the lost authentication device is in the hands of the attacker, it ceases to be applicable immediately. Or if the user later finds the device he/she can use his/her replica to activate it again and continue to use it.

While doing so the whole time he/she can use his/her backup device to authenticate to the target service and continue to use the target service without downtime and complicated recovery.

4.4 Personal Factor

A Personal Factor is a new approach to solution of strong multi-factor authentication. Its aim is to maximally simplify the use of multi-factor authentication while maintaining or increasing the level of security.

The basic idea is that the second factor is a means of verifying that the authentication device is being used by the correct person. The second factor is not necessary for strengthening the security of a cyber identity. Security of the cyber identity in cyberspace is ensured by means of strong automatic authentication of the cyber identity managed by the authentication device, which is supported by a security analysis of the difference between the real world and cyberspace and the properties of authentication factors applicable in the real world and in cyberspace [Neum12a].

One of the results of additional analysis is the fact that the usual requirements for entropy in the present cyberspace are more than 10^{20} times higher than is the achievable entropy of authentication factors in common real world. In other words, in order to increase security it is pointless to add 1 to 10^{20} and thus complicate the lives of the users.

At the same time the idea of replicas was respected, namely the fact that the user has more authentication devices. The Personal Factor is designed as a single universal factor used by one person as a second factor on any of his/her authentication devices and to authenticate with any service provider. At the same time, the use of the second factor is minimized only to situations where it is required to protect the target assets. The second factor is not always necessary at each startup of the authentication device or even for each use of the authentication device but only if it is for reasons of security requested by the service provider. E.g. during payment transaction with a higher amount.

For such a solution of the Personal Factor it was necessary to solve a wide range of operational and security challenges.

One of the challenges was how to verify the Personal Factor in an environment that does not rely on a secure hardware. This was solved by dual authentication technique, in which the secret of the Personal Factor is not stored anywhere. Personal Factors can only be verified with the cooperation of the authentication device and the authentication server. In addition it is possible to nearly arbitrarily increase the entropy used to verify the Personal Factor in cyberspace.

Another challenge was to handle synchronization that would allow the right changes at the right time to manifest itself on all replicas and at the same time the synchronization must not be a security weakness. The result is implementation of the Personal Factor with new security features, using precisely the fact that the Personal Factor is the same on all the authentication devices.

As an example we can use a comparison of success rate when using the Personal Factor on different replicas of the same user. When it is detected that during the same period the Personal Factor is entered right on one replica and wrong on another one, it is possible to immediately automatically block the replica where the Personal Factor is entered wrong.

The implementation enables the user to choose the technology of Personal Factor that suits him/her more. There is a secure picture or numeric keypad, the use of NFC tags or Bluetooth personal devices (watches, bracelets, ...) available. The user can change his/her Personal Factor, including the change of technology. The change will be performed on all replicas automatically.

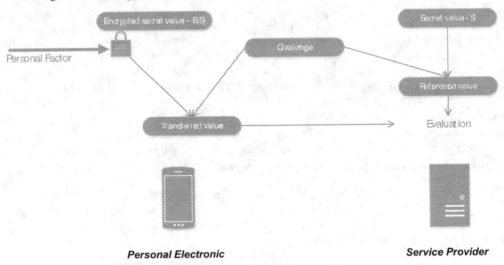

Personal Electronic   **Service Provider**

Fig. 4: Personal Factor Dual Authentication

Dual authentication of the Personal Factor operates as follows: at the time the Personal Factor is set a shared authentication secret S with high entropy, which is known to the authentication device and the authentication server, is utilized. The S is stored on the authentication server and the S encrypted by Personal Factor E(S) is stored on the authentication device.

During verification the value E(S) is decrypted by specified Personal Factor and a value derived from the challenge and decrypted value (see Figure No. 4) is forwarded to the server for verification.

The use of identical Personal Factor for multiple service providers carries the risk of a potential brute force attack. This is prevented by using time lock of the authentication device, which takes into account all attempts to use the Personal Factor for any service provider and at the same time ensures compliance with the parameters of the time lock set separately by each security administrator of service provider.

4.5 Vector Authentication

To implement the previously described partial or additional authentication, a unified flexible apparatus of vector authentication has been designed. It allows performing a whole range of sub-authentications tied to the primary authentication in a homogeneous and simple way.

After a primary strong and mutual authentication of the cyber identity is performed using 2 pairs of asymmetric keys, a single secondary authenticated shared secret SAS is established.

The individual elements of the additional authentication are processed as elements of an authentication vector. Client authentication device processes each element of the vector by using a SAS derivative as a challenge or a key and the product is passed on for evaluation to the authentication server. The authentication server evaluates each vector element separately using SAS and based on the results, it generates an overall authentication result. Since SAS is an authenticated secret, each component of the evaluated vector is also authenticated.

Since each component or group of components is evaluated separately, the result of evaluating contains a range of useful information. For example the evaluation of a dynamic anti-copy also includes an evaluation of potential failure on the part of client authentication device or authentication server.

In actual implementation [ADUC15], the following components of authentication vector are used:

- Two components are used to verify the binding and anti-attack via binding
- One component is used to verify Personal Factor (if required)
- One component is used for static detection of copying
- N components (e.g. five) are used for dynamic detection of copying.
- In case of replica generation, two additional components are used for anti-attack during replica generation.

Therefore 9 or 11 components of vector are typically used. In addition to the primary authentication 9 or 11 additional authentications tied to the primary authentication are thus performed.

Authentication result includes not only overall success or failure but also additional information, for example that neither attacker nor a copy of client authentication device was identified, that the correct client authentication device is used but the user mistyped his personal factor, etc.

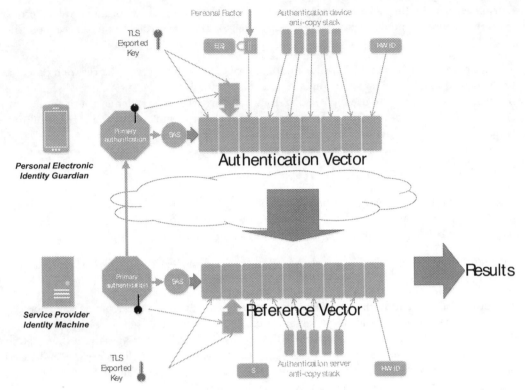

Fig. 5: Vector Authentication Schema

5 Conclusion

Measured by conventional understanding of factors, this is an adaptive multi-factor authentication, e.g. 10-factor authentication, in which the user only enters the second factor and additional authenticated information is collected automatically.

Since it is not a classic use of factors and a uniform method of processing and evaluation by vector is used, the title of the paper uses the term multidimensional authentication.

The described method brings new options and features. In conclusion, let us repeat the most important ones.

- User authentication via an external authentication service could be strongly linked with the authentication of the data channel to the target assets without inconveniencing the user and without relying on his knowledge and attention.
- It is possible to use conventional hardware, the protection of authentication secrets is dynamic. Every time the utilization of a copy is evaluated and if the copy is detected, the cyber identity on all copies is immediately blocked without human intervention. At the same time failures are tolerated to an extent managed by security administrator.
- The user can use hardware which he/she has chosen himself/herself and which he/she likes to use and uses it out of his/her own choice (BYOD). This eliminates additional costs for eID hardware and prevents overcoming of user barriers.

- The user has the option to use more than one eID device and has a self-service option to recover from emergency situations without failure of the target service.
- Burdening of the user with entering the second factor is minimized. The second factor is common for all replicas and all service providers. The user can choose the technology of the second factor and easily change it if he/she wishes to.
- An active anti-attack is used in a way invisible to the users. This additionally increases the power of authentication and provides a new system property of the eID ecosystem. The more it is used, the more secure it becomes.
- The eID ecosystem can be also used for the IoT as it provides fully automated lifecycle of eID for things as well, including anti-copy on common hardware.

References

[ADUC15] ADUCID: "ADUCID", ADUCID web page, ANECT a.s., 2015, http://www.aducid.com/.

[HuLE09] B. Hulsebosch, G. Lenzini, and H. Eertink: "D2.3 – Quality authenticator scheme", STORK – Secure Identity Across Borders Linked, 27 February 2009.

[Leyd11] Leyden J.: "RSA explains how attackers breached its systems", The Register, 4 April 2011, at http://www.theregister.co.uk/2011/04/04/rsa_hack_howdunnit/

[NeKl11] Neumann, L., Klíma, V.: "Universal Cryptographic protocol – a new way of cryptographic security management", Smart Event 2011 – World-eID, Nice, France, 23 September 2011.

[Neum08] Neumann, L.: Anonymous, Liberal, and User-Centric Electronic Identity – A New, Systematic Design of eID Infrastructure, In: e-Challenges e-2008, 22-24 October 2008, Stockholm, Sweden.

[Neum12a] Neumann, L.: "Cyber Identity is NOT Human Identity – A System Weakneses Analysis of Current eID Technologies", European Journal of ePractice, No 14 – January/February 2012, pp 79-89.

[Neum12b] Neumann, L. at.al: Strong Authentication of Humans and Machines in Policy Controlled Cloud Computing Environment Using Automatic Cyber Identity, In: ISSE 2012 Securing Electronic Business Processes, Highlights of the Information Security Solutions Eu-rope 2012 Conference, Springer Vieweg, 2012, pp 195-206.

[Neum13] Neumann, L.: Security Challenges of Current Federated eID Architectures, In: ISSE 2013 Securing Electronic Business Processes, Highlights of the Information Security Solutions Eu-rope 2013 Conference, Springer Vieweg, 2013, pp 21-32.

[Neum14] Neumann, L.: "Redefining Authentication Within a Full Cyber-Security Strategy", World-eID Congress, Marseille, France, 24 September 2014

[WiBu11] William E. Burr, at all: "Electronic Authentication Guideline", Special Publication 800-63-1, NIST- National Institute of Standards and Technology, December 2011

[Zett15] Zetter K.: "Gemalto Confirms It Was Hacked But Insists the NSA Didn't Get Its Crypto Keys", Wired, 25 Feb 2015, at http://www.wired.com/2015/02/gemalto-confirms-hacked-insists-nsa-didnt-get-crypto-keys/

Bring Your Own Device For Authentication (BYOD4A) – The Xign–System

Norbert Pohlmann · Markus Hertlein · Pascal Manaras

Institute for Internet-Security
Westphalian University of Applied Sciences
{pohlmann | hertlein | manaras}@internet-sicherheit.de

Abstract

The paper proposes an innovative authentication-system called Xign that is very easy to use, easily integrated in existing infrastructure, while offering strong multifactor-authentication for different domains of application, like web applications and physical access control. A QR code is all that is needed to provide an entry point of authentication to the user. The system comprises a smartphone application (Xign App), a server-component (Xign Authentication Manager) and a smartcard-applet (Xign SC). A NFC token contains a special smartcard-applet and a keypair which is protected through a user-selected PIN. To use this token for authentication, it must be paired with the users smartphone. To achieve that, the smartphone is also equipped with corresponding certificates. The Xign-system is backed by a Public Key Infrastructure (PKI). As trust-anchor the PKI depends on the attributes of the new German identity card or similar identity verification systems, which are used to generate a derived identity, that is subsequently stored into token. As a consequence the Xign-System also takes steps to ensure anonymity of the user, while preventing tracing over multiple authentications.

1 Authentication in Organisations

This chapter focuses on problems during authentication in organisations and shows two improvements and its limitations.

1.1 Problems

Mobile devices, such as tablets and smartphones, are on the rise to an extent, that they are used in nearly every situation in our daily lives. They are used personally, but also during work, resulting in a need to establish some form BYOD-Policy for the use in corporate networks containing sensitive data. Compromised personal devices, thus endanger the security of every network, which grants access to them.

In this context secure authentication and authorization of a user are as crucial as the use of strong cryptography to protect the user's personal information and in the end the security of the whole infrastructure involved.

Today authentication is primarily done via passwords. Password authentication is vulnerable to many attacks like Phishing or Bruteforce attacks and thus considered as insecure. The main problem is that the chosen passwords are often too easy to guess. Additionally a password is often used for more than one user account, adding to the insecurity of password protected user accounts.

There are not only problems regarding authentication and authorization, but also social problems regarding the privacy of every user in general:

In recent years IT security gained relevance, as there were several high-profile security breaches, such as the attack on Lockheed Martin in 2013. The secret operations of intelligence agencies have never before reached such a high level of intrusion into the personal lives of citizens, as shown by the documents revealed by Edward Snowden.

In general the trust in IT security, especially in IT security solutions provided by US businesses, is heavily shaken. Reports of NSA-backdoors, the deliberate use of weak cryptography and the tampering with hardware of Internet service providers to spy on users, are the most prominent reasons for this kind of distrust.

1.2 Approaches

Over the past years, there were many attempts to solve the security problems in connection with password authentication. As a result, several security solutions have found their way into the market.

Mainly there are two types of approaches: The field of One-Time-Passwords (OTP) and the field of X.509-Tokens and smart cards.

OTPs, as generated by the RSA SecurID Token, rely on a shared secret and can be used as single or second factor. OTPs especially improve the security if used as second factor. If, however, the secret is stolen, an attacker can easily generate his own OTPs, as shown in the hack of Lockheed Martin in 2013.

X.509 Token or smart cards use certificates and public key pairs. Because of the tamper proof design of smart cards, the private key is never exposed or transferred. As a result authentication is only possible, if the user has control over two factors: knowledge (PIN) and possession (smart card; the token itself). The X.509 Token has an advantage over OTPs: Because of contained digital certificates it is also possible to enable authentication across different organisations (bridging).

As shown, both approaches can be used for improving security during authentication in different realms. Since both approaches often require to align existing infrastructures appropriately, they are not easy to integrate. As a consequence the proposed system supports multiple protocols as well as direct integration, while maintaining usability.

2 Base Technologies

This chapter explains both established technologies, QR-Code and PKI, and how they are used to build an easy to use and modern authentication system.

2.1 QR Code

Quick Response codes (QR codes) are crucial for the Xign-System. They offer an easy way to contain information in a machine-readable fashion and are used to transfer the necessary information to start the authentication process, from the server to the smartphone application. The QR codes, as issued by the Xign Authentication Manager, contain compressed JSON-objects structuring the information. These codes are subsequently read by the smartphone's camera and processed by the smartphone application. A QR code's payload can be described as follows:

```
QRCode{
      String url;
      String signature;
      String id;
}
```

The url property points to the corresponding endpoint at the authentication manager, the application needs to communicate with. The id property is required to match the client-session and the corresponding authentication-session. The signature property is used to ensure the legitimacy of the QR code and is verified by the application before starting the authentication process.

2.2 Public Key Infrastructure

The PKI consists of a Certification Authority (CA) and a corresponding Registration Authority (RA), which represents a user interface for administration and user management. An administrator is able to enrol new, delete old or manage existing users. Furthermore certificates of existing users can be revoked, ultimately preventing successful authentication with the system, this way providing a mechanism for efficient risk-management.

The RA is able to communicate with the CA to enrol users and to retrieve user certificates needed for token personalization, while providing an interface for smartphones to securely personalize software tokens.

3 Xign

This chapter gives an overview of the Xign-System and its components comprising the four core actors (Fig.1) authentication server, smartphone app, security token and service provider.

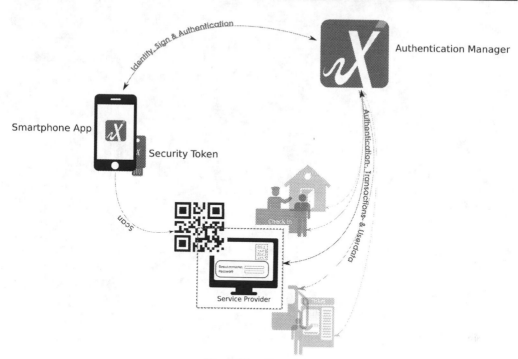

Fig. 1: Xign Overview

3.1 Concept

The Xign-System comprises of four actors: the smartphone application, optionally extended with a hardware token, the authentication server and the service provider. A service provider could be a Webshop and other Websites, an ERP system, a VPN server, the local workstation or a physical access control systems or any other system, that needs to grant access to its users.

The service provider represents a service the user wants to authenticate with. To enable the user to authenticate, the service provider retrieves a QR code from the authentication server and presents it to the user.

The user scans the QR code to start the authentication. The smartphone application processes the information contained and communicates with the authentication manager to authenticate the user.

The authentication manager mediates between smartphone application and service provider. It is responsible for delivering authentication events and QR codes to service providers and communicates with the corresponding smartphone clients to authenticate users. Authentication is done by using a PKI-backed challenge-response-protocol.

3.2 Components

Figure 2 shows the architecture of the Xign-System and their integration. It illustrates how the main components act together.

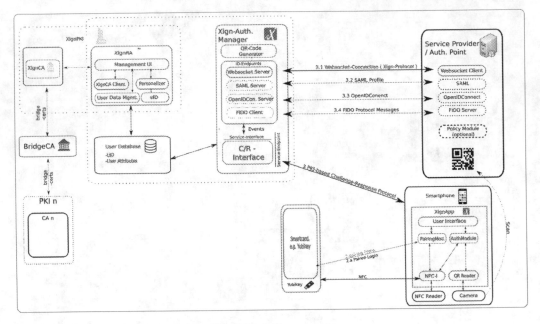

Fig. 2: Xign Components

3.2.1 Authentication Manager

ID-Protocols for Integration

Since existing solutions often require to align existing infrastructures appropriately, they are not easy to integrate. As a consequence the proposed system supports multiple protocols as well as direct integration.

As cloud computing becomes more prevalent, authentication with cloud services is crucial for every service provider. As a result it is important to support cloud based protocols:

- **SAML**
  The Security Assertion Markup Language (SAML), developed by the Security Services Technical Committee of OASIS, is an XML-based framework for communicating user authentication, entitlement, and attribute information. As its name suggests, SAML allows business entities to make assertions regarding the identity, attributes, and entitlements of a subject (an entity that is often a human user) to other entities, such as a partner company or another enterprise application [Adva].

- **OpenID Connect**
  OpenID Connect 1.0 is a simple identity layer on top of the OAuth 2.0 protocol. It allows Clients to verify the identity of the End-User based on the authentication performed by an Authorization Server, as well as to obtain basic profile information about the End-User in an interoperable and REST-like manner.
  OpenID Connect allows clients of all types, including Web-based, mobile, and JavaScript clients, to request and receive information about authenticated sessions and end-users. The specification suite is extensible, allowing participants to use optional features such

as encryption of identity data, discovery of OpenID Providers, and session management, when it makes sense for them [Open].

- **Xign-Protocol**
  The Xign-Protocol is the proprietary protocol used by the Xign-System. It relies on the websocket-protocol for transport and uses JSON-Messages as payload. This protocol is also used by service providers to directly integrate Xign into their systems.
- **FIDO**
  The FIDO Alliance has two sets of specifications, U2F and UAF. The FIDO UAF strong authentication framework enables online services and websites, whether on the open Internet or within enterprises, to transparently leverage native security features of end-user computing devices for strong user authentication and to reduce the problems associated with creating and remembering many online credentials. The FIDO UAF Reference Architecture describes the components, protocols, and interfaces that make up the FIDO UAF strong authentication ecosystem [PhSS14].

Larger businesses typically manage their users using LDAP, RADIUS or other protocols. Because of that, it is mandatory to provide appropriate interfaces for these kinds of services, eliminating the need for duplication or transformation of existing user data.

Service Protocols – Authentication

The challenge-response protocol is used between smartphone/token and authentication manager to authenticate the user with the authentication manager, while taking account of Phishing and MIT-attacks. Since there are no passwords, the whole system is secure from Phishing attacks. Furthermore the system is even secure against Man-In-The-Middle Attacks due to its PKI. Another benefit in using the PKI lies in the capability to authenticate with other Xign Authentication Managers through a process called bridging. The whole protocol consists of a set of JSON messages and thus is independent of its underlying transport-protocol.

3.2.2 Smartphone Application

The smartphone app acts as user interface, as QR-Code scanner and as token reader for the NFC Security Token. It is equipped with a public-private key pair and corresponding certificate. Because of the key pair and the need for a PIN, the smartphone can be used as soft-token providing two-factor authentication. If the smartphone is used as Security Token reader the key pair is used for pairing.

While authenticating, the smartphone provides contextual information, like location data. This information helps the user and the Authentication Manager to proof the validity of the authentication process.

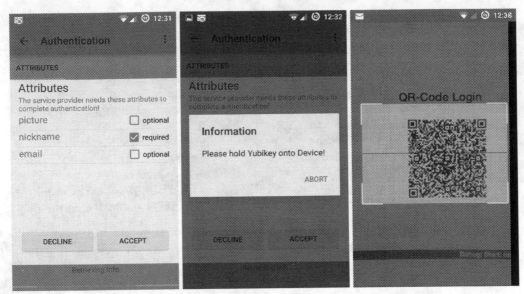

Fig. 3: Smarthpone Application Screenshot 1   **Fig. 4:** Smarthpone Application Screenshot 2   **Fig. 5:** Smarthpone Application Screenshot 3

3.2.3   Security Token

The system supports hardware tokens as well as software tokens. These tokens are so called X.509 tokens, containing a distinct key pair for each user.

At first the tokens need to be personalized. While hardware tokens can be personalized by authorized personnel, using the capabilities of the Registration Authority (RA), the software tokens need to be personalized with the help of the smartphone application, since software tokens are stored on the user device itself.

Additionally the hardware tokens can be paired with the user device to further enhance security. By pairing the hardware token with the device, the system ensures that authentication can only succeed, if the user uses both of these particular factors.

The keys stored in these tokens are used for signing the challenge, which is transmitted by the server. The Security Tokens are connected through Near Field Communication (NFC) or Bluetooth. NFC is the first choice on Android and Windows Phones, while Bluetooth is used on Apple's iPhone, since it lacks proper NFC-support.

3.2.4   Service Provider

There are different ways a service provider can integrate Xign into his systems. First of all Xign can be integrated directly, using the Xign Client Library. The Library offers a set of methods and objects to communicate with the corresponding authentication manager endpoint.

To facilitate integration in several scenarios and existing systems, Xign also supports several well-known protocols, such as OpenIDConnect, which is widely used even by large enterprises like Google and Facebook, as well as a set of SAML profiles. If the service provider already uses one of these technologies, integration is done by directing the authentication requests to the corresponding endpoint at the authentication manager.

3.3 Features

These are the main features of the Xign Authentication System:

3.3.1 Strong Authentication

End-2-End Encryption

Most protocols rely on SSL/TLS for encrypting the connection between two parties. Recent attacks and security issues showed that the dependence on SSL/TLS alone is not sufficient for establishing a secure encryption. Thus the proposed system implements an end-2-end encryption independent from the channel used.

To achieve that, the smartphone application, authentication server and service provider own a distinct keypair of its own. These key pairs are used to establish a session key between the communicating parties, based on a Diffie-Helman key exchange. The session key is used for encrypting each message. Additionally each message is also signed with the corresponding private key of the actor.

Pairing

Pairing is an extra feature provided by the smart card of the hardware token. During the pairing process the smart card and the smartphone are cryptographically bound together by calculating a secret, using its elliptic curve private key and the counterpart public certificate. The pairing protocol is based on the ECDH algorithm, AES encryption and mutual authentication.

A benefit of pairing the smartphone and the token is the realization of different security levels. Pairing results in a higher security level due the combination of two-times possession (personalized smartphone & paired hardware token) and one- or two-times knowledge (smartphone and/ or token PIN) or in a higher usability level through two-times possession (personalized smartphone & paired hardware token) without any user input. The level of security can optionally be requested by the authentication point.

3.3.2 Multirealm Authentication

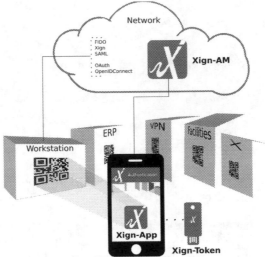

Fig. 6: Xign Multirealm Examples

The authentication system relies on QR codes as triggers to start the authentication process. This design enables authentication without the need for extra peripheral devices, such as monitors or pin pads, resulting in a broader range of use cases.

The QR code can be displayed anywhere using stickers, monitors or even a sheet of paper, this way extending the domain of application beyond authentication with web applications. Imaginable use cases (Fig. 6) are ranging from physical access to premises to check-in systems in hotels, but also include claiming reservations in restaurants or at ticket terminals.

3.3.3 Authentication Across Organisations

The fact that the whole authentication process is PKI backed not only leads to a quick and comfortable risk management, but also enables the feature of 'authentication across multiple organizations'. For this purpose the certificates of organizations offering authentication to one another are signed by a bridge CA. The certificate signed by the bridge CA becomes the new trust anchor for these organizations. Thereby the only requirement is to negotiate a policy between the organizations. There is no need for further software or hardware changes.

3.4 Functions

These are the current main functions of the Xign Authentication System:

3.4.1 Registration

Before users can be authenticated, they must be registered with the system. Registration can be done in different ways: For existing user data which is typically managed via LDAP or similar technologies, registration can be done automatically by using special adapters, effectively integrating the existing data sources.

New users are generally registered using the Registration Authority component of Xign. During registration the necessary user data is collected and stored. The stored information is then derived into a digital identity, a so called derived identity, which is subsequently stored into a X.509 token and used for authentication later on. The process of storing the derived identity together with its corresponding key material is called personalization. Alternatively registration can be done using id cards, such as the new German identity card. These cards are suitable for the use in this context, as they contain sovereign information about a person, which is machine readable.

3.4.2 Authentication

The authentication process can be described as follows:

The user wants to authenticate with service provider in the realm of online services. To achieve this the service provider retrieves a QR code from the authentication server and presents it to the user. The user scans the QR code using his smartphone and the client smartphone application. The smartphone client communicates with the authentication server to authenticate the user and displays any information necessary to complete the procedure. Once the authentication process is finished an appropriate event is sent to the service provider, containing status information. Upon this information the service provider grants or denies the access to its system.

4 Threats

Phishing and similar attacks are not a threat, because there is no user interaction. Even a "stolen" QR-Code, that is placed at a different authentication point, will be detected by the system due the use of contextual information.

Using additional end-2-end encryption instead of only using plain TLS bears the advantage, that there are only the known threats, such as attacks on the PKI itself or on the infrastructure of the Xign-System (e.g. DDOS).

5 Outlook

The system can be extended in some different ways. First of all the system can be extended to support triggers different from QR codes, such as NFC tags or Bluetooth, to support devices lacking a suitable camera or to enable new use cases. NFC, for example, is commonly used for building and facility access and in automotive solutions.

As other smartphone applications may want to integrate smartphone-based two-factor-authentication, an API can be exposed to provide corresponding entry points to the calling application. Same goes for authentication in smartphone browsers.

The system also can be extended to support qualified signatures for different domains of application. In the domain of financial Services, e.g. Online Banking and Payment Services, the Xign-System can be used to accelerate and secure the execution of transactions. In a business environment Xign helps to securely digitalize the paper-based processes. Since the smartphone is used to sign data with the personal key of the user, it is particularly suitable for this use case, because any signature can be matched to a specific user and a corresponding authentication, thus providing non repudiation.

6 Conclusion

To enable the authentication of users by using their personal devices, the authentication system needs to be designed to be flexible. Since most enterprises use a well integrated infrastructure, the system needs to be easily integrated into the target system without the need to align the existing infrastructure.

Ideally the system does not depend on passwords, as the problems regarding that type of authentication are well-known. Most passwords are either easy to guess or, if password policies are in effect, not easy to remember. Systems that are not easy to use, typically won't be used as frequent as their easier, maybe more unsafe counterparts.

A more suitable approach is the use of X.509 tokens for authentication as there is no symmetric secret that can be stolen. The whole system relies on two factor authentication.

Usability is achieved by the ease of use of the proposed system, as the user only needs to scan a QR code and remember a simple PIN, if any, instead of a complex password.

References

[DSBL10]   Dodson, Ben, Sengupta, Debangsun, Boneh, Dan, Lam, Monica S.: Secure, Consumer-Friendly Web Authentication and Payments with a Phone. In: Processdings of MobiCASE 2010, the Second International Conference on Mobile Computing, Applications, and Services, p. 17-37.

[FePo08]   Feld, Sebastian, Pohlmann, Norbert: Security analysis of OpenID, followed by a reference implementation of an nPA based OpenID provider. In: Information Security Solutions Europe (ISSE) conference, Madrid, Spain, 2008.

[Tech]   Technology Nexus AB: Mobile PKI Security, Potential, Challenges and Prospects. In: https://www.nexusgroup.com/contentassets/0b5f8d23e4be466bb698b6f91769bb8f/nexus-white-paper-mobile-pki-en.pdf

[LiWe05]   Liang, Wei, Wang, Wenye: On performance analysis of challenge/response based authentication in wireless networks. In: Computer Networks, Volume 48, Issue 2, 2005, p. 267–288.

[PhSS14]   Philpott, Rob, Srinivas, Sampath, Kemp, John: UAF Architectural Overview. In: https://fidoalliance.org/specs/fido-uaf-overview-v1.0-rd-20140209.pdf, 2014.

[Pint12]   Pintor Maestre, David: QRP: An improved secure authentication method using QR codes. In: https://www.grc.com/sqrl/files/QRP-secure-authentication.pdf, 2012.

[Bund13]   Bundesamt für Sicherheit in der Informationstechnik, BSI: Überblickspapier Consumerisation und BYOD. In: https://www.bsi-fuer-buerger.de/SharedDocs/Downloads/DE/BSI/Grundschutz/Download/Ueberblickspapier_BYOD_pdf.pdf?__blob=publicationFile, 2013.

[Mtit]   MTI Technology: Bring Your Own Device. In: https://mti.com/Portals/0/Documents/White%20Paper/MTI_BYOD_WP_UK.pdf.

[Open]   OpenID Foundation: What is OpenID?. In: http://openid.net/connect/.

[Adva]   Advancing open standards for the information society (OASIS): OASOS Security Services (SAML) TC - Overview. In: https://www.oasis-open.org/committees/tc_home.php?wg_abbrev=security.

Addressing Threats to Real-World Identity Management Systems

Wanpeng Li · Chris J Mitchell

Information Security Group, Royal Holloway, University of London
Egham TW20 0EX, UK
Wanpeng.li.2013@live.rhul.ac.uk
me@chrismitchell.net

Abstract

Recent practical studies have revealed that, in practice, widely used identity management schemes such as OAuth 2.0 and OpenID Connect are often poorly implemented by relying parties, and as a result very serious vulnerabilities can result. In any event, any system relying on browser redirections, as is the case for OAuth 2.0 and OpenID Connect, is vulnerable to web-spoofing and phishing attacks. Many of these vulnerabilities would disappear if the user's browser (or other agent under user control) remained in charge of what credentials are divulged to whom, and when. We outline a system known as Uni-IdM, which has been successfully prototyped, which provides a generic service of this type. Through the installation of a simple JavaScript plugin, the user is provided with a unified means of managing and using all his or her credentials via a simple and intuitive interface, which will work with a multiplicity of identity management systems. This not only reduces the risk of credential and/or account compromise, but also greatly simplifies the work of the user in credential management as well as providing a much clearer view to the user of which end parties are being sent user information.

1 Introduction

There is clearly a pressing need for better ways of handling user credentials than expecting users to remembers tens of individual usernames and passwords. The end user demand for improved solutions to practical identity management can be seen from the rapid growth in adoption of services provided by Facebook, Google and others, primarily relying on OAuth 2.0 and its variants (in particular OpenID Connect). However, recent practical studies, as outlined in this paper, have revealed that in practice these schemes are often poorly implemented by relying parties, and as a result very serious vulnerabilities can result. In any event, any system relying on browser redirections, as is the case for OAuth, is vulnerable to web-spoofing and phishing attacks. Many of these vulnerabilities would disappear if the user's browser (or other agent under user control) remained in charge of what credentials are divulged to whom, and when.

In this paper we outline a system known as Uni-IdM, which has been successfully prototyped, which provides a generic service of this type. Through the installation of a simple JavaScript plugin, the user is provided with a unified means of managing and using all his or her credentials via a simple and intuitive interface, which will work with a multiplicity of identity management systems. This not only reduces the risk of credential and/or account compromise, but also greatly simplifies the work of the user in credential management as well as providing a much clearer view to the user of which end parties are being sent user information.

The remainder of the paper is organised as follows. In section 2, we first briefly describe how OAuth 2.0 works, and then go on to outline issues which have arisen in real-world implementations, and that have given rise to serious security weaknesses. We also consider equally serious problems arising in real-world OpenID Connect implementations. In section 3 we outline the rationale for, and operation of, Uni-IdM, and explain why it can help to address some of the problems we have observed in practice. We conclude in section 4 with a discussion of ways forward for practical identity management.

2 OAuth-based Identity Management

OAuth 2.0 had rapidly gained huge traction as a means of simplifying the user authentication process. It has been adopted by Facebook and many others as a means of providing identity management services, and these services have been very widely adopted. OpenID Connect, which builds additional functionality on top of OAuth 2.0, has also seen widespread adoption for the same purposes, not least involving Google as identity provider. We next describe briefly how these systems work, and at the same time consider some of the serious security threats arising from their use.

2.1 OAuth 2.0 – a Brief Introduction

Since OAuth 2.0 was published in 2012 [Hard12], it has been used by many websites worldwide to provide single sign-on (SSO) services. By using OAuth 2.0, websites can ease password management for their users, as well as saving them the inconvenience of re-typing attributes that are instead stored by identity providers and provided to relying parties as required.

OAuth 2.0 involves four roles. The *resource owner* is a host acting on behalf of an end user, which can grant access to protected resources. The *resource server* is a server which stores the protected resources and consumes access tokens provided by an *authorisation server*. The *client* is an application running on a server, which makes requests on behalf of the resource owner (the client is the Relying Party (RP) when OAuth 2.0 is used for identity management purposes). The authorisation server generates *access tokens* for the client, after authenticating the resource owner and obtaining its authorisation (the resource server and authorisation server together constitute the Identity Provider (IdP) when OAuth 2.0 is used for identity management).

Fig. 1 provides an overview of the operation of OAuth 2.0. The client initiates the process by sending (1) an authorisation request to the resource owner. In response, the resource owner generates an authorisation grant, and sends it (2) to the client. After receiving the authorisation grant, the client initiates an access token request by authenticating itself to the authorisation server and presenting the authorisation grant (3). The authorisation server issues (4) an access token to the client after successfully authenticating the client and validating the authorisation grant. The client makes a protected source request by presenting the access token to the resource server (5). Finally, the resource server sends (6) the protected resources to the client after validating the access token.

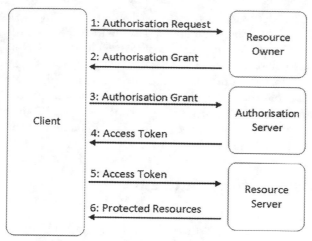

Fig. 1: OAuth 2.0 Protocol Flow

OAuth 2.0 was designed to provide a way of allowing controlled access by an application to resources protected by a resource server on behalf of the resource owner. The application is given the necessary rights in the form of an access token issued by the authorisation server, and this token is consumed by the resource server. The underlying goal is to allow the application to gain access to resources independently of the resource owner, after the resource owner has initially given consent, without being given the resource owner's credentials. That is, OAuth 2.0 is not a conventional identity management system, but is nevertheless used as one, as we describe below.

In order to use OAuth 2.0 for identity management, and in particular for SSO, the resource server and authorisation server together play the role of the IdP, the client plays the role of the RP, and the resource owner corresponds to the user. OAuth 2.0-based SSO systems build on web browser (or, more generally, user agent) redirections, where a user wishes to access services protected by the RP which consumes the access token generated by the IdP. The IdP provides ways to authenticate the user, asks the user to allow the RP to access the user's attributes, and generates an access token. The RP uses the access token to access the user's attributes using an API provided by the IdP.

OAuth 2.0 does not support identity federation as defined in identity management systems such as Shibboleth or SAML, although federation is necessary if SSO services are to be provided. In practice, a commonly used means of achieving identity federation involves the RP locally binding the user's RP-managed account with the user's IdP-managed account, using the unique identifier for the user generated by the IdP. After binding, a user is able to log in to the RP-managed account using his or her IdP-managed account.

Such a federation scheme typically operates as follows. After receiving the access token, the RP retrieves the user's IdP-managed account identifier and binds the user's RP-managed account identifier to the IdP-managed account identifier. When the user next tries to use his or her IdP-managed account to log in to the RP, the RP looks in its account database for a mapping between the supplied IdP-managed identifier and an RP-issued identifier. If such a mapping exists, then the RP simply logs the user in to the corresponding RP-managed user account.

In real-world OAuth 2.0 SSO systems supporting federation, RPs typically use one of two ways to perform the binding. Firstly, suppose a user chooses to log using SSO. After finishing the authorisation process with the IdP, the user is asked either to bind the IdP-managed account to his or her RP-managed account or to log in to the RP directly. The user will need to provide his or her RP-managed account information (e.g. account name and password) to complete the binding. Alternatively, after a user has already logged into an RP, he or she can initiate a binding operation. After being authenticated by the IdP and granting permission to the RP, the user can bind his or her RP-managed account to the IdP-managed account. After binding, many RPs allow users to log in to their websites using an IdP-managed account.

2.2 Practical Issues with OAuth 2.0

A number of authors have analysed the operation of OAuth, and have identified issues in real world implementations. To understand the real-world security of OAuth 2.0, Wang, Chen and Wang [WaCW12] examined a number of deployed SSO systems, focussing on a logic flaw present in many such systems, including OpenID. In parallel, Sun and Beznosov [SuBe12] also studied deployed systems. Both these studies restricted their attention to systems using English. Indeed, until recently, very little research had been conducted on the security of OAuth 2.0 systems using other languages, some of which, like those in Chinese, have very large numbers of users. Indeed, OAuth 2.0 is very widely used on Chinese websites, and there is a correspondingly rich infrastructure of IdPs providing identity services using OAuth 2.0. For example, some RPs, such as the travel site Ctrip, support as many as eight different IdPs. At least ten major IdPs offer OAuth 2.0-based identity management services. RPs wishing to offer users identity management services from multiple IdPs must support the peculiarities of a range of different IdP implementations of OAuth 2.0. To try to redress this imbalance, Li and Mitchell [LiMi14] reported on an analysis of Chinese-language OAuth 2.0 systems.

This latter study identified a number of serious security issues in these implementations. The security of 60 implementations of OAuth 2.0 for federation-based SSO, as deployed by leading Chinese websites, was studied. Nearly half of these implementations were found to be vulnerable to cross-site request forgery (CSRF) attacks against the federation process, allowing serious compromises of user accounts. These attacks allow a malicious third party to bind its IdP-managed account to a user's IdP-managed account, without knowing the user's account name or password. Logic flaws were also discovered in real-world implementations of federation, which again allow binding of an attacker's IdP-managed account to a user's RP-managed account. These latter issues arise primarily because of the lack of a standardised federation process.

More generally, CSRF attacks are only possible because the operation of the identity management system is invisible to the user and to the browser. That is, all the actions of the user's browser are controlled by remotely controlled mechanisms such as the use of HTTP redirects and JavaScript code downloaded from the RP. We return to this issue in section 3 below.

2.3 OpenID Connect

OpenID Connect 1.0 [SBJ+14] is built as an identity layer on top of the OAuth 2.0 protocol. The functionality that it adds enables RPs to verify the identity of an end user by relying on an authentication process performed by an OpenID Provider (OP), i.e. it adds identity management functionality to the OAuth 2.0 system. In order to enable an RP to verify the identity of an end user, OpenID Connect adds a new type of token to OAuth 2.0, namely the *id token*. This complements the access token, which is already part of OAuth 2.0. These two types of token are both issued by an OP, and have the following functions.

- An access token contains credentials used to authorise access to protected resources stored at a third party (e.g. the OP). Its value is an opaque string representing an authorisation issued to the RP. It encodes the right for the RP to access data held by a specified third party with a specific scope and duration, granted by the end user and enforced by the RP and the OP.
- An id token contains claims about the authentication of an end user by an OP together with any other claims requested by the RP. Possible claims within such a token include: the identity of the OP that issued it, the user's unique identifier at this OP, the identity of the intended recipient, the time at which it was issued, and its expiry time. It takes the form of a JSON Web Token [JoSB14] and is digitally signed by the OP.

Both access tokens and id tokens can be verified by making a call to the web API of the issuing OP.

OpenID Connect builds on user agent redirections. Suppose that an end user wishes to access services protected by the RP, which consumes tokens generated by the OP. The OP provides ways to authenticate the end user, asks the end user to grant permission for the RP to access the user attributes, and generates two types of token: an access token and an id tokens, where the latter contain claims about a user authentication event. After receiving an access token, the RP can use it to access end user's attributes using the API provided by the OP, and after receiving an id token the RP is informed about the authentication of the user.

Even though OpenID Connect was only finalised at the start of 2014, there are already more than half a billion OpenID Connect-based user accounts provided by Google, PayPal and Microsoft. This large user base has led very large numbers of RPs to integrate their services with OpenID Connect, and the Google service alone is being used routinely to protect many millions of user accounts, as well as sensitive information stored at both RPs and the Google OP server.

2.4 Practical Issues with OpenID Connect

Given the clear and growing practical significance of OpenID Connect, it is clearly important to understand its security in real-world deployments. A very recent study [LiMi15], conducted in early 2015, has sought to address this by conducting a large scale survey. The operation of all one thousand sites from the GTMetrix Top 1000 Sites providing services in English was examined. Of these sites, 103 were found to support the use of the Google's OpenID Connect service. All 103 of these websites were then further examined for potential vulnerabilities. In the study, all the RPs and the Google OP site were treated as black boxes, and the HTTP messages transmitted between the RP and OP via the browser were analysed to identify possible vulnerabilities. For every identified vulnerability, an exploit to evaluate the possible attack surface was implemented and tested.

This study revealed serious vulnerabilities of a number of types, which either allow an attacker to log in to the RP website as the victim user or enable the compromise of potentially sensitive user information. Google has customised its implementation of OpenID Connect by combining SDKs, web APIs and sample code, and as a result the OpenID Connect specification only acts as a loose guideline to what RPs have actually implemented. Further examination suggests that the identified vulnerabilities are mainly caused by RP developers misunderstanding how to use the Google OpenID Connect service, and by making design decisions which sacrifice security for simplicity of implementation. Many of the attacks that were discovered use cross-site scripting (XSS) and CSRFs, well-established and widely exploited attack techniques.

As was the case for the vulnerabilities identified in OAuth 2.0 implementations, these problems would not have arisen if the system did not rely on a completely 'passive' browser, which simply executes remotely provided JavaScript and performs redirects as requested. Of course, in all cases so far identified, careful implementation of the schemes would also have avoided the problems, but the possibility of further flaws remains, and it seems inherently risky for users to rely on all the many RPs implementing identity management systems as carefully as is necessary.

3 Uni-IdM: a New Approach to ID Management

3.1 Rationale

Identity management systems are in many cases based on web browser redirections, as is the case for OpenID Connect and OAuth 2.0; as a result such systems are vulnerable to phishing attacks [Jaru03]. A means of mitigating such attacks is therefore needed. One general approach to mitigating such phishing attacks is to incorporate a client-based user agent into the identity management system, e.g. as is the case for the now-defunct CardSpace and Higgins. It is also possible to equip a redirection-based identity management system with a client-based user agent, which can help to reduce the threat of phishing attacks [AlMi12]. Recently a new scheme has been proposed [LiMi15b] which adopts this latter approach by integrating the OpenID Connect identity management system with client functionality both in order to reduce the risk of phishing attacks and to improve the usability of the system.

As noted above, since OpenID Connect is based on web browser redirections, and does not depend on any client-based components, it is therefore vulnerable to phishing attacks; e.g. a malicious relying party could redirect a user to a fake OpenID Connect provider which is under the control of the relying party. This would enable the relying party to collect sensitive user information, such as the account name and password of the user's OpenID Connect account at the impersonated provider. The effects of user credential theft could be very serious, potentially enabling unauthorised access to all the RP user accounts which the user has linked to the OP. Moreover, as we have observed above, many widely used practical implementations of both OAuth 2.0 and OpenID Connect possess vulnerabilities exacerbated by the lack of control on the user platform.

In some identity management systems, e.g. CardSpace and Higgins, a client-based user agent is used. Such an agent has a range of practical advantages including ease of use, greater user control, and resistance to certain classes of phishing attacks. However, it would appear that no systems of this general type have been widely adopted; indeed, Microsoft no longer supports CardSpace. Also these schemes typically require the use of specific protocols between the main parties, preventing their use with other identity management systems. Instead, identity management schemes based on web browser redirections have become widely used, not least because of their ease of deployment. Given the security advantages of client-based functionality, there is a potentially significant benefit to be gained from devising a way of adding client-based functionality to these widely used redirect-based systems, particularly as it offers the possibility of combating phishing fraud and other frauds arising from RP implementation vulnerabilities (e.g. allowing CSRF attacks).

3.2 Uni-IdM – How it Works

Al-Sinani and Mitchell [AlMi12] proposed a client-based identity management tool which they called IDSpace. The idea underlying IDSpace is to provide a client-based environment which can operate with a wide variety of identity management protocols, and can also replace the Card-Space and/or Higgins agents. The primary goal of IDSpace is to provide a single, consistent and user-comprehensible interface to a wide range of identity management systems, and, through the deployment of trusted client functionality, to reduce the threats of phishing and other attacks.

For a variety of reasons the IDSpace architecture requires two separate software components: a browser extension and separate client software which executes independently of the browser. This complicates both installation and operation because of the need for the two components to intercommunicate. The newly proposed Uni-IdM scheme [LiMi15b], implements the same concept as IDSpace but follows a somewhat different architectural approach by implementing all the functionality within a browser extension. As a browser extension written in JavaScript, Uni-IDM is inherently portable, and could be implemented on a range of browsers, host operating systems and platform types with minimal modification. The Uni-IdM scheme has been prototyped for OpenID Connect [LiMi15b], but is designed to operate with a multiplicity of identity management systems.

Uni-IdM stores information about individual relationship between the end user and an IdP in a logical entity known as a *uCard*. A uCard specifies the type of identity management system with which the uCard can be used, and also the types of personal information held by the IdP on behalf of the end user. It does not contain potentially sensitive personal information, such as an account name or password. uCards are stored in the protected Uni-IdM *card store*. The *credential store* stores sensitive data associated with the uCards in the card store, such as personal information, user account names and passwords, and certificates. A variety of measures could be used to protect the card store and credential store, such as authenticated encryption, logical protection and/or physical protection.

The Uni-IdM *content scanner* searches the login page of an RP web-site in order to discover which identity management systems it supports. It sends the results of the search to the Uni-IdM *card selector*, which provides an interface enabling the user to interact with Uni-IDM. It displays the identity (address) of the RP website to the user, and if it is the first time that the user has visited the RP website (possibly indicating phishing) it enables the user to either terminate or continue. It further allows the user to manage his or her uCards, including creating, reviewing, modifying and deleting them, and it indicates which identity management systems are supported by the RP (in the case of the prototype, only OpenID Connect is supported). If the user has previously visited the RP website, it displays all the available uCards to the user; otherwise it requires the user to choose an identity management system and then create a uCard for the user-selected system.

The system automatically manages the submission of user credentials to the OP, and also the transfer of the id token from the OP to the RP. That is, HTTP redirections and the operations of any RP-provided JavaScript are controlled by the Uni-IdM plug-in, inherently protecting against certain classes of attack. These functions enable the user to achieve control over what information is sent to whom, and also prevents a range of attacks of the type discussed above.

3.3 Analysis

As the URL of the OpenID Connect OP is known to the Uni-IDM, once support for OpenID Connect is detected by Uni-IDM, it compares the known URL with the URL of the OP to which the browser is directing the user; only if the two URLs share the same domain will it submit the user's credential to the OP on behalf of the user. If a malicious RP website tries to redirect the user to a 'fake' OP under its control, Uni-IDM will terminate the process and will warn the user of a potential attack. This effectively mitigates the threat of phishing attack.

Many RPs put a specific OpenID Connect logo on their login page to indicate that they support OpenID Connect. In normal use the user must find the logo and click it in order to first initiate log-in to the RP using OpenID Connect; subsequently log-ins will take place automatically and, as a result, the user loses all control over the process. However, each RP designs its own website, and so the precise details of how a user initiates an OpenID Connect login will vary. This has the effect of downgrading the user experience because of the lack of a consistent login procedure, compounded by the subsequent lack of any control over continued use of the chosen OpenID Connect OP. However, Uni-IDM inherently provides a consistent user experience through the use of the card selector interface, and enables continued control over the login process. Whenever a user visits a RP which supports OpenID Connect, Uni-IDM will scan the DOMs of the login page and, assuming OpenID Connect support is identified, Uni-IDM will trigger its card selector; the user does not have to examine the website to find the OpenID Connect button, and always interacts with the card selector for the purposes of identity management. This improves the user experience for RP websites which support identity management systems, and also provides a consistent interface for the user. Moreover, it also gives the user a simple way of understanding exactly which authentication system is being used at all times.

As the Uni-IDM browser extension must scan every browser-rendered web page to find whether the page supports OpenID Connect, this might affect the performance of the web browser. However, tests using a Uni-IDM prototype have shown that this is not a big issue.

Perhaps the most serious possible limitation of Uni-IDM relates to the need for it to automatically detect whether or not RP websites support OpenID Connect. As websites implement support for the system in a range of different ways, e.g. using tags such as 'iframe' or 'img', the indicators used by the content scanner to search for support of OpenID Connect will also need to vary. As a result it is challenging for Uni-IDM to be designed to correctly detect all RPs which support OpenID Connect, requiring extensive testing on a site by site basis. Further details of experiments testing this are given in the paper describing the system [LiMi15b].

4 Conclusions

We have briefly reviewed the operation of the OAuth 2.0 and OpenID Connect systems, both of which are widely used today to support identity management services, notably those provided by Facebook and Google. We also summarised some of the recent findings regarding vulnerabilities in real-world implementations of the many websites which rely on these services. Whilst the problems we have discussed could be mitigated by more careful implementations, serious risks remain. Firstly, phishing attacks are not addressed by OAuth 2.0 and OpenID Connect, even when correctly implemented. Secondly, CRSF and XSS attacks can be performed in many ways, and vulnerabilities to such attacks are difficult to completely eradicate. As a result, some other method of improving the security of the operation of these systems is required, not least because of their very widespread use.

We have further described the operation of one system designed to mitigate these vulnerabilities, namely the Uni-IdM system [LiMi15b]. This is an evolution of the IDSpace system, proposed in 2012, [AlMi12]. Uni-IdM seeks to give users greater control over the identity management process through a simple browser plugin. This both enables the user to exert greater control over the identity management process, and mitigates a range of possible attacks, whilst remaining completely transparent to both RPs and IdPs.

This is, of course, just one possible approach to the long-term problem of improving operational security for identity management systems. As observed above, in practice these systems appear to be far from secure despite their widespread use, and hence this area is in urgent need of further research and development.

References

[AlMi12]   Al-Sinani, Haitham S. and Mitchell, Chris J. A universal client-based identity management tool. In: Proc. EuroPKI 11. Editors: S. Petkova-Nikova, A. Pashalidis and G. Pernul, Springer-Verlag, 2012, p. 49-74.

[Hard12]   Hardt, D. The OAuth 2.0 Authorization Framework. IETF RFC 6749, 2012.

[Jaru03]   Jarupunphol, P. A critical analysis of 3-D Secure. In: Proceedings of the 3rd Electronic Commerce Research and Development (E-COM-3). 2003, p. 87-94.

[JoSB14]   Jones, M., Sakimura, N., and Bradley, J. JSON Web Token (JWT). IETF RFC draft, 2014.

[LiMi14]   Li, Wanpeng and Mitchell, Chris J. Security issues in OAuth 2.0 SSO implementations. In: Proc. ISC 2014. Editors: Chow, S. S. M., Camenisch, J., Hui, L. C. K., and Yiu, S.-M., Springer-Verlag, 2014, p. 529-541.

[LiMi15a] Li, Wanpeng and Mitchell, Chris J. Analysing the security of Google's implementation of OpenID Connect. arXiv:1508.01707v1, August 2015.

[LiMi15b] Li, Wanpeng and Mitchell, Chris J. Enhancing user security for OpenID Connect. Preprint available from the authors, 2015.

[SBJ+14]   Sakimura, N., Bradley, J., Jones, M., de Medeiros, B. and Mortimore, C. OpenID Connect Core 1.0. The OpenID Foundation, 2014.

[SuBe12]   Sun, S.T. and Beznosov, K. The devil is in the (implementation) details: An empirical analysis of OAuth SSO systems. In: Proc. CCS '12. Editors: Yu, T., Danezis, G., and Gligor, V. D., ACM, 2012, p. 378-390.

[WaCW12] Wang, R., Chen, S., and Wang, X. Signing me onto your accounts through Facebook and Google: A traffic-guided security study of commercially deployed single-sign-on web services. In: Proc. IEEE Symposium on Security and Privacy 2012. IEEE, 2012, p.365-379.

Regulation and
Policies

Information Security Standards in Critical Infrastructure Protection

Alessandro Guarino

StudioAG
a.guarino@studioag.eu

Abstract

The standards applicable to Information Security are legion, from the purely technical, low-level specification of crypto protocols to the high-level organisational management frameworks. Industrial Control Systems - among them the Information Systems in Critical Infrastructure - still present their own set of challenges and quirks, despite the convergence trend towards mainstream information technologies and networking. Among these challenges we can recognise the still widespread use of legacy and proprietary systems with a long life and often poor documentation, the geographical spread, the fact that ICSs control physical equipment with all the related consequences (safety risk, difficulty of testing), the lack of IT and especially security training among the personnel, the legal and regulatory environment. The paper analyses the application of standards in Critical Infrastructure Information Protection, both from an organisational and technical perspective, their choice, their implementation and economic cost and benefits, in the context of the existing legal landscape, in particular in the European Union context. A brief theoretical excursus will examine a cost-benefit model for policymakers called to formulate the best policy in mandating - or not - the use of standards.

1 Introduction

Industrial plants, factories and infrastructures – be they "critical" or not – have become today heavily dependent on Information and Communications technologies for their control and operations. This holds true even for traditional sectors like for instance freshwater delivery or railway transportation. ICTs used in this applications can be labeled in general as Industrial Control Systems (ICSs) and are quite different in many ways than office networks and mobile appliances.

While ICSs are widely used in many context, we are concerned here in particular with their use in operating infrastructures and even more specifically, "critical" infrastructures. According to the common definition infrastructures constitute the basic framework needed for a society to function properly. It goes without saying that modern, developed countries need more than a basic road network and freshwater wells to function, all the way up to airports and air traffic control, oil and gas distribution, smart power grids, wide-area information networks – of which the Internet is the ultimate example. Among infrastructures, "Critical Infrastructures" are informally defined as those systems the failure of which could seriously impair the lives of the citizens or the national security of a country. While the exact list varies by country, even inside the EU, some are unanimously considered critical: the power grid, energy supply, transport systems, water supply. In European legislation Critical Infrastructure are defined as follows:

> *[...]an asset, system or part thereof located in Member States which is essential for the maintenance of vital societal functions, health, safety, security, economic or social well-being of people, and the disruption or destruction of which would have a significant impact in a Member State as a result of the failure to maintain those functions.*

Standards and best practices are one of the means used to elevate information security levels and their implementation is more and more mandated, in various ways by governmental policies. Policies however can assume many different forms and they are not always chosen by rational means. The tools provided by economics can help policymaker to make rational choices; economics applied to the formerly purely technological field of information security has already helped better understand many phenomenons and behaviours.

2 Available Standards

The world of standardisation is very fragmented and complex. As a broad overview standards can be categorised along two variables: technical level and the presence of certification schemes. In the information security field specifications of cryptographic algorithms are examples of technical standards and risk assessment schemes are examples of organisational standards. Some organisational schemes are certifiable, meaning that a third party independently assesses the organisation and declares that the it is in compliance with the standard requirements: ISO/IEC 27001 is an example of such a standards. A standard for which a certification scheme is not establishes is commonly referred to as a "guideline", but this is not at all a usage accepted by everyone and many non-certifiable guidelines as termed standards as well.

Among the standard developing organisations ("SDOs") the most relevant in the European context are the European Committee for Standardisation (CEN), the European Committee for Electrotechnical Standardisation (CENELEC) and the European Telecommunications Standards Institute (ETSI). These are also officially recognised by the European Commissions and can legally be the recipient of standardisation requests. Their area of competence can overlap – information security and cyber security being a case in point – but their constituency and operations are quite different. While CEN-CENELEC membership is composed of national standardisation bodies part of the ISO system, ETSI membership is mainly industry-based, while also including academic institutions and national administrations. All operate by trying to reach a consensus among members. The ETSI process and products tend to be more technically-oriented, market driven and faster. In the cyber security field however, ETSI is a comparative newcomer, having formed a dedicated group in 2014. A Cyber Security Coordination Group [CSCG13], fathered by all three European SDOs, has been established to help reduce overlaps and duplication of efforts.

The American effort in cyber security standardisation has been comparatively more directly driven by the government, in the wider context of national security. Executive branch involvement in Critical Infrastructure Protection began with the Presidential Decision Directive 63 (PDD-63) in 1998, later superceded by HSPD-7 in 2003 [DHS03]. The standardisation bodies most relevant to CI protection are the National Institute of Standards and Technology (NIST) and The North American Electric Reliability Corporation (NERC).

In the next section we'll review the standards most relevant to cyber security and critical infrastructure information protection, with a bias toward the organisational frameworks.

2.1 ISO/IEC 27001

ISO 27001 [ISO13] is a governance framework specifying the requirements for the security management of information systems. It's based on the concept of risk management and a continuos cycle of risk assessment, than treatment reassessment. It's by design a generic framework, flexible enough to be applicable to organisations of any size and kind. While risk management is the core of the implementation, the process and its requirements are not well-defined in the standard itself: its very flexibility implies that adapting it to real cases requires a lot of work, especially in the case of industrial systems and infrastructures, with all their peculiarities. This trait can be considered a weak point but it actually allows implementers to select the risk assessment method that suits best their use case. It must be remarked that no generally accepted risk management framework exists for ICSs and SCADA systems anyway, and that the ISO 31000 framework for risk management – also developed by ISO – can be considered the natural complement of ISO 27001.

The set of controls described in the document are the base for risk treatment, via their selection and implementation. It is a bit lacking in the physical security, environmental threats and safety areas, which are all very relevant in systems geographically spread like infrastructures. The most recent 2013 version of the standards widened its definition of assets to anything "[...] associated with information and information processing [...]", a language that allows for physical assets to be included in its scope. All considered however the framework is applicable to CIs and it is a worldwide recognised document. Moreover it is a certifiable standard.

Other guidelines are part of the 27xxx series and relevant, for instance ISO/IEC 27032 on cyber-security, the multipart ISO/IEC 27033 on network security and – pertaining to incident response and forensics – ISO/IEC 27037, 27041 and 27042.

2.2 The Common Criteria (ISO/IEC 15408)

This work – well-established in the military sector – were developed to ensure that the process of specification, development and implementation of security products is conducted in an accountable mode. While not directly relevant to the operations of a CI at a systemic level, they are used to ensure the level of security of products used. A caveat is necessary here: while it is important to assure the security of single elements, this does not make by itself the system as a whole secure. Critical Infrastructures information systems – it is useful to stress again – are complex, both socio-technical and cyber-physical.

2.3 U.S. Standards

Cyber security and the protection of Critical Infrastructures from cyberattacks is well-developed in the United States and even considered by the government a national security priority. This is in part due to the higher level of ICT sophistication of the U.S. when compared to other countries, even developed ones, that on the flip side provides adversaries with a wider attack surface. Standard frameworks are more developed and mature also because SDOs had to respond to direct policy input from the executive branch, starting with the Presidential Directive 63 in 1998, later updated in 2003 as Homeland Security Presidential Directive 7. More recently Executive Order 13636 in 2013 called for the development of a voluntary Cybersecurity Framework "Improving Critical Infrastructure Cybersecurity"

2.3.1 NIST

NIST 800-53 [NIST14a] is a risk assessment framework developed by NIST – a federal agency, so part of the executive branch – targeted to federal government entities and their contractors. It is developed from an American perspective but it as widely accepted also outside the U.S. by its own merit and the influence of its developers. As a small footnote it has to be remarked that all NIST documents are freely available, while ISO standards are not. NIST 800-53 – which can be considered on a parallel with ISO 31000 for instance – is a very consolidated and mature framework, constantly updated and kept up to date. It is structured on a three-levels security baseline and consequent set of controls to implement, based on the systems risk level: low-impact, moderate-impact and high-impact. It is quite generic like ISO 27001 but, once the impact is sized, provides a way to select controls from the complete set provided. Moreover, it includes a guide to selecting controls, based on several examples and use cases. So, some details of the implementation are provided, contrary to the ISO documents. An appendix gives moreover guidance on how to adapt adapt controls to ICSs, which are as we have seen different from general purpose systems in many ways.

More important for Critical Infrastructure Protection is the result of EO 13636, the "Framework for Improving Critical Infrastructure Cybersecurity", released by NIST in 2014 [NIST14]. The guideline, in its own words, does not substitute risk assessment models but complements them (in particular of course NIST's own 800-53). It provides a mechanism for organisations (CI owners and managers) to assess their posture in terms of cyber security, identify the gaps with the target state and the activities needed to reach it, all in a cycle of continuous improvement common to basically all standards and guidelines. The guideline notably provides table referencing the other existing documents and standards.

2.3.2 NERC

North American Electric Reliability Corporation is the government-supervised corporation responsible for the bulk electric system supply chain. The power grid has a key role among Critical Infrastructures because it represents a necessary enabler for almost all the others and its fails could trigger large scale domino effects. NERC CIP 001-009 is a series of nine documents applying to all actors in the sector: reliability coordinators, balancing authorities, interchange authorities, transmission service providers, transmission owners, transmission operators, generator owners, generator operators, load serving entities, regional reliability organisations, and NERC itself. The scope is understandably strictly North American; extensive reworking and adaptation would be needed to implement in the European Union. No compliance metric is present, so it is difficult to estimate compliance costs. This represents the only example of mandatory standard implementation, enforced in the U.S. and Canada. When initially developed adoption was voluntary but, due to the cost estimation difficulty, several actors chose not to comply. Controls provided are based, and are in fact a subset of the moderate baseline set from NIST 800-53. In july 2015 FERC (the regulatory commission overseeing NERC) proposed to direct NERC to develop a new version of its CIP series.

2.3.3 ANSI/ISA 99

The security guidelines and user resources for Industrial Automation and Control Systems developed by ANSI (a private SDO), were later submitted to IEC as IEC 62443. Here compliance metrics are present and considered fundamental, so increased security can be measured. In its vision revenues should be increased to cover for security costs, so the implementation should be cost neutral for the operator, but costs are reverted on end users. Few of this multipart series has been published by IEC so it is still premature to judge its validity.

3 Standardisation Policies

As Critical Infrastructures Information Protection is prominent in public policy, standardisation adoption policy options may usefully be studied leveraging a tool common in economics, the cost-benefit analysis. The question facing regulators is how to incorporate standardisation in security policy and to what extent: mandating the adoption of existing standards to CI operators, regulate directly, leave complete freedom. To date, NERC CIP is the only example of mandatory standard. In Europe especially the standardisation policy effort appears uncoordinated and lacking a strategic vision – more reactive than strategic.

3.1 Cost-benefit analysis

A Cost-benefit Analysis model could be used by policymakers in order to select the correct standardisation policy. CBA has a long standing and tradition in policymaking, however it was usually employed in the selection of infrastructural investment projects rather than in choosing regulatory options, or in other words, chosing how – and if – to incorporate standard compliance in legislation and regulations in a context where both public and private interests are at stake, from the economic well-being of operators, to a fair and open market for services, even to national security and safety of populations. Cybersecurity is notoriously hard to define but no doubts exist that it involves the security of interconnected systems: the convergence of ICSs to mainstream IT technologies like IP networks and general-purpose Operating Systems brought them squarely under the information security umbrella. When studied from the standpoint of economics, information security of large-scale networked systems is a public good, i.e. non-excludable and non-rivalrous.[Ande01]. One recognised as such, it has been demonstrated [Vari04] that cyber security is explained largely by a lest-effort model, i.e. the level of security of the system is as high as its weakest element. This reality, coupled with the so-called "free-rider problem" - where elements in a network can benefit of others' investments in security without cost – makes the case for some sort of regulation when industrial systems and infrastructures are involved and become part of the general network. Regulation options can be studied employing a cost-benefit perspective: costs and benefits to all stakeholders are considered, especially societal ones; according to the model benefits must exceed costs for the policy option to be viable and, when several options are available, the choice entailing the biggest net benefits is chosen.

Underpinning CBS is economic utilitarianism, where benefits to society are simply the sum of individual benefits, and measured in monetary value. Generated externalities should be included and expressed in monetary terms too, but extremely complex. The economic value of information security is not easily measured.

A simplified version of the model considers three policy options, as follows:

1. No mandatory standardisation for security (non-intervention);
2. Voluntary standardisation, possibly with economic incentives;

3. Complete regulation or compulsory standards adoption.

Table 1: Costs, benefits and externalities

Actor	Cost	Benefit	Externalities generated

CI operators (public and private)	• Participation in the developing of standards
	  • personnel (2,3)
	  • overhead (2,3)
	• Implementation of standardisation programs for their systems (could be high) (2,3)
	• Maintaining of compliance (2,3)
	  • Overhead
	  • Administrative
	  • Operative
	  • Audits
		• Reduced number of attacks (higher security) (2,3)
		• Speedy disaster recovery (2,3)
		• Lower costs of communication with partners (esp. cross-borders) and authorities (2,3)
		• Lower liability and reduced insurance costs (2,3)
		• Incident reporting standards, threats catalogs can foster collaboration, reduce costs
			• "saner" and more predictable cyberspace in general (2,3)
			• environmental benefits and safety of CIs (2,3)
			• knowledge/experience sharing (2,3)
			• (negative) More rigid markets, less competition (3)

Societal	• (possible) Participation in the developing of standards (consultation, editing etc) (2,3)	• Less downtime for users/clients (2,3) • (possible) Lower costs of services (shared with operators) (2,3)	• Heightened trust in institutions by citizens • National security and resilience (2,3) • Standardisationsupplies a common base and increases trust among international partners.

The model presented is still simplified: the existence of different categories of standards is not considered for instance; the policy options list can be refined, especially when considering the EU where regulation can be both at the Union and at the national level. More importantly we should solve the problem of how to economically evaluate cost, benefits and externalities; this is the crux of the implementation of Cost-Benefit Analysis. To do that, better empirical data is surely needed – costs of actual attacks, their absolute frequency, a reasonable estimate of the probability of occurrence, and so on. However, while much is still needed, a workable model for rational economic policy decisions is very much a necessity, especially in the general field of security and national security where the last decades saw more of a fear-driven reaction to threats than meditated choices.

4 Case Study

Power grids are the ideal case study for information security as applied to Critical Infrastructures for several reasons. They have a key role in the ecosystem because electricity is a necessity for many other CIs and blackouts can trigger significant chain failures in other domains (energy, transport, health...). Deregulation and liberalisations make for a system where a plurality of actors are involved, both vertically along the supply chain and as competitors at the same level. The transition towards renewable sources and, self-production and flexible architectures ("smart grids") significantly elevated the complexity level of the system when compared to the old-style uni-directional, "waterfall" structure. Smart grids have an absolute need of ICT technologies and the grid itself can be repurposed as a wide area information network – the rapid deployment of smart meters is an example.

The NERC CIP series, developed for the american bulk electric supply chain, is an interesting policy case study, as it is the only example of compulsory information security standard implementation. When initially deployed, the scheme was merely voluntary, but with penalties imposed for non-compliance. The resistance to adoption by operators was widespread and many self-reported violation reports were registered, as they preferred the incur the (known) cost of the penalty rather than the (largely unknown) cost of implementation, hard to forecast. Penalties had to be increased and later on a compulsory scheme was introduced. While the supply chain landscape in Europe is in many ways different than in North America – the market is somewhat less fragmented and liberalised, this experience strongly suggest that regulation probably is necessary in order to overcome economics mechanisms that work against voluntary investments in information security standardisation.

5 Conclusions

In Critical Infrastructure Protection, the benefits of technical standardisation are fairly evident, those of high-level management and risk-management much less so. Opportunities however very possibly overcome costs, even if the exact balance is not so simple to quantify and study. In a multinational setting like the European Union the adoption of a common baseline for the management ans assurance of information security in such important systems would certainly increase trust across borders – a factor widely recognised as fundamental in enhancing general cyber security and ease fast reactions to attacks – data exchange and interoperability. Unfortunately strong economic mechanisms hinder the adoption of information security schemes just like information security investments in general. Voluntary schemes proved not so effective if the objective is widespread adoption, and att least a basic mandatory implementation policy is probably needed. Europe, with fewer big operators and still several state-owned actors, even after rounds of privatisations and liberalisations, should be a more receptive testbed than North America. At the same time work, in academia, industry and standardisation bodies alike is still needed, especially on better security and compliance metrics and the associated costs.

References

[Ande01]   Ross Anderson: "Why Information Security is Hard – An Economic Perspective", 2001

[CSCG14]   CEN/CENELECT/ETSI Cyber Security Coordination Group: "White Paper No. 01 - Recommendations for a Strategy on European Cyber Security Standardisation", 2014

[DHS03]   Department of Homeland Security: "Homeland Security Presidential Directive 7: Critical Infrastructure Identification, Prioritization, and Protection", 2003

[FiRS13]   Ugo Finardi, Elena Ragazzi, Alberto Stefanini: "Considerations on the implementation of SCADA standards on critical infrastructures of power grids", CNR-CERIS 2013

[ISO13]   ISO/IEC: "ISO/IEC 27001:2013 - Information Technology – Security techniques – Information security management systems – Requirements"

[NIST14]   National Institute of Standards and Technology, "Framework for Improving Critical Infrastructure Cybersecurity", 2014

[NIST14a]   National Institute of Standards and Technology, "NIST Special Publication 800-53 - Revision 4 - Security and Privacy Controls for Federal Information Systems and Organizations", 2014

[Vari04]   Hal Varian: "System Reliability and Free Riding", 2004

Data Protection Tensions in Recent Software Development Trends

Maarten Truyens

University of Antwerp
maarten.truyens@uantwerpen.be

Abstract

Privacy by design and data protection by design focus mostly on product/service features, high-level design, security measures and organizational practices. However, low-level implementation details can also have a data protection impact that may need to be taken into account. This contribution discusses three emerging software development trends (immutability, schema-less databases and reactive programming) that are not yet well-known outside the software development sector. Each of these trends relies on ideas that may at first glance seem discordant with fundamental data protection principles (such as data quality, data minimization and data retention limitations). Even so, upon closer inspection, they also offer direct or indirect data protection benefits. Depending on the circumstances, the use of these trends may therefore be beneficial or even advisable from a data protection perspective. It nevertheless remains difficult to assess to which extent the new Data Protection Regulation will require these aspects to be integrated into data protection impact assessments and data protection by design/default compliance processes.

1 Introduction

Similar to how legislation typically plays catch up with technology, legal experts tend to lag behind, by not studying technology trends until these trends have already become well-entrenched in the industry. Indeed, it seems that the legal community only focuses on technologies that have already reached the "peak of inflated expectations", or are even already going the "trough of disillusionment" in Gartner's hype cycle of information technology trends[1]. This happened with cloud computing *(currently going through the trough)*, happened again with Big Data *(already beyond the peak)*, and may happen again with the Internet of Things *(currently at the peak)*.

This contribution wants to break this trend, by focusing on three emerging software development methodologies that have a direct impact on privacy and data protection point. All of these trends are already used in practice, but have not yet reached – and may very well never reach – the hype cycle, and have therefore remained out of the legal community's sight.

After a brief technical introduction, each of these trends will be matched against general data protection requirements, and in particular the new requirements of "data protection by design" and "data protection by default".

---

[1] First described by consultancy company Gartner, and kept up-to-date on http://goo.gl/4Bxvp.

2 Data protection by design/default

2.1 Current regulatory status

Data protection by design/default (DPDD) is one of the most prominent novelties in the proposed Data Protection Regulation[2], which will replace the current Data Protection Directive (95/46/EC). A final text should be adopted by the end of 2015 or early 2016.

According to the Commission's proposal, *data protection by design* implies that appropriate technical and organizational measures must be taken upfront to ensure that the data processing complies with all the requirements of the Regulation[3]. The amendments of the European Parliament[4] further emphasize that data protection must be embedded in the entire life cycle of a product or service.

According to the principle of *data protection by default*, the data controller must ensure that the principles of data minimization, data retention and purpose limitation are respected, both with respect to the amount of data that is collected and the duration of the storage[5]. The amendments of European Parliament clarify that it requires privacy settings on services and products which should by default comply with the data protection requirements.

Interestingly, the amendments of the European Parliament also state that DPDD should not only apply to the data controllers, but also to data processors (such as service providers). Similarly, the Council's amendments state that "producers" of the products, services and applications that are used to process personal data *"should be encouraged"* to take into account the various data protection requirements when developing, designing, selecting and using applications. Even when this – rather softly worded – amendment would not be adopted, software developers will likely be indirectly targeted by DPDD requirements, because data controllers and data processors will have to choose products that incorporate DPDD.

In the Commission's proposal, the Commission would itself be tasked with issuing technical standards and delegated acts to further clarify the implementation of these principles[6]. Conversely, in the Parliament's amendments, such tasks would instead be assigned to the European Data Protection Board. Whoever takes on these tasks, specific standards and elaborated guidelines are indeed very welcome, taking into account the vagueness of the DPDD requirements and the harsh consequences of not complying with them (fines of up to 5% of the annual worldwide turnover).

---

2 Proposal for a Regulation on the protection of individuals with regard to the processing of personal data and on the free movement of such data, COM(2012) 11 final.
3 Recital 61 and article 23.1.
4 First Reading of the European Parliament, 12 March 2014, available on http://goo.gl/R2XCYQ, recital 61 and article 23.1.
5 Recital 61 and article 23.2 of the proposed Regulation. Article 23.2 further adds that the mechanisms implemented must ensure that by default personal data are not made accessible to an indefinite number of individuals (a requirement obviously targeted at social networks).
6 Recitals 129, 130 and 131, as well as articles 23.3 and 23.4.

2.2 General contents

Although "privacy by design" does not entirely coincide with "data protection by design", it can be assumed that the EU legislator will adhere to the seven foundational principles of privacy by design, as first formulated by the former Canadian privacy commissioner Ann Cavoukian[7], and later on adopted in a resolution[8]. These principles state that (1) the privacy approach must be proactive instead of reactive; (2) privacy must be the default setting; (3) privacy must be embedded into the design and architecture of IT systems and business processes; (4) unnecessary trade-offs between privacy and other legitimate objectives must be avoided; (5) end-to-end security must be offered; (6) visibility and transparency must be ensured in order to establish accountability and trust; and (7) a user-centric approach must be taken.

These seven principles of privacy by design rightfully emphasize that privacy by design is a holistic concept that is broader than information technology alone, and should be applied end-to-end to all operations and processes of an an organization. Nevertheless, from a software developer's practical perspective, the seven high-level objectives offer very little practical guidance on the technology that must be chosen, or the way an information system must be designed. Indeed, the principles remain rather vague for practical application when effectively engineering systems[9], so that it should not surprise that DPDD has so far been largely ignored by traditional engineering approaches[10].

While, in addition to some general literature[11], fragmented case studies and guidelines have been published[12], as well as research into security-related aspects (in particular the development of privacy-enhancing technologies / PETs)[13], these do not cover the entire spectrum and/or remain on a fairly theoretical level. Instead, software developers should have access to methodologies, best practices and software design patterns that offer concrete building blocks for dealing with PBDD in their day-to-day tasks and technology choices.

---

7   See the many publications on http://privacybydesign.ca/

8   *Resolution on Privacy by Design*, October 29, 2010, http://goo.gl/ZV54ML.

9   S. GÜRSES, C. TRONCOSO and C. DIAZ, "Engineering Privacy by Design," *International Conference on Privacy and Data Protection Book*, 2011, https://goo.gl/ZTKxYx, 2; J. VAN REST, D. BOONSTRA, M. EVERTS, M. VAN RIJN and R. VAN PAASSEN, "Designing Privacy-by-Design," in B. PRENEEL and D. IKONOMOU (eds.), *Privacy Technologies and Policy*, Springer Berlin Heidelberg, 2014, 68.

10   ENISA, *Privacy and data protection by design — from policy to engineering*, December 2014, http://goo.gl/Kwy76Y, iv.

11   C. BETTINI and D. RIBONI, "Privacy protection in pervasive systems: State of the art and technical challenges", *Pervasive and Mobile Computing*, 2014; Privacy and data protection by design — from policy to engineering; S. GÜRSES, *o.c.*; J.-H. HOEPMAN, *Privacy Design Strategies*, ICT Systems Security and Privacy Protection (29th IFIP TC 11 International Conference); B.-J. KOOPS, J.-H. HOEPMAN and R. LEENES, "Open-source intelligence and privacy by design", *Computer Law & Security Review* 2013, 29; M. POCS, "Will the European Commission be able to standardise legal technology design without a legal method?", *Computer Law & Security Review* 2012, 28, 2012; S. SPIEKERMANN and L.F. CRANOR, "Engineering Privacy", *IEEE Transactions on software engineering* 35, 1, February 2009.

12   See http://privacybydesign.ca/ (e.g., on RFID, biometrics, body scanners, in-home sensors, smart grids, etc.) as well as J. AUSLOOS, E. KINDT, E. LIEVENS, P. VALCKE and J. DUMORTIER, ICRI, *Guidelines for Privacy-Friendly Default Settings*, February 18, 2013, http://goo.gl/XdbxVd; P. BALBONI and M. MACENAITE, "Privacy by design and anonymisation techniques in action: Case study of Ma3tch technology", *Computer Law & Security Review* 2013, 29, 2013.

13   See, for example, M. DENG, K. WUYTS, R. SCANDARIATO, B. PRENEEL, and W. JOOSEN, "A privacy threat analysis framework: supporting the elicitation and fulfilment of privacy requirements", *Requirements Engineering Journal*, 16(1):3–32, 2011.

3 First trend: immutable design

3.1 Background: programming with variables

Programming languages traditionally rely on the concept of *"variables"*: locations in the computer's memory to which the developer assigns an easy-to-remember label. To keep software manageable, a developer will typically split the program into many small parts. When executed, such *"subroutines"* [14] *perform certain calculations and update variables if necessary. For example, a subroutine "calculate_total"* would calculate an invoice's total, and would update the variable *"invoice_total"*.

For small programs, it does not cause any concern that each subroutine may update variables. However, in large programs with possibly tens of thousands of subroutines, the number of places where a variable may be updated becomes difficult to remember[15]. Moreover, large programs are created by teams of developers, whereby each additional developer and each additional subroutine multiplies the likelihood of errors. For example, the person who uses an existing subroutine may be unaware that such subroutine happens to call a third subroutine, which itself calls a fourth subroutine that unexpectedly modifies a certain variable.

Over time, traditional programming languages have introduced or extended facilities to manage these complexities. However, such facilities are typically optional, and because they typically require extra planning, the temptation to use normal variables remains very high. After all, the drawbacks of using normal variables only surface in the long term.

Variables also make it much more complex to perform *concurrent processing* of data, *i.e.* splitting data in different parts and performing calculations in parallel. Such concurrent processing has become necessary due to the evolutions in hardware, which – due to physical limitations – cannot be made faster by simply increasing the computer processor's clock speed (mega/gigahertz). As an alternative to increasing the number of instructions per second, multiple CPUs ("cores") are now combined that can execute tasks concurrently[16].

Unfortunately, programming a task to be performed concurrently is very complex, similar to how it is challenging to ensure that a single task gets properly distributed over, and subsequently executed by several persons. One of the single most difficult aspects is ensuring that two concurrent tasks do not step onto each other's toes, for example when the first task would update a variable, go on with performing some calculations, and come back to that variable, only to find out that it got inadvertently changed by another task. Such situations lead to bugs that are very difficult to track by the developer[17].

---

14 Depending on the programming language, they can also be called "functions", "methods" or "procedures".
15 J. HUGHES, "Why functional programming matters," *Research topics in functional programming*, Addison-Wesley, 1990, 2.
16 J. LAIRD, "Is multi-core the new Mhz myth?", 4 January 2008, *Techradar*, available on http://goo.gl/UmPqyW.
17 A. PROKOPEC, *Learning concurrent programming in Scala*, Packt Publishing, 2014, 15.

3.2 Functional programming

An alternative to programming with variables is found in so-called *"functional"* programming[18], which either eschews variables completely, or isolates them to just a few parts of the source code. All other parts of the software work with immutable values, so that subroutines never modify existing data in the computer's memory, but instead always work with copies of previously existing data. Because the addition and use of new subroutines has little effect on the other parts of the software in functional programming languages – unlike other programming languages, where using new subroutines may cause unwanted side-effects – functional programming can also increase the reuse of code[19], better testing of subroutines (because subroutines are more isolated), as well as facilitate better "reasoning" about the software by the developer.

Storing several versions of (almost) the same data may seem wasteful, but immediately solves the two drawbacks of programming with variables. First, it is never a problem for a subroutine to pass data to other subroutines, because other subroutines will not be able to change the initial data. Secondly, tasks can be more easily executed concurrently, because they will not step onto each other's toes by simultaneously updating the same variable.

Functional programming is not new, but up to recently, their practical use was very limited, due to limited memory capacity, and due their counter-intuitive concepts. However, the necessity to execute tasks concurrently and better manage software errors have now pushed functional programming languages to leave their academic use[20].

3.3 Append-only databases

Similar immutability ideas are found in database design. When traditional databases need to reflect changes, they update the existing information, effectively removing any trace of the old version. Developers need to undertake additional work to keep the old version, for example by copying it to a table with historical data.

New "append-only" databases (also called "immutable data storage")[21], deliberately append to existing information, instead of updating existing information. As a consequence, old versions of the data remain easily accessible in the dabase.

An append-only design is claimed to provide many benefits[22]. First, it maintains an inherent audit trail, because the entire flow of information updates can be retraced. Secondly, data that does not change is easier to synchronize between devices (*e.g.,* between a server, desktop and mobile device). Third, searches that involve time elements become much easier than would be the case

---

18 The word "functional" refers to the fact that the subroutines resemble mathematical functions, which inherently work with immutable data.

19 J. BACKFIELD, *Becoming Functional*, O'Reilly, July 2014, x.

20 As a result, there is now a revived interest for older functional programming languages (such as Haskell, OCaml and Erlang), while simultaneously new languages specifically focused at functional programming (such as Scala, F# and Clojure) have emerged. At the same time, languages that were traditionally non-functional (such as C#) are receiving functional features, while new general languages (such as Swift and Rust) are immediately announced with functional features.

21 See "The imminent revolution of functional append-only databases", available on http://goo.gl/Dct8Ww. Example append-only database products include Datomic and Event Store.

22 *Contra*: see the blog post "Immutability, MVCC and garbage collection", 28 December 2013, available on http://goo.gl/gzurDX.

with traditional databases, because an append-only database can always "go back in time" to get a view on a historic situation. Fourth, backups of running append-only databases are much easier to implement and take up less disk space.

Once again, this idea of append-only databases is not new, and has in fact been around for a long time[23], although it was never truly exploited in commercial products due to storage constraints. Similar to functional programming, however, the append-only design is now gaining ground.

3.4 New file systems and version control

The immutable design theme is also surfacing outside the realm of software development practices — for example in file systems, which manage the storage of all files on a computer's hard disk.

Traditionally, such file systems store one copy of each file on the hard disk, and overwrite that copy with a new version when the file needs to be updated. However, there are several problems associated with this approach. First, the risk of file corruption is no longer negligible due to the enormous capacity of today's hard disks: the risk that a few bits get inadvertently changed due to a hardware error or software glitch, has become a statistic reality[24]. If a file system overwrites the old version of a file, then it can no longer retrieve that old version in case of corruption.

Secondly, also outside the scenario of data degradation, users may want to retrieve an old version of a file because they would like to revert some changes made to it.

Third, a file system that overwrites old versions of files makes it more difficult to take backups. In an active server, at any given moment, several files may get updated. Taking a backup takes at least several minutes (but possibly several hours), so that it becomes difficult to take a consistent "snapshot" of the contents of a hard disk, unless if the server would be made inactive during the backup period.

While mainstream file systems adhere to the old "overwrite on save" design, new file systems (such as the ZFS, BRTFS and ReFS) are being developed where a new version of a file no longer overwrites the old version, but is instead written to a different location on the hard disk ("copy-on-write") and safeguarded there until certain conditions are met. The advantages of this design include better protection against data degradation, reduced exposure to data loss, backups and restores with minimal downtime, as well as storage-saving backups because the file system carefully tracks which parts of a file were not updated and therefore do not require to be included in the backup. Due to the low overhead associated with backups, they can be taken much more frequently than is the case with the old design[25].

From the end-user's perspective, one of the most interesting features of a new file system such as ZFS is the creation of snapshots. At any point in time, the current version of a set of files can be saved into a "snapshot" that can easily be restored ("rolled back") later in time. By creating multiple snapshots, users can experiment with different versions of a document.

---

23 See www.element84.com/technology-radar-2014.html. By way of example, the idea of "log structured storage" originated in the 1980s.
24 See J. SALTER, "Bitrot and atomic COWs: inside "next-gen" filesystems", *Ars Technica*, 15 January 2004, available on http://arstechnica.com/?p=396065.
25 See www.ibm.com/developerworks/tivoli/library/t-snaptsm1/index.html.

This idea of snapshots and rollbacks is also used outside file systems. Since many years, developers use this same idea for managing their source code in "version control systems" such as Git, CVS and Perforce. These systems not only allow creating, inspecting and rolling back different versions of files, but also allow users to annotate each version (who performed changes and for what reason), merge different versions of a file into a new version, and even create different parallel file sets that evolve differently over time. Because version control systems store new versions of a file instead of deleting files, they allow developers to experiment with changes to the source code and different "branches" of the code. For example, while new features can be implemented in version 2.2, developers can easily go back to version 2.0 of the software in order to resolve a software bug that was discovered for a customer who still uses that version.

3.5 Immutable infrastructure

The technology of virtualization allows multiple "virtual" servers to be run in parallel on one single physical machine, fully isolated from each other. Together, these virtual servers can better exploit the full hardware capacity of a physical machine, because many typical server operations tend to consist of a combination of periods of low load and peaks of high load. In addition to making better use of capacity, virtualization also allows for easier management and better availability, because virtual servers can be easily created, copied and moved across physical machines.

Immutable infrastructure combines the ideas of virtualization and immutable programming, by arguing that the configuration of a virtual server should never be changed. Instead, virtual servers should be built in such way that they can be easily thrown away and rebuilt when a configuration change becomes necessary. Similar to how variables in a programming languages invite developers to make changes to them which lead to software bugs in large programs, servers also attract configuration changes that over time result in increased operational complexity and unpredictable behaviour. With an immutable infrastructure, however, servers are frequently rebuilt, creating a situation that is akin to pushing a very hard "reset" button. It also becomes easier to test software, because servers are guaranteed to be in a certain state[26].

4 Second trend: schema-less design

Traditional (so-called "relational") databases are highly structured, with a strict design ("schema") containing multiple "tables" with one or more "fields" of ordered information. Designing such a schema requires significant upfront planning to ensure that all data can be stored in the table, in a way that minimizes the amount of duplication across all tables.

While providing stability and predictability, this rigidity does not fit well with the often-changing requirements of IT projects, which causes relational databases to become a hurdle for change. This will especially be the case when a database system is already in use, because changing the schema of a database with millions of records may lock the database for hours.

---

26   J. STELLA, "An introduction to immutable infrastructure", *O'Reilly Radar*, 9 June 2015, available on http://radar.oreilly.com/?p=77715.

Relational databases also suffer from the problem that data must perfectly match the database structure, making it difficult to fit in data shape variations[27]. For example, a typical contact database may foresee commonly used fields (*e.g.,* "street", "city" and " phone number"), but can obviously not foresee all fields that may eventually be required by a particular user, such as a contact's musical preference or partner's name. While there are ways around this limitation, such workarounds tend to undermine the virtues of strict relational database design. Moreover, these workarounds do not resolve the difficulty to store data that is by nature very unstructured, such as the body of an email, presentation or web page — which can essentially take any shape. It is estimated that 80 to 90 percent of the data in any organization is unstructured[28].

Another drawback of relational databases is that the way they store data is very different from the way programming languages express that same data. Programmers therefore have to mentally switch between, on one moment, working with the data in the memory of the software they are developing and, on another moment, storing that same data in a very different way in the tables of the relational database software they happen to use. This so-called "impedance mismatch" complicates the source code and hampers easy reasoning about the software[29].

In order to accommodate these challenges, the "NoSQL"[30] trend advocates a schema-less design that does away with these upfront design requirements, and allows data to be stored in an unstructured format, which can accommodate any type of data and corresponds much closer to the way data is presented by typical programming languages. When NoSQL databases are used in the right way, they can significantly increase a developer's productivity, and allow him to more easily respond to the ever changing design requirements of a software project. This increased flexibility does, however, come with increased responsibility for the software developer, because the shape of the data is no longer fixed, and is less predictable than data stored in relational databases. Instead of a situation where one central component (the database server) ensures that all software components that access the data retrieve and deliver this data in a predefined format, NoSQL database servers typically provide no such guarantees, so that all software components will themselves have to take on this responsibility.

The increased freedom of many NoSQL databases is not only visible in the *shape* of the data, but also in the consistency guarantees for the data. While relational databases go to great lengths to ensure that data is at all times consistent, such consistency guarantees lead to complexity in the database software and, often, performance problems when data is distributed across multiple servers[31]. After all, if a database is split across several servers, then each server will have to inform all the other servers about any changes it is about to make to the data, which will cause delays in all of the pending operations for all the other servers. Because of the way they are structured,

---

27 E. REDMOND and J.R. WILSON, *Seven Databases in Seven Weeks: A Guide to Modern Databases and the NoSQL Movement*, Pragmatic, May 2012, 308.

28 D. STEWART, "Big Content: The Unstructured Side of Big Data", *Gartner Blog Network*, 1 May 2013, available on http://goo.gl/Nm61y.

29 J. ATWOOD, "Object-Relational Mapping is Vietnam of Computer Science", *Coding Horror blog*, 26 June 2006, available on http://goo.gl/qt0tlG.

30 The name intends to illustrate the shift away from databases using the SQL programming language, which is used by the vast majority of traditional relational databases. The label "NoSQL" is nevertheless misleading, because several new types of database products can also be queried with the SQL programming language (similar to how some NoSQL databases will allow the enforce a predefined data scheme). The label "NoSQL" is nevertheless used as an umbrella term for all databases that deviate from the standard relational databases.

31 A. MEHRA, "An introduction to NoSQL & Apache Cassandra", *Java DZone*, March 10, 2015, https://goo.gl/4j3nBC.

relational databases therefore scale best *vertically* (by increasing the memory size, disk speed or processor performance of a single server) instead of *horizontally* by adding new servers.

For many types of data (*e.g.,* financial and medical data), it is indeed mandatory to ensure that a server will never return outdated data. For other types of data (*e.g.,* databases that log simple events, marketing tools and general search engines), however, this requirement is not mandatory, because small errors and inconsistencies in the database can be tolerated. By relaxing the strict consistency requirement, as done by several NoSQL databases, much higher performance can be achieved[32], in particular when a database is distributed across several servers. An additional advantage is that, in return for the risk that limited data inconsistencies may occur, an individual NoSQL server can be allowed to continue working even when the connection with its peers is temporarily lost[33].

For these reasons (flexibility, performance, network interruption resilience and scalability), NoSQL is often preferred for web databases and very large databases — such as those used by Big Data applications, where quantity and speed are more important than absolute consistency[34].

5 Third trend: reactive programming

No matter which programming language is used, errors will occur in software. Even if no bugs are present in one's own source code, bugs may creep in, due to upgrades of the environment in which the software operates, or due to unexpected interactions with third-party components. And even if the source code would not exhibit any bugs, then network errors, hardware failure and user errors (such as accidentally unplugging the wrong network cable) need to be accounted for. The result is that software can crash, hang, produce incorrect results or lead to data corruption.

Almost all programming languages provide mechanisms to deal with such unexpected situations. Essentially, they require developers to "guard" those parts of the source code that may trigger errors, and then indicate how each type of error should be handled. In principle, this should be sufficient to allow the software to gracefully handle errors and continue execution if possible. In practice, however, there are several drawbacks which render error handling code less than optimal.

First, developers are often too optimistic, and tend to forget or omit to guard source code parts against error. Secondly, even for those places where developers do guard source code with error handling mechanisms, developers often rely on one-size-fits-all error handling routines that do not differentiate between the various types of errors, which can lead to suboptimal error handling. Third, and somewhat paradoxically, error handling source code can itself make software more complex – and thus more prone to causing themselves errors – because the error handling code is intertwined with the normal source code, resulting in more complex source code.

In other words, error handling is difficult. Over the years, several "defensive" programming methodologies have emerged that try to provide a solution, either by including more checks in the source code (e.g., *"programming by contract"*, where each subroutine specifies which conditions

---

32 E. REDMOND, *o.c.*, 308–311.
33 A. MEHRA, *o.c.*
34 *Ibid.*

the incoming data must meet), or by accompanying source code with numerous tests (*"test driven development"*). Furthermore, new programming languages are often designed in such way that the most common types of errors can simply not occur[35].

Recently, however, a completely different error-handling methodology has emerged — or rather re-emerged[36] – as part of the "reactive programming" methodology, which combines scalability and error-prevention into a distributed software system[37]. Instead of the traditional main flow of linearly executing code intertwined with error-checking code, reactive software is fundamentally composed of thousands of lightweight subroutines called "actors" that execute concurrently. Actors can easily monitor each other, for example to check whether a crash has occurred in another actor, or whether another actor is unresponsive or delayed, in which cases a new actor will be started to take over and the work.

Reactive programming adheres to a "let it crash" philosophy: write source code that assumes optimal executing conditions and therefore has as little defensive code as possible. It lets actors crash when those assumptions are not met (or when other errors would occur), and dedicates separate actors to error-checking[38]. Through this separation of concerns, cleaner source code can be achieved, which on itself also reduces programming errors.

The key notion of reactive programming is to aim at *fault tolerance* instead of *fault avoidance*, by isolating the different components of a system in order to increase reliability. Individual components might fail, but the probability that all components will fail at the same time can be made arbitrarily small by having a sufficiently large number of replicated components[39].

Moreover, actors can be easily distributed across different (possibly thousands of) machines[40], by merely changing a few configuration parameters, so by changing no or only limited parts of the source code. This distribution of actors allows for massive scalability and performance, while simultaneously protecting the software against hardware failures. Hence, reactive programming moves away from linearly executing software that runs on a single machine – or with significant effort on a few machines – to distributed software composed of potentially thousands of independent actors that are easily spread over many machines. In a certain way, this "monolithic to distributed" move[41] aligns with a similar trend that has been witnessed in hardware: where com-

---

35   For example, as discussed above, functional programming languages minimize mutability, so that software errors caused by mutable variables are less likely to occur. As another example, new programming languages include features to deal with situations where the output of a subroutine is undefined (typically called "null" or "nil"). While developers are traditionally required to always check whether the output of a certain subroutine is undefined, they may simply forget or ignore to do so. This error may sound trivial, but was dubbed the "billion dollar mistake" by Tony Hoare (the inventor of the first programming language that allowed to return an undefined value), who apologized that *"[returning an undefined value] has led to innumerable errors, vulnerabilities, and system crashes, which have probably caused a billion dollars of pain and damage in the last forty years"*. It should therefore not surprise that many new programming language avoid undefined return values, or force the developer to cope with such values.

36   Similar to functional programming, this concept has existed for many years (first described in 1970), but remained confined to a few use cases, most notably the Erlang programming language. Erlang is primarily used for telecommunication equipment and other situations where uninterrupted availability is a key feature of a computer system.

37   See the Reactive Manifesto, version 2.0, available on http://reactivemanifesto.org/

38   J. ARMSTRONG, "Erlang", *Communications of the ACM* 53, 9, September 2010, 70.

39   *Ibid.*, 69.

40   See P. NORDWALL, "Large Akka Cluster on Google Compute Engine", 22 January 2014, available on goo.gl/8L3xgM (where up to 2400 separate servers were combined, each hosting many thousands of actors).

41   This is also called the move from vertical scaling (more powerful single machines) to horizontal scaling (more but less powerful machines).

panies once opted for few very powerful servers (such as a mainframes) that were each loaded with redundant hardware to avoid downtime at all cost, they will now gravitate to the alternative of having many cheap and easily replaceable servers for which periodical failure is simply assumed and dealt with by redistributing the workload.

6 Legal analysis

6.1 General

The software development trends discussed above trigger several data protection perspective questions. Among the many data protection requirements that should be taken into account, the following will in particular be investigated:

- The *purpose limitation* requires data to only be used for the specific purpose(s) for which it was collected[42].
- The *data minimization* requirement demands to minimize both the amount of personal data collected[43] and the number of persons that have access to the data[44].
- The *data retention* requirements demand that personal data is only kept for as long as necessary, and deleted afterwards[45].
- The *data adequacy* requirements demand that the data that is processed, is adequate, relevant and not excessive[46].
- The *data quality* requirement demands that the data is accurate and kept up-to-date[47].
- The *data security* requirement requires data to be sufficiently protected against losses, unauthorized access, unintended changes, integrity issues, etc.[48]
- The *accountability requirement* demands that data controllers can demonstrate that the processing meets the various legal requirements[49]. Article 28 of the Regulation also requests the controller to document the processing operations.
- *Data protection by default* requires that the default options are non-privacy invasive[50].

By way of example, the limited literature that is available on this topic[51] suggests the following "privacy design patterns" to implement these requirements:

---

42   Article 6.1.(b) of the Data Protection Directive.

43   Article 6.1.(b) and 6.1.(c) of the Data Protection Directive. Note that the principle of data minimization is not, as such, set forth in the Data Protection Directive, but instead implicitly emanates from the combination of the purpose limitation in article 6.1.(b) and the data quality requirements of article 6.1.(c). In the proposed new Regulation, the data minimization principle is explicitly set forth in article 5.(c).

44   Article 17 of the Data Protection Directive.

45   Article 6.1.(e) of the Data Protection Directive.

46   Article 6.1.(c) of the Data Protection Directive.

47   Article 6.1.(c) of the Data Protection Directive.

48   Article 17 of the Data Protection Directive.

49   Implicitly set forth in the Data Protection Directive, explicitly set forth in article 22 of the proposed Regulation.

50   Article 23.2 of the proposed Regulation.

51   The examples were primarily based on J.-H. HOEPMAN, *Privacy Design Strategies*, ICT Systems Security and Privacy Protection (29th IFIP TC 11 International Conference). See, however, also P. BALBONI and M. MACENAITE, "Privacy by design and anonymisation techniques in action: Case study of Ma3tch technology", *Computer Law & Security Review* 2013, 29, 2013; J. VAN REST et al., "Designing Privacy-by-Design," in B. PRENEEL and D. IKONOMOU (eds.), *Privacy Technologies and Policy*, Springer Berlin Heidelberg, 2014.. With respect to privacy in general, see M. HAFIZ, "A collection of privacy design patterns", in *Proceedings of the 2006 conference on Pattern languages of programs*, PLoP 2006,

- Data collected for one purpose should be stored separately from data stored for another purpose (implements purpose limitation, data minimization and data security).
- Privacy policies should be enforced during the processing of personal data (implements accountability).
- The interrelationships between personal data should be hidden if possible (implements data minimization).
- Personal data should be processed in a distributed fashion, in separate compartments when possible. In particular, data from separate sources should be stored in separate unlinked databases, while separate records of the same type should be hard to link to each other (implements the purpose limitation and data security).

Data should be aggregated over time if possible: instead of consistently recording all inputs, inputs should be cumulatively recorded over time – *e.g.*, every hour (implements data minimization).

6.2 Negative data protection impact

Assuming that the data that is processed by the software at least partially consists of personal data, the three software development trends can be argued to be at least partially discordant with said data protection principles and privacy design patterns. The level of discordance varies however.

For example, in the case of functional programming, many copies of (almost) identical data will be stored in the computer's memory when the software is executing. Depending on the specificities of the software and the environment it is running in, irrelevant old copies may get deleted immediately, after a few minutes, a few hours, or perhaps only when the software is terminated[52]. While this could be argued to run against the data minimization and data retention requirements, the data protection impact of all these copies will in practice be almost completely negligible, because the copies are volatile (only stored in temporary memory — RAM) and will in any case get deleted when the software terminates. Moreover, all these copies are automatically managed behind the scenes by the programming language, and are therefore out of reach for the developer. The number of persons having access to these copies is therefore not increased by the use of a functional programming language.

This negligible data protection impact may not hold true for the new generation of file systems discussed above. Similar to functional programming, they keep around old copies of data (files), but these old copies are obviously not volatile, because they are kept on a hard disk instead of in the computer's temporary memory. In addition, the old copies are usually accessible by the end-user, often through a friendly user interface. Depending on the file system and its precise configuration, old copies of personal data may therefore remain accessible on the hard disk months or even years after they have become irrelevant[53]. In general, this will not be desirable from a purpose limitation, data minimization, data adequacy and data security protection point of view.

7:1–7:13; S. PEARSON and Y. SHEN, "Context-aware privacy design pattern selection", in K. SOKRATIS e.a., *Trust, Privacy and Security in Digital Business*, 7th International Conference, 2010, p. 69-80.

52 These deletions are performed by the so-called "garbage collector". For a general description of the garbage description of the OCaml functional programming language, see https://goo.gl/04zPtM.

53 For example, in the case of ZFS, the default configuration is to keep 3 frequent, 23 hourly, 6 daily, 4 weekly and 12 monthly snapshots. Snapshots are deleted, however, when space is needed (see http://goo.gl/KVE1kr).

The alleged discordance can be even more significant for append-only databases, because the possibility to go back in time is one of their main features. It goes without saying that allowing end-users to go back many years in time risks to breach the data retention requirement. In fact, probably the largest data protection criticism against append-only databases is that they continue growing without limitation, thereby reflecting the view that it is often much easier to simply keep gathering new data instead of cleaning up data.

Whether reactive programming has a negative data protection impact will depend on the circumstances. Because the thousands of actors that execute concurrently will all get copies of a part of the data that is processed, possibly thousands of copies of the same data may be in use in parallel. As long as these actors are all executed on the same machine, their data protection impact will be negligible, because the copies are volatile and will be lost when the software is terminated. Conversely, if the actors are distributed across hundreds of servers, data security questions may arise (in particular when the servers are spread across the globe), despite the volatile nature of all these copies.

The use of schema-less databases may be argued to more easily lead to data quality issues, because the data that is stored will not match a predefined scheme, so that software components may store incomplete data or data in the wrong format. This risk may be limited during the early stages of a project, but may significantly increase when either the number of independent software components that access the database increases, or when the number of developers involved rises. In addition, as pointed out above, some NoSQL databases also allow to trade data consistency for higher speed and/or more independence in a distributed network environment. In such cases, it may happen that software components receive data that is slightly outdated or not coherent with the rest of the database. Depending on the circumstances, this may also be difficult to reconcile with the data quality requirements.

In addition, schema-less databases may result in data minimization and data adequacy issues, because their flexibility (as well as their marketed targets of big data) allows to more easily "dump" any kind of unstructured data into the database, as compared to highly structured relational databases with a rigid data model. Similarly, NoSQL databases' focus on quantity instead of quality means that NoSQL databases are ideal for storing huge amounts of small records (such as each action of every user, or each small physical event that takes place). Conversely, one of the privacy design patterns discussed above advocates to aggregate incoming data if possible, instead of storing each and every input separately.

Finally, schema-less database may make it harder to meet the accountability requirements, given that it can be less easily demonstrated which kinds of data are actually stored in the database.

6.3 Positive data protection impact

At first glance, the design trade-offs made by NoSQL databases – higher speed, flexibility of data storage and ease of development in return for possibly reduced data quality consistency – should result in an overall negative data protection impact. Such is, however, not necessarily the case, for a variety of reasons.

- NoSQL databases are also claimed to lead to more simple software designs[54]. Because the amount of bugs tends to be proportional with the overall complexity of the software[55], the use of NoSQL databases may indirectly also be beneficial from a data protection point of view. The impact of a simple design should not be underestimated, because software bugs are assumed to be one of the main causes of data losses and data breaches[56], which themselves lead to significant data protection issues.
- Relational databases, from their side, may conflict more easily with the privacy design pattern of hiding the interrelationships between personal data. As suggested by its name, relational databases are all about relationships between tables of similar records. While many NoSQL databases also offer relational features, these are more "bolted on", instead of a core aspect of the nature of the database.
- Due to their more recent arrival, NoSQL databases were designed with *horizontal* server distribution in mind, while SQL databases are typically more suitable for the *vertical* scaling of a single server. From a data security point of view, distributed NoSQL servers may therefore be preferable, because a successful attack on a single NoSQL server will only result in a partial data breach.

Nevertheless, taking into account that the database that is used is only one element in the entire system setup, it would be an exaggeration to claim that, across the board, NoSQL would be beneficial from a data protection point of view.

For the other software development trends, the data protection benefits will be equally mixed.

Functional programming, for example, is claimed to lead to less complex software designs and significantly less software bugs, due to the immutability restrictions imposed on the developer. Such will in particular be true for concurrent programming tasks, which strongly benefit from a functional programming approach. Considering that the detrimental data protection impact of functional programming is negligible (see above), functional programming could therefore be argued to be very beneficial from a data protection perspective.

The same applies to reactive programming, for which one of the two alleged main benefits is the better resilience, due to the better error-handling. From a data protection perspective, this benefit may very well outweigh its possible negative impact of having actors distributed across many servers.

The data protection benefits of the new "copy-on-write" file systems are more pronounced: while the storage of outdated information will, in general, not be desirable from a data protection point of view, the protection against data degradation and the enhanced backup facilities will on the contrary be very desirable. Furthermore, the possibility to compare the current version of a file with a previous version, may in certain circumstances also facilitate better data quality. Across the

---

54   Thoughtworks technology radar May 2015, available on http://goo.gl/WBgNp7
55   T.M. KHOSHGOFTAAR, "Predicting software development errors using software complexity metrics", *IEEE Journal on Selected Areas in Communications*, 1990, 8:2, 253-261; D. STURTEVANT, "Technical debt in Large Systems: Understanding the cost of software complexity", MIT webinar, May 2013, available on https://goo.gl/n43Qpt.
56   T. OLAVSRUD, "Most data breaches caused by human error, system glitches", *CIO*, 17 June 2013, available on http://goo.gl/KlPoJE.

board, we therefore see solid reasons why the new file systems may generally be preferable from a data protection perspective, if their parameters are configured correctly[57].

Append-only databases go beyond simple file comparisons, because they inherently keep an audit trail of all update and delete operations applied to certain records. From a data security point of view, having such an audit trail "by default" is a very useful feature, which can furthermore be argued to match the idea of data protection by default. Data quality may also benefit from append-only databases, because the audit trail allows to reconstruct all database records in order to track down where inconsistencies occurred or errors were inputted. Accordingly, while the facility to go back to any point in time may conflict with the data retention limitations, it simultaneously provides substantial other data protection benefits. When properly configured to purge old records as from a certain age, append-only databases may therefore be very beneficial from a data protection point of view.

7 Conclusion and outlook

In the trend towards a holistic view on data protection, it is frequently stated that a product/service's high-level features and data processing operations are not the only factors. In addition, the accompanying business processes, security controls and the human factor should also be take into account. It may, however, be useful to also integrate some "lower-level" technical implementation details — such as the programming language that is used, the style of database or the file system of the server.

While the three software development trends we discussed in this regard claim to offer significant benefits to developers (such as higher performance, simpler designs, increased productivity and increased software robustness), some of their features and ideas also conflict, in varying degrees, with various data protection principles. At the same time, these very same trends may also bring along significant data protection benefits, such as enhanced accountability and reduced data breach risk.

Even a software development trend that has a trivial data protection impact (such as the use of a functional programming language) may trigger the use of other technologies and methodologies that may, in turn, have a significant data protection impact (such as reactive programming, or the use of an append-only database). In other words, while functional programming itself may be neglected during data protection impact assessments, its choice may not be completely neutral. Nevertheless, it would be a severe stretch to consider functional programming to be out of line with EU law's data protection requirements. In fact, we think that the opposite is true: when properly configured and used in the right context, both functional programming languages and the other trends we identified can be, overall, very beneficial for data protection.

---

57   Similarly, note that the use of version control systems for storing source code is very useful (if not even necessary) to comply with the accountability requirements.

Seen from a broader perspective, these nuanced views (this contribution tries to stay away from strong claims) should obviously not come as a surprise, because subtle shades, fine lines and paradoxes seem inherent in data protection[58] [59].

It remains to be seen to which extent these lower-level technical implementation details will need to be taken into account once the new Regulation is adopted and the data protection by design/default requirements become applicable. Based on its proposed wording (*"implement appropriate technical and organisational measures and procedures"*), data protection by design/default will likely primarily target processes, high-level decisions and company policies. The way these processes and high-level decisions will then be technically implemented does not seem to be the main focus of the Regulation. Even so, given their impact, it may be the case that over time some of the "lower-level" technical aspects will also trickle in.

Unfortunately, in light of the legislation's principle-based approach, the current data protection by design/default requirements remain very vague, and little guidance exists on how data protection by design/default will need to be implemented in practice. More multidisciplinary investigations into privacy engineering will therefore be required, if possible accompanied by relevant standards.

Acknowledgements

This contribution was created in the context of the Flemish IWT-SBO project nr 110067.

---

58 For example, collecting very few information about a data subject may contribute to the goal of data minimization, but at the same time risks to endanger the data quality requirement, similarly, storing an extensive audit trail in a database system may lead to higher security and better data quality, but may also conflict with data retention limitations if taken too far.

59 *Contra:* the fourth privacy-by-design principle warns not to see privacy as a trade-off for other objectives, or to oppose privacy in a "false dichotomy" against other objectives such as security.

Changing the Security Mode of Operation in a Global IT Organization with 20000+ Technical Staff

Eberhard von Faber

T-Systems
Eberhard.Faber@t-systems.com

Abstract

In response to technical developments (cloud services) and radical changes in IT production (industrialization) a leading IT service provider has developed a new architectural framework. This paper describes how the new methods, procedures and standards are introduced throughout the organization. Best practices or proven practices are presented that help IT organizations to manage the introduction of new guidelines. The best/proven practices also help to cause the necessary fundamental change sustainably ("transformation"). They provide guidance how to deal with complexity in security programs and provide several tips for genuine security management activities. This paper reports real-world experience gained during the "transformation" performed in a global IT organization with business in 20 countries and more than 40,000 employees in total. The IT service provider maintains a comprehensive service offering portfolio and maintains a complex IT. Security managers are given deep insight into the specific situation and the challenges on the one hand and in the solutions developed to change the security mode of operation sustainably on the other hand.

1 Background and subject

This chapter 1 describes the background and defines the subject only. The best practices are provided in chapter 2 which builds the main part of this paper. Understanding the background is important since it shows why our program is so intricate.

1.1 Why this is not a usual program

This paper is about the introduction of new methods, procedures and standards in a large global IT organization.[1] Organizations initiate and execute programs in order to introduce such new methods, procedures and standards. We have called our program "Transformation":

> [Definition] Transformation is the act of revising or altering into a different form (involving reconsideration and modification). The change (revision or alteration as meant here) has a significant effect so that the starting and the ending point significantly differ in terms of maturity or attainment. The change lasts a period of time

---

1 We use the term "IT" (information technology) although "ICT" (information and communication technology) would have been more appropriate. However, "ICT" does not seem to be a common term.

and usually has an anticipated ending as projects have. So, the Transformation is not considered to be a continuous process nor it is repeated. The expected changes are massive.

Fig. 1 shows that the program described in this paper differs from "usual programs". There are four differences:

- "Usual programs" may run continuously. Security or risk management programs are examples. Continuous improvements are also executed in this way. Our "Transformation" is planned to be executed only once.
- "Usual programs" may also be repeated. E.g. a security awareness program is usually repeated to order to make sure that the required knowledge is still available and standards are adhered to. Our "Transformation" will not be repeated. It is designed to introduce a new set of methods, procedures and standards in one project.
- This relates to the fact that in our "Transformation" we aim to *cause a massive change* in the organization. The security mode of operation shall be changed. "Usual programs" mostly have a limited scope and aim at causing limited changes only.
- There is another difference which makes our "Transformation" more difficult. In "usual programs", organizational units and employees use to work through pre-defined material. They execute what has been prepared. In our "Transformation" we want the organizational units *to refine on working methods by themselves:* They shall identify necessary roles and assign them. They shall identify interfaces to other organizational units (and suppliers and customers as well) and find out what they like to receive and what they have to deliver. They shall understand security in their business and learn how to develop and apply security standards. This means that the organizational units shall take part in shaping the division of labor and in refining the processes.

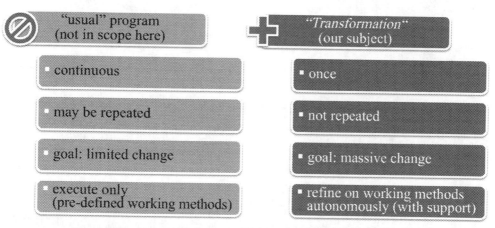

Fig. 1: Subject is a "Transformation" (right) not a "usual program" (left)

1.2 Why we had to induce massive changes

There are fundamental changes in the IT industry [Abolh2013]. Technical developments (e.g. cloud) and other changes (e.g. industrialization of IT) require to reorganize the Security Management of large IT organizations (especially IT service providers acting on the market).

Cloud computing and industrialization lead to a change of the provisioning processes: The interface between the provider and the user organization changes, and the IT organization must modify and optimize its internal provisioning processes. This results in a situation where "traditional" security management no longer works. Large IT organizations have to change their internal security mode of operation and introduce new methods, procedures and standards. That's why we had elaborated the *Enterprise Security Architecture for Reliable ICT Services (ESARIS)* which was the subject of the authors' previous contributions in this series (see [EvFWB12], [EvFWB13b]). The models and standards of ESARIS were developed for large-scale IT production, which is characterized by resolute division of labor and by resolute process orientation. In terms of security, there is the challenge to implement the right division of labor and to shape the processes appropriately.

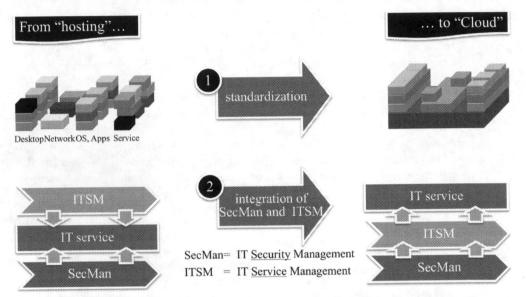

Fig. 2: Fundamental changes requiring to reorganize the Security Management

The three most important changes of the new methodology ESARIS are as follows. Refer to Fig. 2.
- Consequent standardization of security measures including all those in processes and procedures necessary to implement and to maintain technical security measures. Today's technology and provisioning processes are highly standardized. Security can only be ensured if it is also standardized [EvF2014].[2]
- Consequent integration of IT Security Management (SecMan) and IT Service Management (ITSM). The IT production is organized according to the ITSM processes as stipulated in ITIL and ISO/IEC 20000 [ISO20000]. Security can only be ensured if the security management becomes part of the IT Service Management [Abolh2015].
- Modified role and mission of the Security Management organization. This is a direct consequence of the last point. One can no longer solely rely on security experts who care for security. Security can only be ensured if the security measures are applied by the IT staff.

The modified role and mission of the Security Management organization is shown in Fig. 3. The Security Management organization concentrates on setting requirements and on verifying if

---

2 Note that an industrialized, large-scale IT production is considered.

standards are applied so that the requirements are met. The business units and the IT staff must apply the security standards and implement security measures in technology and processes.

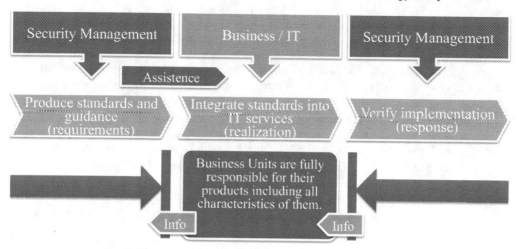

Fig. 3: New role and reorganization of the Security Management

This fundamental change is important in our context, since all IT people are now the audience for the "Transformation". They are provided with very detailed material and must learn to care for security autonomously.

1.3 What are the results?

Obviously, such fundamental changes (see above) need to be actively managed and the introduction of the new guidelines etc. needs to be organized accordingly. Hence, a "Transformation program" needs to be designed, and set-up and progress must be measured continuously.

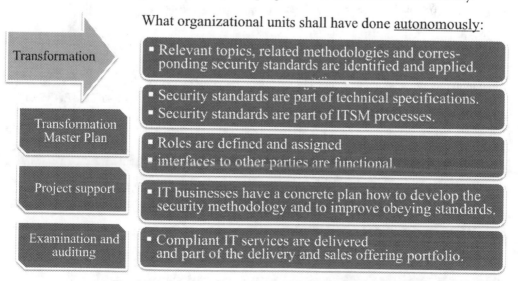

Fig. 4: Input (left) and results (right) of the Transformation

Fig. 4 summarizes why our "Transformation" is so special and complex. It is not only a common training. The Transformation runs for more than two years and by now addresses more than 20,000 people in IT. The figure (right hand side) shows what the organization (IT business units) must have done in the Transformation autonomously. The left hand side shows the central support.

The program is quite comprehensive and the expectations are challenging. The business units take the responsibility to secure their IT services and to identify what is required to do so. The IT staff (not primarily security experts from the Security Management organization) applies the security standards that are made centrally available. The business units identify the roles and tasks necessary to do so and assign these roles to teams and individuals. They analyze the supply chain and their own business and organize the collaboration with other units so that security aspects get considered as required. The business units develop their own plan to develop the security methodology and to improve obeying standards. Finally, the IT services shall be compliant with the security standards and security is considered in the IT service catalogs (delivery and sales offering portfolio). – This seems to be a perfect world. The Transformation program must deliver accordingly.

As support (left hand side of Fig. 4) the business units receive guidance in form of a master plan as well as project support from a central office and a competence team. Examination and auditing help them to keep on track and to actually work on the right things.

2 Best practices for managing the massive changes

Of course: It's common knowledge that training material such as videos, flyers, and a websites is needed. It's well-known that a project management etc. have to set-up.

But: We had no clue how to distribute our information, how to organize the Transformation process with more than 40,000 employees in hundreds of organizations in 20 countries and how to ensure that people learn the right things. But we developed several concepts that helped us to manage the massive changes in our corporation:

In the remaining of the paper, best practices or proven practices are described that have been developed in order to manage the massive changes that became necessary in the organization. This paper reports real-world experience gained while introducing the new architectural approach (called *Enterprise Security Architecture for Reliable ICT Services (ESARIS)*, [EvFWB13a]) with new methods, procedures and standards in a global IT organization with more than 40,000 employees. The list comprises several best/proven practices that help CISOs and other security managers to manage introducing new methods, procedures and standards and to establish a new security mode of operation in a larger IT organization. The best practices are organized in the following three fields or areas
- General organization of the Transformation (section 2.1),
- Training and communication (section 2.2), and
- Management of security (section 2.3).

The text provides many recommendations and practical tips organized in 16 subsections.

2.1 Organizing the Transformation

The organization of the Transformation covers best practices related to project structure, split into the Transformation of organizational units (people) and the Transformation of IT services (service delivery), the provisioning of master plans and their use by the organizational units, performance review and KPI as well as tool support and certification.

2.1.1 Set-up

Obviously, one has to start with the elaboration of the new methods, procedures and standards. Refer to Fig. 5. Then, a Transformation plan must be elaborated. Before starting realizing the change, it is absolutely necessary to have the explicit support from the top management. Our Board of Directors issued the "Directive for the Adoption and Use of ESARIS". Hereby the board also formally decided that the organization undergoes the Transformation and that every organizational unit must support the Transformation program which includes provisioning of the required budget and resources as well as the execution of the activities which were pre-defined to be done.

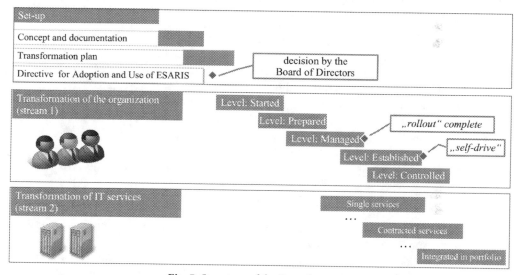

Fig. 5: Structure of the Transformation

2.1.2 Split into Transformation of organization units and Transformation of IT services

We had to train the employees and enable the organizational units to work with ESARIS and to apply the security standards. However, the main goal is to produce IT services according to our standards. This covers all phases of the life-cycle including service strategy, service design, service implementation, service operations and maintenance.

As a result, the Transformation is split into two streams. Refer to Fig. 5. The preparation of organizational units is seen as pre-requisite for "overall ESARIS compliance" and therefore started first. This process (stream 1, called Transformation of organizational units) has to establish processes and create the necessary conditions for the delivery of secure IT services according to ESARIS. In this stream the organization and the people working there learn how to use the methods, procedures and standards of ESARIS in order to produce IT services that are compliant with the security standards and produced efficiently. After having achieved a reasonable maturity level (see below), organizational units can start with stream 2, the Transformation of IT services. This means that the IT production starts to use ESARIS. Methods, procedures and standards of ESARIS are applied. Note that this needs to be done also step-by-step since during ingoing operations only a few practices can be changed at a time. Hence, the second stream also takes time so that the overall Transformation has two streams both taking considerable time to be completed. Refer to Fig. 5.

2.1.3   Staged approach: ESARIS Maturity Levels and ESARIS Attainment Levels

Both Transformation processes use a staged approach. There are five levels in each process (or stream). The levels in the Transformation of organizational units are called *ESARIS Maturity Levels*, and the levels in the Transformation of IT services are called *ESARIS Attainment Levels*. This simplifies both processes and eases the organization of the overall process.

The *ESARIS Maturity Levels* relate to the achievement of milestones and a defined ranking with five stages: started, prepared, managed, established and controlled. Refer to Fig. 5. The levels were developed using input from the Capability Maturity Model® Integration (CMMI®) and the Systems Security Engineering - Capability Maturity Model (SSE-CMM®, [ISO21827]). The CMMI is built to implement and improve processes. Processes coordinate three things: (i) people with their skills and motivation, (ii) tools and equipment they are using, and (iii) procedure and methods that organize and manage individual tasks. The CMMI levels are not used as is. On the one hand, the Transformation towards using ESARIS is not only implementing processes. New working methods are introduced, skills are developed and even the products of the IT service provider are changed. On the other hand, the ESARIS Transformation is not a continuous course of action; it is a project having a planned starting time and an anticipated ending.

The *ESARIS Attainment Levels* relate to the achievement of milestones in delivering IT services according to the methods, procedures and standards of ESARIS. The first three levels are related to more technical tasks (IT engineering and implementation). Level 1: The technical components integrate the security measures that are stipulated in the ESARIS security standards. Level 2: The IT Service Management processes also integrate security as defined in the ESARIS security standards. Level 3 is "successfully delivered" which means that the IT service has at least once been provided to a customer with security measures as defined in the ESARIS security standards. The last two stages are related to the management of the service portfolio (called catalog management in ITIL). Level 4: integrated into delivery portfolio means that ESARIS is part of the IT service description provided by the delivery units. Level 5: integrated into sales portfolio means that ESARIS is part of the IT service description provided to customers. Refer to Fig. 5.

2.1.4 Start with smaller organizational units and step-by-step increase the scope

The whole company is partitioned into many organizational units, departments or teams. This allows to start with smaller entities. After having achieved higher *ESARIS Maturity Levels* the scope is increased so that finally all relevant organizational units are enabled and cooperate efficiently.

Each organization unit assigns a so-called Transformation Manager who organizes the Transformation in his or her organization. Note that there are hundreds of such entities in a very large company. The execution of the Transformation needs to be organized centrally which requires a central team performing the overall project or program management. A Sponsor is also assigned for the Transformation of an organization unit. This ensures the necessary management attention and support.

2.1.5 Provisioning of master plans and their use by the organizational units

At this stage we are facing a inconsistency. On the one hand, we want the organization to act autonomously while adopting ESARIS with the new methods, procedures and standards. This is required since the IT staff shall take over tasks that will no longer be conducted by security experts from the Security Management organization. It is also true, that no one can actually anticipate all situations and define the best solution for each of them. On the other hand, it is clear that organizational units require assistance and guidance to step-by-step adopt the new methods, procedures and standards of ESARIS. We also planned to verify the achievement of milestones and certify the related levels (*ESARIS Maturity Levels*, refer to above). Such a certification requires the definition of concrete requirements as the basis. One cannot start an assessment without having defined the target.

Activity number and name	Goal, scope	Description of activity
S1.2: Create conditions	Before starting the transformation you must define the scope (the unit with its business that start the process) and the people who must make their contribution (sponsor, security management, business units or teams).	• define scope (unit, business) • set-up *ESARIS Transformation Core Team (ECT)* • name program sponsor (one person from senior management) • identify major roles and responsibilities in this process; identify other stakeholders; define who has to be actively involved or consulted only • consult the *Security Management Delivery* in Germany (more specifically the *ESARIS Program Management*)
Further remarks	**Notes by the Transformation Manager**	**Evidence expected from the Transformation Manager**
Don't make the unit too big. It may be helpful to split larger organization into small parts which run their own program. In later maturity levels these can be reunited.	• Unit specifics • Roles and responsibilities • Due date; completion date / status • Evidence	• unit name and total number of employees; • in case that the unit is a virtual one or if it comprises more than one organizational units: a list of real organizational units is required together with their number of employees; • the name of the Transformation Manager, his or her deputy, and the name of the sponsor; • description of the organizational unit's business (including typical services being delivered, customers or the unit's services that are delivered). Description of typical roles and an outline of the role of security for the services. • Note that the above information must also be included into the ETS
Activity number and name	**Goal, scope**	**Description of activity**
S1.3: Planning	The main content of this activity is project or program management. These are basics which are not very specific to ESARIS transformation.	• elaborate the *ESARIS Transformation Plan (ETP)* in a first version by making unit specific adaptations of the ETMP; set milestones, identify supporting factors and obstacles as well as strategic success factors • verify resources • schedule achievement of *ESARIS Maturity Level* "Started"

Fig. 6: A small and simple part of the ESARIS Transformation Master Plan (stream 1)

The way out of this situation turned out to be straightforward but was not easy to go. A so-called *ESARIS Transformation Master Plan (ETMP)* was developed and given to all organizations in the Transformation. This plan actually comprises five individual plans, one for achieving one *ESARIS Maturity Level*. The levels are reached subsequently; a level must not be skipped. Each plan is organized in different activities or steps and described in one table. Refer to Fig. 6 which shows a small and very simple part of the ETMP. Each activity is given a number and name. Then the major goals are described which shall be achieved. This part also describes the motivation and can be considered as a rationale too. The field "Description of activity" enlists things that are demanded to be done. The field "Further remarks" provides explanations etc.

As mentioned above, each organizational unit has its Transformation Manager. This role organizes the Transformation in one organizational unit. A main task for him or her is to create a unit-specific *ESARIS Transformation Plan (ETP)* using the master plan (ETMP) as the basis. The cell describing the information to be added is entitled "Unit specifics". Refer to Fig. 6. This unit-specific information includes for example the following: "Roles and responsibilities" to determine who should do what, "Due date" and "Completion date/status" are for planning to describe the progress made, and "Evidence" refers to things that have to be delivered (documented) by the Transformation Manager in order to complete the *ESARIS Maturity Level* and get certified to have achieved this milestone. The field "Evidence expected from the Transformation Manager" provides the details.

2.1.6 Performance review and KPI as well as tool support and certification

Technically the Transformation of an organizational unit is supported by a well-defined process and central roles. An organizational unit registers for the Transformation process or is asked to do so. Here general information is recorded. Refer to Fig. 7. The Transformation Manager performs the planning. Hereby he or she uses the *ESARIS Transformation Master Plan (ETMP)* as described above. The Transformation Manager must demonstrate that the activities and sub-activities have successfully been conducted. To this end, he or she must provide evidence. The necessary evidences are also described in the ETMP. Training of employees is e.g. an important part of conducting the Transformation (refer to below). So, evidence that employees attend the trainings is required. After having performed all activities and sub-activities, the Transformation Manager can request for certification, i.e. formal approval of the achievement of an *ESARIS Maturity Level*. The ETP, specifically the evidences, are checked and verified by the central ESARIS Transformation Program Management. Other people help to organize the overall process: they do normal project management for the Transformation of the whole company and especially take care that the entities keep to the schedule. This team is called ESARIS Transformation Project Management.

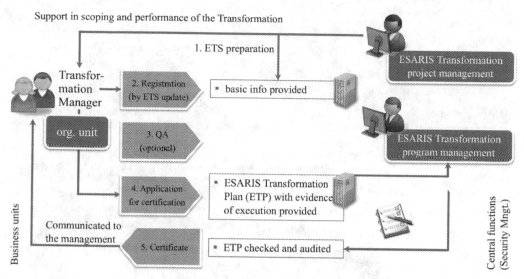

Fig. 7: Verification of execution and certification

KPIs are used to manage the overall project were the individual organizational units have to provide key figures. The process described above is supported using tools: there is a workflow tool and electronic filing of all information including the unit's plans with the evidences. Also certification reports are filed which are generated using templates with a questionnaire.

2.1.7   Can this be managed at all? Estimating the costs

How many organizational units must pass how many certifications? This seems to be an easy question but its analysis shows the real challenge. This Transformation program is huge and difficult.

It is really a question if an organization can actually manage such a process. In order to find out if this can realistically be managed and how, some estimations are performed. Refer to Fig. 8. Three simple questions guide us through the analysis which is necessary for the detailed planning:

- Path: How can we work through the whole corporation? What are the units to begin with? How do we know if we have actually covered the whole organization?
- Size: What is the best or realistic size of an organizational unit that performs the Transformation according to one *ESARIS Transformation Plan (ETP)* as described above? If the units are small, their business is homogeneous which facilitates the process. However, the smaller the units the higher the number of certifications (called cases in Fig. 8).
- Costs. What are the overall costs for the central ESARIS Transformation program/project? Is it realistic at all to perform the Transformation under the given circumstance as planned? Note that we do not consider the costs for the business units in detail. We primarily estimate the extra costs for the central team. The central team must spent time for kick-off meeting, for support during the Transformation and for the certification process which includes the management of the registration information and of the ETP as well as the evaluation of the ETP and the provisioning of the result.

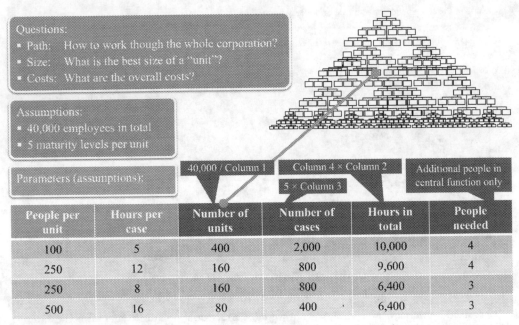

Fig. 8: Four scenarios for which the costs are calculated

Fig. 8 shows the assumptions: It is assumed that there are 40,000 employees. There are also five *ESARIS Maturity Levels* so that each unit must go through five processes. The number of cases the central team must manage is "5 × number of units". We assume that one expert can spent 1,400 hours a year and that the Transformation lasts two years.

Fig. 8 shows a specimen calculation. The parameters are "people per unit" which determines the "size" of a typical organization under consideration and the "hours per case" to be spent by the central team for kick-off, support and the certification process.

As an example, three values for the average "size" of a unit are taken for the calculation: 100, 250 and 500 (refer to Fig. 8). The "hours per case" which must be spent by the central team are related to the size. It is assumed that the larger the unit the more complex and inhomogeneous its business. As a result, the effort for the central team is higher. We take absolute minimum values: 5 hours only for a rather small unit and only 16 hours for a larger unit with 500 people in average. For the units with 250 people we take the assumption in the specimen calculation that 12 or 8 hours are required for kick-off, support and the certification process.

The results show the challenge. The number of cases varies between 2,000 and 400. Note that for each case the unit needs to be registered, the process needs to be started which requires a kick-off meeting (usually using the Web), support during the execution of the Transformation, some project management activities like scheduling and corrective measures in the case of delays, and the evaluation of the *ESARIS Transformation Plan (ETP)* including the certification as well. Hence, 5 to 16 hours per case are not much.

Here are some other numbers:

- Is it realistic to manage 2,000 cases in two years? Or, is even 400 too much? We wanted to take smaller units at the beginning, since the process is easier for both the unit and the central team. But the number of cases must be reduced to a minimum.
- The total effort for the central team varies between 10,000 and 6,400 which relates to about four or three extra people. These people only provide project support. The Transformation activities are executed by the people in the organizational units. If every employee would spend two hours a year this would sum up to additional 80,000 hours equivalent to 45 people equivalents (full time).
- Each unit has a Transformation Manager. If we assume that he or she spends only 25% of the time for the Transformation, this sums up to 100 to 20 people equivalents (full time).

The total costs range approximately between 70 and 150 people equivalents (working full time) which would only work for the Transformation from its start to the end. This does not only mean that the Transformation is complicated It also means that the standardization produced by ESARIS leads to savings in development and operations that are higher than the effort spent for the Transformation. ESARIS is also the basis for the secure IT service delivery in a industrialized, large-scale IT production. That's why the company introduced ESARIS.

A calculation as the one shown above also provides important information on how to organize the Transformation. There are three things we had to do to manage the complexity and to reduce the effort:

- Prioritization: A list that helps to choose the right units have been developed. Depending on its business one organizational unit may have higher priority to participate in the Transformation than another. High priority units are "leaders" or "centers of gravity" in a larger organization. Operations management or units that provide infrastructure services may be more important to start with than others.
- Nomination: Finally, ESARIS is used along the whole supply-chain. We started with some "single units". Then the scope is increased so that "several units" are involved and reach the same *ESARIS Maturity Level*. Finally, all units that are involved in businesses along the internal supply-chain are working with ESARIS. To achieve this, each organizational unit must nominate other organizational units during the Transformation which provide or receive relevant services to or from it. The nomination of "neighbors" helps the unit to apply the ESARIS security standards and to reach a higher *ESARIS Maturity Level*.
- Aggregation: As already mentioned it is best to start with smaller organizational units. The effort for higher *ESARIS Maturity Levels* is higher than for the lower ones. Therefore, the number of certifications (cases) especially in higher levels should be reduced. That why, only large organizational units are accepted in higher *ESARIS Maturity Levels*.

2.2 Training and communication

Training and communication covers best practices related to target group definition using avatars, video production and distribution, integration of video clips into Office documents, the provisioning of navigators as well as a central repository for leaflets, posters, FAQ etc.

2.2.1   Target group definition with avatars

It is a real challenge to distribute the right information to the right people. We underestimated the difficulties. For the team that developed the material, it was obvious that a certain information is e.g. for designers or operations personnel. However, in a large organization terms like "design", "engineering", "realization", "implementation", "production", "delivery" or "operations" are not as clear as one may expect. If a certain information is e.g. labeled with "design", many employees may ignore it since their unit is not labeled "design" even if they are working in projects were something is designed. Additionally, the internal supply-chain is complicated: there are organizational units which perform tasks in different phases of the supply-chain. Moreover, experts get involved in tasks which are usually not performed by the unit they belong to. Names and titles also change when the company is reorganized.

We started with organizing the material in working areas. The working areas had more or less understandable names which were not clear to everybody and maybe too long. In addition, people do not necessarily associate a working area with people doing this work independent from the name of their organizational unit. That's why we introduced the avatars Adrian, Betty and Chris representing the three major work areas as shown in Fig. 9. Each avatar representing a work area / function is then split into three sub-avatars as shown for Adrian in Fig. 9. Short names facilitate communication; the names a gender balanced since Chris may be male or female.

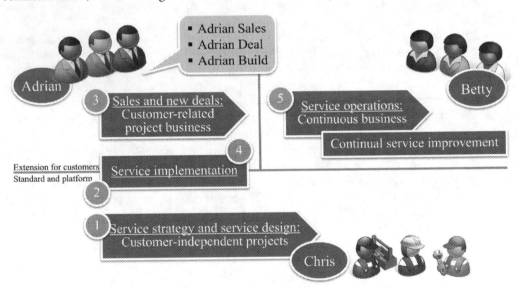

Fig. 9: Avatars are introduced to specify the audience

Note there is a high volume of information. The organization has to manage a large number of corporate security documents, but due to the high degree of division of labor every team only requires specific security documents although these teams also need to have a complete picture to some extent. There is a huge number of recipients and the audience is inhomogeneous. The organization has to distribute the content not only to some security experts but to almost all people who are engaged in the design, implementation and delivery of IT services. Note additionally that in a global organization specific roles and teams with a dedicated deliverable exist many times. The avatars help to bring the message right to the people.

2.2.2 Cost efficient provisioning of training videos

It is common practice to use multimedia to train people. Companies engage agencies which produce high quality video material based upon the specialist input being provided. The advantages are perfect content and professional performance. The disadvantages are high effort since an external agency needs to be provided with all information and results need to be reviewed in review cycles. In addition, our organization would not have paid this amount of money since a large number of videos is required. Another problem is that the videos get outdated and mistakes cannot easily be fixed.

Our solution was that experts use of-the-shelf software that captures the screen and records the voice on a PC. In this way training videos and video instructions are produced. Refer to Fig. 10. The training videos (run time 15, 30 or 45 minutes) are stored in a central repository and therefore available to all employees.

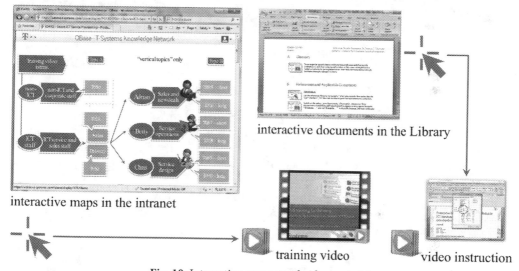

interactive documents in the Library

interactive maps in the intranet

training video

video instruction

Fig. 10: Interactive content and video material

2.2.3 Presentation of training material and navigators

How do employees know what video to watch? We integrated interactive maps in Intranet sites and our knowledge base. These maps provide an overview of a specific topic. The maps show the available content and guide employees to the content they are looking for. A click on a graphical element of the map opens a list or directly the video. The interactive maps are called ESARIS Navigators internally. They are created from PowerPoint slides which are converted into HTML 5 or Flash using a special software. These formats make it possible to seamlessly integrate the maps into a web site.

We have also produced video instructions (Fig. 10) which for instance explain how to work with a document. Guidance is given e.g how to fill in required information. These video instructions are played if one clicks onto a graphical element in the document. This approach allows employees to get the best support working with ESARIS documents.

In order to ensure sufficient quality, one must develop a training concept. The training concept describes all content on a general level and provides a structure that is necessary to make sure all target groups and all topics are addressed in the right way. Each video is characterized by six parameters as shown in Fig. 11. Of course, all videos are assigned a unique reference number (ID). For each topic a range of reference numbers (IDs) is reserved. In addition to the six parameters (Fig. 11), a short description of the content and of the use case is provided. The training concept is provided in form of an interactive map (see above).

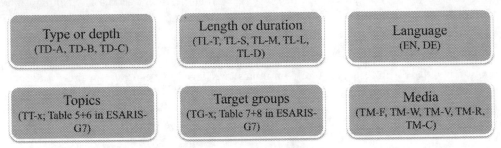

Fig. 11: Parameters that characterize a video

2.2.4   Communicating with codes: Document IDs

One of the big challenges is to ensure that people are able to find and identify documents. ESARIS is a fully hierarchical, structured and modular approach to organize information about how to secure IT services. Every ESARIS content that is electronically filed for general use throughout the company is assigned a unique document ID. This document ID is composed of letters and numbers which allow to identify

- The nature of the document and location within the hierarchy,
- The topic or area as organized by the *ESARIS Security Taxonomy*,
- The use and purpose of the document.

This facilitates the identification of documents. References to documents can be made with the document ID only. Mixing up is avoided. The document ID also makes it possible to create Navigators as mentioned above. The interactive maps (Navigator) can indicate one document or a group of documents with a specific topic and/or purpose. Document IDs are very space-saving which is important for many multimedia applications.

2.2.5   Central repository for leaflets, posters, FAQ etc.

Not all content can be made available in one repository. The storage media are still optimized to serve specific purposes. Official documents of the company are filed in its Document Library. There is a Knowledge Base to share associated information. A social media platform is optimized for the communication between people and not to store structured content.

One central repository was used for leaflets, posters, FAQ etc., i.e. all information that cannot be stored in the Document Library. However, there are still different sites and people use to start with one of them and may be confused not to see the content they are expecting to see. To this end, each site has been equipped with the same interactive map that provides links to the other sites.

2.2.6   Bring it down to a set of known messages

Though this is maybe considered to be common practice, we think it is not. It is complicated to get the message: people concentrate on the content and there is no time to simultaneously consider why the content is important. However, motivation is important. We have tried to relate all our new methods, procedures and standards to at least one of three key messages. Refer to Fig. 12. The three messages are also related to a request since we want people to act.

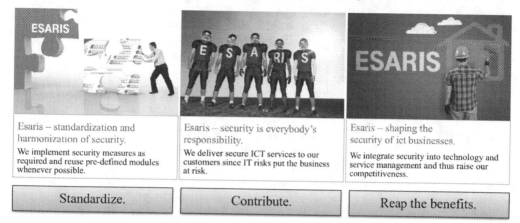

Fig. 12: Each information is linked to one of the three key messages

2.3 Management of security

Finally, the security management itself had to be adapted. Best practices relate to balancing activities in the transformation project on the one hand and those in the day-to-day, continual security management on the other hand, redefinition of responsibilities (refer to section 1.2), definition of processes to secure IT service on the one hand and those to verify compliance with internal standards on the other, as well as the introduction of so-called Aces (see section 2.3.2) to inform about attained compliance levels and to facilitate re-use of IT elements that are compliant.

2.3.1   Security is everybody's responsibility

ESARIS is introduced to respond to the fundamental changes in IT. Refer to section 1.2. The new approach aims at the consequent integration of IT Security Management (e.g. ISO/IEC 27001) and IT Service Management (e.g. ITIL or ISO/IEC 20000). The modified role and mission of the Security Management organization is shown in Fig. 3 at the beginning of this paper. This has a major effect.

The IT staff (and not only people from the security organization) implements the security measures that are stipulated in the ESARIS standards. The business units are responsible to secure their IT services which includes the provisioning of required resources (technology, people etc.). The IT experts shall also participate and strongly support the development and maintenance of the security standards.

We have summed up this new approach with the (elder) slogan "Security is everybody's responsibility". In practice, this is a massive change in roles and responsibilities requiring a quite different mindset of many employees and managers. But also people from the Security Management organizations must learn that standardization alters their way of acting [EvF2014].

2.3.2   Link the Transformation to the day-to-day Security Management activities

As described above, the Transformation is split into two streams. The Transformation of organizational units (stream 1) has to establish processes and create the necessary conditions for the delivery of secure IT services according to ESARIS. In this stream the organization and the people working there learn how to use the methods, procedures and standards of ESARIS in order to produce IT services that are compliant with the security standards and produced efficiently. After having achieved a reasonable maturity level, organizational units can start with stream 2, the Transformation of IT services. This means that the IT production starts to deliver IT services meeting the ESARIS security standards.

The Transformation of IT services (stream 2) is also initiated by the unit's Transformation Manager. Refer to step 1 in Fig. 13. The business unit (represented by the "service owner") designs, implements or operates the IT service (step 2) and must thereby take the ESARIS standards into account. ESARIS defines a methodology (*ESARIS Compliance Attainment Model*) for documenting the level of compliance of an IT service with the ESARIS security standards. The result is called Ace and produced by the business in step 3 as shown in Fig. 13. This attainment information is collected (step 4) and then checked and verified (step 5) by the Security Management organization. They assess the risks associated with deviations (step 6) and request mitigation (step 7) if required. In this way, stream 2 of the Transformation initiates a process that will later run in the same way without support from a Transformation Manager.

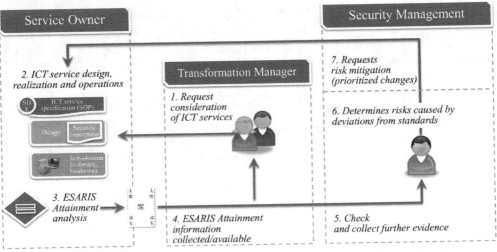

Fig. 13: Transformation and day-to-day Security Management activities are linked

2.3.3 Deviations identified during Transformation get managed in day-to-day security management

Note that the steps 2 through 7 are fully independent from the Transformation. Though introduced with ESARIS, Aces are the basis for our day-to-day security management.

People from the Security Management organization can also inspect an *ESARIS Transformation Plan (ETP)* of an organizational unit. The Transformation Manager is required to describe critical success factors as well as obstacles and supporting factors for the use of ESARIS in his or her organization. Obstacles and supporting factors are an important source of information. The Security Management organization can use such information to plan and initiate corrective measures (as a part of Transformation or not). In addition, a quality gate with an extensive audit is scheduled before the *ESARIS Maturity Level 4* ("established") is actually performed. The audit is performed with considerable support from the Security Management organization.

3 Summary

It is well-known that large IT departments and leading IT service providers must (a) handle a variety of security documents due to their complex IT business, (b) distribute the information to the right teams in their organization, (c) train the staff so that they can appropriately use these documents, and (d) verify and track the results.

There are fundamental changes in the IT which were the trigger for the development of a new architectural approach called *Enterprise Security Architecture for Reliable ICT Services (ESARIS)*. This paper reports real-world experience gained while introducing the new architectural approach with its new methods, procedures and standards in a global IT organization with more than 40,000 employees. We have called our program "Transformation".

The recommended and proven practices described in this paper should help CISOs and other security managers to manage introducing new methods, procedures and standards. The best practices should also help to cause a necessary fundamental change sustainably and to bring a large IT organization into a new security mode of operation. They also provide guidance how to deal with complexity in security programs and provide several tips for genuine security management activities.

References

[ISO21827] ISO/IEC 21827 – Information Technology – Systems Engineering – Capability Maturity Model (SSE CMM)

[ISO20000] ISO/IEC 20000 – Information technology – Service management – Part 1: Service management system requirements, Part 2: Guidance on the application of service management systems

[Abolh2015] Ferri Abolhassan: Standards für die IT-Sicherheit schaffen Transparenz; Datakontext, 21 April 2015, http://www.datakontext.com/index.php?seite=artikel_detail&navigation=356&system_id=268609

[Abolh2013] Ferri Abolhassan (Hrsg.): Der Weg zur modernen IT-Fabrik, Industrialisierung - Automatisierung – Optimierung; Springer Gabler, Wiesbaden, 2013, ISBN: 978-3-658-01482-7

[EvF2014] Eberhard von Faber: In-house standardization of security measures: necessity, benefits and re-al-world obstructions; in: ISSE 2014 Securing Electronic Business Processes, Highlights of the Information Security Solutions Europe 2014 Conference, Springer Vieweg, Wiesbaden, 2014, ISBN 978-3-658-06707-6, p. 35-48

[EvFWB13a] Eberhard von Faber and Wolfgang Behnsen: Secure ICT Service Provisioning for Cloud, Mobile and Beyond, A Workable Architectural Approach to Equilibrate Buyers and Providers; Springer Vieweg, 2013, ISBN-978-3-658-00068-4

[EvFWB13b] Eberhard von Faber and Wolfgang Behnsen: A security taxonomy that facilitates protecting an industrial ICT production and how it really provides transparency; in: H. Reimer, N. Pohl-mann, W. Schneider (Editors): ISSE2013 – Securing Electronic Business Processes; Springer, ISBN 3-658-03370-5, pp. 87-98

[EvFWB12] Eberhard von Faber and Wolfgang Behnsen: A Systematic Holistic Approach for Providers to Deliver Secure ICT Services; in: H. Reimer, N. Pohlmann, W. Schneider (Editors): ISSE 2012 – Securing Electronic Business Processes, Springer Vieweg (2012), ISBN: 978-3-658-00332-6, p. 80 – 88

Index

A

B

C

E

F

G

H

I

K

L

R

S

T

U

V

W

Printed in the United States
By Bookmasters